The Arts in Children's Lives

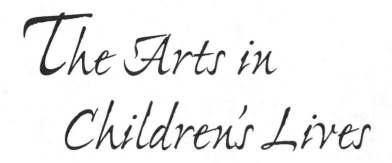

The Arts in Children's Lives

Aesthetic Education in Early Childhood

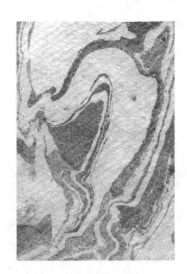

Mary Renck Jalongo
Indiana University of Pennsylvania

Laurie Nicholson Stamp
Indiana University of Pennsylvania

Allyn and Bacon
Boston   London   Toronto   Sydney   Tokyo   Singapore

Series Editor: Frances Helland
Editorial Assistant: Cheryl Ouellette
Marketing Manager: Kathy Hunter
Production Editor: Robert Tonner
Editorial Production Service: P. M. Gordon Associates
Interior Text Design and Composition: Glenna Collett
Composition Buyer: Linda Cox
Manufacturing Buyer: Suzanne Lareau
Cover Administrator: Suzanne Harbison

A list of photo credits appears on page 269.

Copyright © 1997 by Allyn and Bacon
A Viacom Company
160 Gould Street
Needham Heights, MA 02194

Internet: www.abacon.com
America Online: keyword: College Online

Library of Congress Cataloging-in-Publication Data

Jalongo, Mary Renck.
     The arts in children's lives : aesthetic education for early
childhood / Mary Renck Jalongo and Laurie Nicholson Stamp.
         p.   cm.
     Includes bibliographical references and index.
     ISBN 0-205-14567-1
     1. Arts—Study and teaching (Early childhood)—United States.
2. Aesthetics—Study and teaching (Early childhood)—United
States.   3. Early childhood education—United States—Curricula.
4. Early childhood education—Parent participation—United States.
I. Stamp, Laurie Nicholson. II. Title.
LB1139.5.A78J35   1997   96-37323
                                                 CIP

Printed in the United States of America
10 9 8 7 6 5 4 3 2 1   01 00 99 98 97

In Memoriam
Clyde Johnson Miller
A colleague and a friend to children

Brief Contents

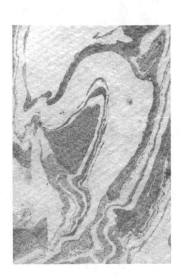

Detailed Contents

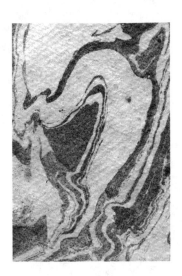

EIGHT   *A*wakening the Artist Within   **221**

 *Appendixes*

Preface

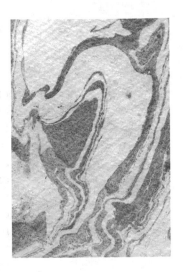

In a 1977 *New York Times* article, David Rockefeller, Jr., advocated a new policy for the arts in education. He identified a desperate need to expand our concept of literacy to include drama, music, movement, art, and craft. In *The Arts in Children's Lives* we propose to answer this long overdue call to action and translate it into sound early childhood practices.

Few teachers of young children have confidence about their backgrounds and teacher preparation in the arts. Over and over again as we work with teachers, we hear objections like these:

> "I can't carry a tune or play an instrument. How could I ever sing with children?"
> "I can't draw a straight line and I know nothing about art. I think that is why art in my classroom is pretty much easels and clay."
> "If I feel awkward and uncoordinated myself, how can I be expected to lead children in creative dance?"

In each of these common protestations, the message is the same: "I am not a performing artist; therefore, I cannot make much of a contribution to young children's growth in art." In this book, we argue that all of these objections are wrongheaded. In the first place, teachers do not need to be performing artists in order to share enthusiasm for art and craft, music and movement, play and enactment. The three foundations for arts experiences in early childhood are process, enjoyment, and participation. To the extent that teachers can create environments for the exploration of arts processes and media, encourage children to associate enjoyment with the arts, and foster fuller participation in the arts, teachers are capable of providing better arts experiences for young children. As Nellie McCaslin says about drama, "Remember, you're teaching children, not selling tickets." Likewise, we don't sing or dance *for* children; we sing or dance *with* them. We don't draw or paint or construct *for* them, by giving them models to imitate; we create the conditions for them to do these things themselves. Thus, contrary to widely held opinion, being an effective teacher of the arts in early childhood depends more on being an enthusiastic consumer of the arts than on being a talented performer in the arts.

For those teachers who have access to the services of specialists in arts and crafts and music and dance, the common solution to feelings of inadequacy in the arts is to delegate all the responsibility for arts education to somebody else. This too, we argue, is inappropriate. Although it is a definite asset to have the support of colleagues skilled in the arts, they typically provide only thirty minutes of instructional time per week, and that is not enough. We contend that when arts experiences are restricted to the art room or music room, children's aesthetic development suffers as a consequence. For when the arts are wrung out of the daily curriculum, teaching becomes routine, monotonous, and spiritless. The arts are not the "dessert" that is offered after children consume their "main course" of academics. Nor are the arts a "frill" to be dispensed with when education gets serious about basic skills. We submit that the arts are an integral part of authentic learning; the heart and soul that complement mind and body, a powerful integrative force that teaches the whole child—social, creative, emotional, intellectual, and physical.

GOALS FOR THE BOOK

In order to unify the arts into a holistic concept of aesthetic education for young children, we have identified several important purposes for this textbook:

- We want to convince teachers that the arts are for everyone, not just children who are privileged, precocious, or potential prodigies.
- We present the argument that the arts are basic to the total curriculum, as essential as reading or mathematics or composition.
- We show teachers, even those who have access to the services of specialists in art and music, that the arts must play an integral role in the overall, daily curriculum—that the arts build children's interest, motivation, and learning in all subject areas.
- We demonstrate to teachers with a limited background in the arts that they can draw upon a wide array of resources to provide a more arts-enriched curriculum.
- We expand teachers' understandings about developmentally appropriate expectations in the arts for each of the age levels encompassed by the field of early childhood education: infant/toddler, nursery, kindergarten, and first or second grade.
- We describe how the arts can support the goals of multicultural education, showing how the arts affirm the worth of each individual, yet encourage respect for cultural diversity.
- We provide many examples of teachers who have designed arts-based curricula, even with limited financial resources and minimal preparation in the arts.
- We offer teachers practical, concrete suggestions about evaluating children's growth in key areas of the arts: music and movement, art and craft, play and enactment.
- We guide both new and experienced teachers of young children in formulating a philosophy of aesthetic education and reconceptualizating the early childhood arts curriculum.

UNIQUENESS OF THE BOOK

$\mathcal{M}$ost of the available publications about the arts in early childhood education are devoted to one aspect of arts education—music and movement *or* art and craft *or* creative dramatics—presumably because the breadth of each one of these areas requires an entire book to do justice to the subject. Yet, as with other areas of the curriculum, separating the arts from one another can lead to fragmentation and trivialization. Just as social studies and whole language were a step forward over isolated bits of curriculum, so too will the arts benefit from a perspective that unifies aesthetic education, combining music *with* art *with* creative movement *with* drama and *with* craft. The best way to explain this perspective is to show, rather than tell. Throughout *The Arts in Children's Lives,* we illustrate what an integrated, arts-based curriculum looks like and explain how it functions. We offer an integrated approach, one that shows early childhood educators teachers how to "put the arts back together again."

Unifying the arts is more than a trend or a whim on our part. It is a respectful response to the way that young children learn and grow. Young children do not separate the arts from daily activity or "academic" subjects. Rather, they can be observed spontaneously integrating the arts with other experiences. A twelve-month-old will invent a nonsense chant to accompany the back-and-forth motion of a swing; a three-year-old will dance about the room with something fashioned from clay as if it were alive; a six-year-old will closely examine the illustrations in a picture book while learning to read. In each of these situations, learning for the very young is all of one piece, not the little compartments of time, space, and subject matter that adults frequently prefer.

We recognize that reconceptualizing the arts curriculum in this way is a departure from what is ordinary, popular, and commonly practiced in classrooms across the United States. It is the rare early childhood teacher who has abiding confidence in her or his own arts background, much less a thorough preparation in the arts for young children. Even those teachers with good preparation in the arts can be pressured by parents and colleagues to reduce the arts to busywork. Even faculty responsible for teaching an early childhood arts course can find themselves mired in textbooks and other materials that push children into making products before giving them the opportunity to explore processes. In consideration of all these factors, *The Arts in Children's Lives* deliberately counteracts the "cute" arts and crafts activities that now predominate in classrooms. As an alternative, we advocate authentic arts experiences that recognize the artist within every child.

AUDIENCE FOR THE BOOK

$\mathcal{T}$his book is intended for beginning and experienced early childhood educators enrolled in a course in the arts for early childhood. We envision it as a primary textbook in a methods course that integrates the arts, such as an undergraduate aesthetics or creative activities course. The book also has value for practicing teachers who are involved in in-service education or who are seeking a refresher course in the arts. Among the groups for whom we feel the book is most appropriate, we include day care teachers, Head Start teachers, and early childhood education majors in two- or four-year degree programs. *The Arts in Children's Lives* is also particularly well suited to teachers who were previously certified in other areas, such as elementary or special education, and who seek a second certification in early childhood education in response to the increasing demand for qualified teachers of children from nursery school through second grade.

Our book will support this diverse group of learners in several important ways represented by the textbook features. We begin each chapter with "Chapter Reflections," questions designed to encourage thoughtful consideration of the topics addressed. This emphasis on reflective teaching practice is in keeping with the latest research on teachers' professional development. The reflection questions can also be used by the instructor to introduce the chapter or during class discussion. In order to show teachers what to look for as they observe children engaged in the arts, we introduce the chapter content through vignettes we call "The Child Artist at Work" and follow with related theory and research ("Theory into Practice").

Every chapter concludes with five components that are designed to build early childhood educators' understanding of the arts: "Learning about the Arts from Children," "The Artist in You," "Situations and Solutions," "Integrating the Arts," and "Individual and Group Projects for Teachers." "Learning about the Arts from Children" is a case-study type of profile focusing on a particular child or a class engaged in meaningful arts experiences. "The Artist in You" provides perspective on how teachers' personal experiences in the arts influence their attitudes and behaviors in classrooms. "Situations and Solutions" presents several difficult, real-life incidents that challenge teachers' thinking and call upon them to apply what they have learned and articulate a philosophy of art. Solutions based on the chapter content are included in the instructor's manual. We included "Situations and Solutions" because we know that teachers are often in the position of having their decisions questioned, thus explaining why we do what we do in support of children's creative expression and artistic growth is an important professional skill.

Teachers are always searching for more effective ways to teach, and we have been careful to incorporate suggestions for high-quality arts experiences to children, infancy through age eight, in a section we call "Integrating the Arts." Finally, each chapter concludes with "Individual and Group Projects for Teachers." These are in-class and out-of-class activities that we have used in our own college-level teaching and have found to be particularly useful in building awareness of and appreciation for the arts in early childhood.

Initially, some of our readers will be disappointed to see that there is no appendix filled with patterns for teachers to copy and use with children. We contend that these adult-constructed, teacher-made, teacher-directed "recipes" do little to develop teachers' creativity, much less children's. As a result, patterns do not appear in our book, not only because they are available everywhere, but also because they conflict with our philosophy of art. We urge readers to keep an open mind and hope that they will arrive at a basic precept we have embraced after many years of struggling with these issues ourselves: that arts education in early childhood is not something that you do for or in front of children, but how you encourage young children to respond through the arts. The visual arts supply a good example. With an authentic arts orientation, there is little room for the prepackaged, follow-the-directions, imitate-the-teacher's-model type of activity seen in so many classrooms. We are opposed to activities that push children into products before they ever explore processes—"refrigerator-door art" patterns that they merely color, cut and paste, or assemble rather than create. Why? Because these activities give children the message, loud and clear, that only the adults have good ideas, that it is best for children to settle into the role of imitators and spectators.

If readers doubt that this message is getting across to large numbers of children in the United States, they need only to look at the result—American adults. Even though Americans spend more money on the arts than on sporting events, they typically function as spectators at both. Even when they look at works of art, they are often embarrassed to discuss their responses because they have not learned ways of talking about art. If they attend a dance, they often sit on the sidelines when they really feel like dancing; if they attend a concert, they are self-conscious about clapping or singing along when the performer invites them to do so. Unlike people in other cultures around the world where the arts are participatory, Americans tend to equate talent in the arts with superstardom and a background in the arts with wealth and privilege. For example, most American adults see themselves as "left out" of music, other than singing in the shower, all alone with the car radio, or walking around with headphones.

For all these reasons, we oppose prefabricated art for the very young. As an alternative, we endorse genuine arts experiences that affirm a child's ownership of his or her own work, cast the child in the multiple roles of artist, musician, dancer, player, and actor, and cast the teacher in the supporting roles of facilitator, encourager, responder, questioner, and observer.

OVERVIEW OF THE CONTENTS

The Arts in Children's Lives is organized into three parts: "Young Children and the Arts," "The Home and School Arts Environments," and "Planning, Assessing, and Rethinking the Arts Curriculum."

In Part I, Chapter One explains the concept of aesthetic education and the arts in early childhood. Chapter Two builds a case for the many ways in which the arts contribute to the quality of children's lives, including their ethnic and cultural identities. In Chapter Three, we take a more integrated approach to the areas of the arts and describe a developmental sequence for children's aesthetic in three major areas of the arts: art and craft, music and movement, and story and enactment.

In Part II, we focus on home and school arts environments. We appreciate that parents exert a powerful influence on children's artistic growth, so Chapter Four focuses on those influences as well as providing guidance in interacting more successfully with parents. Chapter Five describes the creative teacher's multiple roles in providing an early childhood classroom arts environment.

Part III focuses on three key aspects of the arts curriculum—planning, assessment, and philosophy. In Chapter Six, we show what an integrated arts curriculum looks like for infants/toddlers, preschoolers, and children in the primary grades. One reason the arts have been neglected is that they have always had the reputation of being more difficult to assess. Yet now, with the emphasis on portfolio assessment—a method borrowed from the arts—teachers can use authentic assessment strategies to assess young children's growth in art, as Chapter Seven details. Chapter Eight, the final chapter, offers some practical suggestions for building readers' confidence and skill as they complete the book and work with children, families, and communities.

Some readers may find that this sequence of chapters is not the one that they would choose, yet, because each chapter stands alone, it is not difficult to rearrange them to suit a particular course or personal preference. We have addressed the key issues, and we leave it to individual instructors to decide the best approach for their students.

The appendixes are designed to support both novice and experienced teachers in locating high-quality curriculum resources. We find that many of the materials we use are ordered from catalogs or purchased at conferences. To support teachers in their search for curriculum resources, the appendixes include sources for toys, recording, and musical materials; a list of song picture books; a compilation of traditional early childhood songs and discography; published curriculum resources; a list of professional organizations that support the arts in education; guidelines for a documentation project; and suggestions on how to use artworks in the classroom.

Welcome, then, to *The Arts in Children's Lives: Aesthetic Education in Early Childhood.* We hope that this book contributes to our readers' appreciation for the artistry in children and supports them as they strive to create classrooms where young children's creativity can flourish.

The Arts in Children's Lives

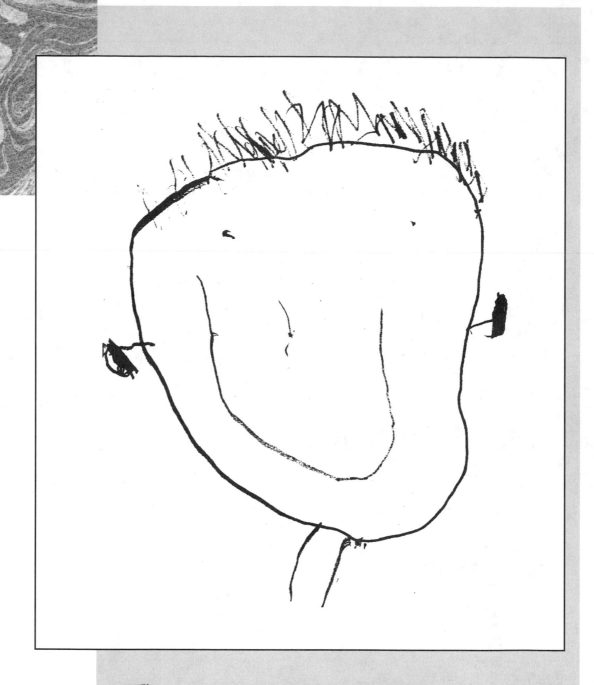

*A*rt is increasingly accepted as a basic form of understanding. It seems only reasonable, then, to say that one of the principal functions of schooling should be the provision of instruction in aesthetic knowing.

—Ralph A. Smith (1992, p. 52)

Aesthetic Education and the Arts

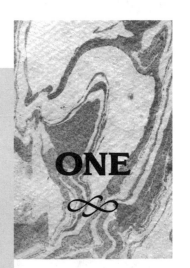

ONE

Chapter Reflections

- ☞ How would you define aesthetic education?
- ☞ What differences would you identify between experiences that are "artful" and those that are not?
- ☞ What challenges do you anticipate as a teacher of the arts in early childhood?
- ☞ Where do the arts "fit" into the total early childhood curriculum?
- ☞ How have your arts experiences as a child and as an adult differed?

UNDERSTANDING AESTHETIC EXPERIENCE

*W*hen you read the subtitle of this book, perhaps your first question was "What is an aesthetic experience?" The word "aesthetics" comes from a Greek word, *aisthetikos,* that refers to the ability to perceive through the senses. Depending upon each human being's sensory capacity and acuity, everyone is capable of sensory perception to some extent. In fact, it has been argued that the sensory perceptions of young children are particularly keen, even more intense than those experienced by adults. One reason why this assertion might be true is that young children do not "sort out" their sensory impressions as adults do. We have seen toddlers trying to scratch a delicious-looking food off a magazine picture, running around the room expecting to see the musical note they hear, or attempting to pick up a pattern printed on a brightly colored carpet. For the very young, sensory input is interconnected. Herbert Read (quoted in Keel, 1972) comments on the power and influence of early childhood aesthetic experiences by remarking:

> The echoes of my life which I find in my early childhood are too many to be dismissed as vain coincidences, but perhaps it is my conscious life which is the echo, the only real experiences in life being those lived with virgin sensibility—so that we hear a tone only once, only see a color once, see, hear, touch, taste and smell everything but once, for the first time. All life is an echo of our first sensations. But it is more complicated than that, for the senses apprehend not only colors and tones and shapes, but also patterns and atmosphere, and our first discovery of these determines the larger patterns and subtler atmospheres of all our subsequent existence. (p. 4)

When we watch and listen to children, perhaps these speculations about first experiences being so influential are not as outlandish as they first appear. Consider the sublime smile from Maria who sits in her high chair and puts her first fistful of birthday cake into her mouth or preschooler Jason's delight at the first sensation of warm beach sand on his bare feet. Evidently, early sensory impressions—those first *aisthetikos*—are memorable, are integrated, and have lasting significance.

Over the years, aesthetics has evolved into a branch of philosophy and curriculum dealing with artistic sensibilities. Aesthetics focuses on determining what is beautiful and good as well as on appreciating these things. Although not everyone becomes an artist, everyone participates in aesthetic experiences (Broudy, 1988). There is an aesthetic sensibility in ordinary tasks—dressing for work, deciding what music to play in the car, or arranging our home and work spaces. Moreover, special events without that aesthetic quality are no longer special. What would a wedding, a holiday gathering, or a graduation dance be like without considering aesthetics? Attention to and appreciation for what is beautiful "is not limited to things in galleries and museums, it's a way of addressing the world" (Eisner, 1992, p. 5). It is attention to what art experts like Samuel Hope (1990) call "mixtures and balances"—a skillful blending of elements—that makes something beautiful. Clearly, when the aesthetic dimension is ignored, much of human experience becomes bland and uninteresting. The same thing is true of education. Without attention to aesthetics, life in schools is routine and monotonous, for both children and their teachers.

Throughout this book, we will be using four key words (Consortium of National Arts Education Associations, 1994):

- **Aesthetics**—"a branch of philosophy that focuses on the nature of beauty, the nature and value of art, and the inquiry processes and human responses associated with these topics" (p. 82).
- **Creativity**—the flexible and fluent production of ideas that are unique, complex, or elaborate.
- **Process**—a complex operation using a number of methods or techniques.
- **Art**—creative works and the process of producing them. Art also refers to all of the art forms that have been produced throughout human intellectual and cultural history.

As you read the following description of a kindergarten project in action, think about the focus on aesthetics, the emphasis on creative processes, and the ways in which the arts enriched the child's experiences.

The Child Artist at Work

A downtown movie theater within walking distance of Ms. Lemley's kindergarten class is under renovation, and children have been watching excitedly as the work progresses. They had the opportunity to tour the building just before it was closed and will tour the building again, ten months later, when the work is nearly finished. Ms. Lemley has looked upon this construction project as a learning opportunity because the children are intrigued by the old building's restoration. In order to build upon the children's interests, a wide array of classroom activities have been planned with the children's input. Before their first visit to the theater, the children completed a K-W-L-S chart like the one in Figure 1.1 (Ogle, 1986; Sippola, 1995). In the first column, Ms. Lemley writes down the *K*—what the children already *know*—about theaters. Under this heading, she writes children's remarks

Aesthetic experiences begin with sensory input. This toddler explores beach toys at home, arrives at the shore, and fully experiences sun, sand, and water.

Figure 1.1   Sample K-W-L-S Chart

What we KNOW	What we WANT to know	What we LEARNED	What we STILL want to learn

Source: Ogle, D. (1986). *K-W-L: A teaching model that develops active reading of expository text.* Englewood Cliffs, NJ: Merrill/Prentice Hall; Sippola, A. E. (1995). K-W-L-S. *The Reading Teacher, 48*(6), 542–543.

such as "You go there to see movies instead of watching them on TV at home"; "They have candy and popcorn there"; "They sell tickets"; and "You aren't supposed to talk." In the second column, she writes the *W*—what the children *want* to know— and the children raise questions like "How much do tickets cost?" and "What movie is playing there?" During their initial tour (before the construction began), the kindergartners were asked to be careful observers, and their teacher kept a list of the things they noticed, both good and bad. Children commented, for example, that the seats were lumpy and the velvet curtain had big holes in it. They admired the art deco light fixtures, the inlaid marble floor, and the wide staircase that led to the balcony. After their tour, the children completed the *L* column of their K-W-L—what they *learned*—back in the classroom. Numbered among the things that they learned were "Sometimes buildings need to be fixed up"; "The movie place I go to isn't as fancy"; "We will get to see how it looks when the workers are done"; and "They play music all the time there."

As a result of the children's interest in the movie house, many daily classroom activities have taken on new significance, and new activities have been planned. The block area became a miniature theater, complete with a "balcony" created by placing a board on top of six cylindrical blocks. Seats were made with square blocks arranged in a semicircle, and the children shuttled miniature plastic figures to and from the theater in toy cars and buses. In the drama center the children lined up chairs in front of the puppet stage, and they created a ticket booth from a large cardboard box. The housekeeping area table was converted into a refreshment stand, and the teacher and children collected empty paper cups, popcorn boxes, and candy boxes as well as a toy cash register and play money to use as props. In the writing center, several children used construction paper to make signs for the refreshment stand and posters about the food items available there.

Finally, the children completed the *S* column—what they *still* wanted to know (Sippola, 1995). Sarah wanted to know how to find out what movies are going to be shown. All of the children had been impressed by the marquee when the manager turned the lights on for them to see. Brian wondered how they got the lights to move in rapid sequence. One day, Ms. Lemley brought in a cardboard box and presented them with two challenging questions: "How can you use this to make a marquee?" and "What information does the marquee give?" The children suggested that they paint the box and print the titles of their current movie favorites. When they wanted to know how to spell some movie titles, Ms. Lemley showed them how to look in the entertainment section of the newspaper to find out what is playing and the times movies will be shown. The children referred to the newspaper often in creating and changing their marquee from day to day. Then they decided that they needed picture posters of their favorite films for the lobby of their theater, so they worked on them at the easels in the art center. The kindergartners taped their posters onto the freestanding classroom mirror and displayed them next to the ticket counter. They also selected some tapes of instrumental music from the listening center to play in the background. When the marquee was finished, they balanced it on top of the ticket booth. Some children mentioned that the marquee had lights, so Ms. Lemley brought in a set of Christmas lights (ones that remain cool to the touch for safety's sake). She supervised as the children draped them carefully around the box. When the room was darkened and the lights were turned on, the children were delighted by the results of their efforts.

After two weeks of concentrating on this project, the children's attention had begun to wane, so Ms. Lemley announced that she would be showing the movie of

Maurice Sendak's Really Rosie: Starring the Nutshell Kids (Sendak, 1976). This announcement prompted the children to plan their grand finale to the project. They created, then purchased "tickets," made popcorn at the refreshment stand, sat in rows in front of the screen, and watched the movie while munching their popcorn. *Really Rosie* is a musical that includes songs by Carole King, and the children enjoyed it so much that they frequently selected the audiotape of the music, both as an individual listening activity and as a group sing-along. During this project, the teacher also read several children's books about theater and film-making: *Mouse TV* (Novak, 1995), *Lights! Camera! Action!* (Gibbons, 1989), and *The Bionic Bunny Show* (Brown & Brown, 1985). She displayed books of photographs borrowed from the public library about theaters, movies, and the art deco era. Finally, when the theater was finished, the children reviewed their K-W-L-S chart and the list of observations they had made so many months ago. They toured the refurbished theater again, and the theater manager even arranged for them to sit in the balcony and watch a short film for free. When they returned back to the classroom, the children drew pictures inspired by their visit to the theater and wrote thank-you notes to the theater manager, which he displayed in the lobby.

The description that you have just read of Ms. Lemley's kindergarten class is an example of a classroom project for young children that focuses on and integrates the arts. As these five-year-olds participated in the project, they had experiences in art, craft, music, architecture, drama, puppetry, song, and literature. Just think of the many ways that children learned about beauty and the arts through their experiences with this single project! Projects like the one in Ms. Lemley's kindergarten are what aesthetic education during the early childhood years is all about. Her project was successful because she understood and met the eight basic conditions for learning that we will discuss in "Theory into Practice."

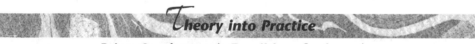

Theory into Practice

Brian Cambourne's Conditions for Learning

Think for a moment about your most unsuccessful learning experience, a time when you felt frustrated or inept or defeated. Now try to analyze *why* that experience was so terrible. What went wrong? Next, turn your experience around. What would it take for you to try again with any measure of confidence and really learn? Finally, answer this question: "How do you learn best?" Try to visualize the process. Draw something that depicts the way that you learn. It could be a map, a web, a spiral, a diagram, a flow chart, a path, a storyboard, or any format you choose. As you read about Brian Cambourne's theory about learning, keep in mind your ideas about what enables you to learn.

Brian Cambourne was originally trained in the arts and applied his understandings about the arts to literacy. In this theoretical model, Cambourne proposed eight different conditions for learning and used them to describe the process that most human beings use to learn. Figure 1.2 is an overview of the elements that are necessary for a person to learn and feel good about the learning that is taking place. In order to provide the young children in your classes with education in the arts and aesthetic experiences, you will need to keep each of these conditions in mind as you plan, teach, and evaluate. Now take a moment to compare/contrast Cambourne's model with the learning process that you attempted to describe. Maybe your model contained some of the conditions he mentions stated in other terminology. How would you revise your model after looking at the one in Figure 1.2?

Figure 1.2 Conditions for Learning

ᗌ **Immersion**

Children need to be immersed in
aesthetic experiences.

ᗌ **Demonstration**

Children need many demonstrations of
the arts and their uses.

ᗌ **Engagement**

Engagement occurs when the learner reaches the following conclusions:

"I can participate in what I have observed—I am an artist, actor, dancer, musician, singer."
"These arts experiences are important to me and my life."
"If I try something new, I will not be punished or ridiculed if it isn't perfect."

ᗌ **Expectation**

All children need teachers who
are creative role models and have high
expectations for the creative abilities of
their students.

ᗌ **Responsibility**

Children need child-initiated and child-
directed aesthetic experiences—they
need to make their own decisions about
when, how, and what to learn.

ᗌ **Use**

Children need the time and opportunity
to use the arts in meaningful ways.

ᗌ **Approximation**

Learners must be free to work at a task,
gradually approaching their desired goal
without becoming overly concerned
about "mistakes."

ᗌ **Response**

Children need useful feedback from others—it should be relevant, appropriate, timely,
readily available, and nonthreatening.

Source: Based on Cambourne, B. (1988). *The whole story: Natural learning and the acquisition of literacy.*
Auckland, New Zealand: Ashton/Scholastic.

In the next section, you will gain a fuller understanding of how aesthetics are a special way of understanding and a way of knowing about the world.

AESTHETICS AS A WAY OF KNOWING

*I*f the arts and aesthetics permeate our lives, then how do we differentiate between these experiences and other kinds of experiences? According to experts in the arts, the aesthetic way of knowing is unique in several ways.

The aesthetic way of knowing looks beneath the surface and pays attention to underlying significance.

In science, for example, the goal is to describe, in the most objective fashion possible, what is seen or experienced. In the arts, the goal is to connect thoughts with feelings and ideas. Art is something of a paradox in that it simultaneously teaches that details are important while maintaining a focus on the whole. This is one reason a choreographer will watch a dance in its entirety to decide whether or not it "works"—the artist is just as concerned with the full effect as with the individual components. In art—unlike mathematics—the whole is *more* than the sum of its parts. As a concrete example, think about the difference between two things: listening to the song sung by an amateur with a karaoke machine or hearing the song sung by your favorite vocalist with a live band. At the most superficial, "objective" level, these things are the same—the same music, the same lyrics. But your favorite singer actually interprets the mood of the song and performs it in a distinctive style, while the amateur merely attempts to imitate someone else's style. Additionally, the musical accompaniment from the machine is hollow and thin, while the live band sounds full and rich. It is these "beneath the surface" differences that cause one performance to "work" and the other to fall flat.

The aesthetic way of knowing focuses on a particular category of symbols.

In the arts, there is a focus on what is fundamental. In dance, dancers use body movements; in music, musicians use sound; in the visual arts, artists use images; and in drama; actors use speech and gesture. These basic ways of symbolizing things are called "first-order representations" (Goodman, 1968). In other areas of the curriculum, it is common to use "second-order" representations or symbols that are further removed from the original experience, such as words and numbers (Goodman, 1968; Davis & Gardner, 1992). One kind of representation is not "better" than the other. Numbers are no better than images, nor are letters of the alphabet superior to speech and gesture. First-order and second-order representations are clearly *different,* yet they are equally important and equally expressive. As Carol Seefeldt (1995) points out, "Because producing art requires that children think of an experience, idea, or feeling and then find symbols to express it, it is a highly symbolic activity. Being able to think about something not present and then find a way to express it is a major cognitive accomplishment" (p. 40). Even though activities surrounding letters and numbers take center stage in many educational programs, these symbols are not the only or the best ways of representing experience. The arts are every bit as symbolic and sophisticated as the sciences.

The aesthetic way of knowing focuses on features that have significance.

If children play with the food on their plates, that activity does not qualify as an aesthetic experience. Why? Because there is more to aesthetics than pure sensory input. A true aesthetic experience suffuses knowing with feeling (Goodman, 1968). It also emphasizes what is significant in our experiences, not only from an individual perspective, but also from a cultural one. Take, for example, Ms. Babich, a new first grade teacher who goes to school before classes begin to prepare her classroom. In order to arrange the room, make it aesthetically pleasing, and make it inviting to the children, she will need to do much more than staple a couple of pictures up on the bulletin board. She will need to plan ways to make the room operate smoothly and consider such things as traffic patterns and where to locate quiet, noisy, and messy activities. Two traditional goals of early childhood education are to promote independence and build responsibility, so Ms. Babich will need to arrange materials so that children can locate them readily and take responsibility for putting them back in place. To make her classroom more welcoming and homelike, Ms. Babich has brought in several large pillows, her collection of art prints, an old rocking chair that she purchased at a garage sale and refinished, and a vase for flowers. Display areas for children's work are another consideration in making the classroom aesthetically pleasing. Ms. Babich has covered some low shelves with plastic shelf liner so that children can display their clay creations.

She also has covered her bulletin boards with paper in dark hues so that the children's crayon self-portraits will stand out, and she has strung a plastic clothesline with plastic clothespins so that paintings done at the easel can be admired as they dry. She has made a display case for the children's wood sculptures out of a shelf that is positioned on top of a low bookcase. In all of this aesthetic decision making, we see evidence of a child-centered philosophy as well as a concept of what is beautiful and functional.

ISSUES IN AESTHETIC EDUCATION

In spite of everything that is known about aesthetic experiences, the misconception persists that young children are merely dabbling when they participate in the arts. Therefore, many Americans contend that the arts and aesthetics are not really significant types of learning. Yet if we visit the schools in a northern municipality of Italy called Reggio Emilia, we would find that just the opposite view exists (Edwards, Gandini, & Forman, 1993). In these high-quality early childhood programs, children create wondrous works of art that teachers from around the globe flock to see. Children produce such impressive work because creativity and the arts are the very heart of the curriculum rather than an "extra" that is allowed if there is time, something that is very different from the situation in many American classrooms.

More specifically, where young children are concerned, aesthetic experiences deal with such issues as the following:

How do children develop an appreciation for beauty?
How do they derive pleasure from experiences in the arts?
What are the essential features of an aesthetic experience?
How do the very young learn to express themselves through the arts?

Each of these important questions has to do with aesthetic education. In early childhood, **aesthetic education** is the deliberate effort of teachers.

- to provide young children with experiences in the arts.
- to nurture an awareness of the arts.
- to foster appreciation of various art media.
- to learn about mixtures and balances.
- to develop skill in evaluating art forms.

These may sound like lofty goals, but early childhood education meets them in concrete, active ways. In the arts—to borrow a phrase from Jacob Bronowski—there is nothing in the head that was not first in the hand. Nor is there anything in the child's heart that was not first experienced directly. But what, exactly, should those initial experiences in aesthetics be? Imagine a five-year-old named Alyssa who comes rushing out of the woodworking corner, creation in hand. "Look!" she announces proudly while swirling her wooden sculpture through the air, "I made an airplane!" This kindergartner's response illustrates the two components of aesthetics identified by Albert Einstein. The first is the creation of something perceived as complete and whole; the second is a sense of profound satisfaction that comes from creating that whole (Rico, 1991). Surely Alyssa not only has invented something but also has derived immense pleasure from the object of her efforts.

Contrast this example with the activity in another classroom. One of the children's grandparents has donated twenty-five identical Christmas tree shapes cut out of wood scraps, and the children are dutifully painting them green. There is no originality involved in this activity for adult or child. The tree pattern was copied from a book by the woodworker and repeated twenty-five times. He did not enjoy making the cutouts. It was a bit of drudgery he endured because he wanted to be involved in his grandson's education. There is no real joy in this for the children, either—just a job to be done, a product to please adults who will instantly recognize what the green shapes are "supposed to be."

Of course, the teachers needed to be gracious and accept the gift. But they could have done more. They could have tried to open up the activity by inviting the children to decorate their trees any way they wished rather than insisting that everyone's look alike. They could have invited the grandfather to come to school with his wood scraps and some simple tools and show children how to use a hammer and nails safely and properly. Perhaps most important, they might have asked him to become a volunteer and share his enthusiasm for working with wood while helping children to make their own creations out of wood, nails, and white glue.

As educators of the very young, it is imperative that we supply rich and varied experiences in the arts for the children in our care. To do otherwise will deprive children of opportunity, and it is this lack of opportunity that jeopardizes art in society. In every decision an educator makes to provide authentic, appropriate aesthetic experiences for young children, he or she will find it necessary to challenge what is routine, commonplace, and generally accepted. Unfortunately, the arts and aesthetics are seldom taught or understood well by the "average" teacher. It is the rare early childhood educator who knows how to make the arts come alive for young children. Our goal in writing this book is to enable you to become one of the teachers who know how to integrate the arts and aesthetics throughout the early childhood curriculum so that more young children can benefit from an arts-enriched early childhood experiences. To further clarify what we mean, the next section will elaborate on the features of aesthetic experiences.

FEATURES OF AESTHETIC EXPERIENCES

After a visit to the farm, Jerri decided to make folded paper replicas of all the animals she had seen on the second grade field trip. She carefully drew, colored with crayons, and cut out the shapes of a cow, a horse, and a pig on recycled cardboard. Then Jerri called out to her teacher, "Look, Mrs. Rice, I have every animal we saw at the farm on my desk." In response to this comment, Mrs. Rice stopped by Jerri's desk to admire her cardboard creations. Then it was time for art class. It was springtime and the teacher brought in several branches from the blossoming trees and shrubs in her backyard. The activity was to draw black branches that imitated the teacher's sample on a piece of blue construction paper, then glue pieces of popcorn or puffed wheat onto the branches with white glue. The children were cautioned to hold each piece of food on the paper for a count of fifteen to make sure that it would adhere. If you observed them during their art class, you could overhear them counting aloud and sense the impatience rising in their voices.

Contrasting these two experiences—the one that Jerri invented and the one that the teacher required—highlights some very important features of aesthetic experiences in early childhood classrooms. In the following paragraphs, we list each key feature and elaborate on its meaning.

Aesthetic Experiences Are Open-Ended and Voluntary

In the "official" art activity, each child's spring branches looked like every other child's picture. Their responses were stereotypic and repetitive rather than unique and creative. There was one "right" way to respond, so it was a closed activity. Clearly, the art experience would have been much more open-ended if all the children had crafted their own spring branches rather than imitating an adult model. Jerri's farm animals, on the other hand, were an open activity. Why? Because she invented them, chose her materials, and created a one-of-a-kind product. Real art, as Marcuse (1977) points out, is committed to freedom of creative expression. Using this criterion, Jerri's spontaneous activity was art, while Mrs. Rice's planned activity was not.

Aesthetic Experiences Make Appropriate Use of Materials

Jerri's activity made appropriate use of resources. She relied mainly upon recycled materials to create her collection of animals. The teacher's activity, in contrast, wasted good food. Educators must be sensitive to this issue of using food for art. It is not uncommon to visit an early childhood setting and see children making macaroni necklaces or using a container of rice for sensory play or creating collages with beans, seeds, and dried corn or painting on bread with food coloring and then throwing it away. In families and societies where food is scarce or expensive or where these foods are staples, it would be unthinkable to squander food in this way. Out of respect for those families and cultures, American educators should reexamine this practice. In order to understand why the use of food for art projects is potentially offensive, think about how you would react if someone planned an "art" activity using something that costs about ten dollars a pound, like Belgian chocolates or macadamia nuts, as the material. Mainly, your objections would be based on the value of the foods—they are precious commodities, reserved for human consumption. The negative reaction you have to the use of these foods as art materials is comparable to the one that many people have to wasting food in the classroom. In the United States, where thousands of children arrive at school without having breakfast, it simply does not make sense to waste food.

As these children pretend to prepare a meal, they use their imagination as well as their actual experiences.

A second issue with the appropriate use of materials has to do with enabling the child artist to select materials rather than "assigning" them. Aesthetic experiences should not be contrived products of some adult's mind imposed on the child—like insisting that popcorn be used to represent flower blossoms. Of course, some teachers will protest, "But it's such a cute idea!" In answer to that objection, we would do well to take the advice of a leader in the field of early childhood education, James Hymes. He once suggested that we think of "cute" as a four-letter word with the negative connotation of child*ish* rather than child*like*. Childlike is fresh, spontaneous, captivating; childish is stale, contrived, predictable, and glaringly immature. When you are teaching, give children some choices about which materials to select and how to use those materials. "Cute" ideas that do all the thinking for children are frequently an insult to children's intelligence.

Aesthetic Experiences Forge Connections with the Child's Experiences

Although Mrs. Rice attempted to make the art experience concrete for the children by bringing in the tree branches for them to examine, the children saw little connection between gluing food on paper and the branches displayed in the vase at the table. The teacher was too busy setting up materials to mention the relationships or, better yet, to invite the children to examine them closely. In fact, after the activity was over, one child looked at the fragrant, flowering branches and remarked aloud, "These are pretty. What are they? Where did they come from?" How much better it would have been to have the children examine the branches closely throughout the day, then respond to them in an *original* way of their own choosing—paints, crayons, clay, collage, printmaking!

In a true aesthetic experience, children come to understand the referent, the material, and the correspondence between the two (Smith, 1982). In Jerri's case, the *referent* was her direct experience with the farm animals. The *materials* were the cardboard and crayons she selected. The *correspondence between the two* was the translation and interpretation of her experience at the farm into a work of the visual arts—her stand-up, brightly colored barnyard scene. Jerri's original activity made these aesthetic connections; the teacher's "canned" activity did not.

Aesthetic Experiences Encourage Originality and Break Stereotypes

Interestingly, Jerri transformed even the teacher's closed activity into an original response. Instead of making a branch as directed, she made "a tree on an island." She giggled aloud as she used green and blue crayons to create "weeds . . . yeah, weeds. They always draw grass and flowers, but an island would have weeds. And a shark in the water" (she hums the theme from the movie *Jaws*). In some classrooms, Jerri's original response would be treated as failing to follow instructions or even as misbehavior. Yet Jerri's spontaneous activity was superior to the one provided by her teacher in every respect. If you interviewed her teacher about the art experience she would say, "Oh, I got that idea from a teachers' magazine." But many of the "art" ideas promoted in magazines and books are busywork, not art. The ideas recommended may be classroom tested, but they would not be endorsed by anyone with training in the arts. It is for this reason that we introduced this section by warning you that you will need to go against what is typically done in the name of art or craft in order to provide the young children in your care with education in the arts and aesthetics. When teacher-made projects (like Mrs. Rice's flowering tree branches) are abandoned, many teachers wonder what to do. They are like the person who is urged to go on a more healthful diet and wonders, "What's left to eat?" Actually, providing genuine opportunities for children's creative expression is not very difficult once you understand the underlying principles that you have just read about. More concrete suggestions for activities that foster creative expression, build aesthetic judgment, and support education in the arts for the very young child are contained in Figure 1.3.

Figure 1.3   Recommended Activities

३ For Infants and Toddlers

Human face mobile—Research with infants suggests that they scan and study the human face more intently than other objects. They seem to be particularly focused on the eyes. Make a mobile out of magazine photographs that show human faces with prominent eyes. Position it 8 inches–12 inches from the baby's face (the optimal focusing distance), and watch the baby's response. As the baby matures, try some other interesting visual experiences such as blinking lights.

Multicultural lullabies—We know that children's musical preferences are shaped during the early years, so the infant and toddler years are a good time to expand children's horizons (and your own). Begin collecting cassette tapes of lullabies from around the world such as *Lullaby: A Collection* (Music for Little People, 1994). Play them in the background during quiet times with infants and toddlers.

Texture obstacle course—Use large scraps of fabric with interesting textures, such as velvet, corduroy, silk, nylon net, satin, lace, and so forth. Stitch the pieces together, and encourage babies who are crawling to move across it. Observe the babies closely to see which textures capture their attention.

३ For Three- and Four-Year-Olds

Child-constructed feely box—The idea of a feely box is to collect objects that will be obscured from view by a box or bag and then invite another child to guess what they are without looking at the object. The child reaches inside and uses touch alone to figure out what the object is. Instead of making a guessing game with objects for the children, invite them to create their own. Encourage them to select some common household or classroom objects, particularly items with distinctive textures such as a piece of crumpled aluminum foil, a button, a small candle, a small stuffed toy, a rubber band, a pine cone, a straw, a piece of yarn. Invite children to find something that feels soft and fuzzy, sharp and prickly, smooth and slippery, and so on (Carr, 1992).

Splatter-paint outlines—Be certain to show the children how to use a plastic trigger-type spray bottle and direct the spray away from them. Paint a directional arrow on top of the bottle with nail polish the night before and allow it to dry. Explain that the arrow always points at the picture, not at people! Let them practice with plain water first to get the technique of a light, sweeping spray. Fill the bottle about half full with a thin mixture of tempera paint. Invite the children to locate interesting leaves outside and pin the leaves to a piece of paper on the easel. The children spray lightly around the leaves, allow them to dry briefly, and then remove the leaves to see the outlines created. Show children the outlines of some other familiar objects, and see if they can guess what the objects were. Invite them to experiment with spray painting around other objects or to create arrangements of objects.

Crayon rubbings—Put a flat, raised-texture object under a piece of construction paper, and let the children rub over it with a crayon until a pattern appears. Try this technique with lace, nylon net, leaves, embossed paper, and so forth.

३ For Five- and Six-Year-Olds

Day/night collage—Tape together two pieces of paper, one black and one white. On one side, encourage children to draw or glue on objects that are associated with nighttime, on the other, objects or drawings that are associated with daytime.

African masks—Use Verna Aardema's (1977) *Who's in Rabbit's House?* to show children African-style masks. Then look at some additional examples of African art, such as those in *African Designs of the Congo* (Caraway, 1986), and discuss its features.

Illustrated poem or song—Invite children to choose a poem and illustrate it in a style that matches the mood of the poem. Encourage them to examine collections of poems illustrated by well-known picture-book artists such as *Sing a Song of Popcorn* (de Regniers et al., 1988). Have them look at examples of Japanese art before illustrating a haiku. A similar activity can be done with the lyrics of a song. Children can examine several song-picture charts or books (see Appendix D) and create their own as individuals or in groups.

Apron story—Encourage children to use pieces of felt or Pellon to create the main characters of a familiar, simple story such as a folktale. Then give them the opportunity to retell the story while wearing a flannel apron. A similar activity is to use a pizza pan and tagboard story figures with magnetic tape attached. This gives the child an individual magnetic board to work with.

Figure 1.3 **Recommended Activities, continued**

↪ *For Seven- and Eight-Year-Olds*

Class quilt—After reading several books about quilts (Ernst, 1983; Flournoy, 1985; Guback, 1994; Johnston, 1984; Karas, 1995), invite each child to design one square for a quilt using a piece of fabric.

Diorama—Collect shoe boxes, and invite children to create scenes inside. They can depict such things as a scene from a picture book or a scene from a historical era, or they can design their dream bedroom.

Filmstrip—Get blank filmstrips and permanent fine-line markers so that children can create their own filmstrips of their original stories. This project requires drawing in miniature, so give the children some practice making tiny drawings on paper before they attempt to draw on the film.

Actually, it is easy to avoid some of the worst activities masquerading as art by asking four simple questions:

- *Are the children's responses predetermined?* If so, it is not art. A teacher who distributes patterns to color, trace, copy, or cut out in some designated way is not providing an art activity, no matter how clever it might be. It is an exercise in following directions, not an aesthetic experience.
- *Will one child's work look nearly identical to another's?* If so, it is not art. When you can scan a display of children's work and see nothing original or surprising, it is not really *children's* work. Young children are naturally imaginative and creative. If their efforts do not reflect this quality, then the activity was not an aesthetic experience.
- *Who is the activity for?* If it is simply to convince parents that their child is keeping busy at school or to fool parents into believing that their child is doing something precocious, it is not art.
- *Will the child's efforts lead to the creation of a new form that is satisfying to the child at his or her level of development?* If a child is being pushed, it is not art. An adult who grasps a three- or four-year-old's hand and forces the child to produce a stick figure is *not* "teaching" the child to draw! Most young children will strongly resist such impositions, and understandably so. When a child is at the scribbling stage, scribbles are satisfying because they are something new and interesting. When adults have to do an activity for the child, it is not suited to the child's developmental level, and it is definitely not art.

Aesthetic Experiences Are Multisensory

Jimmy is in a three-year-old class where the children are cooking cinnamon modeling dough using the picture recipe in Figure 1.4. As he works with the material, he pauses, inhales the aroma deeply, and calls out, "Hey! This is warm an' it smells like . . . it smells like *breakfast!*" "Hmmm," the teacher replies, "I'll bet your mom sprinkles cinnamon sugar on your toast sometimes." "Yeah," Tommy says, while squishing the playdough through his fingers and licking his lips, "It tastes good . . . but you can't eat this playdough, right?" Later, this three-year-old tries to roll the dough out and uses a plastic knife to cut out some shapes. Not only do Jimmy's responses to the cinnamon dough involve all of his senses, but they also combine and recombine

Figure 1.4   **Cinnamon Playdough Recipe**

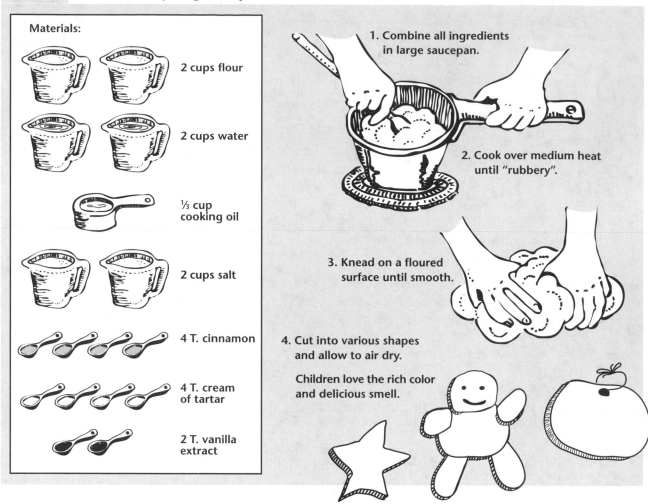

Materials:

2 cups flour

2 cups water

⅓ cup cooking oil

2 cups salt

4 T. cinnamon

4 T. cream of tartar

2 T. vanilla extract

1. Combine all ingredients in large saucepan.

2. Cook over medium heat until "rubbery".

3. Knead on a floured surface until smooth.

4. Cut into various shapes and allow to air dry.

Children love the rich color and delicious smell.

his sensory input. He not only connects the aroma at school with the smells and tastes at home, but also connects words with actions. Jimmy even examines the social appropriateness of behavior by inquiring about eating the modeling material. As this three-year-old's responses illustrate, aesthetic experiences integrate sensory input with thought and language as well as using those experiences to link past, present, and future.

When children respond aesthetically, they engage in three types of activity: (1) expression through various artistic media, (2) dialogue or communication centered on arts experiences, and (3) acceptance of artistry in self and others (Henkes, 1989). Research suggests that a child's aesthetic responses are affected by external influences—things like the physical environment, prior experience, cultural opportunity, and the responses of significant adults in the child's life. Aesthetic responses are also influenced by characteristics within the child. These include such things as sensory perception, mental capacity, and psychomotor skills (Henkes, 1989). As educators, we wield a tremendous influence over the external influences on artistic growth and ultimately shape even those characteristics within the child.

Aesthetic Experiences Are Natural

Children participate in and respond to the arts spontaneously. An infant can be observed moving to music, a preschooler can be observed creating different forms with wet sand, and a second grader works on creating an original picture book—all without adult insistence or persuasion. Real art uses the child's own experience as a source material. It trusts children by valuing child-initiated and child-directed activities. **Child-initiated** means that the idea originates with the child. **Child-directed** means that the child monitors his or her own progress and does not need excessive adult intervention to complete the desired task. In order for children to initiate and direct arts activities, classrooms must create conditions for learning in the arts.

Aesthetic Experiences Are Social

The arts are shared, enjoyed, and shaped within the company of others. Arlyss's favorite song is a train song from the country and western tape that her father plays while riding in the truck, Johnny Cash's "Orange Blossom Special." When Alex, a three-year-old, is asked about his favorite music, he says "Beethoven," and then imitates the beat and pitch of the composer's fifth symphony with a "Dah dah dah DAH." In both of these situations, the children's musicality is being affected, not simply by the musical selections provided, but also by the people they share them with. Children learn practically anything, including the arts, "from the company they keep" (F. Smith, 1992). Ideally, the school should put children in the company of others who appreciate beauty and value the arts.

Aesthetic Experiences Are Integrative

The arts unify body, mind, and spirit. Consider, for example, Ms. Hilty's enactment activity with her kindergarten class. They know the "The Three Bears" story well, and today she poses a different sort of challenge. She supplies toy bears, chairs, bowls, beds of three different sizes, and a doll to play the role of Goldilocks. Then she invites them to help her tell the story as they play with props on a tabletop. As the children participate in this informal activity, they are using their bodies to manipulate the props, using their minds to invent dialogue, expressing their feelings through their voices, and responding to classmates' words and actions. As this example illustrates, the arts integrate different types of learning as well as integrating the traditional school subject areas.

Aesthetic Experiences Lead to the Creation of New, Satisfying Forms

There is an old "Family Circus" cartoon in which one of the children calls out, "Mom, I need more destruction paper!" This child's confusion of *con*struction and *de*struction is humorous, yet the distinction in some classrooms is difficult to detect. Occasionally, teachers go too far with the notion of creative freedom and assume that the arts are simply an "anything goes" type of activity, a free-for-all with arts materials. These same teachers also mistakenly believe that they are allowing a child to express creativity if they stand idly by watching the child flit from one activity to another. Effective teachers are more like musical conductors who pay attention to each section of the orchestra while keeping the total performance and group in mind. Carol Wein (1996) gives a good description of a teacher named Jill who works with two- and three-year-olds. As you read the following excerpt from Wein's observational notes, notice how Jill manages to meet individual needs and give children choices, all the while gently guiding behavior.

> After group time, Jill puts Raffi on the record player and joins the children to march and sing. Trevor bangs the drum with a confident beat, Lisa bangs the sticks randomly, and Jill marches with them, clanging sticks as she goes. Then she tells them they can do something in the rest of the room now, if they wish, or they can stay and dance. Suddenly, she crosses the room and sets out three paint pots and brushes at places around a table. Three girls follow her and paint; two boys stay to drum and dance. . . . Several children draw, after painting, replacing the marker tops carefully. Jill joins a child who asks, "Can I have the rain song?" They sing with the song, and as the others finish drawing, they come, drawn by the sound. Three girls and Jill sing the "pawpaw patch" song, each with a turn to hide and be found. They insist Jill take a turn hiding, too, and she crawls under the big loft. All three run to find her, falling into her arms for a big hug. (pp. 25–26)

Jill supported her students in creating new, satisfying forms by continuously demonstrating "the techniques for doing things. . . . Constantly, through paying attention to aspects of children's development, she modeled how she wanted things done and people treated in her room—with respect, good manners, gentleness" (Wein, 1996, p. 26).

Figure 1.5 **Arts Continuum**

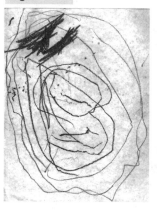

Formless
All process

Child-Made Forms
Exploration of processes that lead naturally into products

Teacher-Made Forms and Stereotypes
All product

Now think back to Ms. Lemley's kindergarten project that introduced this chapter. She followed the children's lead and allowed them the freedom to create, but their activity was both focused and constructive. Ms. Lemley functioned as a facilitator, environment arranger, appreciator, questioner, and observer. The children were actively involved in inventing things and using their inventions—their marquee, ticket booth, popcorn stand, miniature theater, and simulated movie house. In Ms. Lemley's class, children *were using art processes to accomplish things that were important to them*. Artists refer to this feature of the arts as "creating new and satisfying forms."

Because this way of looking at children's art is a departure from the usual, it might seem confusing at first. Try conceptualizing it as a continuum such as the one in Figure 1.5. At one end is formlessness (aimless activity). At the other end, premade adult forms (patterns). What is acceptable and desirable are the "mixtures and balances" that bring us to the midpoint on the continuum. In the middle of the continuum is where children are inventing new forms without being teacher dominated. To illustrate this distinction further, consider working with clay. At the formless extreme is the teacher who looks on as children smash the clay into the carpeted area, bring small wheeled toys over to the clay and gum up the wheels by rolling them through it, or put the clay in another child's hair. At the opposite extreme is the teacher who puts a container of clay and a box of cookie cutters on the table and encourages children to pound and roll the clay in the same ways, day after day. Teachers who have a firm commitment to the arts do not err by going to either extreme. Mr. Brody, a student teacher, is a good example. During his semester-long assignment in a multiage preschool class, he has

Aesthetic experiences give children a sense of something that is whole, complete, and satisfying.

- encouraged children to select their best clay creations, allowed them to air dry, put them on a display table, and labeled them with the children's names.
- involved the children in experimenting with different modeling materials and following recipes to create different modeling clays and materials such as those in Figure 1.6.
- developed children's vocabulary of art by discussing their work with them.
- brought in books of sculpture borrowed from the public library.
- taken the children on a walking field trip to a high school art room that has a pottery wheel and kiln.
- borrowed some simple clay sculpting tools from his roommate and showed the children how to use them.
- brought in some real clay, dug from the earth, for children to work with.

By sharing his enthusiasm for art with the children (rather than by being a professional artist himself) Mr. Brody has contributed to children's aesthetic education. With each of the activities listed, he watched children's interest in modeling and sculpting renew and expand.

Figure 1.6 **Sample Rebus Recipes**

Quick Modeling Dough

3 cups flour
½ cup salad oil
½ cup water
food coloring

1. Mix the food coloring in the water.
2. Add remaining ingredients.
3. Knead until smooth.
4. Store in an airtight container.

Long-Lasting Dough

½ cup salt
1¾ cups water
food coloring or powdered tempera paint
2 cups sifted all-purpose flour
2 T. salad oil
2 T. alum

1. Boil water and salt together until salt dissolves.
2. Add food coloring or powdered tempera paint to color the mixture.
3. Stir in the flour, salad oil, and alum.
4. Allow mixture to cool, then knead.
5. Store in an airtight container.

Permanent Plaster Pulp

4 cups newsprint, torn into small pieces
water
1 t. white glue
1 cup plaster of paris

1. Add enough water to the newsprint to make a soupy mixture.
2. Let the water/newsprint mixture stand overnight.
3. Add glue and plaster of paris until the mixture has the consistency of modeling clay. (Cover your mouth and nose when mixing plaster of paris. Do not allow children to breathe in the dust.)
4. Shape the mixture into various forms.
5. Use torn or cut pieces of tissue paper to decorate the item—they will stick to it while it is still wet.
6. Let the items air dry.

Sawdust and Wheat Flour

cold water
1 cup whole wheat flour
4 cups sawdust

1. Add cold water to the flour until it makes a creamy paste.
2. Mix in sawdust.
3. Shape into objects.
4. Let them air dry.

Source: Adapted from Eagan, R. (1994). *Kid creations.* Carthage, IL: Teaching and Learning Company.

To summarize, an aesthetic experience is an open-ended activity that encourages discovery, exploration, experimentation, and invention (Schirrmacher, 1988). It is natural, social, and integrative. Authentic early childhood arts experiences lead to the creation of new, satisfying forms. When teachers provide high-quality experiences in the arts and aesthetics, young children's learning is enriched in many significant ways. Reflect back for a moment on the kindergarten project that was described at the beginning of this chapter. Through their investigation of the movie theater, the children learned

- to observe carefully and record their observations.
- to organize ideas and to express feelings.
- to work with purpose and maintain a focus.
- to solve problems through trial-and-error methods.
- to respect themselves through their own achievements.
- to communicate ideas and feelings with others.
- to discover their own points of view.
- to appreciate different viewpoints and cultures.
- to create change in their environment using a wide range of media.
- to make aesthetic discoveries and judgments (adapted from Cohen & Gainer, 1995).

For all these reasons, you owe it to your students to deepen and widen your background and understanding about the arts and aesthetics.

DEVELOPING AN AWARENESS OF AESTHETICS

*L*ook around classrooms and you will immediately recognize that there is considerable confusion where the arts in early childhood education are concerned. This confusion usually occurs for three reasons: uncertainty about what qualifies as art, insecurity about one's own arts background, and difficulty in matching art activities to children's developmental levels. In this section you will meet some early childhood teachers who are faced with aesthetic education dilemmas in each of these areas.

In a toddler child care program, two teachers are discussing an activity—finger painting with instant pudding. One teacher contends that the activity will cause the children to confuse food with paint and that it is wasteful. The other teacher says she has used this idea successfully before. They finally agree to another art experience described in the National Association of the Education of Young Children's journal *Young Children* (Clemens, 1991), cornstarch and water, which is also called ooblique and slime. Figure 1.7 gives the recipe. They decide that it is preferable to the pudding for several reasons. First, cornstarch and water appears to be a solid after it is left standing, but becomes a liquid when it is mixed with the hands. The teachers feel that children would be intrigued by this transformation and be more likely to use their vocabulary of art. Second, the two teachers feel that providing another sugary snack is not in the best interest of the children's health. Third, they feel that they could get the children more involved in making predictions about the mixture of cornstarch and water than with the pudding because most children have already had some experience with pudding at home. This teaching team faced and successfully resolved the first dilemma in aesthetic education: *uncertainty about what counts as art.*

Figure 1.7   Cornstarch and Water Recipe (Also Called Ooblique and Slime)

1 cup cornstarch	bowl
1 cup water	plastic tablecloth
green food coloring	

1. Mix food coloring and water.
2. Put about half of the cornstarch into a bowl and slowly add water, a few drops at a time.
3. Continue adding water until the mixture becomes a thick liquid, then add the remaining cornstarch, mixing it with your hands.
4. After the material sits, it will become a solid. Mix it with your hands to make it liquefy.
5. When you are finished with it, allow it to dry out; then throw it away.

Source: Adapted from Eagan, R. (1994). *Kid creations.* Carthage, IL: Teaching and Learning Company.

In a Head Start program, the teacher's aide is seeking a Child Development Associate Credential. During the process of preparing her portfolio, she recognizes some gaps. What experiences does she provide for children in music and movement? In all honesty, she must admit that music in her classroom is mostly listening to records—and just a few scratchy ones, at that. This teacher feels that she is poorly qualified to provide musical experiences, yet she knows that supporting young children's musical development is an important role, one that will probably remain unfulfilled unless she takes responsibility for it. In this Head Start classroom, the teacher has confronted and resolved a second major difficulty in aesthetic education: *insecurities about personal qualifications in the arts*. She has made the improvement of her music curriculum a professional development project and has taken every opportunity to learn more about early childhood music at conferences, training sessions, in her college coursework, and in her professional reading (Isenberg & Jalongo, 1996; Jalongo, 1995).

Meanwhile, a first grade teacher recognizes that she does little with drama in her classroom and decides to attend a workshop on creative drama. Even before participating in the workshop, the teacher realized that the one play a year she provided was insufficient. After the workshop she recognized that it is not only the *amount* of drama but also the *kind* of drama that was inappropriate. The annual, formal, scripted play she planned was a big production that taxed her patience and took too much time away from other activities. Now she sees that creative drama—drama in which the children invent the dialogue based on their familiarity with the story—is better suited to young children and could be much more fully integrated into her curriculum. This teacher gained insight about the third key issue in arts education for the very young—*designing arts activities to meet the young child's developmental level*.

All of these teachers have taken responsibility for children's aesthetic education. By evaluating the quality of the experiences provided for children in art, music, drama, and dance, these teachers have also allowed the arts to take their rightful place in the early childhood curriculum. For while there can be an inferior or ordinary program without aesthetics, there can never be a good or great program without aesthetics (Surace, 1992).

Even though the three teachers just described are ready to make significant changes in their curriculum, each remains unclear about where to go next or how far to go. This indecision is partially attributable to persistent stereotypes about the arts and aesthetics in society. In the past, there was a tendency to view the arts and aesthetics as pure emotion, intuition, compulsion, inspiration, or even irrational behavior—activities that had no connection to reflective thought. "In doing so, they promoted some unwelcome stereotypes. Student involvement in the arts has often been tarred with the suspicion that it is a matter of deviant personalities engaging in compulsive behavior. . . . Such views also went hand in hand with a *laissez faire* approach to teaching, an approach that has prejudiced many against education in the arts" (Geahigan, 1992, p. 7). One of the challenges that you will face as a teacher of young children is counteracting the negative stereotypes about creativity, artistry, and aesthetics that are pervasive in society. You will need to be very clear about how the arts contribute to children's overall development and knowledgeable about the manner in which that growth proceeds. Chapters 2 and 3 will provide you with that information so that you can begin your new role as an advocate for the arts in early childhood.

CONCLUSION

*W*hen early childhood educators understand aesthetic education, they become staunch advocates of the arts for young children. Eventually, they arrive at the same conclusion as Susan Grilli (1987):

> There is absolutely nothing stopping us from taking more care and courage in every choice we make for our children. We simply must choose fewer and better activities for children and leisurely explore with them those few chosen programs in far greater depth. There is also nothing stopping us from setting an example for children of determination to do something—anything—well, with energy and good humor, especially if it does not at first succeed. (p. 80)

The arts are an area where teachers must apply this philosophy of quality, depth, enjoyment, and risk taking. By so doing, we will contribute to every child's life in enduring, significant ways and guide each child's growth in "artful knowing."

Learning about the Arts from Children

Profile of Matthew: "I Making Music"

Matthew Dunn is three years and eight months of age. His mother, Ruth, is an early childhood education major who has been observing his musical responses over a period of several weeks. Excerpts from the observations that she recorded are reported in the following paragraphs. As you read through Ruth's anecdotal records, reflect on the following questions:

- What are the different ways that Matthew responded to music in his environment?
- How did these musical experiences contribute to Matthew's development in all areas—physical, cognitive, social, emotional, and aesthetic?
- How does Matthew use and interpret different types of symbols, including objects, pictures, drawings, and words (spoken and written)?
- How does Matthew respond to music? When you are observing young children's responses, what would you look for? Why?

- What sort of musical experience would you try next with Matthew? Why?

Ruth Dunn's Observations

The first song picture book that we shared was *Over in the Meadow* (Keats, 1971). During the song, Matthew asked questions like "Where is the mommy?" or "Why is that one bigger?" Some of the words were unfamiliar to Matthew, including "dragonfly" and "bask." When I asked Matt what he thought "bask" meant, he said, "The sun." He also seemed to enjoy counting the babies and matching one of his raised fingers to each baby on the page. Although Matthew liked talking about the different animals, he had no desire to learn or sing the song. I brought up the song several times, but each time I did, Matthew found some reason not to sing it.

1

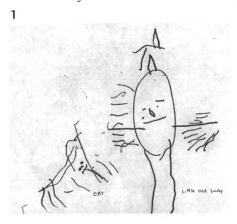

2

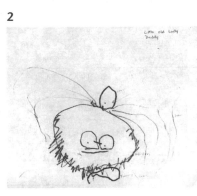

3

The second story/song that we shared was *I Know an Old Lady Who Swallowed a Fly* (Karas, 1995). Matthew had many questions about this song, including "How her eat them?" and "Where her tummy go?" He clapped his hands and swayed his body to the music as well as joining in at the refrain, "I guess she'll die." Next, we moved to the flannel board. Matthew liked playing with the pieces and placing them in the old lady's stomach. Later, Matthew looked at the book again and said, "See, mommy? See what the book says? Her needs a web in her tummy." He then began to draw pictures of the old woman, the dog, the cat, and many different spiders (drawings 1–4 on p. 22 and below).

Matthew did not attempt to sing all of the lyrics of "I Know an Old Lady" the way it was in the book, but he liked to sing parts of it or, better yet, he invented his own version of the song by substituting words. In one of his renditions of the song, Matthew had the old lady swallow a potato, a hammer, a pencil, and a bunny. Interestingly, the item that led to the old lady's demise was swallowing his baby sister Nicolle! His nickname for Nicolle is "Colzer," and his made-up song concluded with "Little old lady swallowed a Colzer, her dead of course."

The third song we shared was "Five Little Speckled Frogs" (Monet, 1986), and it was clearly Matthew's favorite of the three. I had made a log, frogs, and flies for the flannel board, and on the first time through, Matt clapped his hands, jumped the frogs from the log, and began singing along with me. Later, I heard him singing the song aloud, and even though he sometimes had trouble with the numbers, he had mastered most of the lyrics: "Three little speckled frogs. Jump in the water eating some wishous [delicious] bugs. Yum! yum! One jump in the pool where it nice and cool. Now, uh, now uh two speckled frogs. Glub, glub. And, uh, jump in the water now it two speckled frogs. Glub, glub. One jump in the pool where it nice and cool eating most wishous bugs. Yum, Yum. And uh jumped in the pool where it nice and cool now there are two speckled frogs. Boo-hoo, boo-hoo. Bye."

Later, Matthew used this song as the basis for dramatic play. He used the kitchen rug for water, then pulled his shirt down over his bent knees and said, "See my speckles, mom? My is a speckled frog.

Wroget, wroget." Then he sang as he jumped in the water. Another time, he said, "Let's try it again. You put the frogs on and my put the water on. Where it was nice and cool. Me going to sing them a whole bunch!" On another occasion, the song led to making pictures because Matt decided that the frogs needed more bugs to eat: "You draw some bugs. Us can draw one here and here and here. Okay? Cause frogs find them and eat them. [sings] Three little speckled frogs jump in the water. One way up the sky, see? One here, one here, one here. Need three, two see, one, two, three, four. That three frogs."

The next week, Matthew drew a frog picture. When I asked him about it, he said the frog was angry. When I asked him why, he said, "Frog angry. What you think? Some frogs is happy, some is not" (drawing 5, below).

At one point, he picked up a kazoo and started playing the speckled frog song. I got another kazoo and started to hum along with him. I decided to see how Matt would do with repeating after me. I tried a number of different melody patterns, and he was able to replicate whatever I produced. Then he turned the game around, and *I* was instructed to imitate *his* patterns.

Following these musical experiences over the course of three or four weeks, I was awakened one morning by rhythmic tapping on my arm—tap, tap-tap, tap-tap, tap. I asked Matthew what he wanted and he said, "Nothing, Mommy. I making music." Then he got one of his musical toys that plays "Twinkle, Twinkle Little Star" and sang along: "Tinkle little star. How I love you. Where are you? Tinkle tinkle, shining in, in the sky a tinkly tink. Tinkle, tinkle little star. How my love you—where are you?"

4   5

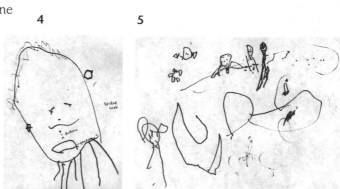

The Artist in You

The Effects of Early Experience on Later Experience

Reflect upon your early experiences with art, music, drama, dance, and craft. Are there any incidents that stick out in your mind?

Here are two incidents, one positive and one negative, described by former students:

Guadalupe's Story

When my parents immigrated to the United States from Mexico, I attended kindergarten at the local public school. I

spoke very little English, but I wanted so much to be a part of what was going on in the classroom! My teacher seemed to sense this, and one day she put me in charge of directing the rhythm band. I was so proud to be the leader. It let me communicate with the other kids without having to rely on words. Now that I am in college, I can see how that experience influenced me. I play the clarinet, and I have joined the marching band.

Jerry's Story

When I was in first grade, we were practicing for the spring musical performance. We were singing a song that I really liked, and I was really getting into the music and singing my heart out. All of a sudden, I realized that the classroom teacher and the regular teacher seemed to be talking about me, and I

overheard one of them say, 'Yes, but they'll sound a lot better if Jerry is absent.' Then they both laughed. I was so humiliated that I stopped singing altogether. I would move my lips to keep from being criticized, but their ridicule hurt me, and I didn't sing again until I was an adult.

Discussion Questions

- How did the arts offer a "universal language" to Guadalupe? Can you think of other examples where the arts communicate without words?
- How would you respond to a colleague like Jerry's teachers? What could you do to tactfully express the opinion that every child has the right to participate?
- What messages did your school experiences give you about participating in aesthetic experiences?

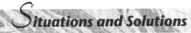

Situations and Solutions

Is It Art?

For each situation described in this section, use the knowledge that you have gained from the chapter to decide whether the activity is an authentic arts experience. Be certain to explain *why* you do or do not consider the activity to qualify as art.

Situation 1

The scene is a kindergarten classroom in late October. The student teacher has distributed a pattern on folded construction paper that looks like Figure 1.8.

Children are instructed to cut along the straight lines without going all the way to the edge of the folded paper, although several of the them fail to do so. Now the teacher demonstrates what the finished product—a "lantern"—should look like by twisting it into a cylindrical shape and stapling edges together. The children are then instructed to cut a long, thin strip of paper to be the handle. A five-year-old who has followed instructions walks by and asks the teacher, "What's this supposed to be again?" What do you think? Is this art?

Situation 2

Paulo has been assigned to begin his sophomore-level field experience by volunteering for at least three hours per week at a school. When he makes arrangements to work at a nearby preschool, the teacher tells him that she would like him to begin

Figure 1.8   Pattern of Art Project

by planning an art and music activity each day. Paulo observes the children to see what they are doing now. Mostly, art is just paper and crayons or paint at the easel, and music is singing along with a record. He decides to add to the materials available during a weekend trip home and gets permission to send a letter to the children's parents requesting donations of "beautiful junk." In this letter, Paulo asks for

Scarves or lengths of fabric—for moving to music, for creating simple puppets, for inventing dramatic play props and costumes (hair, tails, skirts).

Paint stirrers and plastic utensils—for magic wands, to support masks, to use with clay.

Plastic bottles, caps, and lids—for water play, as playing pieces for child-made games, to make puppets and dolls, for graduated sizes as the Three Bears' chairs.

Cardboard boxes—small boxes to create dollhouse furniture, buildings for cities and farms, and puppet heads and bodies; large boxes to create playhouses or a drive-through bank or restaurant; ice cream boxes to make dioramas.

Recycled and special papers—to use in making posters, collages, books, letters, banners, big books, and greeting cards.

Food containers—such as microwave dishes, yogurt containers, pretzel cans—to use for castles, puppets, picture frames.

Wallpaper samples or wallpaper books—to use for collage, textural interest, developing aesthetic judgment.

Cardboard tubes—to use for rolling up pictures to take home, to use in construction and as dramatic play props.

Packing materials—such as shredded paper, styrofoam

shapes—to use for collage, construction, puppet features.

Styrofoam meat trays—to use as picture frames, paint trays, sculpture platforms.

After a good collection of materials has been assembled, Paulo encourages the children to create collages, puppets, pictures, dramatic play props, and presents for one another using the materials. Is this art?

Situation 3

Coreen is an exchange student from England who is attending an American teachers' college during her junior year. When she is out at the schools at Thanksgiving time, she sees turkeys, pumpkins, Pilgrims, and Native Americans everywhere—things that are very surprising to her. One of the classrooms she visits is a kindergarten, and the children are being instructed to trace around their hands, then make the drawing into a turkey. The teacher demonstrates on a piece of paper taped to the board and tells the children to be sure to use brown for the turkey's body and color the "feathers" red, yellow, or orange. This whole idea is new to Coreen, but very familiar to her classmates. She is wondering if it is a good idea and debating about whether or not to use it when she teaches. Is it art?

Situation 4

In a first grade class, the teacher has brought in a variety of pasta. The children are coloring the pasta with food coloring, allowing it to dry, and then using it to make "jewelry." Most children are stringing a few multicolored rigatoni into necklaces. Some are trying to make earrings without much success. One child has made a necklace with a pendant. The teacher encourages the children to wear their necklaces throughout the day, then to take them home. Is it art?

Integrating the Arts

A Garden Center Project in the Kindergarten

Nancy Cecil and Phyllis Lauritzen (1994) offer the following guidelines for projects:

1. Projects can be completely child-initiated, as when children "discover" something of interest, or more teacher-initiated, as when the teacher uses knowledge of children's lives, developmental characteristics, and the community context to suggest a topic or area of study. Even if the teacher initiates the project, children must exercise choice and help to plan.
2. The project should evolve creatively and be negotiated among the participants.
3. Academic skills are integrated into the project by the teacher's awareness of their potential usefulness to the project participants. Such goals as reading to obtain information (a display of related picture books), using visual art to communicate (creating a storefront and advertising), and calculating mathematical problems (making change for a customer) are integrated into the play surrounding the topic.
4. Because the project extends over a period of time, it requires long-range planning, a flexible environment, and the use of a variety of resources.
5. The evaluation of the project is ongoing and is performed cooperatively with the students. The goal is to encourage children's creative problem solving and critical thinking.

The project described in this section has two parts: Sue Ann's original version and her professor's suggestions on how to make what was clearly a good idea even better. As you read Sue Ann's ideas and her professor's commentary, think about the following questions:

1. Does the project meet the criteria that were set forth? What suggestions do you have for making it more effective?
2. How does the project support children's creativity? What can you infer about their growth as artists, actors, writers, dancers, and musicians?

Sue Ann Mack is a student teacher in a public school kindergarten. As spring approaches, she realizes that a garden center is opening up near the school; in fact, the children can take a walking field trip to the center. She asks the children about it, and they have noticed the brightly colored flowers on their way to school. They are very excited about it. So, rather than doing the tired old "spring" theme, Sue Ann decides upon the garden center as her project.

Project Goals

- To provide children with firsthand knowledge about how plants grow.
- To develop children's understandings of basic economic concepts.
- To give children role-playing experiences with the role of grower, clerk, cashier, and customer.
- To encourage a variety of self-expressive behaviors as children describe what goes on in a garden supply

store, interview the owner, and create maps, signs, and letters.

- To develop responsibility as children care for their plants properly.
- To build social skills as children interact with one another in the center and workers at the garden center.

Sue Ann's Introduction

1. Refer to previous unit on butterflies and talk about the stages in metamorphosis.
2. Ask children if they know how vegetables and flowers begin.
3. Invite children to share their experiences with gardens and growing plants (flowers, trees, grass, fruits, vegetables).
4. Read Jeanne Titherington's (1985) *Pumpkin, Pumpkin* and Ruth Kraus's (1945) *The Carrot Seed*.

Professor's Comments: Sue Ann, why not incorporate creative dramatics with your stories? You could invite children to use their bodies to show the growth cycle from seed to plant. Also, try experimenting with some different styles of presentation, such as telling The Turnip *using the flannel board. Children can enact this simple tale as you read it aloud. They will also have good ideas for creating simple costumes for the characters in the story. When I told this story to five-year-olds, for example, they decided on an apron for the mother, a hat for the father, and ears, tails, whiskers (etc.) for the animals in the story. Another idea is to compare two different variants of the story (e.g.,* The Carrot Seed *[Kraus, 1945] and* The Enormous Turnip *[Parkinson, 1986]). We used a Venn diagram to compare and contrast the two. Also, try some newer books about gardens such as* Home Lovely *(Perkins, 1995),* Anno's Magic Seeds *(Anno, 1995), or* It's Pumpkin Time *(Hall, 1994). You may want to create a song chart for Maria Muldaur's (1990) "Garden Song"—it describes all the work and care that go into maintaining a garden, as well as the satisfactions that come from having a garden of your own. At first, you might want to teach the children only the chorus while you sing the verses.*

Sue Ann's Introduction, Continued

- Tell them we will be planting seeds, and ask if they know where we can obtain seeds and plants.
- Discuss a greenhouse and garden center. Talk about who works there.
- Show and name some supplies used at the garden center (trowel, watering can, seed packets, planters).
- Plan the center with the children by asking for suggestions on how we could have a garden center in our room.

As a result of this introduction, the children suggested that they bring whatever they could from home to stock their play center and decided to make some of the props from materials already available in the classroom. Child-made materials included signs with prices on them, paper flowers to decorate the store window, and a sign with the store's name and hours on it. To their materials the teacher added aprons, baskets, a terrarium, potting soil, plant food, live plants, flower pots, garden tools, flower seeds, vegetable seeds, dried flowers, a cash register, a pencil and pad of paper, and plastic fruits and vegetables. She also contacted gardeners and the family members of children who had experience with gardens or growing things.

Professor's Comments: Because the children were so impressed by the rows of flowers, why not capitalize on this response? Bring in works of art that portray flowers in different styles. Included in my collection are poster-sized prints of Georgia O'Keeffe's "Red Poppy," Van Gogh's "Irises," Picasso's "Hand with Flowers," and Monet's "Water Lilies." Other good sources are the public library, art museum catalogs, and art postcards. Gardening books, flower and bulb catalogs, and art books like Georgia O'Keeffe: One Hundred Flowers *(Callaway, 1990) are good resources. I once created a bingo-type game using pictures cut from my bulb and flower catalogs. Soon children were talking about tulips, roses, daffodils, and carnations instead of just flowers.*

Another day, I picked flowers from my garden and bought several others at the grocery store. The children were enthralled by the colors and variety of forms. They made connections with their experiences, like these: "Hey, my grandma has these growing in her yard" (daffodil), "I saw these ones before at my cousin's wedding, but they was pink, not red" (carnation), and "They have these at church sometimes" (lilies). There were so many flower paintings that day at the easel!

Sue Ann's Activities

- Sue Ann encouraged children to bring in items for the store by sending a letter home.
- She modeled the behaviors of people connected with the store during dramatic play.
- She suggested activities involved in maintaining the store and keeping it neat and attractive to the customers.

The Children's Activities

The children took a walking field trip to the garden supply store. The owner gave each child a marigold plant, and they were surprised and delighted. When we came back to the classroom, they suggested that we write an experience story about their trip to the garden center. Several children commented about how really nice the garden center owner had been. The children sent drawings, which were put on display.

Professor's Comments: *Sue Ann, I read an article recently about a Jack and the Beanstalk project. One of the goals was to encourage children to make predictions on a chart about which one would grow. They planted a red jelly bean, a dried kidney bean, a cooked lima bean, and a bean seed. Maybe you could incorporate some of their ideas into your unit.*

Sue Ann's Notes

Sue Ann also made observational notes about the children's interaction at the center. Here are some brief examples of dialogue at the center:

Teacher: Today we are going to practice how we behave when we go into a garden supply store. I need someone to be the cashier, someone to be the clerk, and someone to be the customer. The customer is the person who wants to buy something. The clerk is the person who helps customers find what they want. The cashier is the person who takes the money from the customers when they pay for what they want from the store.

Winter: I'd like to buy this.
Samantha: Pay the cashier, please.

Elyse: Look, Mrs. Mack, I found one of those little papers in my bag.
Teacher: Do you know what it is called?
Elyse: I know that it tells you what you bought.
Teacher: It's called a receipt. It tells what you bought and also how much you paid for your items.

Professor's Comments: *Here is a good opportunity to follow the child's lead. Make receipts part of the center.*

Clinton: How much is this plant?
Elyse: $2.00. All of your stuff is $5.00. Do you have $5.00?
Clinton: Yes.
Elyse: Do you want a bag?
Clinton: No, I'll just carry it.

Professor's Comments: *Once again, follow the child's lead. Bring in some different types of containers—bags, flats, plastic baskets, cardboard boxes. Have the children seriate, classify—which ones would we use for one plant? for six? for a dozen? They can match individual flowerpots to the number of sections in the holders, too. Another idea—encourage them to look at the flower garden diagrams in catalogs and books. Invite them to plan their dream garden using the plants they saw at the garden center. How will they decide how many plants they will need? See if you can use a little area of the schoolyard to actually plant and tend some hardy annuals.*

Individual and Group Projects for Teachers

Exploring the Arts

1. The German philosopher Goethe once said, "One must ask children and birds how cherries and strawberries taste." What did Goethe mean by this statement? Discuss your ideas in your groups.
2. Reread "The Artist in You" in this chapter, then conduct an interview with an artist you know. In what ways did the interviewee's experiences during early childhood exert an influence on his or her later artistic pursuits?
3. If you could instantly acquire extraordinary talent in any of the arts, which would you choose and why? Ask several other people you know the same question, and be prepared to report on your findings to the total group. Which artistic pursuits seem to be most popular?
4. Arrange to speak with any parent who is encouraging a child to take lessons in the arts. Ask the parent questions like these: How did you make the decision to get your child involved in this particular experience? Are you satisfied with what your child is learning? Why or why not? Can you share any examples of what your child has achieved (artwork, photo of dance performance, audiotape of song/music)? What are you hoping these experiences will do for your child?

REFERENCES

Broudy, H. S. (1988). Aesthetics and the curriculum. In W. Pinar (Ed.), *Contemporary curriculum discourses* (pp. 332–342). Scottsdale, AZ: Gorsuch Scarisbrick.

Callaway, N. (1990). *Georgia O'Keeffe: One hundred flowers.* New York: Knopf.

Cambourne, B. (1988). *The whole story: Natural learning and the acquisition of literacy*. Auckland, New Zealand: Ashton/Scholastic.

Caraway, C. (1986). *African designs of the Congo*. New York: International Design Studio.

Carr, M. (1992). Easels and beyond: Everyday arts experiences for 3 to 5 year olds. *PAEYC Newsletter, 17*(3), 5–8.

Cecil, N. L., & Lauritzen, P. (1994). *Literacy and the arts for the integrated classroom: Alternative ways of knowing*. New York: Longman.

Clemens, S. G. (1991). Art in the classroom: Making every day special. *Young Children, 46*(2), 4–11.

Cohen, E. P., & Gainer, R. S. (1995). *Art: Another language for learning* (3rd ed.). Portsmouth, NH: Heinemann.

Consortium of National Arts Education Associations. (1994). *National standards for arts education: Dance music theatre visual arts: What every young American should know and be able to do in the arts*. Reston, VA: Music Educators National Conference.

Davis, J., & Gardner, H. (1992). The cognitive revolution: Consequences for the understanding and education of the child as artist. In B. Reimer and R. A. Smith (Eds.), *The arts, education, and aesthetic knowing* (pp. 92–123). Chicago: University of Chicago Press.

Eagan, R. (1994). *Kid creations*. Carthage, IL: Teaching and Learning Company.

Edwards, C., Gandini, L., & Forman, G. (1993). *The hundred languages of children*. Norwood, NJ: Ablex.

Eisner, E. (1992). Arts can counter school reform's standardizing aims. *ASCD Update, 34*(5), 5.

Geahigan, G. (1992). The arts in education: A historical perspective. In B. Reimer and R. A. Smith (Eds.), *The arts, education, and aesthetic knowing* (pp. 1–19). Chicago: University of Chicago Press.

Goodman, N. (1968). *Languages of art*. Indianapolis: Bobbs-Merrill.

Grilli, S. (1987). *Preschool in the Suzuki spirit*. Tokyo: Harcourt Brace Jovanovich.

Henkes, R. (1989). The child's art expression. *Early Child Development and Care, 47,* 165–176.

Hope, S. (1990). Technique and arts education. *Design for Arts in Education, 91*(6), 2–14.

Isenberg, J. P., & Jalongo, M. R. (1997). *Creative expression and play in early childhood*. Englewood Cliffs, NJ: Merrill/Prentice Hall.

Jalongo, M. R. (1995). Awaken to the artistry of young children! *Dimensions of Early Childhood Education, 23*(4), 8–14.

Keel, J. S. (1972). The roots of aesthetic experience. *Art Education, 24,* 4–7.

Marcuse, H. (1977). *The aesthetic dimension: Toward a critique of Marxist aesthetics*. Boston: Beacon Press.

Ogle, D. (1986). K-W-L: A teaching model that develops active reading of expository text. *The Reading Teacher, 36*(9), 564–570.

Rico, G. (1991). Writer: Personal patterns in chaos. In M. Schwartz (Ed.), *Writer's craft, teacher's art: Teaching what we know* (pp. 3–20). Portsmouth, NH: Boynton/Cook.

Schirrmacher, R. (1988). *Art and creative development for young children*. Albany, NY: Delmar.

Seefeldt, C. (1995). Art—serious work. *Young Children, 50*(3), 39–45.

Sippola, A. E. (1995). K-W-L-S. *The Reading Teacher, 48*(6), 542–543.

Smith, F. (1992). Learning to read: The never ending debate. *Phi Delta Kappan, 73*(6), 432–435, 438–441.

Smith, N. R. (1982). The visual arts in early childhood education: Development and the creation of meaning: In B. Spodek, (Ed.), *Handbook of research in early childhood education* (pp. 87–106). New York: The Free Press.

Smith, R. A. (1992). Toward percipience: A humanities curriculum for arts education. In B. Reimer & R. A. Smith (Eds.), *The arts, education, and aesthetic knowing* (pp. 51–69). Chicago: University of Chicago Press.

Surace, E. (1992). Everyone wants to join the chorus. *Phi Delta Kappan, 73*(8), 608–612.

Wein, C. A. (1995). *Developmentally appropriate practice in real life: Stories of teachers' practical knowledge*. New York: Teachers College Press.

Children's Books and Recordings

Aardema, V. (1977). *Who's in rabbit's house?* New York: Dial.

Anno, M. (1995). *Anno's magic seeds*. New York: Putnam.

Brown, M., & Brown, L. K. (1985). *The bionic bunny show*. New York: Little, Brown.

de Regniers, B. S., Moore, E., White, M. M., & Carr, J. (1988). *Sing a song of popcorn: Every child's book of poems*. New York: Scholastic.

Ernst, L. C. (1983). *Sam Johnson and the blue ribbon quilt*. New York: Mulberry.

Flournoy, V. (1985). *The patchwork quilt*. New York: Dial.

Gibbons, G. (1989). *Lights! Camera! Action! How a movie is made*. New York: HarperCollins.

Guback, G. (1994). *Luka's quilt*. New York: Greenwillow.

Hall, Z. (1994). *It's pumpkin time*. New York: Scholastic.

Johnston, T. (1984). *The quilt story*. New York: Putnam.

Karas, B. G. (1995). *I know an old lady*. New York: Scholastic.

Keats, E. J. (1971). *Over in the meadow*. New York: Four Winds.

Kraus, R. (1945). *The carrot seed*. New York: Harper.

Monet, L. (1986). "Five little speckled frogs." On *Circle time*. Redway, CA: Music for Little People.

Muldaur, M. (1990). Garden song. On *On the sunny side*. Redway, CA: Music for Little People.

Music for Little People. (1994). *Lullaby: A collection*. Redway, CA: Author.

Novak, M. (1995). *Mouse TV*. New York: Orchard.

Parkinson, K. (1986). *The enormous turnip*. New York: Whitman.

Perkins, L. R. (1995). *Home lovely*. New York: Greenwillow.

Sendak, M. (1976). *Maurice Sendak's really Rosie: Starring the Nutshell Kids*. New York: Harper. (Video: Weston Woods.)

Titherington, J. (1985). *Pumpkin, pumpkin*. New York: Greenwillow.

Kaylee wore her yellow cats, yellow cats, yellow cats.

Kaylee wore her yellow cats all day long.

The arts are not pretty bulletin boards. They are not turkeys and bunny rabbits. They are not frivolous entertainment. The arts are our humanity. They are the languages of civilization through which we express our fears, our anxieties, our hungers, our struggles, our hopes. . . . This is why schools that provide students with the means and the encouragement to explore these realms provide a better education. This explains, too, why the arts are a mark of excellence in American schooling.

—Charles Fowler (1994, p. 9)

Contributions of the Arts to Children's Lives

written with Hollis Hall

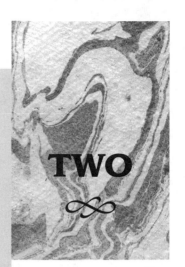

TWO

Chapter Reflections

ॐ How have the arts contributed to your development? How can the arts contribute to a child's overall development?

ॐ How are ideas, experiences, and feelings expressed through the arts?

ॐ As a teacher, how can you adapt arts experiences to meet the needs of every child?

ॐ What role do the arts play in promoting acceptance of diversity and multicultural appreciation?

THE ARTS AND CHILDREN'S LEARNING

*E*arly childhood educators around the globe share a philosophy that puts needs of children first, that looks at children's learning holistically, and that regards the curriculum in an integrated, play-based fashion. For these reasons, we often hear references to being a "child-centered" teacher, to teaching the "whole child," and to the value of a "total" curriculum, one that addresses social, emotional, cognitive, physical, and aesthetic growth. Nothing could be more consistent with this perspective than education in the arts (Jalongo, 1995). By their very nature, the arts are child-centered, holistic, and integrated. For all of these reasons, aesthetic education makes a major contribution to the young child's learning, as this chapter will detail.

The Child Artist at Work

The scene is a spring elementary school concert, and Teresa, a twenty-four-month-old, is in the audience. The family members and teachers look on with pride as the children play songs on their instruments. Some adults are snapping pictures or running videotape equipment. Teresa has a very different response. The toddler is standing on a chair so that she can see, and as soon as her brother participates in playing a lively song, she kicks the sandals off her chubby feet and begins to dance. Her body and sundress skirt sway in response to the music. The final song is about a bird, and Teresa moves her arms and hands expressively, like a bird gliding through the air. She is completely unself-conscious in her response even though many adults in the audience are pointing her out and smiling at her reaction to the tunes she

Young children are less inhibited than adults—just look at these responses when children are asked to act like lions and tigers!

has heard her brother practice at home so often. Teresa has not been taught to dance, she simply allows her feelings to be her guide. This toddler's response illustrates some important assets of early childhood, some characteristic ways in which the typical young child is actually superior to the typical adult.

First, as discussed in Chapter 1, young children are particularly sensitive to the sensory and aesthetic qualities of objects and experiences—objects and experiences that they are often encountering for the first time in their lives. Second, young children are less inhibited in their responses than most older individuals. Most adults would be far too embarrassed to dance, even if they felt like it, when no one else in the room was dancing. Third, the very young have active imaginations and unique ways of expressing the mental images their minds produce. Usually it is only the most creative of adults who feel confident with self-expression; most adults keep their flights of fancy to themselves. Fourth, the young child's responses are appealing and engaging even before they are exposed to formal training. A young child like Teresa responds intuitively to her experience; she moves physically to what moves her emotionally.

Although Teresa's response is charming and uninhibited, many adults feel uncertain about what good it might be doing Teresa to dance, both now and in the future. Adults often wonder, "What good is it?" One way of answering that question is to ask older students who have had their first opportunity to pursue their interest in dance about how dance has contributed to their lives, something that Susan Stinson (1992) did in a study of North Carolina high school students. These were some of the students' explanations of what they learned from and through dance:

Afrika: It gives you a whole 'nother way of mind, a whole 'nother way of thinking.
Damien: [Dance is] discipline, it's not just go crazy.
Dionne: It kind of helps in everything 'cause I learn how to concentrate and focus—even like—focusing more in class.
Kristen (referring to her dance teacher): She's teaching us how to be ourselves, how to . . . give everything you've got, instead of keeping it all within yourself. . . how to work with others . . . and have patience and understanding, cooperation—things you can't learn in world history.
K.G.: Just to be able to be there and to be able to do the work together, as a group, and to be able to produce something from nothing, is, you know, really a lot of fun . . .
Kristen: In geometry, who cares what the guy next to you is doing? . . . But in dance, you want to make sure what they're doing is good—help them out, if you can.
Mercedes: When you start to know everybody, you're in an atmosphere where you feel safe—and secure. It's kind of like . . . when you have a security blanket when you're little. . . . After a couple of years the blanket is part of you. And dance—that's what it was like. You get to feel like part of each other. So you feel like, when you dance in front of them, it's like dancing in front of your grandma or something. (Stinson, 1992, pp. 23, 24)

As these students recognize, the arts are not simply a pleasant diversion or lighthearted fun. Rather, aesthetic education experiences should be taken seriously because they are authentic learning opportunities that make enduring contributions to emotional, social, cognitive, and physical abilities. These contributions of the arts are summarized in Figure 2.1.

Figure 2.1   **How the Arts Contribute to Children's Development**

Emotional—providing pleasure, building self-confidence, and developing pride in ethnic and cultural heritage.

Perceptual—developing sensory awareness—visual, auditory, tactile, kinesthetic.

Psychomotor—mastering gross and fine motor skills, such as learning to move the body in interpretive ways or using a paintbrush.

Vocal—increasing vocal range and flexibility; improving communication skills.

Social—encouraging participation, sharing, and cooperation.

Cultural—becoming familiar with the art of various regions, ethnic groups, and eras.

Cognitive—contributing to knowledge, understanding, problem solving, analysis, and judgment.

Aesthetic—developing "sensitivity for the feelings, impressions, and images" (McDonald & Simons, 1989, p. 2) that the arts convey and building appreciation of the arts.

Source: Adapted from McDonald, D. & Simons, G. (1989). *Musical growth and development: Birth through six.* New York: Schirmer/Macmillan.

Theory into Practice

The Symbolic Function of the Arts

When people speak of the arts, they generally associate them with feeling rather than thinking. Moreover, the general public tends to view the arts as "mindless, nonacademic fare, more related to the hand than the head" and to "associate the arts with entertainment and play, academic subjects with the serious business of life and work" (Fowler, 1988, p. 5).

Increasingly, however, arts experts are arguing that the arts are grounded as much in thought as they are in emotion. As Parsons (1992) points out, art is based upon a very disciplined and attentive kind of perception. It is a different way of seeing and understanding from the detailed observations conducted in a scientific experiment because in scientific observations you tend to pay attention to surface qualities and focus on practical purposes (Smith, 1989). If a child is maintaining an observational log on a classroom pet, the focus is on keeping an accurate record of the animal's observable behavior. As Herbert Read (quoted in Keel, 1972), a respected British aesthetician and critic, observed, "Art is the representation, science the explanation—of the same reality." As teachers of the arts, we want to encourage children to link seeing with feeling, to read the medium, and to interpret the meaning of the symbols represented. So, as children examine the intricate weaving of a tapestry, we would encourage them to verbalize their responses to it, to discuss who might have made it and how it might have been made, and to infer reasons why the work of art was created in the first place. Very young children might come away with the feeling that the horse "looks big" or that the man looks "proud of himself." They might assume that the tapestry was made by machine and infer that it was "made a long time ago" to "be pretty" and "put up on the wall." Their teacher asks questions that urge them to think more deeply about what they have seen, such as "Brian, you think that this might be old. What did you see that helped you to decide about whether it is old or new?" As they talk more, the children might learn that the tapestries were used to insulate the walls of the drafty castles as well as to beautify. Tapestries were created on a loom, a very simple wooden machine operated by hand, and the pictures were made by weaving thread or yarn into patterns that resulted in pictures. To further develop children's interpretation of these symbols, the teacher might have a variety of art books on display from the library that show other tapestries, old and new. As children attempt to do some simple weaving of their own back in the classroom, their responses would deepen into appreciation for this intricate art form when they get a sense of how much work is involved. Following this experience, the large tapestry with the detailed picture is all the more impressive to the children who have been studying it.

For the young child, understanding that one object can represent something else is a remarkable discovery. A significant breakthrough occurs the first time a child "reads" a scribble saying, "It says . . . ," or names a scribble with "It's a. . . ." After many experiences in the arts and aesthetics, children come to recognize that symbols can express meaning that is metaphorical rather than literal; it is possible to speak of "sad music" or a "happy story" even though a song or a drawing cannot possess these emotions in the objective, literal sense (Davis & Gardner, 1992). As children mature, they further realize that "not only can symbols function alone, they can also be used in concert with other symbols to construct a more intricate web or system of symbols. From such spidery webs are spun the products of symbolic functioning: the drawings, the songs, the poems, the mathematical proofs, and the rituals which shape and define human culture(s)—the aesthetic form that humans strive to impose on experience" (Davis & Gardner, 1992, pp. 101–102). It is this new theoretical emphasis on the cognitive, symbolic aspect of the arts that has revolutionized modern conceptualizations of what art is and what artists do. Today, the artist is not a person who relies purely on inspiration. Rather, the artist in today's society is regarded as a meaning maker who knows how to communicate through the multiple symbol systems of the arts (Davis & Gardner, 1992).

THE ARTS AND YOUNG CHILDREN'S DEVELOPMENT

*B*ecause young children bring imaginative and creative assets to the arts, early childhood is the ideal time to expand their abilities. As with other areas of the curriculum, the early years are the time when children are forming dispositions, or "habits of mind," that will serve them throughout their lives (Katz, 1988). Just as young children's reading instruction needs to originate with the enjoyment of literature, their initial experiences with aesthetic education should emphasize enjoyment of the arts. As teachers, we need to build upon children's delight in what they see, hear, taste, smell, and feel; we need to capitalize upon their enjoyment of things as new, fresh, and vivid (Smith, 1992). Have you ever watched a young child's delight in the sensory experiences that adults take for granted? If you look, you can observe a child twirling among the brightly colored fall leaves as they drift down in an autumn breeze or see a child dash outdoors to catch big, fluffy snowflakes on his tongue or express pure pleasure and excitement while splashing through mud puddles after a spring rain. The next step, of course, is expanding those naive sensibilities into aesthetic and artistic ones. Through the arts and aesthetics, children develop understandings and insights that have far-reaching implications for their overall development (Eisner, 1991, 1992a, 1992b; Grumet, 1988; Smith, 1992).

1. *In the arts, meaning is communicated through medium, form, and content.* When young children learn the African song "There Come Our Mothers" (Ladysmith Black Mambazo, 1994), they learn about medium, form, and content. Children realize how the medium of musical notes and words can be used to create melody and lyrics. Additionally, they notice that the song has a form—repetitive verses that the children are aware of after they have listened to the song, participated in singing it, moved to its rhythm, or seen the words printed on paper in two languages. Children also recognize that the song has content—its subject matter is children greeting their mothers as they return home from shopping bearing presents and special foods. All three of these elements—medium, form, and content--combine to enable children to interpret the song's meaning. As children participate in all of these activities surrounding the song, they are gaining important insights about how medium, form, and content interrelate to make meaning through the arts.

2. *In the arts, details are important.* Think about three posters advertising an upcoming event on campus. The first was hastily scribbled onto a piece of paper, the second copied graphics and lettering from computer software, and the third was an original silkscreen design carefully crafted by a student. Objectively speaking, all posters contain exactly the same information—what the event is, who it is for, when and where it will be held. What makes two of these posters an ordinary sign, and what makes the other one a work of art? The computer-generated sign was a cut-and-paste operation. It isn't art. The hastily scribbled sign is not a copy, but it has no craftsmanship. It isn't art. *How* the poster has been created and crafted makes all the difference. An important learning that children acquire through arts experiences is that craftsmanship matters. Craftsmanship is more than being talented or competent. A person can be talented and skilled, yet fail to demonstrate those abilities. The word "craftsman" implies not only a high level of skill, but also attention to even the tiniest detail as well as a sense of pride in and identification with work. Craftsmanship is the opposite of shoddy work—products that are thrown together, flawed in many ways, and dismissed by the person who produced them as insignificant. Reimer (1992) explains it this way: "Craftsmanship includes skill but transcends it; craft is the ability to think in terms of meaningful material—material which has taken on and is taking on meaning as a function of its created structure. To know how to create art is to know how to think in this mode. . . . one's ability to 'think art' is tied directly to one's ability to control the material within which one is thinking" (p. 41).

To illustrate how the arts teach craftsmanship, look at Figure 2.2. Divonna Mohr Stebbick, a junior-level early childhood education major, did a special art project with Chelsea, a first grader. When Divonna interviewed the seven-year-old, she asked her what she would like to create, and Chelsea talked about her interest in horses. Because owning a real horse was not a possibility, Chelsea decided that she would like to make a stuffed toy of a horse. She designed the pattern, selected all the materials, and did all of the construction. The only part Chelsea needed help with was using the sewing machine to stitch along the outline she had drawn on the fabric. You can sense Chelsea's sense of accomplishment as she poses with the finished product and proudly holds it before her. She has paid attention to details and craftsmanship. Just look at how she has used contrasting fabric to create a saddle, put a bow in her horse's mane like those she has seen at the fair, created ribbon reins, given her horse a flowing tail, and used strong thread to create hooves. As a result, Chelsea feels a sense of completeness and satisfaction in the results of her object-making activity.

3. *In the arts, individuality and imagination are celebrated.* Every year, UNICEF produces a wall calendar of art by children from all over the world. Often the drawings are centered on a particular theme, like families. When adults or other children examine these drawings, the immediate impression is that there are similarities in theme, yes, but that the ways of responding are original, individual, and influ-

Figure 2.2 **Chelsea's Stuffed Toy Horse**

enced by the physical and social environment in which the artist lives. If we look at children's paintings and drawings from around the globe, we can see these influences on the child artist. Because the arts celebrate individuality, the arts teach children to appreciate human diversity.

4. *In the arts, problems have multiple solutions.* In the real world, right and wrong answers are seldom as clear-cut as they are in the classroom. More often than not, there are several possible options, each with its particular set of advantages and disadvantages. When a child goes to the art center with the intention of creating a puppet, there are many choices and possibilities, and few of them are wrong, strictly speaking, yet some of them are better than others. Craig, a third grader, participated in a puppetry workshop sponsored by the public library. During that experience, Craig became fascinated by the Bunraku puppets he had seen demonstrated. Part of the appeal of these puppets was the challenge involved. Unlike the hand puppets with which Craig was more familiar, the Bunraku puppet is very large and dramatic, and considerable skill and coordination are required to operate it. It also has the flowing robes and almost ethereal quality that Craig wanted to capture for his performance of *The Little Old Lady Who Was Not Afraid of Anything* (Williams, 1986), a ghost story. But now, there is a creative problem to solve. The Bunraku puppets Craig saw demonstrated used an empty plastic milk jug for the head, but Craig wants his puppet to have a round head. He does some exploring in books and sees other possibilities for the head—a large styrofoam ball, a balloon covered with papier-mâché (it is allowed to dry, then the balloon is popped), and soft sculpture heads made from polyester fiberfill with a nylon stocking stretched over it. Then he has a brainstorm. He could use the plastic pumpkin bucket he got for Halloween last year as the head if he can think of a way to secure the dowel rod inside. After much experimenting, he decides to stuff the bucket with polyester fiberfill and use a cardboard tube for the puppet's neck. Figure 2.3 is a sketch of the Bunraku puppet that Craig used to dramatize *The Little Old Lady Who Was Not Afraid of Anything.* Projects like Craig's puppet help to balance a school curriculum where "one right answer" type of tasks often dominate. The arts help children to solve problems and to make good choices when the answers are not obvious. Both of these abilities are important throughout life.

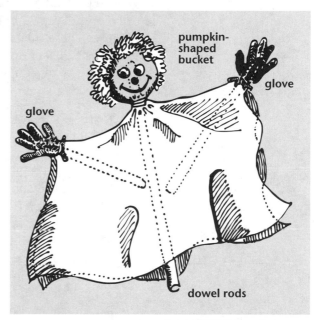

Figure 2.3 **Craig's Bunraku Puppet**

5. *In the arts, judgment is a part of responding to works of art.* Artists often refer to whether or not something "works" as a shorthand way of judging the overall quality of a film, a scene from a play, or a musical composition. What they are really saying is that all of their skill, knowledge, and experience have been used to create a set of internalized criteria. These standards enable artists to make a value judgment about the work of art under scrutiny. Young children are practicing this important skill when they decide which of the stories they have written is the best and select one to be made into a book. Look, for example, at Elizabeth's choice of material for her culminating activity in second grade—producing a hardcover book. In the book you see that Elizabeth has decided to sing the praises of her beloved dog, Brittany.

My dog tried to fly. It was very very funny.

II.

Everyone—Elizabeth, her peers, and her teachers—thinks that this is a good book. The ability to make appraisals of something's relative value and quality is considered to be a high-level thinking skill, one that is an important aspect of virtually all human endeavors. Ability in holistic evaluation is developed through arts experiences and aesthetic education.

6. *Creative processes and products in the arts engage us in dialogue and social interaction.* As Cortines (1994) points out, the arts are fundamentally social: "Remember that line that used to appear on our own report cards— 'Works and plays well with others'? We rarely see that judgment explicitly stated in student evaluations today. But that is precisely the skill, the talent, the state of mind . . . taught most effectively in and through the arts, through group painting, sculpture, and collage projects; team productions in dance, theater, and film; class trips to studios, performance halls, and museums" (p. 10). Melanie Carr (1992), who works with the Carnegie Museum of Art, recommends teaching children about texture by creating a texture board— a piece of heavy cardboard with many different materials affixed such as small pieces of yarn, fabric scraps, straws, pine needles, tree bark, flower petals, a birthday candle, a rubber band, a paper clip, buttons, stickers, aluminum foil, burlap, nylon net, paper of various sizes, textures, and colors, and so forth. Then the items on the board can be discussed using questions that focus on texture, color, and line:

- **Texture:** Can you find something that feels sharp and prickly? Something that is soft and fuzzy? smooth and slippery? Which one do you like to touch the best? Why?
- **Color:** Can you find something that has blue on it? What different blues are there? Name another color that you see. Can you find one of the colors you are wearing on the board?
- **Line:** Can you find something with a straight line? with curvy lines? How about a jagged line? Is there anything with lots of little lines?
- **Shape:** Do you see anything that is round? How about a large shape? a small one? Are there any shapes that seem to go together? Can you find any shapes in the room that are on the board too?
- **Arrangement:** Choose several items from the board and arrange them on this small piece of cardboard. Move the items around until you like the way they look. How did you decide what to put together? How did you decide where to place things on the board? Let's have someone else try.

One teacher who read about this idea invited the children to make a texture house with a large cardboard box that was big enough for preschoolers to crawl inside. The children spent several days attaching fabric samples and scraps to the outside walls of the house with glue and staples. As they collaborated on the project, there was much excitement and social interaction. The completed house was used for further discussions about texture and as a special place to do quiet activities. In this way, the children's investigations into textures promoted dialogue and social interaction.

7. *Artworks share and preserve what a social group values most.* One important learning that takes place in an early childhood classroom is respecting other people's work. Most teachers have rules governing when it is acceptable to knock down someone's block tower or squash a classmate's clay creation back into a ball. Usually, those rules emphasize getting the person who made the work to give his or her permission for it to be destroyed. When you visit classrooms, you will often see signs posted on work that children want to keep, such as a representation of an ice-breaking machine that a group of preschoolers designed from blocks (Figure 2.4). After children have invested much time and effort in creating a representation of their ideas and experiences, the sensitive teacher will take the time to explain about the need to respect others' work. Often, they will assist the children in posting signs that read, "Please do not touch," or, "Do not disturb," or, "Mattie, Jane, Tomas, and Kelli are still working on this." These are early understandings about classmates' works of art. All of this is a precursor to understanding that works of art are so special that society carefully displays, maintains, and restores pieces of artwork. After children have learned to become appreciative members of the audience when their classmates are performing, they are more likely to understand why the performing arts are so valued that we create special places in which they can be shared—auditoriums, concert halls, outdoor amphitheaters.

What the children are learning in and through arts activities is not always obvious to the uninitiated because most of what the children are doing looks like play. But the learning is there nevertheless if you look carefully and know what to look for. To illustrate, imagine the following activity in a preschool classroom. The teacher is going to involve the children in making their own sidewalk chalk using the recipe in Figure 2.5. Because the dust from the plaster of paris should not be breathed in, the teacher uses a mask to cover her face when pouring it into the bowl and cautions the children to step back so they will not breathe in the dust. She uses this demonstration as a safety lesson about working in dusty conditions. Some of the children have seen adults wearing a mask like the teacher's when they are using a sander or working on a construction site. The children assist in the remaining steps of making the chalk, and, after it has dried, they pull off the cardboard covering and take it out to the playground to test it. Some three-, four-, and five-year-olds use sidewalk chalk to create huge scribbles; others create shapes and designs; still others make drawings. Carlos, a three-year-old, is making "a circle bigger than me." When he is finished, he stands in the center of the circle, then lies down to

Figure 2.4 **An "Ice-breaker" Constructed from Blocks**

Figure 2.5 **Sidewalk Chalk Recipe**

1 part water	cloth or face mask
2 parts plaster of paris	mixing bowl
powdered tempera paint	spoon
small paper tubes, plastic wrap, rubber bands	

1. Cover the bottom of each paper tube with plastic, and secure with a rubber band.
2. Mix powered tempera paint in the water until a bright color is reached.
3. Pour water into bowl.
4. Put on face mask.
5. Gently pour plaster on top of water and let sit until plaster settles to the bottom.
6. Stir mixture with spoon or hands until it forms a creamy mixture.
7. Pour into paper roll forms.
8. Let the mixture dry until hard—at least one hour.
9. Peel off the paper form, and use the chalk.

make sure he fits inside, then writes the first letter of his name next to it, admires it for a moment, then calls to his teacher, "Mrs. D., look at mine!" Meanwhile, four-year-old Rhiannon, who is in a wheelchair, has the idea of "making a running line." She leans out of her chair and holds the chalk down at her side to touch the asphalt as she goes around the outer edge of the playground. After surveying the result, she gets the idea that she could do the same thing for every color of chalk and make "a rainbow." When it is complete, she invites other children to go around the rainbow with her, and they happily oblige, singing the names of the colors as they follow each line. Five-year-old Loretta is using her sidewalk chalk to outline "a big dinosaur—a stegosaurus. It says in the book I have at home that we don't know what color they were because we never saw their skin, but I'm gonna use green and brown and purple together."

After exploring the medium of chalk, the children's teacher has planned some special experiences in the classroom. They will also have a visit from the high school art teacher who will be demonstrating how he uses chalk to create what he is most noted for—pictures of the flowers he has picked from his garden and arranged with other objects. Several of his works have been on display at the local bank, and a few children recognize them. As he talks with the children, the professional artist demonstrates such techniques as using the side of the chalk for making broad marks, gently rubbing the chalk with a tissue to soften the lines, and dipping the chalk in water to make the colors more intense. Now the children are really excited about trying some of these techniques themselves. The teacher has provided all of the materials and encourages them to choose their own subject matter, but to be sure to use the techniques that they have learned. Note that from this art activity, children are

- exploring multiple uses of a medium.
- meeting new challenges and working at their own paces and levels.
- using their imaginations and taking intellectual risks.
- developing a sense of form, content, and style.
- engaging in dialogue with others about creative processes and works.
- exploring the ways that artistic objects are used to represent other objects, experiences, and feelings.
- building skills in self-evaluation and in responding to aesthetic objects.

Clearly, from the discussion thus far, children do learn something of value from the arts. As you imagine these preschoolers at work, you can see that the arts involve the mind as well as the emotions, the head as well as the hand (Fowler, 1994). Increasingly, experts in the field of aesthetic education are emphasizing that "aesthetic knowing" is a special type of understanding that enables children to use and interpret symbols in a different way.

AREAS OF THE ARTS

$\mathscr{A}$rts expert Harry S. Broudy (1988) says the arts are all about connections: "Briefly, this relation can be considered in three forms: The relation of images to language, to thought, and to feeling" (p. 335). Where young children are concerned, these connections may be conceptualized as three broad, interrelated areas. **Art and craft** include all works of the visual arts such as picture making (drawing, painting) and object forming (modeling with clay, constructing from paper, wood, fabric, etc.). **Music and movement** include listening to music, singing, and making music, as well as responding to music with the body through creative dance. **Story and enactment** include puppetry, story writing, creative dramatics, and dramatic play.

Art and Craft

Go to an arts and crafts show, and you will see hundreds of patterns purchased, cut out, and assembled by adults. Often there is more evidence of following directions than of originality! This is one reason why most artists feel that even though children's art work is not technically superior to that of an adult, it is often creatively superior. Think for a moment of all the things that you created as a young child. Maybe you made a puppet, a pinwheel, a greeting card, or a picture using string dipped in paint. Maybe you made a clay pot, a crayon etching, or a doll bed from a shoe box.

During the early childhood years children engage in a variety of visual arts activities. Some of these activities result in one-dimensional forms such as paintings, drawings, murals, and prints. Other activities, such as constructing puppets, making dioramas, using papier-mâché, or modeling clay, result in three-dimensional forms. Some objects that children construct have moving parts, while others remain stationary. In virtually every early childhood classroom we can observe children forming objects from modeling clay or dough, wood scraps and white glue, construction paper and paste, and so forth. Why are these activities so much a part of a developmentally appropriate early childhood curriculum? Is it simply because we are trying to keep children occupied? Actually, picture-making and object-forming activities are the primary means that young children use to reveal what they see, feel, and understand (Baker, 1990). Thus arts and crafts have a clear symbolic function. In many ways picture making and object forming can be thought of as a language in the broad sense of that word—as a means of communication. Children can usually tell a story through pictures before they tell a story using words. They can describe their processes as they form objects ("I'm rolling the clay out like a pizza") as well as their products ("See, this is our camper that I made out of wood").

Many teachers are constantly on the lookout for arts and crafts ideas for children to do. After they locate these ideas, teachers often restrict children to some very specific, predetermined outcome, such as making half a walnut shell into a turtle. Yet if children are given the freedom to create their own forms, their work is far more interesting. How much better it would be to provide children with an assortment of nutshells and let them form what *they* see in the shapes! Whenever children are robbed of ownership of their own work and forced to follow an adult's predetermined agenda, the goals of arts and crafts are lost in the process. True, children may learn to "stay in the lines" when they color or follow directions during these "crafts" projects, but what else do they learn? Most arts experts in early childhood feel that children who are given predetermined crafts projects to follow are getting one message loud and clear—"Your art and crafts ideas aren't good enough. Follow this instead. The things you can buy, trace, or copy are always better than the things you can make." After many years of such messages, creativity begins to diminish. When Pablo Picasso was asked why his work continued to improve as he got older, he replied, "It has taken me a lifetime to draw as a

child." By this he meant that children's art and drawings have a freshness and originality that is frequently lost as they mature. As an example, look at the drawings above. If you are like most adults, you will identify the work that has been done by first graders as being the "best" because it is immediately recognizable and uses many of the conventions of cartooning that we see in American culture. But the stylized cartoon is not the best from an artist's point of view because it is less original.

Any activity that claims to be art or crafts for young children should give them a chance to be themselves and to express themselves. In all of these ways, authentic art and crafts activities contribute to development during the early childhood school years.

Music and Movement

From the earliest days of life, young children respond to music through bodily movement. Even newborn infants, for example, become more active when lively music is played and calmer when soft music with a slower tempo—such as a lullaby—is played (Wilcox, 1994). As the child matures, music and movement continue to be nearly inseparable. Look in on any high-quality program from toddler through the primary grades, and you will see children chanting, singing, clapping, swinging, tapping, marching, skipping, doing simple dances—all in response to music. For the very young, dance "begins with an awareness of the movement of the body and its creative potential. At this level, students become engaged in body awareness and movement exploration that promote a recognition and appreciation of self and others" (Consortium of National Arts Education Associations, 1994, p. 23).

How do music and dance for young children differ from the experiences provided for older children and adults? Dance for the very young is often referred to as creative movement because a young child's physical responses to music are more spontaneous and free-form than the kinds of dance typically performed by trained adults. Similarly, where music is concerned, there is less emphasis on performing music and more on simply enjoying it (Jalongo, 1996). You should not become concerned if young children sing off-key or have difficulty clapping in time to the beat of the music. It is more important that they express their enjoyment and build confidence in their ability to participate. Too often, in both music and movement, young children are pushed to attain higher levels of performance skill at the expense of their enjoyment in the arts activity. They may be enrolled in dance classes or private music lessons in an attempt to accelerate their performance skills. Children may have a teacher who lacks any understanding of early childhood and tries to push the child to perfection. But that drill can kill a child's love of music and dance, convincing her or him to cease that pursuit at the earliest possible opportunity. Over and over again, when famous musicians and dancers are asked to identify what influenced them to become artists, they cite relaxed, pleasurable participation in music and movement activities, encouragement by enthusiastic adults, and opportunities to pursue their interests during the early childhood years.

Both music and movement are unique ways of communicating through symbols. Movement depends upon the ability to create thought about motion and to communicate that thought through body movement (Morningstar, 1986). The ultimate goal of early childhood dance activities is for children to express inner thoughts, ideas, and feelings through their bodies. When children engage in movement, they coordinate thought, feeling, and action. A young child engaged in a creative dance activity does not move in the wrong way or take a wrong step (Stinson, 1990). However, haphazard jumping and swaying of young children is not creative dancing. Children need to be guided in the essence of dance—expressing emotion through movement and gesture. Before young children begin to move, you need to get them focused on the feelings and ideas that they want to express through their dance. You can accomplish this purpose by suggesting a theme, such as looking outdoors on a snowy day and inviting children to first think about how snowflakes move on a day that is calm versus one that is blustery. Another way to focus on the expression of thoughts and emotions is to listen to a piece of music first, then create a dance to go with it. For older children, creative dance can be approached as an interesting puzzle to be solved. One dance expert described how she posed an interesting dance challenge to her elementary school students (Williams, 1992). They were told to work with a partner and create a dance that involved starting apart, traveling to meet, moving in contact, and then parting again. After giving this assignment, she observed and listened as children worked on this assignment. Two boys worked at the task beyond the practice time allocated in class, determined to create something that would appear smooth and graceful. Williams says that dance enables children to function as problem solvers who meet interesting challenges through movement until they arrive at an understanding of dance composition.

> They discover through exploration, the body's capabilities in releasing and controlling energy, in traveling through space, in forming static and moving shapes, and in cooperating and synchronizing with other children and with outside factors such as rhythmic patterns, words, or musical accompaniment, in

order to achieve an aesthetically satisfying resolution. . . . As children become more mature, the phrases of the sequence acquire more dancelike qualities arising from a clear point of departure, proceeding and arriving at a point of completion with the children showing understanding of rhythmic flow and design, texture and balance, all principles of artistic form that characterize good dance composition. (Williams, 1992, p. 114)

Of course, expert teachers connect music and movement with a wide variety of developmental skills. In terms of social development, when children participate in movement or creative dance, they need to adjust to the group as they lead, follow, and interact with one another. As children participate in music activities, they learn the importance of sharing. Waiting for turns and cooperating with others may be developed through singing games and playing instruments. Teaching songs that educate about numbers, letters, and colors enhances children's concept development, memory/sequencing skills, listening comprehension, and vocabulary development (Feierabend, 1990). The bodily/kinesthetic activities associated with music and movement meet the young child's need for activity and thereby enhance his or her motor skills. When children learn an action song, they are linking music and movement to enactment. If the words of the song are on a chart or in a book, then music and movement have been connected to the symbol system of written and oral language as well. These music and movement activities contribute to the young child's cognitive, emotional, physical, and social growth.

All areas of children's development—physical, social, emotional, and cognitive—are supported through arts experiences.

Story and Enactment

How do story and enactment support the child's aesthetic education and artistic development? Story and enactment use the symbol system of words (written and spoken) and gesture to communicate ideas and feelings. From the earliest days of life, babies discover that language has patterns and rhythm. As infants mature and can sit on an adult's lap or knee, they learn action rhymes with accompanying actions like pattycake. As toddlers, they sit with loving adults and look at simple "point and say" books or simple stories about familiar events. Later, as preschoolers, they become involved in folktales and picture story books and use those stories in their play. They pore over the pictures and recognize the work of favorite illustrators. And finally, as first and second graders, they begin to see that they too can be users of language—readers, writers, storytellers, playwrights.

Enactment is the natural companion for story because it is based on play and make-believe. What is drama like for the very young? Mostly, it is like their spontaneous, free play. Drama for young children should not cause you to think of scripts, stages, and theatrical performances. Rather, it should be grounded in children's play and the inspiration that props provide. Take, for example, a teacher of three-year-olds who wanted children to enact the book by Eric Hill (1987) *Spot*

Goes to the Farm. She took a stuffed toy of Spot, and the children helped her to gather the plastic animals that Spot saw on his visit. Then she demonstrated how to tell the story with a stuffed dog visiting each animal. Several of the three-year-olds were delighted by this type of enactment. They played with the stuffed dog and the other toys repeatedly while saying parts of the story that they remembered. As children mature into the later preschool years, drama remains "ad-lib" rather than memorized, rehearsed, and performed for large audiences. A more developmentally appropriate choice is for teachers to begin with some simple props like cardboard bricks, real straw, and real sticks and then invite the children to enact a very familiar story like "The Three Little Pigs" in their own words. As this example illustrates, in early childhood, there is a strong connection between play and dramatization. Of course, puppetry is another way to get children involved in drama. When children invent their own puppets, they are combining the symbol system of the visual arts with the symbol systems of language and gesture. Note that in all of these forms of drama, the emphasis is on playing the role and deriving pleasure from taking on a different persona. If a teacher has to "wait in the wings" and whisper lines to children who are struck by stage fright, then it is no longer *children's* drama, and children's feelings are being disrespected in the push to perform. This brief introduction to the arts in early childhood provides a rationale for including the arts as part of a basic, developmentally appropriate curriculum for the very young.

THE ARTS FOR EVERY CHILD

*W*hen we examine the role of the arts in education, we also uncover some of the aspects of American society that make it inhospitable to the arts. Five key issues are recognizing the artistry of children, counteracting stereotypes about the arts and artists, providing access to all children, meeting special needs, and celebrating human diversity.

Recognizing the Artistry in Children

When Ezra Jack Keats, the renowned children's book author and illustrator, was a boy, he drew a picture on his mother's tablecloth. But Mrs. Keats didn't punish the preschooler. Rather, she treasured the cloth and used it daily. Another children's book author/illustrator, Tomie de Paola (1989), describes his discouraging school experiences in his picture book *The Art Lesson*. Tomie was instructed to use just one sheet of paper, to be careful not to break the points on the school crayons, and to copy the art teacher's drawing. In every imaginable way, his school experience contradicted what he knew and admired about artists. Had it not been for the support of his family, we might have been deprived of the most popular children's book author/illustrator in the United States. Ezra Jack Keats and Tomie de Paola are famous illustrators and authors, but artistic expression is not the exclusive property of celebrated individuals. In fact, effective teachers of young children know that there is artistry in every child.

Lynn is a good example. At age five, he used a small screwdriver to disassemble the turn signals on the family car. By sixth grade, he was helping out at an electronics repair shop, and when the family got a new television set, Lynn took it apart to see how it worked. His father did not get angry, he simply said, "That thing better be put back together and working when I get home." It was. As an adult, Lynn became the head videotape engineer for a major television network.

It is only recently that we have democratized creativity to include respect for "ordinary creativity," the creative efforts of individuals who are not famous but devise clever solutions to everyday problems, who are highly imaginative and have many ideas, and who are more open to experience and therefore more willing to take risks (Ripple, 1989). In early childhood, we find the origins of both ordinary and extraordinary creativity. The apparently small things that teachers do have enduring consequences. Take, as an example, the child's musical development. Research suggests that both the vocal range and musical preferences are well formed by about age seven (Boyd, 1989). What, then, are the consequences of arts deprivation during early childhood? At the very least, it means wasted human potential and diminished sensibilities. With regard to musical experiences, Feierabend (1990) summarizes the research in this way: "In the upper grades, a teacher can teach more music literature or present more information about music, but in kindergarten the teacher can change the children's music intelligence for life" (p. 17).

Furthermore, we can imagine how the potential of children who have become artistic adults might have been affected by negative reactions to their early efforts. Yet every day, all over America, children are being discouraged from pursuing their unique forms of artistry. It might be in fairly subtle ways, like the teacher who has children copy a letter from the board rather than drawing and using invented spelling. It might be in very destructive ways, such as adults who publicly criticize students who "dare to be different." As you work with young children, remember that it is important to respect the child's unique forms of artistry.

Resisting Stereotypes about the Arts and Artists

When adults think about the arts, they frequently confront many stereotypes. If you are a student on a college campus and an eccentric-looking student walks by, it would not be unusual to remark, "Hmmm. Let me guess—art major." Here, the stereotype of the artist as eccentric is at play. But this sort of remark fails to see that attitude, not appearance, is the hallmark of the artist. There is also a tendency to associate the arts with highbrow activities such as sipping champagne at a New York gallery or a gala evening at the opera. Here, the stereotype is that enjoyment of the arts is a privilege reserved for the cultured, refined, and wealthy. Yet this viewpoint disregards the artistry in carpentry, ceramics, or computer science. Even more damaging and pervasive than either of these stereotypes is the one that is applied to children's behavior. Mainly, it falls into the realm of "childism"—the belief that children's ideas and feelings are somehow inferior to those of adults. A group of six-year-olds will draw pictures, and the teacher will single one out saying, "Look, this one is really good," meaning that it is a good copy of a popular cartoon character. Yet, as we have seen, this imitation has very little to do with creativity and even less to do with art.

Equity and Access to the Arts

Consider, for a moment, all of the young children who have never attended a live musical performance, touched a piece of sculpture, or seen a real oil painting. For some children, particularly rural children, it may be a question of access—there are simply very few places where they can go to do these things. Yet that same child may be very rich in experiences with folk art and craft, whereas a city child may be deprived of the experience to see a beautiful handmade quilt, touch a wood carving, or see a folk instrument built and played. Clearly, there are inequities in access to the arts.

Proximity alone still does not guarantee access. Children need interested adults to share their enthusiasm for art with them. Many children are surrounded by works of art in museums, lavishly appointed buildings, or public parks, yet remain deprived of the opportunity to share those aesthetic objects with an interested adult or to have their responses acknowledged. As Ramon Cortines (1994), the chancellor of the New York City public schools, observes, "In a city as filled with art and culture as New York City, home to so many of the world's most distinguished museums and performing arts companies, our students are languishing for lack of high-quality, ongoing, developmentally appropriate, dependable arts education in their schools. While there are a number of extraordinarily talented teachers and powerful programs in some schools, very few schools offer sequential arts education to all of their students on a regular basis" (p. 6).

Schools have a responsibility to democratize the arts and be the great equalizer where aesthetic education is concerned. In order to achieve equity and access, the school must supply not only art objects, materials, and experiences, but also people who care deeply about the arts. Too often, artists and other adults who are enthusiastic about the arts are available only to those children who are labeled early on as gifted and talented in the arts or reserved for those who can afford private lessons in a studio (McLaughlin, 1988). In a democratic society, the quality and quantity of children's opportunities to learn about the arts "must not depend upon their geographical location, social status, racial or ethnic status, urban/suburban/rural residence, or parental or community wealth" (Music Educators National Conference, 1991). If we examine who is "allowed" to participate in the arts, we find that, all too often,

> the arts are something to be enjoyed *after* one is "successful," to be supported after one becomes affluent. Artists are to come into full flower by some form of immaculate conception, not through being nourished in public schools. Likewise, the ability to enjoy art blossoms late, when one has the time and money to participate in those experiences that hone appreciation. Cultivating the arts becomes a kind of finishing school for the much educated and well positioned, and has little place in the lives of the masses, presumably. (Goodlad, 1992, p. 193)

These attitudes pervade public education as well. Children who struggle with the three Rs are frequently excluded from the arts as well because of the misguided notion that the arts are "extras" reserved for those who have time left over from the academic pursuits that are considered to be the "basics." As early childhood educators, we have a responsibility to change this situation by bringing arts experiences to every child.

Meeting Special Needs through the Arts

Too often there is a tendency to assume that high intelligence is synonymous with creativity. In a study of preschool teachers' judgments of children's creativity, the researchers found that teachers often overlooked the creativity of those children who were less advanced developmentally than peers, even though the research team had identified these children as exceptionally creative using a variety of measures (Nicholson & Moran, 1986). But being able to do something before most peers is precocious, not necessarily creative. You may have been one of the first children in your kindergarten class to learn to tie your shoes, for instance, but that is not a creative achievement. The same principle applies to intelligence. Most measures of intelligence focus on one right answer, or convergent thinking, whereas most measures of creativity do just the opposite and focus instead on generating many possible answers, or divergent thinking. So high intelligence, at least as it is defined by standardized tests, and high creativity are not one and the same.

As we strive to give every child experiences in the arts, particularly in today's inclusive early childhood settings, teachers need to make many adaptations in arts activities. Basically, the categories of modifications necessary to meet special needs are adaptations in planning, in preparing the physical environment, and in assessing children's participation. In terms of planning, it is not enough to hurry and make adjustments in an activity after it has begun. Planning needs to be done in advance. In music, for example, you can plan to have the hearing-impaired child gently touch the speakers on the record player to feel the vibrations associated with the beat of the music. A teacher would also need to develop new ways of talking to children about their artwork. Thinking and planning ahead will make these modifications proceed smoothly.

In adapting the physical environment, you would need to do such things as helping a child who has been born without arms to figure out the best way to draw—with a crayon, a marker, a brush, on the table, on the floor, and so on. At the Garderie de Papillon school for children with physical limitations in Canada, children who use walkers and wheelchairs are equipped with protective gear and taken to the ice-skating rink, where they can experience a type of fluid motion that is only possible on the slippery surface of the ice (Driscoll, 1995). There are also many technological aids available to children that enable them to write, draw, speak, move, hear, or see better than they would without these devices. Whatever the adaptation that is made in the physical environment, the focus needs to be on the individual child's abilities. No two children are exactly alike, even if they have the same physical condition, such as cerebral palsy. One child might have a stronger left side than right, another the reverse. The same holds true with multiple sclerosis: one child's physical condition might be declining rapidly due to the disease, another's might be stabilized. Similarly, a child with Down syndrome may improve when placed in a classroom with a new and stimulating environment. In all cases, teachers should maintain a focus on what each child *can* do.

As you consider how successful these adaptations have been, you will need to observe children's participation in the activities. Most parents who have children with special needs want to see their child's life normalized. They want to see their child accepted by peers and functioning smoothly within the group. Effective adaptations allow these things to happen. One child with multiple obstacles to overcome had both Down syndrome and leukemia. She had been in and out of the hospital several times and had lost most of her hair because of the chemotherapy. Yet when she was enrolled in a summer program and kindergarten with a child-centered curriculum that allowed her to make choices among activities and decisions about her level of participation, she was able to thrive and succeed. One activity that she found particularly engaging was participating in a dramatic play center with a seashore theme. On the last day of the program, she was able to participate in a program planned and presented by the children in which they sang together, recited a poem, and shared their drawings—all much to the delight of her parents who were excitedly capturing these moments on video. Sadly, this child died two years later. But her parents valued the videotape that showed their daughter more actively involved with her peers than any other school experience she had. If the entire focus of this school had been on the traditional basic skills, the child's special needs would not have been met. By including this child in the arts and making the necessary adaptations, she was better able to express herself, to feel accepted by her peers, and to share in the joy of a performance well done and enthusiastically received.

Multicultural Education and the Arts

The arts capture the essence of the different cultures they represent. "The soul of every people is found in its songs, its images, its dances, its stories. The arts are basic because they are a universal language" (Music Educators National Conference, 1991, p. 13).

We also know that different cultures have different perspectives on the role of the arts in people's lives. Take, for example, music and movement. African culture views the arts as participatory rather than as a spectator sport. The Zimbabwe of Africa have a saying, "If you can talk, you can sing. If you can walk, you can dance." European traditions view the arts as part of a heritage that adults are obligated to share with the young. A good example is the Hungarian early childhood and folk music expert Zoltán Kodály, who said, "Music is everyone's." German music expert Carl Orff and Swiss music expert Émile Jaques-Dalcroze both emphasized that music and movement were inextricably connected for the young child, and many of the practices they endorsed form the foundation for high-quality early childhood programs today. The renowned Japanese early childhood music expert Shinichi Suzuki regarded music within the context of relationships; the more experienced teacher with the less experienced learner, the supportive parent with the preschool child. In all of these cultures, the arts are welcoming and familiar—they are like an invitation into a close friend's home, full of warm, reassuring, comfortable feelings.

This view is in sharp contrast with American perspectives. The approach to the arts in the United States is more like an armed guard at the border of a war-torn country. Americans demand to see credentials and function as gatekeepers who deny access to others. The passport is extraordinary talent and promise—star potential. We need to abandon this rigid, restrictive view of the arts that demands performance skills from participants, a limited perspective that often serves to exclude and alienate.

It is helpful to keep in mind that "the arts are one of the main ways that humans define who they are. They often express a sense of community and ethnicity. Because the arts convey the spirit of the people who created them, they can help young people to acquire inter- and intracultural understanding. The arts are not just multicultural, they are transcultural; they invite cross-cultural communication. They teach openness toward those who are different than we are. . . . It isn't intellect that connects us to other people, it is feeling" (Fowler, 1994, p. 8). When early childhood educators believe in the child artist, fight for equity and access, meet children's individual needs, and recognize the role of art in building cultural understandings, they have the attitudes and values that allow the arts to flourish and to

Figure 2.6 **Contributions of the Arts to Children's Lives and Learning**

- ༃ The arts have both intrinsic and instrumental value; that is, they have worth in and of themselves and can also be used to achieve a multitude of purposes—for example, to present issues and ideas, to teach or persuade, to entertain, and to design, plan, and beautify.

- ༃ The arts play a valued role in creating cultures and building civilizations. Although each arts discipline makes its unique contributions to culture, society, and the lives of individuals, their connections to each other enable the arts disciplines to produce more than any of them could produce alone.

- ༃ The arts are a way of knowing. Students grow in their ability to apprehend their world when they learn the arts. As they create dances, music, theatrical productions, and visual artworks, they learn how to express themselves and communicate with others.

- ༃ The arts have value and significance for daily life. They provide personal fulfillment, whether in vocational settings, avocational pursuits, or leisure.

- ༃ Lifelong participation in the arts is a valuable part of life fully lived, and it should be cultivated.

- ༃ Appreciating the arts means understanding the interactions among the various professions and roles involved in creating, performing, studying, teaching, presenting, and supporting the arts, as well as in appreciating their independent nature.

- ༃ Awakening to folk arts and their influence on other arts deepens respect for one's own and for others' communities.

- ༃ Openness, respect for work, and contemplation when participating in the arts as an observer or audience member are personal attitudes that enhance enjoyment and ought to be developed.

- ༃ The arts are indispensable to freedom of inquiry and expression.

- ༃ Because the arts offer the continuing challenge of situations in which there is no standard or approved answer, those who study the arts become acquainted with many perspectives on the meaning of "value."

- ༃ The modes of thinking and methods of the arts disciplines can be used to illuminate situations in other disciplines that require creative solutions.

- ༃ Attributes such as self-discipline, the collaborative spirit, and perseverance, which are so necessary to the arts, can be transferred to the rest of life.

- ༃ The arts provide forms of nonverbal communication that can strengthen the presentation of ideas and emotions.

- ༃ Each person has responsibility for advancing civilization itself. The arts encourage taking this responsibility and provide skills and perspectives for doing so.

Source: Consortium of National Arts Education Associations. (1994). *National standards for arts education. Dance, music, theatre, visual arts: What every young American should know and be able to do in the arts.* Reston, VA: Music Educators National Conference.

make an enduring contribution to the quality of children's lives. Figure 2.6 summarizes the important contributions that the arts make to children's lives and learning (Consortium of National Arts Education Associations, 1994).

CONCLUSION

*A*s teachers, we know that the arts teach what cannot be taught in any other way. Aesthetic education contributes to the development of the whole child—mind, body, and spirit. The arts teach all learners to delve beneath the surface and discover new layers of meaning. The arts make a contribution to children's lives because "growth in the ways persons know the world and themselves is, after all, the point and purpose of schooling and education. If the young people who pass through our schools are to learn how to realize their full humanity, then opportunities for aesthetic growth must be provided. The development of artistic and aesthetic ways of knowing must become part of the basic education of all students" (Reimer & Smith, 1992, pp. xi–xii).

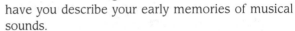

Learning about the Arts from Children

An Interview with Cynthia Sydnia

Cynthia Sydnia is a harpist who performs professionally and also works with young children in a music therapy program that she created. She has been blind since birth. This interview with Cynthia was conducted by another musician and early childhood educator, Susan Lachmann. The text of the interview highlights Cynthia's artistic growth as a child as well as her contributions to the field of early childhood education through art. As you read, consider the following questions:

- In what ways was Cynthia privileged? In what ways was she "at risk"? How do your own early childhood music experiences compare with Cynthia's?
- What influences contributed to Cynthia's love of music and musical development?
- What are the implications of her experience for the classroom teacher?
- Why might we be able to reach children through the arts when we are unable to reach them through other means?
- In what ways have you been privileged or disadvantaged in the arts?

Susan: Cynthia, what can you tell us about your early childhood music experiences?

Cynthia: I come from a rather musical family. My parents both played instruments. My father was a principal at a middle school, and he had access to a lot of materials, plus the instruments that he owned—a mandolin, a slide guitar, a couple of guitars, a zither, and an autoharp. My brothers were older than I was, and they would get together and practice with their bands. They had friends that would come over and play mostly country and fifties kind of music. I could sing before I could talk or walk, actually. My father was Norwegian, and my parents told me that I was in the walker singing a melody, and my grandmother was enthralled because she recognized the Norwegian folk music that I was singing.

Susan: So, there was music in and out of your house . . . in the way that we watch television today, you were ac-

tually hearing and seeing music, live music. It would be interesting to have you describe your early memories of musical sounds.

Cynthia: My earliest memory is when I was about two and a half—I remember sitting outside in a spruce grove in the backyard. There were a lot of animals and birds, and I used to love listening to them. I also recall articulating with the birds.

When I was about 5 or 6, I remember watching television. In fact, I attribute my interest in the harp to Harpo Marx. My father was a real Marx brothers fan, and I became fascinated by the way Harpo's face looked when he played. Here's this very comedic person running around, and all of a sudden he picks up the harp and becomes very angelic. That transformation. I thought, "Wow! I want to play the harp."

Susan: Oh, the Harpo Marx connection is really interesting. Of all things. What caught your attention was that *transformation*. You fell in love with the harp when you got that visual and auditory cue of being transfixed. But there is something that's confusing to me. I don't really know how you see.

Cynthia: I have retinopathy of prematurity, ROP. What I have in my right eye is no vision and approximately 7 percent in my left eye. . . . I see colors, I see you . . . in general, I can watch television if I get pretty close to it, just like with print.

Susan: So, let me recap here. We know that in terms of your earliest childhood development, you operated more from auditory cue and came to know your environment primarily through sound. We also know that in your home, there was a lot of sound, instruments, and live music. There were musicians in your family and friends of your family were musicians. Was this a radio household too? What about musical experiences outside the home?

Cynthia: Yes, absolutely. Radio, record player—we were middle class. . . . Because I grew up in northern New

Jersey, New York was accessible, and we went to concerts in the area. As I progressed in school, we would go to the ballet or opera or whatever. I started vocal training and piano and guitar lessons early, so I was always going somewhere. And of course, plays as well. I had a lot of cultural events to choose from, and my family took advantage of that.

Susan: And when did you get your first harp?

Cynthia: When I was 24. I had started lessons on the piano when I was six, and a year later I started on the guitar.

Susan: You had a piano at home, and you were allowed access even before you were six?

Cynthia: Oh yes, definitely. I picked up things by ear. I was just enthralled with music.

Susan: And nobody said, "Cynthia, get off that piano!"?

Cynthia: No, absolutely not. I was encouraged, again and again. And then of course my brothers' band would come over and practice.

Susan: And you would always sing along?

Cynthia: Absolutely. I'd be right there.

Susan: Hmmm . . . didn't want to miss anything. Well, that says a lot again, for you had access, music was available to you, and you were encouraged.

Cynthia: Yes, by sixth grade I started vocal training. My parents believed in education—the more instruction, the better.

Susan: We know that for you, music was critical in your formation. I wonder, what about normally developing children? Is it very important for them to have this?

Cynthia: Oh, I would say yes. If we can tap into something that really intrigues or interests a child and develop that, we empower and help them empower themselves. And it doesn't matter whether they have a particular challenge or not. Children are children, they're individuals first, they're children first. If we can open them up to be creative and think of options, just think of all the life decision and opportunities they can create eventually from that.

Susan: Well, then, what would you, as a person who loves children and music, say to early childhood educators about the arts?

Cynthia: I'd try to expose children to as much as possible and allow them to be themselves. And as they develop, gently guide them into more focused and directed kind of teachings. I see music as a nurturer, like with the Hug-a-Harp Program. I had been working with pet therapy for a while with my Shetland sheepdog, and some of the children were still not responding, so I decided to bring my harp to a preschool class. When I brought it in, they touched it and I told them that you got to hug it . . . and I thought, what a way to nurture hugging, even though it's an instrument, it's an instrument that's so *alive*. So I had them hug the harp, which is basically what you do in order to play it. And they would draw this energy into themselves, feel the vibrations against their ear, cheek, or body. Even children with attention deficit disorder would be transformed, transmuted, transported by this instrument. One of the children, a five-year-old boy who had lived with so much violence—I believe he witnessed a murder in the household—went over to the harp and began playing all the red strings, which are Cs. I heard it and thought, "Wow, what's he doing?" Then he played the blue strings, which are Fs. And then he'd go back and play the red strings again. Then I thought, "Wait a minute, if he can see this color, and play this particular color . . . then why couldn't we develop some songs by using color?" Once he realized that the sounds were similar in octaves, I think that's what got him really fascinated. He kept playing the Fs and Cs over and over again. So we took a piece of paper and some crayons, some reds and blues and black (some strings are black), and we put the colors in different sequences, and we would show the colors to him and say, "Okay, now do this one." Our idea was to let children look at the paper and do the correct string and play little songs . . . the idea for Hug-a-Harp basically stemmed from this young boy.

Susan: Now, I'm going to ask you to imagine something . . . if music had been absent in your life, how might that have affected you? I know that music is your career and that you have been touring both as a solo and with bands. Can you imagine your life without music?

Cynthia: My life would have gone totally differently, I'm sure. I don't think I would be as creative an individual as I would hope that I now am. I definitely would not be internalized, focusing on the inner self—and I don't mean that egotistically, I mean that spiritually or knowing the self. Traveling, doing journeys within that I couldn't do on the outside. And getting to really know who I am—I think that allows me to open up and be creative.

Susan: It seems that what you are implying is that as far as empowering children goes, what we need to do first is empower ourselves. It's this whole issue about connecting with children and with our own inner child. We've also discussed the importance of accessibility, availability of materials plus access to our own creative fires that will lead us, as leaders of children, to continue to make the environment and the programs and the opportunities. We have a responsibility to make that keep happening for children.

The Artist in You

Stacy's Story

Student teachers often encounter situations that cause them to assess their own ideas about the arts and what they truly value. As you read about Stacy's experience, consider how you might have responded. You may want to discuss the issue with a small group of classmates before arriving at a decision. This is how Stacy began telling her story:

> In the nursery school class I was assigned to for my student teaching experience, the teacher had planned a finger-painting activity for the three-year-olds. There is this one boy, in the group—I'll call him Jay to protect confidentiality—who really seemed to be put off by the activity. I asked him about it and he said, "No, no, no! My mom will get mad if I get my clothes dirty." At first, I didn't know what to say . . .

Some questions to consider include these:

* What value does finger painting have for young children?
* Why might some adults feel better about having children cut out patterns or color in the lines rather than having them finger-paint?
* What does your response to finger painting say about you?

Stacy continued her story, quickly thinking of a response:

> Then I pointed out to him that we always pushed up the children's sleeves and used painting smocks. [The classroom teacher uses her husband's old shirts, cuts the lower portion of the sleeves off, and has the children put them on backwards so that the closed back of the shirt protects their clothing.] He still seemed reluctant, so I didn't push. I talked with the classroom teacher about it, and she suggested

that we mention it to Jay's mother, which we did. Jay's mother said that she would talk it over with him, but also questioned why finger painting was a part of the curriculum. I was really impressed with the teacher's answer. She was not defensive or condescending, just very professional. She said that finger painting was a way for children to explore materials that were new to most of them, to identify colors and experiment with mixing them, and to begin to control their finger, hand, and arm movements, something that was important in many other areas, such as writing. Jay's mother seemed satisfied with that answer and said that she would reassure him about joining in the finger painting. I don't think that finger painting ever became Jay's favorite pastime, but as the year went on, he did feel sufficiently relaxed to participate in a variety of "messy" art projects like the colored chalk mural we did on the cement walk that leads out to the playground, decorating eggs, and making collages out of recyclables during our environmental awareness unit.

Now that Stacy's story is complete, reflect further on your initial responses.

* Are there times when you would choose a different activity over finger painting? When and why?
* How would you deal with nonparticipation?
* If an activity is messy, is that sufficient reason to abandon it?

Imagine another situation where a parent would challenge an aesthetic experience. Try to formulate a persuasive, professional response.

Situations and Solutions

Is It Developmentally Appropriate?

Situation 1

Patricia is a first grade teacher in an inclusive early childhood setting. Gabriel, one of her students, has a neurological disorder, and his motor control seems to be deteriorating of late. She knows that Gabriel enjoys coloring with crayons on his wheelchair tray, but the crayons keep falling on the floor. Patricia tries to think of a solution and finally comes up with an idea—Velcro! She uses an adhesive-backed heavy-duty Velcro strip, affixes it to a

small plastic container, and attaches it to the wheelchair tray. Now Gabriel has more frequent access to his crayons. Is this an appropriate adaptation? Why or why not?

Situation 2

Mr. Brewer has asked for parent volunteers for his nursery school, and today is Jennifer's mother's visit to the classroom. All of a sudden, he hears Jennifer wailing and turns to see her mother giving a lesson on the "right way to draw a cat's face." The mother is gripping Jennifer's hand and forcing her to draw a circle with triangles for the ears and nose, ovals for the eyes, and lines for whiskers. What should Mr. Brewer say and do to help Jennifer's mother understand developmentally appropriate practice?

Situation 3

During the first graders' unit on Native Americans, their teacher and a sixth grade teacher have decided to collaborate. The first graders have become intrigued by the idea of a totem pole and want to create one out of cardboard, paint, paper, and glue. Before they begin, the sixth graders are responsible for researching and locating a wide array of materials on Native Americans, particularly on the topic of totem poles. The sixth graders have been trained to be support people who will offer advice and encouragement without doing the work for the first graders. Is it developmentally appropriate?

Situation 4

Sylvia has a two-year-old son named Daryl who is enrolled in a private child care program. The teacher requests a conference and explains, much to Sylvia's surprise and dismay, that Daryl does not "fit in" with the group because he is "too immature." The teacher reports that Daryl has difficulty maintaining attention during circle time and seldom finishes his art projects. Then the teacher asks that Sylvia remove her son from the class. During the conference, Sylvia is so surprised that she says very little, but afterward she contacts a friend who is studying to be a teacher and says, "This program came highly recommended, but I am beginning to wonder if their expectations for toddlers are unrealistic. They're barely out of diapers [one of the center's entrance requirements], and the teachers there expect them to act like grade school children. Obviously, my husband and I were disappointed by this rejection, but I don't think this is just a case of sour grapes. I honestly wonder if they understand toddlers there." How would you respond to Sylvia's concerns?

Integrating the Arts

The Arts in an Inclusive Classroom

A group of college students who are studying to be teachers are gaining additional experience by working in a summer enrichment program that serves children ages 5–12. One of the student teachers has read about child-made games as a way to encourage creativity and integrate visual/spatial, bodily/kinesthetic, and verbal/linguistic forms of intelligence (Isenberg & Jalongo, 1997). She begins by gathering together several different games: card games, board games, a video cartridge, and so on. After they look at the games, they do some brainstorming on chart paper. She writes the word "games" in the center, then writes the children's ideas around it with their initials next to the ideas they contributed to the discussion. Included among their comments are these:

"You win or you lose." K.D.

"Some games are on video. My brother goes to the mall to play virtual reality." J.C.

"A game could be outside, too, like hide and seek—we play it in the yard in the summer." F. B.

"I like the stuff that comes with some games, like Monopoly." G. G.

"My grandad plays old maid with me sometimes." R. S.

"I play soccer and baseball." J. R.

Next, the teacher asks the children to make a list of some of the games they have played. They include bingo, Candyland, Twister, Sega, go fish, catch, Don't Spill the Beans, and Chutes and Ladders. Finally, the teacher poses this challenge: "Working with your partner, create a game. Give your game a name. Decide together what the rules are. Play the game to make sure it works. Be ready to show and explain your game by the end of the week." Looking around the room you would see two second grade girls working on a board game they call "Visit to Sea World." One is working on making the cards that will sit in the middle that read "lose one turn" and so on. The other is trying to make some playing pieces out of black and white paper that "look like killer whales." A sighted child and a child who is legally blind have agreed upon their own version of pin the tail on the donkey called "Pin the Tail on the Dinosaur." Another team is working on a catch game that is made from a ball of yarn and two plastic milk jugs with the bottoms cut off, an idea that they saw in a book on recycling. One of the boys has attention deficit disorder, but he is managing to concentrate on writing the rules for the game. When the children are finished, their teacher is very impressed by their creativity and the quality of their work. Seeing their classmates' ideas inspires many of the children to create new games at home (or to make revisions in the ones that they developed in class).

Discussion Questions

- Why do you think this lesson was successful?
- How did the teacher go about individualizing?
- What examples could you envision in your classroom that would accommodate individual needs as this one did?
- If a parent complained that the children were "just playing games," how would you respond?

Individual and Group Projects for Teachers

Creating Books with Moving Parts

When most teachers plan, their natural tendency seems to be to separate the arts into specified times. Perhaps this practice is so common because this is the approach that teachers themselves have experienced the most as students. Yet seeking opportunities to combine the arts is supremely appropriate for the very young. Imagine a first grade classroom where the children are involved in a very challenging project—inventing books with moving parts such as lift-the-flap and pop-ups that they will read and donate to a Head Start classroom down the hall. They examine several books with moving parts, including *How Many Bugs in a Box?* (Carter, 1988), *Where's Spot?* (Hill, 1980), *The Christmas Alphabet* (Sabuda, 1995), *The Wheels on the Bus* (Zelinsky, 1990), and *Where Can It Be?* (Jonas, 1986). Aarika is not satisfied with a simple lift-the-flap. She wants "something to pop out," and she experiments with several materials until she finally decides on some stiff paper folded in accordion-style pleats glued on the back of the jack-in-the-box figure she has created. Carl has decided to create a song picture book for his favorite song, a Caribbean tune called "Tingalayo" (Raffi, 1987), and will introduce each new verse with a lift-the-flap. The only trouble is, on his first attempt at creating doors, he cut it out on all four sides instead of just three. As he solves this problem, Carl talks out loud, saying, "I could tape it here . . . no, I'm gonna start all over again, I want it to be really good." Janine is producing a book that is based on a story that she wrote and enacted with other members of the class. As you imagine these first graders at work, you can see that all of the areas of the arts discussed in this chapter are involved: art and craft, music and movement, story and enactment. Combining several areas of the curriculum together like this is referred to as integrating the curriculum. For more on books with moving parts, see *Literature on the Move: Making and Using Pop-up and Lift-flap Books* (Bohning, Phillips, & Bryant, 1993).

Now it's your turn. Working individually or in a group, try to create a project like this one that offers opportunities to integrate the arts rather than teaching them separately.

REFERENCES

Baker, D. W. (1990). The visual arts in early childhood education. *Design for Arts in Education, 91,* 21–25.

Bohning, G., Phillips, A., & Bryant, S. H. (1993). *Literature on the move: Making and using pop-up and lift-flap books.* Englewood, CO: Teacher Ideas Press.

Boyd, A. E. (1989). *Music in early childhood.* (ERIC Document Reproduction Service No. ED 310 863).

Broudy, H. S. (1988). Aesthetics and the curriculum. In W. Pinar (Ed.), *Contemporary curriculum discourses* (pp. 332–342). Scottsdale, AZ: Gorsuch Scarisbrick.

Carr, M. (1992). Easels and beyond: Everyday art experiences for 3–5 year olds. *PAEYC Newsletter, 17*(3), 5–8.

Consortium of National Arts Education Associations. (1994). *National standards for arts education. Dance, music, theatre, visual arts: What every young American should know and be able to do in the arts.* Reston, VA: Music Educators National Conference.

Cortines, R. C. (1994). *The arts: Partnerships as a catalyst for educational reform.* Sacramento, CA: California Department of Education.

Davis, J., & Gardner, H. (1992). The cognitive revolution: Consequences for the understanding and education of the child as artist. In B. Reimer, & R. A. Smith, (Eds.), *The arts, education, and aesthetic knowing* (pp. 92–123). Chicago: University of Chicago Press.

Driscoll, A. (1995). *Cases in early childhood education: Stories of programs and practices.* Boston, MA: Allyn and Bacon.

Eisner, E. (1991). My educational passions. In D. L. Burleson (Ed.), *Reflections: Personal essays by 33 distinguished educators* (pp. 136–145). Bloomington, IN: Phi Delta Kappa.

Eisner, E. (1992a). Arts can counter school reform's standardizing aims. *ASCD Update, 34*(5), 5.

Eisner, E. (1992b). The misunderstood role of the arts in human development. *Phi Delta Kappan, 73*(8), 591–595.

Feierabend, J. (1990). Music in early childhood. *Design for Arts in Education, 91*(6), 15–20.

Fowler, C. (1988). *Can we rescue the arts for America's children? Coming to our senses—10 years later.* New York: American Council for the Arts.

Fowler, C. (1994, January). Quoted in J. O'Neil, Looking at art through new eyes: Visual arts programs pushed to reach new goals, new students. *ASCD Curriculum Update,* 1–8.

Gardner, H. (1993). *Frames of mind: The theory of multiple intelligences*(10th anniversary ed.). New York: Basic Books.

Goodlad, J. I. (1992). Toward a place in the curriculum for the arts. In B. Reimer & R. A. Smith (Eds.), *The arts, education, and aesthetic knowing* (pp. 192–212). Chicago: University of Chicago Press.

Grumet, M. (1988). *Bitter milk: Women and teaching.* Amherst: University of Massachusetts.

Isenberg, J. P., & Jalongo, M. R. (1997). *Creative expression and play in early childhood curriculum* (2nd ed.). Englewood Cliffs, NJ: Merrill/Prentice Hall.

Jalongo, M. R. (1995). Awaken to the artistry of young children! *Dimensions of Early Childhood Education, 23*(4), 8–14.

Jalongo, M. R. (1996). Using recorded music with young children: A guide for nonmusicians. *Young Children, 51*(5), 6–14.

Katz, L. (1988). *Early childhood education: What research tells us.* Bloomington, IN: Phi Delta Kappa.

Keel, J. S. (1972). The roots of aesthetic experience. *Art Education, 24,* 4–7.

McDonald, D., & Simons, G. (1989). *Musical growth and development: Birth through six.* New York: Schirmer/Macmillan.

McLaughlin, J. (1988). A stepchild comes of age. *Journal of Physical Education, Recreation, and Dance, 59*(9), 58–60.

Morningstar, M. (1986). *Growing with dance.* Point Roberts, WA: Windborne.

Music Educators National Conference. (1991). *Growing up complete: The imperative for music education.* Reston, VA: Author.

Nicholson, M. W., & Moran, J. D. (1986). Teachers' judgments of preschoolers' creativity. *Perceptual and Motor Skills, 63,* 1211–1216.

Parsons, M. J. (1992). Cognition as interpretation in art education. In B. Reimer & R. A. Smith (Eds.), (1992). *The arts, education, and aesthetic knowing* (pp. 70–91). Chicago: University of Chicago Press.

Reimer, B. (1992). What knowledge is of most worth in the arts? In B. Reimer & R. A. Smith (Eds.), *The arts, education, and aesthetic knowing* (pp. 20–50). Chicago: University of Chicago Press.

Reimer, B., & Smith, R. A. (Eds.). (1992). Preface. *The arts, education, and aesthetic knowing* (pp. ix–1). Chicago: University of Chicago Press.

Ripple, R. E. (1989). Ordinary creativity. *Contemporary Educational Psychology, 14*(3), 189–202.

Smith, R. A. (1989). *The sense of art: A study in aesthetic education.* New York: Routledge.

Smith, R. A. (1992). Toward percipience: A humanities curriculum for arts education. In B. Reimer & R. A. Smith (Eds.), *The arts, education, and aesthetic knowing* (pp. 51–69). Chicago: University of Chicago Press.

Stinson, S. W. (1990). Dance education in early childhood. *Design for Arts in Education, 91,* 34–41.

Stinson, S. W. (1992). Reflections on student experience in dance education. *Design for Arts in Education, 93*(5), 21–27.

Wilcox, E. (1994). Unlock the joy of music. *Teaching Music, 2,* 34–35, 46.

Williams, G. (1992). Dance, language development, and the young child. *Early Child Development, 79,* 107–124.

Children's Books and Recordings

Brown, M. (1985). *The bionic bunny show.* Boston: Little, Brown.

Carter, D. (1988). *How many bugs in a box?* New York: Simon and Schuster.

de Paola, T. (1989). *The art lesson.* New York: Putnam.

Hill, E. (1980). *Where's Spot?* New York: Putnam.

Hill, E. (1987). *Spot goes to the farm.* New York: Putnam.

Jonas, A. (1986). *Where can it be?* New York: Greenwillow.

Ladysmith Black Mambazo (1994). "There come our mothers." *Music for Little People sampler: Joyful music from around the world.* Redway, CA: Music for Little People.

Raffi. (1987). "Tingalayo." On *One light, one sun*. Hollywood, CA: A&M Records.

Sabuda, R. (1995). *The Christmas alphabet*. New York: Orchard.

Williams, L. D. (1986). *The little old lady who was not afraid of anything*. New York: Crowell.

Zelinsky, P. (1990). *The wheels on the bus*. New York: Dutton.

Rosemarie

First and foremost, art is the key to our humanity. From art we renew our sense of wonder and enlightenment. In a world where the mysterious and wondrous are often removed, where everything is analyzed, categorized, and demystified, we need a place from whence we can search inward for a renewed sense of awe, a sense of uniqueness in harmony with the world in which we dwell."

—Laurie Ball (1989, p. 36)

How Children's Artistry Develops

THREE

Chapter Reflections

- ও How did your attitudes about and abilities in the arts develop?
- ও How do young children use their creative processes? How do they develop artistically?
- ও What phases did you or a child you know go through in music and movement, art and craft, and story and enactment?
- ও What do teachers do that facilitates children's progress through these stages of development?

HOW IMPORTANT IS ARTISTIC AND AESTHETIC GROWTH?

*I*magine that you are sitting on a bench in the hallway of a building where college classes meet. There you will see several students walking by with headphones on, obviously engrossed in their music. Later that morning, you will overhear several students who are talking about how much they enjoyed the performance of an African dance troupe that was on campus the night before. Then two of the secretaries meet, and one of them relates that she had a wonderful time over the weekend when she went to a dinner theater with her husband. That afternoon, a nontraditional student chats with a faculty member and shares the exciting news that her son will be going on a high school band trip and will perform during halftime for a televised football game. That evening, an international student from China brings a magazine to show to her friends before class begins. She plans to get married in the summer and will wear the traditional bridal costume, something that her classmates are anxious to see. As they look at the photographs, they remark on how beautiful the fabrics are and ask questions about Chinese customs. From this one-day imaginary visit to the college campus, you can see that the arts' reputation for being nonessential is undeserved. None of the individuals just described would find their lives very interesting or enjoyable without experiences in the arts and attention to aesthetics. An experience becomes aesthetic when it meets two criteria (Eaton, 1992). First, we must be focused on the intrinsic features of things or events and pay close attention to them. Second, the features that we concentrate on must be traditionally or culturally defined as worthy of our attention and reflection.

Young children have a natural inclination to attend to details, but they do not yet understand intrinsic features, nor do they understand at first how to sort out what is significant from what is insignificant. To illustrate this point, consider an eight-month-old baby who is crawling around on the carpet. Even if the carpet was just vacuumed, the baby will probably be able to find a tiny piece of lint, pick it up, examine it closely, and put it into his or her mouth—all before a watchful adult has time to intervene and grab the piece of fuzz. In order to mature aesthetically, the baby will need to differentiate between things that are worthy of attention, culturally speaking, and those that are not. Additionally, the baby will need to go beyond looking at surface details and begin to focus more on the inner qualities of things and events.

Now think about a preschooler for a moment. If you send young children out into the yard on a summer's day, they are just as likely to bring you a fistful of dandelions or other weeds as they are to bring you cultivated flowers. Yet as children mature aesthetically, they begin to recognize that some things are better, rarer, and more appealing than others. Ray described how his five-year-old daughter expressed her growing awareness of the cultural significance of certain flowers. Her teacher had received a bouquet of roses and baby's breath during the parent/teacher/child gathering that celebrated the children's completion of kindergarten. When Ray asked his daughter what special thing she would like to do after school to commemorate this event, he fully expected that she would ask to go to McDonald's. Instead she said, "I want some of those flowers the teacher had, you know, baby's breath." Apparently this kindergartner was impressed by the fact that these flowers were regarded as a worthy tribute for an admired teacher. She may also have been intrigued by the lovely sounding name. But now, given a choice among weeds and baby's breath, she knows which one is traditionally and culturally preferred.

When we look at the arts and aesthetics through the lens of actual experience rather than thinking about them in abstract terms, many important issues emerge. Among the fascinating yet perplexing questions about the role of the arts in our lives are the following, based on Reimer's (1992) work:

- How are our aesthetic sensibilities learned?
- Why does art exist? How is it used? How should it be used?
- Why is enjoying and creating art so important to us?
- What role does art play in a particular culture? How is that role alike and different from the role art plays in other cultures?
- Why do people disagree on whether education in the arts is essential for all?
- Why do some individuals devote their lives to developing their creative capacities in the arts and aesthetics?

Reflecting on these issues underscores the importance of the arts, aesthetic education, and creative expression in children's lives. In this chapter we will examine the child's unique approach to artistry and the developmental sequence for children's growth in three major areas: music and movement, art and craft, and story and enactment. We begin with the story of Jadran, a first grader who is remarkably mature, talented, and creative.

The Child Artist at Work

Since the 1940s, one of the most common ways of assessing a child's maturity was through the child's drawing of a person. During the first week of first grade, Ms. Happler used an informal draw-a-person activity to get an idea of what her students were like. When most of the other children in the class were drawing circles for a head and lines for arms and legs, Jadran drew a sheriff with boots, spurs, a badge, a cowboy hat, a holster and gun, a checked shirt, and a bandanna. There is no question that his work is precocious, meaning that it is advanced for his age. Mrs. Happler was quite frankly amazed by Jadran's drawing. As further evidence of Jadran's advanced abilities in art, he won the districtwide competition for his oil paintings later that year.

Whenever people who know Jadran's family hear about his artistic inclinations, they immediately say, "Oh, he must take after his mother," because Jadran's mother teaches art at the local high school. But is it logical to assume that Jadran's talent is genetic, as this statement seems to imply? Or would it be more accurate to say that Jadran lives in an environment that fosters creativity, supports the arts, and provides high-quality materials? Unlike any other child in his class, Jadran owns not only crayons and paper, but also brushes, canvas, an easel, and many types of paints. Jadran's mother accepts that art can be messy, and she values originality. Therefore, rather than concluding that Jadran has a genetic predisposition to be an artist, it could be more cogently argued

Providing open-ended activities is one way that teachers support children's creative growth.

that he has the time, the materials, the opportunities, the role model, and the encouragement to express and further develop his talents. In other words, Jadran is privileged.

Thinking about Jadran's advantages in the arts should serve as a reminder of the educator's central role in making the most of every young child's abilities. A teacher's responsibility for developing students' potential is doubly important in the arts and aesthetics because these areas are so frequently neglected elsewhere in children's lives. Thinking about Jadran's case also raises the issue of how we as a society view human potential. No one can predict with great accuracy what a child's creative aptitude is currently or might be in the future. Every day we hear amazing stories about new milestones that people reach. The media celebrate new levels of artistic achievement, like the child violinist and musical prodigy Midori. But what about all of the talents and abilities that remain undiscovered? There could be many situations in which what appears to be the absence of talent is really a lack of opportunity. We may never discover, for instance, the person who has the potential to become an Olympic figure skater because he happens to live in rural Hawaii and has never seen an ice rink, much less skated on one. And we will never know if a child whose family is homeless and living in poverty had a great talent for filmmaking because she was not given the chance to discover her abilities, demonstrate her talent, and produce the award-winning documentary of which she was capable.

When you start thinking along these lines, there are hundreds, thousands, even millions of individual examples. Some people never even suspect their true talents, while others spend a lifetime wondering whether the talent existed or regretting the deterioration of a talent they felt certain was there. As people mature, sometimes even after they have retired, they frequently revisit the arts and try to rediscover their talents. They now have what adults would not give to them when they were children—time, materials, and opportunities to participate in the arts. As we have seen, early childhood is the ideal time for developing artful and aesthetic ways of knowing because young children are naturally observant, curious, imaginative, uninhibited, responsive to stimuli, and profoundly affected by their experiences. As Gharavi (1993) points out, "It is this propensity for imagination and fantasy that is the foundation for the arts and, ironically, the orientation that the adult must stay in touch with or recapture in order to become artful" (p. 29). It is clear that imagination and fantasy are essential elements in the creative process, and it is widely acknowledged that the creative process underlies any authentic arts activity. The Theory into Practice that follows will enhance your understanding about what teachers can do to ensure that children can remain in touch with their natural creativity throughout their lives.

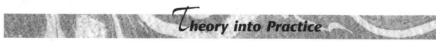

Theory into Practice

E. Paul Torrance on Creativity

Suppose that you were asked to identify exceptionally creative children in your classroom. If you are like most people, you would use the wrong set of criteria to arrive at your decisions. When asked to identify creativity in their students, most teachers name children who perform well on structured, academic tasks; children who are compliant and well-behaved; and those who are advanced for their age (precocious) (Nicholson & Moran, 1986). Based upon his professional lifetime of research on creativity, E. Paul Torrance (1969) suggested a very different set of characteristics that were associated with creative persons. These creative behaviors include

- *intense concentration*—becoming completely absorbed in listening, observing, or doing something while appearing to be relatively relaxed.
- *active involvement*—playful, hands-on participation in a task; voice and manner communicate interest and excitement.
- *expressions of individuality*—a tendency to challenge ideas of authorities and trust one's own ideas even though they sometimes seem wild or silly.
- *careful observation*—taking a closer look at things, seeing beneath the surface and expressing curiosity.
- *interesting connections*—seeing relationships among apparently unrelated ideas; combining or recombining elements to create new forms.
- *insightful commentary*—raising interesting questions and offering penetrating insights.
- *self-initiated learning*—working at a task without prompting from adults and persisting at a task even when it proves difficult.

From this list, you can see that many of the behaviors reinforced in rigidly structured schools and classrooms would undermine creative thought. When teachers support children's creative expression, they supply the conditions that facilitate growth in each of the traits Torrance identifies. This often means substantive changes in four areas: (1) attitudes toward children's art, (2) instructional approaches, (3) classroom practices, and (4) understandings about how children's artistry develops. Each of these points will be discussed in the remainder of the chapter.

CREATIVITY IN EARLY CHILDHOOD

$\mathcal{V}$irtually everyone agrees that early childhood is a time when creativity flourishes. Laypersons often marvel at the young child's imagination, and experts contend that young children are at a creative high point in their lives (Davis & Gardner, 1992). What, exactly, is creative behavior? Children may be said to be engaged in creative expression when they use materials (including language) to express ideas, images, feelings, or experiences (Engel, 1989). To illustrate the creative process in action, look at the samples of Mrs. Lipkin's first graders' artwork (shown on p. 62). Their student teacher, Wendi Cunningham, presented the children with a challenge: to use paper fasteners to produce a human figure with movable, posable limbs, and write a story about the figure they created. In meeting this challenge, Ashlee decided to portray her sister (1); Christine made an imaginary friend named Kimberly (2); Kenny crafted a representation of the rock singer Elvis (3); and Jessica created a figure of her friend who likes to ice-skate, complete with windswept hair (4). Their work has aesthetic merit—it is pleasing to the eye, and it evokes a response from those who see the figures and read the sentences the children composed to accompany their creations. We cannot help smiling at "Elvis the King" or sensing the warm feelings that Ashlee has for her sister, for instance. In all four of these creative products, children have used materials (in this case, yarn, construction paper, and metal paper fasteners) to communicate ideas, images, experiences, and feelings.

Unlike physical growth that usually proceeds in linear fashion from one predictable milestone to the next—for example, from sitting to standing, to crawling, and to walking—creative growth does not follow a steady, predictable pattern. About children's creative development, Engel (1989) remarks, "Children do not develop

smoothly or in a linear fashion. . . . Instead, children experience change in the creative mode in fits and starts. . . . The strands of experience leading up to creative insight or change come from many aspects of a child's life and are both internal and external [such as] . . . personal concerns and feelings, characteristics of home life, general styles of thinking and learning, particular ways of relating to materials, exposure to visual models, the acquisition of new bodies of knowledge, and access to appropriate materials" (p. 17). It is for these reasons that it is so important for teachers to provide open-ended activities for children.

Just imagine how stilted and uninteresting the first graders' responses to Wendi's activity would have been if she had required them to trace a pattern and then use the paper fasteners to assemble it. An opportunity for creative expression would have been missed. And what of those children whose teachers require mindless busywork all year long? What might happen to them? Some children are fortunate. Like Jadran, their lives at home and at school are filled with opportunities for creative expression. Other children seldom get a chance to realize the creative potential that is evident during early childhood because their families and teachers do not value artful ways of knowing.

AESTHETIC ASSETS OF EARLY CHILDHOOD

*S*tandards for child art and fine art are and must be different. In fine art, the final form, the technical skill, and the quality of the performance are critically important. But children's art is different and therefore appreciated in a different way.

> Children produce art in a spontaneous and natural way, yet all children do not become great artists, or even artists at all, when they mature. In part this is because other expressive techniques, such as verbal language, are perfected,

while the skills necessary for the arts are permitted to atrophy. . . . Young children
practice art to express ideas, to explore art media, and to assert themselves. . . .
In child art, adults look for revelations about thought and feeling that may help
them to understand a child and to communicate with him or her. We value the
spontaneity of children's artistic expressions and appreciate the energy, thought,
and joy that went into their productions. (Cohen & Gainer, 1995, p. 21)

Paradoxically, just as the child shapes a work of art, so too is that child shaped by
whatever he or she produces. The composer creates a piece of music, yet that
person, both as human being and as composer, is also defined by the music that
she or he has invented. Michelangelo painted the ceiling of the Sistine Chapel and
created the sculpture of David, but he was also defined and shaped by his works.
Likewise, both the art object and the child artist are affected by aesthetic experiences. The three-year-old who drew the human forms in the child drawing (right)
learned something about herself as she looked and said to herself, "What did I
draw?"

The arts processes of the adult and the child are distinctive, yet similar. Both
begin with significant objects or experiences in their surroundings, both explore
relationships between and within those objects and experiences, and both transform ideas, feelings, and experiences into visual forms that reflect the artist's individual point of view (Cohen & Gainer, 1995). Look, for example, at the three drawings
(below) of bats by first graders Travis (1), Jason (2), and Michael (3). The boys made
these pictures after they studied photographs and realistic drawings of bats. Each
artist's work is unique and reflects not only the outward appearance of a bat, but
also that child artist's perspective on bats. The way that they chose to label their
drawings is equally distinctive. Travis simply wrote "bat," Jason wrote "Imofada"—
("I'm afraid of"), and Michael, who has often seen bats flying outside the third-story
bedroom of his old house and once had one inside his room, wrote,
"Ilvbatsbkzalafrormibed" ("I love bats because they always fly over my bed"). These
boys transformed their ideas, images, feelings, and experiences into a visual form
that reflected their personal perspectives.

As you work with young children, you will need to develop an attitude of abiding respect for child artists and take delight in their artistic endeavors. In order to
fully support children's artistry, you will need to develop a child-centered teaching
philosophy, one that provides a play-based curriculum and that is based upon the
principles of developmentally appropriate practice.

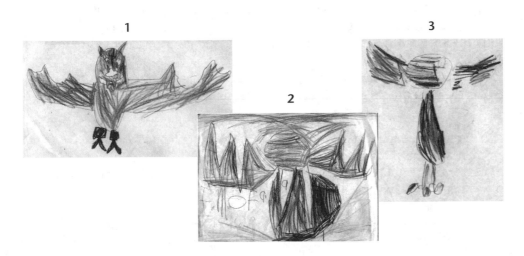

1

2

3

PLAY: THE FOUNDATION FOR THE ARTS
IN EARLY CHILDHOOD

*A*sk most people to define play and they will resort to some version of "the opposite of work." Yet if you investigate theories of play and research on play, you will find that play is the essential style of learning during early childhood (Isenberg & Jalongo, 1997). A child who sits at her desk and dutifully completes a color-by-the-number activity may appear to be doing "real" schoolwork to the casual observer. But early childhood educators realize that the child would be learning much more—in fact, functioning at peak capacity—if she were participating in play-based activities instead. Rather than simply identifying the name of a color, for instance, she might use an eyedropper to mix food coloring with water. She would be encouraged to experiment with water that is tinted the primary colors by mixing it in small, clear plastic cups, thereby discovering the secondary colors. She might use color paddles, which are wooden paddles with tinted plexiglass in the center. By placing the paddles one on top of the other and looking through them, a child can discover which secondary colors are produced by blending primary colors. (A similar activity can be done with color-tinted translucent cellophane or plastic.) Another type of play-based color exploration activity might be working with a prism, mixing paints, dyeing eggs, or working with an artist's color wheel. In every case, rather than simply being told some facts about the relationships between colors, the child is actively engaged in constructing his or her own understandings about color. So, what first appears to be simply playing around (or, as the British say, "messing about") actually has more instructional value than the paper-and-pencil task.

Although people usually assume that play is frivolous and work is serious, our most celebrated creative geniuses report that the line of demarcation between work and play was, for them at least, a rather blurry or dotted one. The most creative individuals among us play with ideas. They do not see hard work and enjoyment as essentially incompatible (Csikzentmihalyi & Schiefele, 1992). In fact, they enjoy the process of arriving at a goal as much as or more than having attained it and look upon their work as playful. Moreover, vestiges of childhood play can be seen in virtually every profession (Isenberg, in press). The child who once transported small plastic toys in wheeled vehicles now, as an adult, designs a scale model of a rapid transit system for a city; the child who once invested many hours in play with dolls now works as the clothing buyer for a department store chain; and the child who once put on plays and puppet performances for family members now works as a children's librarian, sharing stories and puppet plays with young children. As each of these situations illustrates, the play of our childhoods is revisited in our lives as adults.

Play has several features that distinguish it from other types of activity (Fromberg, 1992). These features also connect play to the arts and aesthetic education.

1. *Symbolic*—Play encourages children to use "what if" or "as if" kind of thinking, something that is important for creative problem solving and inventing new forms through the arts.
2. *Meaningful*—Play connects and relates experiences. This type of integrative thinking is important for interpreting works of art and evaluating aesthetic experiences.
3. *Active*—Play, like the arts, is dependent upon active participation. When children are at play, they are actors, not spectators. This intense involvement is equally important for creative expression via the arts.

4. *Pleasurable and voluntary*—Both play and the arts are intrinsically motivating. Children are naturally attracted to both pursuits and enjoy them, if given the chance. Just as there is no need to "assign" play to children, there is no need to make aesthetic experiences and arts experiences a mandatory activity. Children are naturally inclined to join in the arts unless someone has turned the arts into a contest or caused the child to feel incompetent.

5. *Rule-governed*—Although play appears to be unstructured, it has an implicit, underlying structure. The same holds true of the arts because art depends upon technique for expression.

6. *Episodic*—Just as children's play has emerging and shifting goals, so also does their art. Play that begins as enacting family roles can quickly change to a dramatization of a favorite story, and a painting that starts out as the sky can quickly change to a different subject with a stroke of the brush.

As Eisner (1990) points out,

> Both play and art have much in common. Both engage imagination, both require reflection, both profit from skill, both seek to generate new forms of experience, both lead to invention, and both are marginalized in the priorities of American education. In my view both children and the cultures within which they live would be better served if art and play had a more prominent place in our schools. (p. 55)

Perhaps you remain skeptical that play has a central role in the early childhood curriculum. If so, try reflecting on the most interesting and exciting things that you did while you were in school. Whenever we pose this question to our students, they usually say things like, "We got to put on a talent show," or, "We made ice and snow sculptures outside," or, "In preschool, we got big sticks and sheets and made them into a tipi." In virtually every case, the activities that were most enjoyed, appreciated, and remembered were play-based and usually involved the expressive arts. Fauth (1990) reports that we remember approximately

Children need large blocks of time to pursue their interests. This boy wanted to drive a "big rig" and used blocks to reach his goal.

    10 percent of what we read;
    20 percent of what we hear;
    30 percent of what we hear and see at the same time;
    70 percent of what we hear, see, and say; and
    90 percent of what we hear, see, say, and *do* (dramatizing, dancing, painting, drawing, constructing). (p. 160)

On that basis alone, there is justification for a play-based early childhood curriculum that emphasizes the arts.

DEVELOPMENTALLY APPROPRIATE PRACTICE

*A*s you work with young children, keep in mind that "the child is not honored if we always expect him to grow up, because a child is not a grown-up" (Moore, 1992, p. 50). Too often, adults begin to push young children to the next stage before the children have had much opportunity to enjoy the stage they are in. This situation is most glaringly apparent when we see teachers bustling around before an "art" activity begins doing much of the work for the children. One university supervisor observed a third grade lesson that exemplifies developmentally *in*appropriate practice. The student teacher provided the children with red, pink, and white hearts of various sizes that she had traced and cut out for Valentine's Day. She also provided patterns of Cupid for children to trace. Then the children were instructed to assemble a greeting card from the materials the teacher had produced. When one of the children in the class folded a tiny square of paper, cut out a heart, decorated it, and taped it to his ear like an earring, he was reprimanded for misbehavior. Yet this boy's activity was more inventive and more challenging than the one the student teacher had prefabricated for her students.

In the activity planned by the student teacher, none of the elements of art and aesthetic experiences are in evidence. The children did not draw upon their imaginations because they were told exactly what to do. They did not craft anything because they were assembling ready-made components. There was no opportunity to link feeling with knowing because they did not select their subject matter or begin with a personally relevant experience. For all of these reasons, the children in this class were not engaged in art.

After the lesson, when the student teacher met with her supervisor and was asked why she selected this particular activity, she said that she remembered doing something similar when she was in school. This is hardly a sound rationale! Certainly, educators can agree that schools ought to seek continuous improvement, and repeating what has gone on before can hardly be expected to achieve that goal. When the student teacher was asked why she had invested so much of her time in tracing and cutting out heart shapes for the children, she said that she wanted to be sure that the cards would "look nice." This reply highlights a persistent source of confusion about the arts. No teacher would compose stories for students or copy students' papers over into his or her own handwriting so that they "look nice," nor would any teacher consider telling children all the answers in math so that their papers "look better." Why not? Because it would misrepresent the child's real abilities and because it would interfere with real learning. Yet many teachers have a double standard, so that what is unthinkable in reading, writing, and arithmetic is perfectly acceptable to them in the arts. It is time to see this double standard for what it is—an impediment to real learning through quality arts experiences. In order to make this activity developmentally appropriate, the teacher needed to trust children and allow them the freedom to respond in their own ways rather than pushing them to produce something that she already had in mind.

We have seen that developmentally appropriate practices, providing a play-based curriculum, appreciating the child artist, and valuing creativity all play a role in the arts and aesthetics. Another key element is understanding child development.

DEVELOPMENTAL SEQUENCE FOR THE ARTS

$\mathcal{M}$any prominent theorists and researchers have studied children's cognitive development and growth in the arts. The discussion that follows uses several classic sources as a way of organizing the major milestones in artistic and aesthetic growth (Bruner, 1960; Hargreaves & Galton, 1992; Kellogg, 1966; Lowenfeld & Brittain, 1964; Piaget & Inhelder, 1969; Vygotsky, 1978). Remember that the chronological ages are merely rough approximations of when these behaviors typically appear. Every child's prior and immediate experiences will affect the pattern of his or her development in areas of the arts and aesthetics.

Infants: Newborn to Six Months

Meet Dianesha, a four-month-old. Her mother says, "She is a cuddler. When you pick her up, she will put her head right up against your neck, cuddle up, and hold on to your clothes. When I sing to her, she makes little sounds. She moves her mouth when she sees food. She has a musical mobile with nursery rhyme characters that is attached to the side of her crib. When I turn it on, she watches it and moves her arms and legs. Loud, sudden noises usually make her cry. The latest development is that when her dad jiggles her around a bit, she smiles."

As baby Di's behavior demonstrates, a baby's behavior at this stage is dominated by reflexes—grasping, sucking, startling at a loud noise. Infants tend to respond with their entire bodies. Their responses are undifferentiated. If a baby cries, for example, it isn't just the face that looks distressed. The entire body shakes. If, on the other hand, the baby is warm, dry, and in direct contact with the caregiver, the baby's entire body is likely to relax in response to these tactile and kinesthetic sensations. These responses from babies are the precursor of knowing and feeling. Sensory experiences inaugurate the baby's aesthetic and artistic growth.

Music and Movement.   Infants respond to rhythmic sounds while still in the mother's womb. The pumping of the mother's heart is imprinted on the baby's memory, and the opportunity to hear that sound again is reassuring to the newborn. Many hospitals use toys that mimic the beating of the heart or play recordings of intrauterine sounds to calm newborns. An infant's hearing is at mature capacity, so listening is an important sensory channel. We know that babies' activity levels are affected by the kinds of music that they hear. Their activity increases in response to lively music and decreases in response to soft music of a slower tempo, such as a lullaby. As they mature, infants will often babble or coo in response to songs that they hear. It is important for infants to hear pleasing, soothing sounds.

Movement for infants is at the precontrol level, meaning that babies do not consciously and intentionally control or replicate body movements (Graham, Holt/ Hale, & Parker, 1993). It is not until they near the end of this stage that they begin to deliberately grasp objects (rather than relying upon the grasping reflex) and exert some control over their body movements. As they become "lap babies" and can sit with support, they often begin to slap their hands, palms down, on surfaces in front of them. Musical toys that make a sound when touched in this way, such as soft plastic squeeze toys or "keyboards," are appropriate for most six-month-old infants. They also begin to respond more to other kinds of sound makers such as rattles, bells, wind-up musical mobiles, and so forth.

Art and Craft.   Babies are capable of responding to sensory impressions. From the moment of birth they can see, taste, listen, and respond to touch. In terms of visual responses, after about two weeks, most babies are capable of following an object with their eyes, an ability referred to as visual tracking. Infants have definite preferences for certain visual stimuli—patterned over unpatterned, complex over simple (e.g., flashing colored lights versus constant white light), moving over stationary (a mobile rather than a picture hung on the wall). According to research, babies' most preferred object is the human face. As they progress through the first six months of life, they begin to touch and manipulate objects more.

Story and Enactment.   As infants reach the end of this stage, a normally developing baby can distinguish between a song, a rhyme, and regular conversation. The way that this ability is tested is through infant research in which the baby is given a pacifier to suck that is hooked up to a monitor. When the baby gets used to a sound, its rate of sucking is relatively slow. When the sound changes, it gets the baby's attention, and it will begin sucking more rapidly. This ability to distinguish among songs, rhymes, and conversation builds the foundation for responding to stories.

Infants learn the rudiments of enactment through simple games such as peekaboo or "This Little Piggy" and also through the exaggerated facial expressions and gestures adults typically use when interacting with them. If you watch a responsive caregiver interacting with an infant face-to-face, you will see how the dynamic between them works. The caregiver will zoom in close, then pull back and touch the baby at various times. The baby will respond by doing such things as vocalizing, moving arms and legs, moving its head forward with the mouth open, raising and lowering its eyebrows, clasping its hands together, and (if the baby becomes overstimulated) looking away. When you watch this interaction on film, as researchers have done, the interaction between the baby and the caregiver has many of the body movements and gestures that we see during a conversation and appears almost like a dance. When caregivers talk with babies, they tend to use a slightly higher pitched, more animated yet gentle voice. A smile actually changes the quality of a voice, and it is this smile in the voice that loving caregivers use with babies. All of these experiences form the basis for enactment as the baby matures.

Infants: Six Months to Twelve Months

Jamal is a nine-month-old infant. His mother reports that he likes to play hide an object, roll the ball, look in the mirror. She says, "Jamal's favorite game is peekaboo, which we play while I change his diaper. I put the edge of a receiving blanket lightly over his face, then quickly pull it away and say, 'peekaboo!' Recently, he has begun pulling the blanket off for himself. His brother got an old jack-in-the-box out of the toy chest the other day, and when Jamal saw the clown pop out, he didn't just smile, he *laughed*. Jamal likes to drop objects and watch them fall when he is in his high chair. He also tries to pull himself up holding onto our hands or a piece of furniture and stand up, although he is a bit wobbly. He also feeds himself pieces of cereal and has learned to wave bye-bye, but he doesn't always do it when you tell him to. Sometimes, the person is long gone before he starts waving! Jamal also tries to talk. You really can't understand the words, but you can tell if he is excited, angry, or sleepy."

Music and Movement.   As babies gain motor control and can sit or stand with support (usually six to nine months), they will give "whole body" responses to music such as moving the arms and legs rapidly, bouncing up and down on an adult's lap, or flexing the knees to do a torso bounce while holding on to something. They begin to differentiate among specific songs and usually have favorites that relax them or prompt them to move excitedly. Often, babies will vocalize along with a song. They babble, coo, or use expressive jargon—a stream of gibberish that has some of the intonation and qualities of speech. When they have mastered deliberate grasping and have learned to use the thumb to pick up objects, they are able to bang on a toy drum with a mallet. They also have sufficient motor control to learn how to push a button in order to start a cassette tape and play music.

Art and Craft. Sensory impressions of the very young are relatively undifferentiated. As infants mature, they are more aware of and responsive to colors, shapes, and designs. As they reach the end of this stage, they usually become adept at urging adults to repeat some stimulus that they found appealing, such as switching the lights off and on. Infants' intense responses to sensory experiences are evident to the observer—the look of rapture as they first experience wet sand or the faces they make in response to a taste of something sour. Infants at this stage are usually learning some of the fine motor skills, such as the coordinated grasp, that will be important in the toddler stage when the baby learns how to use tools such as a crayon.

Story and Enactment. Near the end of this stage, children are beginning to look briefly at books and attempt to name some pictured objects. Books suitable for this stage are *realistic,* usually containing brightly colored photographs or realistic (rather than cartoon-style) drawings of familiar objects. Books appropriate for babies are also *durable,* typically printed on cardboard, plastic, or cloth. Babies are just learning how to turn the pages, so these heavier materials are easier for them to manage. Usually, babies at this stage learn to "point and say," meaning that they will point to what they see pictured and attempt to name it in a book like *Oh Baby!* (Stein, 1995). Most children at this stage have learned how to enact simple, everyday gestures such as pretending to sleep, eat, or touch a forbidden object.

Toddlers: One Year to Two Years

Meet Melanie, an eighteen-month-old. Her father usually takes care of her, and this is what he has to say, "Melanie is on the move. I have had to 'baby proof' the house big time because she gets into everything. One day, I was fixing lunch at the kitchen counter and had one of the cabinet drawers open. The next thing I knew, she had used the drawer as a step and was up on the kitchen counter! She climbs like a monkey! She loves to race around the house while I chase her and say, 'I'm gonna get you.' When I catch her, I lift her up over my head, then give her noisy kisses. She always laughs and says, 'More.' Melanie sleeps with a wind-up musical toy, and she recently figured out how to wind it up herself after quite a bit of practice. She likes to fill plastic milk bottles and buckets with plastic blocks, then dump them out. Her big brother figured out this game where she gets inside a plastic laundry bushel and he slides her around while she laughs. Melanie also likes push and pull toys. She has favorite songs (one is 'The Riddle Song') and she has started to listen to really simple books—mostly books about other toddlers! Her favorite books are ones that they read at toddler story time: *'More, More, More,' Said the Baby* (V. Williams, 1990) and *So Much* (Oxenbury, 1995). I think I've read them to her about a hundred times. When Melanie is around, there is never a dull moment." As this father's comments illustrate, toddlers have become mobile, and they are driven to practice their newly acquired motor skills.

Music and Movement. During the second and third years of life, most toddlers attempt to sing along with simple nursery tunes. They usually know just a few words or a phrase from a song (for example, they may only say "rind round" when they hear "Ring around the Rosie" and refer to the song in that way).

Manipulation is the first level in music development (Beaty, 1992). It occurs when children are exploring and experimenting with music, such as banging on a toy xylophone or making other kinds of sounds with musical toys, homemade musical instruments, or real musical instruments. Just imagine how a typical toddler might react to a piano. The child would be likely to pound on the keys in a haphazard fashion with fists or palms down—a toddler might even crawl up on the keyboard to see how that action affects the sound. It would be unusual to observe the toddler playing one note at a time unless someone had demonstrated how to do so. Basically, the child's goal at this stage is to find out about the sounds that the object makes through direct manipulation. Even though toddlers may lack the musical vocabulary, they can distinguish among sounds produced by different musical instruments. One way that toddlers can demonstrate what they are learning is to listen to familiar sounds or instruments played on a tape or outside their view and then select the item that made the sound. Two-year-olds will sometimes sing improvisationally during play, such as inventing a lullaby while they rock the baby or singing to themselves before they go to sleep.

Movement during toddlerhood becomes more controlled and coordinated. There are three basic aspects of creative movement: how bodies move (locomotor skills), where bodies move (spatial awareness), and when bodies move (timing, tempo, rhythm) (Pica, 1995). Toddlers have acquired more graceful and coordinated gestures than previously. They may sway in response to music or try to move their arms and hands in a more dancelike way. The typical toddler can move in response to the tempo of the sounds on a rhythm instrument, and children will often "dance" on request while music is playing. When movement activities are very simple and approached in a gamelike fashion, toddlers can learn about their bodies and what they can do with them in response to music. Bob McGrath and Katharine Smithrim (1983, 1985) offer a good, basic collection of toddler music and movement activities on *The Baby Record* and *Songs and Games for Toddlers*. Toddlers use primarily their large muscles—the legs and arms—but these gestures are not necessarily synchronized with the music. They enjoy singing simple tunes, particularly songs that can be adapted to include their own names like "Jim along Josie" (Axton, 1995).

Awareness of music in their environment also increases. Toddlers who own records or tapes usually have favorites that they request and can identify even if there are many others strewn about the room.

Art and Craft.   For toddlers, art is experienced as multisensory input. When they see an object, they may also expect to hear it, touch it, or taste it. It is not unusual to see toddlers looking at pictures of a kitten, stroking the page with their fingers, making meowing sounds, and saying, as if calling a real cat, "Kitty kitty." Because of their multisensory orientation, toddlers have a very different orientation to art and craft experiences. Their goal is not to produce something, but to explore and manipulate the materials. A toddler does not make something out of playdough; a toddler *experiences* playdough. The same holds true for drawing. A toddler does not attempt to draw something; a toddler enjoys the kinesthetic experience of crayons, markers, or fingerpaints as these materials are used on paper (or the walls!). Most toddlers scribble for the first time between fifteen and twenty months. They begin by producing accidental scribbles that are created when the child swipes at the paper with a fat crayon or marker. Wherever the drawing tool happens to make

Figure 3.1 **From Random Marks to Scribbles**

contact with the paper becomes the scribble that they produce. Gradually, they learn to control the writing implement more and manage to keep the point in contact with the surface of the paper, still producing random scribbles. Figure 3.1 shows the progression from random marks to controlled scribbles. Scribbling is essential to the growth and development of all children. As Baker (1990) contends: "It first allows them to act upon their immediate environment, and, as their thoughtfulness about the relationship between mark-making acts and the possibilities that reside in assigning meaning to their markings increases, they acquire the power to shape ideas and share them with others" (p. 21).

Toddlers have a keen yet holistic type of perception. They are capable of identifying favorite objects from among a group of objects using what Heinz Werner called physiognomic perception (Werner, 1957). If several cassette tapes are scattered around the room, a toddler will be able to locate the one that he or she likes by responding to its overall qualities, rather than reading the label as an adult would. Toddlers are capable of differentiating in this fashion even though cassette tapes have a very similar appearance. This ability is the precursor of aesthetic judgment in which choices are made based upon what is good, beautiful, and useful to society.

During preschool years, children begin to participate more fully in music and movement, often combining the two.

Story and Enactment. Literature for the very young generally consists of action-oriented material: fingerplays, action rhymes, nursery tunes, and board books. Toddlers' interest in durable books with uncluttered pictures of familiar objects continues to develop. They can understand simple, action-filled books with large, bright pictures like *Piggies!* (Wood, 1991). Stories with very simple plots like *I Went Walking* (S. Williams, 1990) and familiar experiences like *Jesse Bear, What Will You Wear?* (Carlstrom, 1986) are good choices for toddlers. Their fascination with fingerplays expands, although they usually cannot imitate the entire fingerplay on their own. In response to "Eency Weency Spider," for example, they might try to imitate the hand gestures. Enactment expands to roles suggested by objects, for example, putting on an article of clothing, such as Daddy's shoes. With these real-life props from their everyday experiences, toddlers will change their demeanor accordingly. They also begin to enact familiar child care rituals with toys such as feeding a doll, changing its diaper, rocking it to sleep, washing its hair, and so forth. Writing for toddlers is the same as their drawing—simply marks on paper.

When introducing toddlers to pantomime, it is advisable to begin with everyday actions. As children gain confidence, teachers can introduce new challenges. For example, you might begin with brushing teeth, then add a dimension of difficulty such as brushing teeth very quickly or very slowly. Pantomime with the entire body can be used as a starting point—running, hopping, walking—and later become more specialized. Hensel (1990) suggests introducing new challenges like "Can you sway your arm? head? shoulder? Can you move across the room swaying your shoulder?" and so forth. After toddlers explore some of these basic movements, they can take on new challenges such as moving with music or pantomiming moving objects that they have experienced directly, such as a butterfly, a kite, or a hopping toad.

With all of these impressive accomplishments in place, the baby approaches age three and becomes a preschooler.

Preschool: Three Years to Five Years

The preschool years are a time period when imagination is flowering. Children are capable of deferred imitation—doing something even when the model is no longer present (Piaget & Inhelder, 1969). One of the great intellectual and creative milestones of the preschool years is make-believe or pretend play, an ability that affects all areas of the arts and aesthetics. To illustrate, imagine this visit to a Head Start classroom. As Ms. Farine watches the children at play, she observes and records the following behaviors:

- Amanda and Daphine are playing with dolls in the housekeeping area. Amanda says, "I'm giving my baby a bath." Daphine says, "My baby is getting her picture taken." She puts the baby in a chair and reaches for an empty animal crackers box that she is using as a "camera." Amanda says, "Baby is bathed. Time for bed." Daphine says, "Smile, baby. Just one more picture."
- Jason and Timmy are playing with cars by crashing them together. Timmy says, "My car! My car is broke!" to which Jason replies, "I'll put it back together."
- Venitia is making a cake from playdough. She holds it up when it is finished and sings "Happy Birthday" in a quiet voice, then pretends to eat a slice of cake.

For preschoolers, the world of the imagination is opening up.

Music and Movement.   At the preschool stage of their musical development, children have mastered some of the basics about how to use a variety of musical objects. They know, for example, to shake a tambourine, to strike rhythm sticks together, or to ring a bell. You might observe a five-year-old at a keyboard, for example, playing the individual keys over and over again, almost as if practicing. During the preschool years, children begin to participate more fully in music and movement, often combining the two. They master some simple action songs, both singing and doing the motions for "Head and Shoulders" (Monet, 1986). Preschoolers are also learning to cooperate to produce music, such as participating in a rhythm band. Often they are interested in exploring musical sounds with instruments and sharing songs they have learned with others. Early childhood singing/dancing games such as "London Bridge," "The Farmer in the Dell," and "Shake It to the One You Love the Best" (Mattox, 1989) are another way that preschoolers link music with movement. Figure 3.2 is an example of a singing/dancing game that is appropriate for preschoolers.

By age three, most children have names for their favorite tunes, can recognize familiar songs, and can sing portions of songs with a fair degree of accuracy (Alper, 1992). Preschoolers can "outline" songs, respond to "global" features of music— pitch, contour, tempo, and rhythm. They try to participate in action songs and fingerplays by doing the gestures. Some three-year-olds can play a simple rhythm instrument in ways that reveal an emerging awareness of beat, tempo, and pitch if they are given songs with definite rhythm patterns like "Little Red Caboose" (Sweet Honey in the Rock, 1990). Some good activities for threes include musical fingerplays like "Grandma's Spectacles"; echo songs like "Down by the Bay" (Raffi, 1987), which

Figure 3.2 **Singing/Dancing Game**

help children to listen and then sing on pitch; call and response (question/answer) songs like "Did You Feed My Cow?" (Jenkins, 1991), which encourage independence; and cumulative songs like "The Green Grass Grew All Around" (Watson, 1990), which have many verses sung to the same melody and give the child sufficient practice, yet challenge the child to remember the correct sequence. Threes move in a more coordinated way to music (usually running) and may experiment with many different types of body movements, such as jumping. Their movements tend to be more graceful than previously. Vocal range, rhythmic ability, and musical vocabulary are expanding rapidly. They will sing both original songs and structured songs spontaneously while engaged in other activities, especially play. Activities that suggest rhythm, such as swinging on a swing, are likely to be accompanied by song. This is a time when creative movement props can be used to develop children's basic concepts about dance. Figure 3.3 contains some suggested creative movement props for preschoolers.

Fours usually enjoy group singing games like "Looby Lou" and longer musical fingerplays like "In a Cabin in the Woods" (Weiss, 1987) in Figure 3.4. A typical four-year-old's musical repertoire is more varied than a typical three-year-old's. Most fours are capable of learning some basic musical concepts such as pitch (high/low), duration (long/short), tempo (fast/slow), and loudness (loud/soft). They can use language to express these ideas. Classifying musical instruments by their sounds, shapes, sizes, and pitches is also within the ability of most four-year-olds. They can substitute words or phrases in a familiar song, like "Mary Wore Her Red Dress,"

Figure 3.2 Singing/Dancing Game, continued

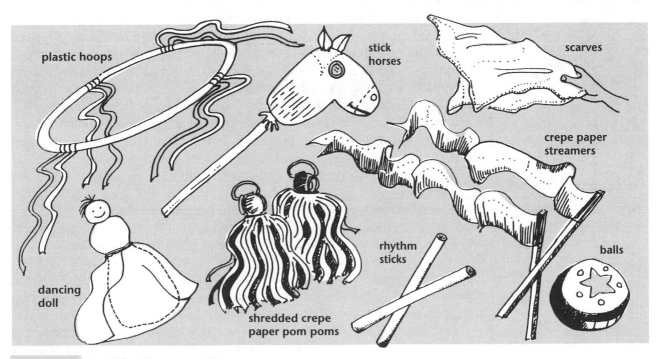

Figure 3.3 Creative Movement Props

Mr. Duck went out for a walk one day in the very best of weather.

He met Mr. Turkey along the way and they stopped to chat together.

(*wiggle finger*)
"Gobble, gobble, gobble"

(*wiggle finger*)
"Quack, quack, quack"

(*have them nod to each other*)

"Good bye"   "Good bye"
(*then move arms apart slowly*)

And they both walked back.

Figure 3.4 **Musical Fingerplay**

sing it, and move to it with adult guidance. Guided listening activities, such as listening to a simple musical story song, are also appropriate for most four-year-olds.

The movement or creative dance of fives also has a more rhythmic, interpretive quality than previously. They can move around in a circle and adjust to changes in the tempo of the music or swirl lengths of fabric in response to a Strauss waltz. They may also be capable of demonstrating their knowledge of the musical concepts they have acquired (fast/slow, high/low, long/short duration) on a small keyboard. Fives understand that music can be represented symbolically--they can conceptualize the musical scale as "stairsteps," for instance. Fives are also better at inventing songs with more melodic qualities.

Five-year-olds learn such concepts as colors, numbers, and letters. Their sense of humor delights in nonsense, slapstick, and incongruity. These features of fives are often reflected in the favorite songs of this age, such as the counting song "Six Little Ducks" (Arnold, 1995b) and the silly action song, "Eye Winker, Tom Tinker, Chin Chopper" (Beale & Nipp, 1983). The typical five-year-old can learn more complicated songs and enjoys singing the chorus while an adult models the singing of the verse. Usually, they are very interested in hearing the song again and again until they have mastered all of the words. Because fives are emergent readers, illustrated song picture books, song charts, or rebus songs such as those in Appendix D are all appropriate.

Art and Craft.   As children enter the preschool years, they continue to think concretely. The figural stage corresponds to what Bruner (1960) called iconic—it is a time when children understand that realistic objects (drawings, photographs, toys, models) can be used to represent reality. They explore and manipulate materials in a playful fashion and are interested in discovering what can be done with color, texture, tools, and techniques. Their drawings gradually become more controlled, and they can recognize and produce basic forms and shapes (e.g., sun, square). Often these shapes are clustered into designs. Young preschoolers usually begin to draw "tadpole people"—a circular shape with some facial features scattered around and lines radiating out to represent first the legs, and later, the arms. Gradually, as children enter the later phases of this time span, they usually begin to draw representationally, meaning that their drawings "look like" whatever it is they are attempting to represent. Figure 3.5 contains some drawings done by preschoolers that illustrate the transition from nonrepresentational to representational art.

Generally speaking, the preschool artist portrays feelings and ideas, including whatever made the greatest impression rather than whatever is seen. Elaboration increases as children's drawings move in the direction of greater detail and preplanning.

As most children reach age five, they are learning the rudiments of crafts— simple weaving, the concept of collage, modeling with clay, and constructing objects out of paper or other materials that are relatively easy to work with.

Story and Enactment.   Preschool is considered to be an exceptionally rapid period of growth in story and enactment. If children have heard stories told and read, they work to make sense out of the words and come to the realization that those marks on paper called writing mean something. With that discovery, children begin not only to listen when a story is read, but also after many experiences with print, they begin to watch the print. During preschool, most children have some favorite books

Figure 3.5 **Preschooler's Drawing of People—from Nonrepresentational to Representational**

that they have committed to memory and ask to hear read aloud over and over again. Reading experts believe that this is the child's way of analyzing print. Preschoolers with prior book experience are generally able to "frame" stories, giving a rough approximation of the story events. One appropriate activity for this stage is to use wordless books (books that tell a story through the illustrations and are textless). Preschoolers can create a text for wordless books and use it to tell the story. Some of the conventions of storytelling are also evident in preschoolers' stories—phrases such as "Once upon a time . . ." or "The End" find their way into retellings.

Enactment also flourishes during this stage. Because their imaginations are blossoming, preschoolers are no longer limited to the literal. They are capable of using fantasy and imagination to cast themselves in myriad roles—a dog one moment, a ballerina the next, and later, a firefighter. Props are usually very simple, and a block can just as easily be an imaginary camera as a spaceship. Children can also use and understand basic pantomimes at this stage if the gestures relate to actions they have performed, such as sipping a beverage from a glass that is very full, chasing a butterfly, or riding in a car over a very bumpy road.

The Primary Grades: Six Years to Eight Years

Seven-year-old Katie is on a car trip with her family. It is a long trip, and she is getting restless. Her parents suggest that they sing, and Katie requests "Grandpa's favorite song that he used to sing with Daddy when he was a little boy, 'Take Me Out to the Ballgame.'" Katie knows many other songs and can sing them "on key." She has brought along crayons, paper, and a plastic tray so that she can write and draw while in the car. Katie makes a sign that reads, "Hi Please wave." As they pass cars, she holds it up in the window and gets very excited when other travelers smile, wave, or even toot their horns. Katie has brought along her favorite books. She likes easy readers, especially the Henry and Mudge series by Cynthia Rylant and Nancy Shaw's (1986) rhyming books about hapless sheep that began with *Sheep in a Jeep*. She can read other predictable books independently, such as *If You Give a Mouse a Cookie* (Numeroff, 1985), and she is excited about demonstrating her new skill in reading to friends and family. Katie also puts on "talent shows" for her family in which she is the talent. She enjoys pretending using dolls from the latest Disney movie, and she likes to play out pretend scenarios. Her latest project was "Katie's Kitchen," a pretend restaurant. She made a menu with prices and pictures of food items, and she created a sign for the door. Katie also took orders on a notepad, set up a table, and served the meals to her customers. She used the toy money from one of her games for customers to pay and for her to make change. Previously, she had a jewelry store that was stocked with junk jewelry donated by her grandmothers. She used the glass coffee table for her counter and provided a bell for customers to ring. Katie made price tags using small pieces of an index card, a hole punch, and string. She also had a toy telephone and boxes to put the jewelry in after it was purchased. As this description of seven-year-old Katie highlights, the thinking of six- to eight-year-olds is more symbolic.

Music and Movement.   It is at this age that children begin to combine music in meaningful ways with other activities—tapping on a drum to accompany their own song, humming along on a kazoo, or playing a simple melody on an electronic keyboard. By the end of first grade, many children are able to sing "in tune." In fact, the singing voices of most adults are not developed much beyond the singing abilities acquired by age six or seven unless they receive voice training (Scott, 1989). Near the end of this stage, most children understand the musical scale as stair steps and begin to make sense of basic concepts about musical notation, such as a whole note lasting longer. The typical six- to eight-year-old can reproduce the melody in an echo song and enjoy the silliness and wordplay of a song like "Iko Iko" (Buckwheat Zydeco, 1994). Children in the primary grades can learn and read the lyrics to the songs which are reasonably complex and place greater demands on memory and sequencing skills such as show tunes like "High Hopes" (Arnold, 1995a) or "Swinging on a Star" (Bartels, 1990).

By the time that most children are in second or third grade, they are developing a sense of harmony. Most can sing a round like Sharon, Lois, and Bram's (1980) "Horsey, Horsey," and some can master two-part harmony with an adult's help. In terms of music concept development, children are more aware of printed music and its relationship to the way that music is sung or played. During the primary grades, children usually have an emerging concept of whether songs are pitched at a key they can sing and whether they are within their vocal range. Many eight-year-olds can learn to read musical notation, and many will show some interest in learning to play a musical instrument.

Physical coordination also improves during the primary grades. Children not only have mastered the different movements such as walking, hopping, galloping, and skipping, but have also become more skillful in matching those movements to the music. They can quickly adjust to changes in the tempo and rhythm of a musical selection, or they can invent their own movements to accompany a piece of music. In terms of small muscle coordination, children can play a rhythm instrument "in time" or clap in time with a square-dance tune like "Turkey in the Straw." Children are more capable of following more complicated instructions and can perform simple folk dances during this phase.

Art and Craft. Most children in the primary grades strive to master new techniques and tackle perspective-drawing challenges such as bird's-eye views or objects viewed from a distance. Objects inside other objects, such as a body inside clothing or food in a dish, often appear to be transparent even though the child recognizes that this is not how they are actually seen. Drawings have baselines and skylines, and show more evidence of planning. Unfortunately, children's drawings during this stage ordinarily move in the direction of imitation and stereotype (Davis & Gardner, 1992). One possible explanation for the loss of the originality and freshness that characterize the preschool years is that children are now more focused on communicating through the abstract symbols of letters and words. Yet while drawings may generally fade as a tool for creative expression, the challenge of crafts is frequently appealing. As Erikson's psychosocial theory suggests, school-age children are industrious and actively seek to develop new skills that contribute to their feelings of self-worth and competence. If given the opportunity and encouragement, many school-age children will seek out and explore a wide array of crafts activities such as making pottery, building things from wood, working with fabrics, creating puppets, and so forth.

Children usually respond first to the subject matter of a work of art. With guidance and opportunity, however, they can begin to identify and experiment with different styles. First, second, and third graders are more sensitive to style and can produce works that possess some of the features of that style. For example, after looking at numerous examples of graphic designs by artists such as M. C. Escher, Gustav Klimt, or Frank Lloyd Wright, they can create a drawing that has some of these characteristics. Likewise, if they examine the works of the Impressionists such as Seurat, Monet, and Degas, children in the primary grades are capable of incorporating some of the soft colors and subdued lines associated with this style into their own work.

Story and Enactment. For six- to eight-year-olds, the interest in fantasy remains, but there is an emerging emphasis on nonfiction accounts of experiences. When composing original stories, most children in the primary grades use standard narrative forms and begin to include the traditional literary elements of plot, characters, setting, theme or motif, and style. Additionally, as they near the end of the primary years, most have learned that stories are interesting only if characters grow and change. Stories that children tell may be a better indicator of these understandings if the child's writing skills are not sufficiently developed to reflect his or her creative expression.

In terms of building skills in enactment, Hensel (1990) suggests that teachers begin with narrated stories that involve group enactments, such as elves making toys or campers on a trip. Gradually, children can move to narrated stories with individual parts, then to stories with dialogue, and finally, to improvisational stories (Hensel, 1990). It is important to emphasize that the goal of the pantomime or improvisation is believability (Hensel, 1990).

At the beginning of this stage, most children are at least beginning to read, and, by the end, most of them can read relatively independently. This ability opens up a much wider range of story influences and often inspires new readers to tell or write their own stories, poems, plays, and performances. Unlike the preschool stage where simple props would suffice, children in the primary grades usually seek rather elaborate props that leave less to the imagination. Because most children in primary grades can read simple texts with expression, they can begin to participate in more formal types of drama such as performing or simple puppet plays that involve a script or inventing their own plays.

As children move through first and second grade, their drama becomes more abstract. An adaptation of Readers' Theater is another type of drama that is appropriate for young children. Rather than relying on memorization, Readers' Theater, as the name implies, is a play that is read aloud in parts, using a script. Typically there is a narrator, and children's assigned parts are highlighted on their copies of the script. For very young children, most of whom do not yet read, a teacher can use a big book version of a predictable book and have the children recite the story from memory (or read it) while other children wear simple costumes they have created and enact the parts. After children are reading independently, they can perform Readers' Theater in the traditional way by reading aloud their parts on a marked script. There are many ways to use written texts as a stimulus for drama and enactment.

As we have seen throughout this book, teachers frequently make the error of expecting children's abilities in the arts to burst forth without much interaction with adults. The art of puppetry offers a good example of how we as teachers can help children to develop their skills and master techniques. Most teachers think

Four first graders' drawings of a lion

that their role in puppetry ends when they display a few puppets for children to play with and show the child how to operate a hand puppet. Under these circumstances, children usually do just one thing—make the puppets fight and hit one another. Then, when children enter the primary grades, they are suddenly expected to produce a polished puppet performance. Just as the young child needs to learn book-handling behaviors—how to turn the pages, hold the book right side up, proceed

Figure 3.6 A Developmental Sequence for Puppetry

⤳ Infants and Toddlers

Characteristic Responses:
Watches puppet intently, tries to grab it or mouth it. May vocalize upon seeing the puppet and try to peer into its eyes or face. Responds to puppets as if they were real and may be frightened by puppets that portray sinister characters or act aggressive.

Appropriate Activities:
Try an "all about you" monologue in which the puppet says the child's name, gives kisses, or shakes hands. The monologues should be short and take advantage of the infant's growing sense of object permanence—the realization that objects continue to exist even when hidden from view. Capitalize on the child's delight in peekaboo by having the puppet disappear and reappear.

⤳ Preschoolers

Characteristic Responses:
Fascinated by simple puppet performances with lots of action and slapstick humor. Give children opportunities to observe live puppet performances as well as puppet plays on film. Puppets that are easy to manipulate, such as mouth-only puppets or stick puppets, are a better choice for children's independent use. Most preschoolers will experiment briefly with hand puppets.

Appropriate Activities:
Consider using masks or toys as a way of building children's proficiency with enactment. For example, you can turn over a wooden rocking boat to represent the bridge in "The Three Billy Goats Gruff" and use paper-plate masks constructed by the children for the characters. Toys can be used as a lead-in to puppets as well, such as first using three teddy bears and a doll to tell "Goldilocks and the Three Bears," then switching to stick puppets. Invite puppeteers from upper grades, the library, or professional puppet troupes to put on a puppet performance. Give children opportunities to observe different types of puppets, such as shadow puppets or marionettes. Consider using a mascot or buddy puppet, one that speaks only to you or is shy and whispers in your ear. Use this puppet to spark children's imaginations, and keep it out of children's reach in a special "house" to maintain its mystique.

⤳ First Grade Children

Characteristic Responses:
As coordination and manual dexterity improve, children are more interested in hand puppets and can operate them reasonably well with practice. Trying to combine speaking with hand movements can still prove difficult, however.

Appropriate Activities:
Consider getting children involved in performing puppet plays where one group recites or reads the story while other children operate the puppets. Another adaptation is to use mouth puppets or stick puppets when novice puppeteers have speaking parts.

⤳ Second and Third Graders

Characteristic Responses:
As children gain skill in reading print, they often begin to experiment with writing scripts for familiar stories based on their experiences. They are also capable of working independently or in small groups to create original puppet plays.

Appropriate Activities:
Give children the time and opportunity to invent and use hand puppets to perform a wide variety of stories rather than having just one puppet play per year. Keep a puppet-making center operating in your classroom throughout the year. To present children with a new challenge, get them involved in using mouth/rod puppets (like many of the Muppets where the mouth is operated by one hand and the arms are operated by rods). Encourage them to watch professional puppeteers (such as reruns of "The Muppet Show") to gain a deeper appreciation for the art of puppetry. Invite puppeteers from other lands to share their unique forms of puppetry, such as the intricate, lacy shadow puppets used in Bali or marionettes, the stringed puppets that originated in France.

from left to right, avoid destroying the pages—children need to learn puppet-handling behaviors (Brady & Gleason, 1994; Long, 1995).

It all begins with the example that the teacher sets for the children. First, select puppetry activities that are developmentally suited to the child's stage of growth. The information in Figure 3.6 will guide your choices. Melissa Renck, a children's librarian, takes a very different and more appropriate approach to instructing children and adults on the art of puppetry. Through her own example of respect for the puppets, she lets the children know that they are for performing. When she works with school-age children, she first gets every child involved by having each one use a swatch of fabric, a rolled-up index card, a 12-by-12-inch square of fabric, and two rubber bands to make a hand puppet as illustrated in Figure 3.7. After the children have decorated their puppets, she walks them through actions and gestures listed in Figure 3.8 from *Making Puppets Come Alive* (Engler & Fijan, 1973). Then the children are given simple tasks to perform with their puppets at the stage while the other students try to guess what is going on—all without words or sounds. By using these strategies, children are actually *taught* the skills of puppetry in ways that respect their developmental levels.

It is a common mistake in teaching the arts to expect children's abilities in art and craft, music and movement, and story and enactment to surface spontaneously. Yet, as you have seen throughout this chapter, teachers have an important responsibility to guide and facilitate children's growth in the arts. Young children need numerous demonstrations of and frequent reminders about how things are done in the arts. By understanding the basic sequence for development in the arts, you can do a much better job of fostering children's growth in all areas of the arts.

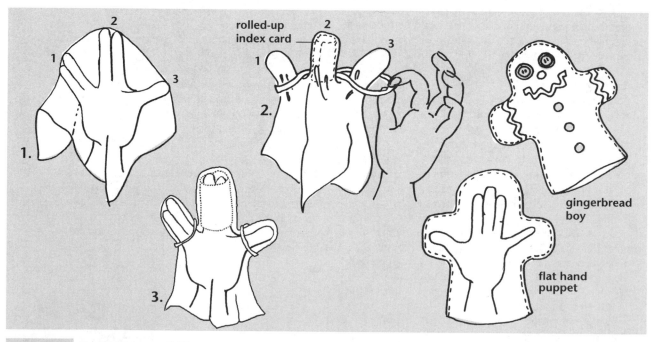

Figure 3.7 **Hand Puppet Skills**

Figure 3.8 **Hand Puppet Actions and Gestures**

Older children can make their hand puppets look alive by learning some basic finger, hand, and wrist movements.

Finger Movements

1. **Nodding/affirmative**—move fingers up and down inside puppet's head.
2. **Point to self**—puppet points to self with either arm; other arm held away from body.
3. **Here**—move puppet's arm toward body; keep other arm near body; combine with slight wrist action for more dramatic effect.
4. **Pointing**—one arm away; slight leaning action to emphasize.
5. **Clapping**—to express joy and excitement bring hands together; can combine with slight up and down motion.
6. **Waving**—one arm in motion; other away from body.
7. **Rubbing hands**—to express anticipation or slyness; move hands back and forth over each other.
8. **Tapping**—to express impatience or anger, tap one hand on stage or self vigorously.
9. **Thinking**—scratch side of head with hand, tap head lightly with one hand, or cross hands and tap one over another.
10. **Creeping**—shift weight from hand to hand while moving across stage.
11. **Crying**—wiggle fingers slightly within head.
12. **Sneezing**—slight jerk of fingers within head.
13. **Snoring**—move head up and down; face away from audience; express intensity by combining with wrist action.

Wrist Movements

1. **Negative**—rotate puppet or rock side to side.
2. **Bowing**—bend wrist; point to self for more emphasis.
3. **Looking**—move wrist back and forth (windshield wipers).
4. **Emphasis**—whack stage with hand.
5. **Reading**—pivot puppet on wrist left to right and move head slightly.
6. **Shyness**—curl in and away from audience.
7. **Sorrow**—put head between hands; combine with slight side-to-side motion.
8. **Picking up**—bow and grasp with hands; straighten.
9. **Sitting**—pivot from front to side view and rest puppet on its seat.

Arm Movements

1. **Walking**—gently move arm up and down in upright position as puppet moves across stage in profile.
2. **Running**—choppy; *not* rapid "zooming."
3. **Hopping**—one deliberate circular motion forward at a time.
4. **Fainting**—fall on back with broad arm movement or slow and comical circular motions.
5. **Falling**—slip; pause for effect; land on back.
6. **Flying**—very broad side-to-side swaying with extended arms.

Source: Engler, C., & Fijan, C. (1973). *Making puppets come alive.* New York: Taplinger.

CONCLUSION

*A*s this chapter has described, children progress through various stages in their artistic growth and achieve many milestones in aesthetic development during the early childhood years. The rate and characteristics of this growth depend upon several factors, including the physical environment of home and school, the role models and encouragement provided by adults, and the individual child's interests, thoughts, and emotions. Few children in the United States are given the time, materials, and support to realize even a fraction of their artistic potential, and, as a result, a cycle of devaluing the arts is set in motion. Parents and teachers who were deprived of the arts as children frequently have allowed their creative potential to decline. Because these adults do not know the arts, they argue that art has no practical value or contend that aesthetics are mere frills instead of realizing that art is a special way of knowing or aesthetics is the heart of the matter. One important goal for early childhood education is to break that cycle and produce a new generation of adults who realize that the arts are just as "basic" as reading, writing, and arithmetic. Without this transformation in attitudes, values, and beliefs about art, the arts will remain a pursuit and a goal only for the privileged. Without the ability to express ourselves creatively, we are diminished in ways that render us less fully human.

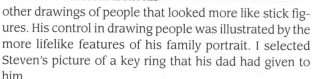

*L*earning about the Arts from Children

Interview with Steven by Dusty Lyn Faber Velesig

For this observation, I chose some of my brother's artwork from this year. Steven is six years old and in the first grade. When we first began to collect some of the artwork he had done throughout this year, I saw a pattern developing. Most, if not all, of the artwork that Steven does in the regular classroom is done in pencil. When I look at his artwork from art class, however, I can tell that he has used a variety of media. I found that difference to be strange, since he told me that they were permitted to use crayons, markers, or pencils to draw. When I asked Steven about it, he said that he liked the way that the pictures looked when they were done all in pencil, "like the ones we saw in high school." Then I remembered how Steven had marveled over the "shadow" drawings that were displayed during my high school graduation ceremony. I was surprised that he even remembered that day, let alone the pictures that we had glanced at for a few moments!

After we collected his artwork, we worked together to create a portfolio of his work. The sample program goals I used were these:

- Uses a variety of media, refines a form.
- Uses art to respond to literature and as a stimulus for writing.
- Gains greater control over artistic media.
- Breaks stereotypes. (Isenberg & Jalongo, 1997)

There was only one piece of artwork that we felt demonstrated the first goal; it was what Steven called his "junk picture"—a collage of scrap materials such as yarn, macaroni, glitter, crayon rubbings, paint, and pencil sketches. Steven loves dinosaurs, and I found two pictures to illustrate his progress in refining the form of a dinosaur. In the first picture, the dinosaur was a circular shape with two eyes, whereas the second picture was much more detailed, with teeth, tail, and spikes on its back. Several pictures could be classified as Steven's progress toward goal three. One pencil sketch of the Plains Indians had been completed during a social studies unit. Another picture was about the fable of the tortoise and the hare and was titled "Tortoise Was Smarter." I believe Steven's picture of his family illustrated the fourth goal. This picture was much different from his other drawings of people that looked more like stick figures. His control in drawing people was illustrated by the more lifelike features of his family portrait. I selected Steven's picture of a key ring that his dad had given to him.

I asked Steven how he gets ready to make a picture, and he said, "Get crayons, paint, pencils, brushes, lids."

Dusty: Lids? What do you use those for?
Steven: For the paint!
Dusty: What kinds of things are there to paint on?
Steven: Cars. And calendars.

Steven is in Cub Scouts, preparing and painting his car for the Pinewood Derby. His reference to the calendar was an item with black-and-white line drawings that I colored in.

Dusty: Tell me about how you decide what it is you will make.
Steven: Well, your brain picks out three or four ideas and then you pick the best one that you like and then you do it.

Steven elaborated on what he selected as his best art project of the year. The picture was a pencil drawing on large construction paper. "This is a big tipi that I made, and this is the horse that I made, and this is the tree that I made, and of course, this is at night with the full moon, and this is the Indians sitting around the fire, and this is a church. You know, church–tipi–ha ha ha." Actually, I think he was confusing the word "tipi" with "steeple."

I was also interested in Steven's music. He seems to have a very special interest in music and musical instruments. Hardly a day goes by without hearing him sing. I asked his mom about his favorite songs, and she said his favorite lullaby is "Jingle Bell Rock." She was singing it one night, and Steven, who was awake at the beginning of the song, fell asleep almost immediately. Even after Christmas was over, the family was using "Jingle

Bell Rock" as a lullaby. Steven's favorite nursery rhyme, according to his mom, is "Sing a Song of Sixpence," his favorite children's song is "I've Been Working on the Railroad," and his favorite popular song is "Friends in Low Places," sung by country musician Garth Brooks.

During the interview, Steven was not at all shy about singing his favorite songs and recording them on a cassette tape. These included "Mary Had a Little Lamb," "I've Been Working on the Railroad," "Friends in Low Places," and "If Your Heart Ain't Busy Tonight." When I asked him who sang the last two songs, he said, "Garth Brooks, and I think, Pam Tillis."

When Steven sang into the tape, I noticed that he was singing in a more restrained and less expressive way on the traditional tunes. But when he began singing the country songs, he began to move around and dance, even adding the country twang into the vocals. For a child of his age, he sings very well both in terms of pitch and tempo. After the interview was over, Steven reminded me that Garth Brooks had sung the National Anthem before the Super Bowl on Sunday. Then he said, "I wish that I could sing like Garth Brooks someday . . . you know, now he's famous an' everybody wants to meet him and sing like him." It was at this point that I realized how strong an influence the media, especially radio and television, have on young children.

*T*he Artist in You

Appreciating the Beauty of Nature: Marissa's Story

Marissa is an early childhood major who is enrolled in two courses in her major this semester, one in science and another in the arts for young children. After she listened to her science professor give a lecture on the importance of nature in children's lives and her arts professor discuss aesthetics, she started to think about an issue that they both mentioned, the child's need to experience nature and its beauty. According to her professors, children address the natural world with a sense of wonder, joyfulness, and creative imagination, and many adults have "ecstatic memories" of special places in the out-of-doors that act like "radioactive jewels buried within us, emitting energy across the years" (Chawla, 1990, p. 18). When Marissa heard this, she thought immediately of her special places—a makeshift tree house she built with her cousins, a pond within walking distance where she spent many joyful hours, and an elderly neighbor's flower garden that included a bird feeder and birdbath. Later, Marissa read Ruth Wilson's (1995) article in which the author stated, "Research also suggests that children seem to have a special affinity, or connection, to the natural world—that they experience a type of 'primal seeing' which, for most people, diminishes with age" (p. 31). She started to think about a child's reaction to a butterfly's wing, a wildflower, or a seashell. Marissa also realized that many children are deprived of contact with the natural world and even fewer have an adult who can share this sense of wonder with them (Carson, 1956). Marissa also located many useful resources (Cole, 1992; Dighe, 1993; Hoot & Foster, 1993; Petrash, 1992; Pope, 1988; Rockwell, Sherwood, & Williams, 1983). She went to the library and discovered that there are beautiful books of drawings by artists who specialized in portraying the natural world—Audubon, Bernard, and Seligman. Based upon all of these experiences, Marissa selected the project of developing an outdoor beauty area at her preschool where children could dig, plant, and tend a small flower garden. Here are some of the learning activities that Marissa and the children engaged in:

- Going on a nature walk to look for flowers that grow in the area.
- Interviewing members of the gardening club.
- Studying reference materials from the agricultural extension office.
- Starting their own compost pile.
- Identifying the plants that provide food for birds and shelter for animals.
- Testing the soil pH.
- Improving the soil with the addition of coarse sand and peat moss.
- Collecting rocks to arrange among the plants.
- Researching the plants that attract butterflies.
- Working with high school students in the vocational education program to build a wooden bench.
- Visiting the sawmill to purchase hardwood bark mulch.
- Weeding and maintaining the space.

Discussion Questions

- Do you think that the project planned here will achieve the goals that Marissa set for it? Why or why not?
- How will this project meet children's individual needs and foster creative growth?
- Read the following quotation and decide whether you agree with it. "Even though our tremendously rich, tre-

mendously mobile society gives far more people access to the more spectacular areas of nature than ever before, nature is not an important part of daily experience. . . . It was nature, and it above all, that was to be discovered, bounteous, mysterious, unmindful, neither judging nor cautioning nor limiting, but mostly, for children at least, infinitely inviting" (Eble, 1966). What examples can you cite from your own childhood that support the contention that nature was "infinitely inviting"?

- The description of this project focuses on activities. What *attitudes* on the part of the teacher would be equally influential in the success of the project?

*S*ituations and *S*olutions

Does This Environment Support Creativity?

Situation 1

The teacher has brought in several prints of abstract paintings. Her teaching goal is for the second grade class to create some abstract paintings of their own after studying several examples. She works to develop the concept that the entire picture is covered with color in each of the paintings that they examine. A child comes up to show her his drawing, which is nothing like the abstract paintings they have been talking about. She holds up the picture and announces to the class, "Look at Jim's picture. Is there white paper showing through? Remember that in all of the paintings we looked at, the artists covered the entire page. Jim, go back to your seat and cover this picture with color. You weren't listening." How would you diplomatically persuade this teacher that her response does not support the students' creative expression?

Situation 2

After their visit to the zoo, Mrs. Krattenmaker's class decides to make a three-dimensional map of the zoo. Using a diagram of the zoo as a reference, the third graders create a tabletop representation of the ideal zoo using paint, clay, stones, crepe paper, and construction paper. Then the children develop a tape that gives a guided tour of their miniature zoo. Does this experience support creativity?

Situation 3

A kindergarten teacher feels that her students' paintings at the easel are not representative of their best work, so she decides to have a contest. The winner will get a helium-filled balloon and some candy. After the winner is announced, many of the children are disappointed, but she tries to console them by saying that everyone tried hard and that all of their paintings will be on display. During recess, one of the children goes back into the room, tears the winning painting off the bulletin board, and rips it up. As a teacher, what would you say if your colleague told you that this happened to her or him? How would you respond to the child whose painting was destroyed? What would you do or say when confronted with the child who tore up the painting?

Situation 4

The computer lab has a new piece of software that children can use to illustrate their stories. After they have typed their stories, they can choose from among several computer-generated images of typical items such as a house, a tree, a dog, and so forth. After the stories are printed out, the children can color the pictures that they selected. Does this activity support children's creative expression? Why or why not?

*I*ntegrating the Arts

An Author/Illustrator Study by Jamie Silk

While enrolled in a children's literature course, Jamie Silk designed an author/illustrator study as one of her projects. Jamie began with her favorite picture-book author/illustrator, Jan Brett, and then consulted the reference book in the library called *Something about the Author* for background information. In collecting this information, Jamie decided to focus on the things about Jan Brett's life that would be interesting to young children. Jamie titled her teaching theme "The Works of Jan Brett" and planned to share the following information with her first grade students:

As a child, Jan Brett wanted to be an illustrator and spent her time reading and drawing. As an adult, Jan Brett lives with her family in the seacoast town in Massachusetts near where she grew up, but during the summer they spend their time at a cabin in the mountains. Jan attributes the inspiration for her work to the environment around her including "the beautiful music, birds, wild animals, and shimmering lake." She says that all her ideas "come from her memory," and she hopes that her readers believe that the imaginary places that she creates might be real.

Jamie has the following activities planned to introduce Jan Brett (1981, 1985a, 1985b, 1989):

1. Have the children look at the covers of the books (*Annie and the Wild Animals, Fritz and the Beautiful Horses, The Mitten, Beauty and the Beast*) that will be used for this unit. Ask them to make predictions about what they think the books will be about. Record their ideas on a web or chart.

2. Ask the children if they notice any similarities in the artwork on the covers of these books, and create a list. Point out that these similarities are part of the artist's style.

3. Invite children to respond to the illustrations. Do they like them? Why or why not?

For the remainder of this teaching theme, Jamie has used the following format:

• Story synopsis
• Reading of the book
• Postreading questions
• Extension activities

Here are two examples from Jamie Silk's project. As you read her plans, try to assess them in terms of how these activities support children's creative, artistic, and aesthetic development.

ANNIE AND THE WILD ANIMALS

Synopsis

Annie is a little girl who becomes very lonely when her pet cat disappears. Annie encounters some very different "pets" when she leaves corn cakes at the edge of the woods in hopes of finding a pet to replace her beloved cat.

Read the Story

Postreading Questions

1. Did you notice anything special about the borders of the pages in this book? How do they differ from other books you have seen? What purposes might they serve?

2. If you were Annie, what would you have done when Taffy disappeared?

3. If Annie had continued to feed the forest animals, what do you think might have happened?

Extension Activities

1. Have the children create stick, sock, or mitten puppets for the characters in the story. They can use these puppets to retell the story or to create their own wild animal story. Children's original stories can be recorded on audio or video tape.

2. Have a class discussion about which animals might make good classroom pets. Establish several criteria and generate a list. Record each child's choice and reasons on a simple bar graph that uses a stick person to represent one vote. Allow children to vote on an animal they would like to buy to keep in the classroom. Before the pet is purchased, the children would be involved in researching pet care. A veterinarian or pet shop owner would be invited to the classroom to explain basic principles of pet care, both for the classroom pet selected and their pets at home.

3. The children will create pinecone bird feeders using large pinecones, peanut butter, birdseed, and string. After the bird feeders are hung outside the classroom, the children can make observations about how birds (or other animals) are responding to the feeders and write/draw their observations in a journal.

FRITZ AND THE BEAUTIFUL HORSES

Synopsis

This is a story about a pony named Fritz who is "kind, gentle, and surefooted." Although Fritz is a hard worker, he is not a beautiful or brilliant jumper, so he must remain outside the city walls. Fritz tries to become more graceful and elegant, but the citizens only laugh at him. When the city bridge begins to collapse, Fritz bravely rushes in and saves the children who were stranded on the other side of the bridge. After rescuing the children, Fritz is rewarded by being given a special place within the city where the children befriend and care for him.

Read the Story

Postreading Questions

1. How do you think Fritz felt after he rescued the children? After he was welcomed into the city?

2. If you could have talked to Fritz when he was left out of the city because he was different, what would you have said?

3. What else could Fritz have done to gain the acceptance of the citizens and the children?

4. How do the citizens' and the children's attitudes toward Fritz change? Why did this happen?
5. You said that Fritz's problem was _____. If you were his friend, how would you help him?

Extension Activities

1. Have the children write about or draw a picture of someone in their lives who they believe is generous, brave, different, or all three. What do they think makes this person this way. Invite them to share their stories/drawings if they wish.

2. Invite children to conduct mock interviews with Fritz, the citizens, the children, and the other horses from the story. Guide children in formulating questions, and give them a choice of format—a talk show–type interview on videotape, an interview that is written/drawn, or a person-on-the-street interview that is taped.

3. The children could read other stories pertaining to the topics of bravery, generosity, and being different. Many of the Native American legends share these themes, such as *The Story of Jumping Mouse* (Steptoe, 1984), *Rainbow Crow: A Lenape tale* (Van Laan, 1989), and *The Legend of the Bluebonnet* (De Paola, 1983).

4. Invite a person with special needs who is willing to talk to the class about the special needs with the class. The guest could discuss experiences with exclusion or access and how these experiences made the person feel. The goal of the presentation is to help the children learn about, appreciate, accept, and respect others.

Discussion Questions

• How successful, in your opinion, was Jamie's plan for integrating art with other subject areas of the curriculum?

• Go to the children's section of the library, and browse through until you find someone whose work is appealing. Check out one or more of that artist's books, and bring them to class. Present your book and your reasons for choosing it to the class. How did your tastes differ?

• Investigate the awards that are given for picture books—the Caldecott Medal, The New York Times Best Illustrated Children's Book of the Year, the Parents' Choice Award, recognition by Reading Rainbow, the Children's Choices and Teachers' Choices of the International Reading Association published in *The Reading Teacher*, and the Children's Editors Choices published in *Booklist* annually. What criteria are used? If you were on the selection panel, what criteria would you use?

• Locate several books that have earned awards for the illustrations. In what ways are these books better, aesthetically speaking, than the books found in discount stores and supermarkets?

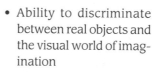

Individual and Group Projects for Teachers

A Photography Project

Mr. Leedy's school has a minigrant program for teachers. A teacher can write a proposal and apply for a grant up to $400 to support a creative teaching project. Mr. Leedy is interested in getting cameras for his twenty-eight second graders because he feels that photography will be a stimulus for writing, class discussion, and arts education. As a start, he reads about photography projects with young children (Osborne, Yocum, & Morgan, 1995). Then he writes a rationale, a statement of the reasons why photography is important. To support his idea, he turns to Lacy's (1986) discussion of visual literacy. She contends that children (particularly in our image-dominated culture) need to learn the following skills of visual literacy:

• Recognition of artistic elements (shape, color, scale, line, proportion, arrangement)

• Ability to discriminate between real objects and the visual world of imagination

• Recognition of likenesses and differences

• Identification of the main idea from pictures.

Next, Mr. Leedy makes a list of pointers he gleaned from his reading.

1. Let children practice with an old camera or one without film before they actually begin taking photos.

2. In the interest of controlling costs, set a limit on how many shots each child can take.

3. Consider developing the shots into one set of prints and one set of slides. The slides can be discussed in a group, and the prints can be kept by each child photographer.

4. Use the new cardboard recyclable cameras to reduce costs.

After developing his rationale and outlining some basic operating procedures in the proposal, Mr. Leedy lists some of the ways that children will use photography throughout the year. On this list of activities he includes recording the first day of school, creating a sequence of photos that depict daily routines, identifying classroom helpers for each day, communicating with parents about the curriculum, using photographs as a way of documenting observations in science, writing and reading stories that accompany photographs, and incorporating three-dimensional projects into portfolios.

As part of his project, Mr. Leedy will use the "Child Care Activity Kit" that he ordered by calling the Polaroid Corporation (1995). He also plans to give children an opportunity to examine the high-quality photographs of several noted picture-book authors, including Tana Hoban, Bruce McMillan, Patricia Lauber, George Ancona, Jane Miller, and Ann Morris. He also plans to share the work of famous photographers such as the black-and-white photography of Ansel Adams and several well-known women photographers (S. Wolf, 1995). He will be sharing a picture book with them called *Boy with a Camera* (Lartigue, 1995) that gives children a sense of how photographers think about their work. Mr. Leedy also knows some resource people. One of his neighbors is a professional photographer who has agreed to make a presentation to the children. Mr. Leedy also knows the instructor for a photography class at the community college nearby, and the instructor has agreed to have the second graders come to campus on a field trip.

REFERENCES

Alper, C. D. (1992). Early childhood music education. In C. Seefeldt (Ed.), *The early childhood curriculum* (2nd ed., pp. 237–263). New York: Teachers College Press.

Baker, D. W. (1990). The visual arts in early childhood education. *Design for Arts in Education, 91,* 21–25.

Ball, L. (1989). Metamorphosis to individual responsibility: A search for curriculum. *Design for Arts in Education, 91*(1), 36–42.

Beaty, J. J. (1992). *Preschool: Appropriate practices.* Fort Worth, TX: Harcourt Brace Jovanovich.

Brady, M., & Gleason, P. T. (1994). *Artstarts: Drama, music, movement, puppetry and storytelling activities.* Englewood, CO: Teacher Ideas Press.

Bruner, J. (1960). *The process of education.* Cambridge, MA: Harvard University Press.

Carson, R. (1956). *The sense of wonder.* New York: Harper & Row.

Chawla, L. (1990). Ecstatic places. *Children's Environments Quarterly, 7*(4), 18–23.

Chawla, L. (1994, August). *Out of the garden, into the world: Preparing children to care for the earth.* Paper presented at the International Symposium on the Prepared Outdoor Learning Environment.

Cohen, E. P., & Gainer, R. S. (1995). *Art: Another language for learning* (3rd ed.). Portsmouth, NH: Heinemann.

Cole, E. (1992). Art and learning: Fostering ecological awareness. *Childhood Education, 68*(5), 285–289.

Csikzentmihalyi, M., & Schiefele, U. (1992). In B. Reimer & R.A. Smith (Eds.), *The arts, education, and aesthetic knowing* (pp. 169–190). Chicago: University of Chicago Press.

Davis, J., & Gardner, H. (1992). The cognitive revolution: Consequences for the understanding and education of the child as artist. In B. Reimer & R. A. Smith (Eds.), *The arts, education, and aesthetic knowing* (pp. 92–123). Chicago: University of Chicago Press.

Dighe, J. (1993). Children and the earth. *Young Children, 48*(3), 58–63.

Eaton, M. M. (1992). Teaching through puzzles in the arts. In B. Reimer & R. A. Smith (Eds.), *The arts, education, and aesthetic knowing* (pp. 151–168). Chicago: University of Chicago Press.

Eble, K. (1966). *A perfect education.* New York: Collier.

Eisner, E. (1990). The role of art and play in children's cognitive development. In E. Klugman and S. Smilansky (Eds.), *Children's play and learning* (pp. 43–56). New York: Teachers College Press.

Engel, S. (1989). *Children's bursts of creativity.* (ERIC Document Reproduction Services No. ED 332 796).

Engler, L., & Fijan, C. (1973). *Making puppets come alive.* New York: Taplinger.

Fauth, B. (1990). Linking the visual arts with drama, movement, and dance for the young child. In W. J. Stinson (Ed.), *Moving and learning for the young child* (pp. 159–187). Reston, VA: American Alliance for Health, Physical Education, Recreation, and Dance.

Fromberg, D. P. (1992). In C. Seefeldt (Ed.), *The early childhood curriculum* (2nd ed., pp.42–84). New York: Teachers College Press.

Graham, G., Holt/Hale, S., & Parker, M. (1993). *Children moving: A reflective approach to teaching physical education.* Mountain View, CA: Mayfield.

Gharavi, G. J. (1993). Music skills for preschool teachers: Needs and solutions. *Arts Education Policy Review, 94*(3), 27–30.

Hargreaves, D. J., & Galton, M. J. (1992). Aesthetic learning: Psychological theory and educational practice. In B. Reimer & R. A. Smith (Eds.), *The arts, education, and aesthetic knowing* (pp. 124–150). Chicago: University of Chicago Press.

Hensel, N. (1990). A developmental approach to creative drama. *Journal of Early Childhood Teacher Education, 36*(11), 7–9.

Hoot, J. L., & Foster, M. J. (1993). Promoting ecological responsibility . . . through the arts. *Childhood Education, 69*(3), 150–156.

Isenberg, J. P. (in press). Play among education professionals. In D. P. Fromberg & D. Bergen (Eds.), *Play from birth to twelve: Contexts, perspectives, and meanings.* New York: Garland.

Isenberg, J. P., & Jalongo, M. R. (1997). *Creative expression and play in early childhood.* (2nd ed.). Englewood Cliffs, NJ: Merrill/Prentice Hall.

Kellogg, R. (1966). Stages of development in preschool art. In H. P. Lewis (Ed.), *Child art: The beginning of self-affirmation* (pp. 3–70). Berkeley, CA: Diablo.

Lacy, L. E. (1986). *Art and design in children's picture books.* Chicago: American Library Association.

Long, T. C. (1995). *Make your own performing puppets.* New York: Sterling.

Lowenfeld, V., & Brittain, W. L. (1964). *Creative and mental growth* (4th ed.). New York: Macmillan.

Moore, T. (1992). *Care of the soul.* New York: HarperCollins.

Nicholson, M. W., & Moran, J. D. (1986). Teachers' judgments of preschoolers' creativity. *Perceptual and Motor Skills, 63*, 1211–1216.

Osborne, J. A., Yocum, L., & Morgan, D. (1995). Ways to use photography in the early childhood classroom. *Day Care and Early Education, 22*(4), 14–17.

Petrash, C. (1992). *Earthways: Simple environmental activities for young children.* Mt. Rainier, MD: Gryphon House.

Piaget, J., & Inhelder, B. (1969). *The psychology of the child.* London: Routledge and Kegan Paul.

Pica, R. (1995). *Experiences in movement.* Albany, NY: Delmar.

Polaroid Corporation. (1995). Child care activity kit. Available from Polaroid Educational Program, Polaroid Corporation, 575 Technology Square, Cambridge, MA 02139; (617) 386-5090.

Pope, J. (1988). *Kenneth Lilly's animals.* New York: Lothrop, Lee, & Shephard.

Reimer, B. (1992). What knowledge is of most worth in the arts? In B. Reimer & R. A. Smith (Eds.), *The arts, education, and aesthetic knowing* (pp. 20–50). Chicago: University of Chicago Press.

Rockwell, R. E., Sherwood, E. A., & Williams, R. A. (1983). *Hug a tree and other things to do outdoors with children.* Mt. Rainier, MD: Gryphon House.

Scott, C. R. (1989). How children grow—musically. *Music Educators' Journal, 76* (2), 28–31.

Torrance, E. P. (1969). *Creativity.* Belmont, CA: Feron.

Vygotsky, L. (1978). *Mind in society: The development of higher psychological processes.* Cambridge, MA: Harvard University Press.

Werner, H. (1957). *Comparative psychology of mental development.* New York: International Universities Press.

Wilson, R. (1995). Environmental education: Let nature be your teacher. *Day Care and Early Education, 22*(3), 31–34.

Wolf, S. (1995). *Focus: Five women photographers.* Morton Grove, IL: Albert Whitman.

Children's Books and Recordings

Arnold, L. (1995a). High hopes. *Sing along stew.* Hollywood CA: A&M Records.

Arnold, L. (1995b). Six little ducks. *Sing along stew.* Hollywood, CA: A&M Records.

Axton, H. (1995). "Jim along Josie" On *Jeremiah was a bullfrog.* Cypress, CA: Youngheart Music.

Bartels, J. (1990). Swinging on a star. On *Sillytime magic.* Van Nuys, CA: BMG Music.

Beale, P. C., & Nipp, S. H. (1983). *Wee sing silly songs.* Los Angeles, CA: Price/Sloan/Stern.

Brett, J. (1981). *Fritz and the beautiful horses.* Boston: Houghton Mifflin.

Brett, J. (1985a). *Annie and the wild animals.* Boston: Houghton Mifflin.

Brett, J. (1985b). *The mitten.* Boston: Houghton Mifflin.

Brett, J. (1989). *Beauty and the beast.* Boston: Houghton Mifflin.

Buckwheat Zydeco (1994). "Iko Iko." *Choo choo boogaloo.* Redway, CA: Music for Little People.

Carlstrom, N. (1986). *Jesse bear, what will you wear?* New York: Macmillan.

De Paola, T. (1983). *The legend of the bluebonnet.* New York: Putnam.

Jenkins, E. (1991). Did you feed my cow? On P. Erikson (Producer) & A. Seeger & S. McArthur (Directors), *Ella Jenkins live! at the Smithsonian* [Videotape]. Available from Rounder Records, 1 Camp Street, Cambridge, MA 02140.

Lartigue, J. (1995). *Boy with a camera.* New York: Simon and Schuster.

Mattox, C. (1989). *Shake it to the one you love the best: Play songs and lullabies from Black musical traditions.* Nashville, TN: GTG Music.

McGrath, B., & Smithrim, K. (1983). *The baby record.* Toronto: Kids Records.

McGrath, B., & Smithrim, K. (1985). *Songs and games for toddlers.* Toronto: Kids Records.

Monet, L. (1986). Head and shoulders. *Circle time.* Redway, CA: Music for Little People.

Numeroff, L. (1985). *If you give a mouse a cookie.* Topeka, KS: Econoclad. (Big book)

Oxenbury, H. (1995). *So much.* Boston: Candlewick.

Raffi (1987). *One light, one sun.* Hollywood, CA: A&M Records.

Sharon, Lois, & Bram. (1980). Horsey, horsey. On *Singin' and swingin'.* Toronto: Elephant Records.

Shaw, N. (1986). *Sheep in a jeep.* Boston: Houghton Mifflin.

Stein, S. (1995). *Oh baby!* New York: Walker.

Steptoe, J. (1984). *The story of jumping mouse.* New York: Lothrop, Lee, & Shephard.

Sweet Honey in the Rock. (1990). Little red caboose. *Family folk festival: A multicultural sing along*. Redway, CA: Music for Little People.

Van Laan, N. (1989). *Rainbow crow: A Lenape tale*. New York: Knopf.

Watson, D. (1990). The green grass grew all around. On *Doc Watson sings songs for little pickers*. Waterbury, VT: Alacazam.

Weiss, N. (1987). *If you're happy and you know it*. New York: Greenwillow.

Williams, S. (1990). *I went walking*. San Diego: Harcourt Brace Jovanovich.

Williams, V. (1990). *"More, more, more," said the baby*. New York: Greenwillow.

Wood, D. (1991). *Piggies!* San Diego: Harcourt Brace Jovanovich.

*P*arents can make a difference: by encouraging their children's participation in art at home, by supporting art programs in their community and by helping to decide how art will be taught in school. Parents can become influential spokespersons for improving school art programs. By working together with school staff, with members of organizations and with other individuals, parents can make sure that art has an important place in their children's education and in the community.

—National Parent Teacher Association (1992, p. 8)

Families' Roles in Supporting Artistic Growth

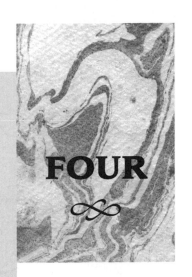

FOUR

Chapter Reflections

- ✿ How have your family experiences affected your self-concept as a creative or artistic individual?

- ✿ What are the characteristics of home environments that support the arts?

- ✿ How can teachers and parents work together in ways that promote every child's talents?

- ✿ What can you do to communicate the value of the arts to families?

FAMILY INFLUENCES ON CHILDREN AND
THE ARTS

As early as 1630, Comenius proposed education for young children that recognized the family as a significant force in children's development and learning (Sadler, 1969). Contemporary early childhood educator Jerry Tello (1995) echoes these traditions when he writes, "Every day, families bring to us the most precious gifts they have to offer—their children. They are the living reflections of their parents' lives, their connections to the past, the legacies of each family's existence—even if they aren't necessarily who we expected, or if we aren't always prepared to receive what they have to offer" (p. 38). What, exactly, do parents have to offer? Figure 4.1 is a summary of the assets that parents bring to education.

A question that has intrigued human beings for centuries is "What conditions during childhood produce artistic genius?" In attempting to answer this question, there has been a tendency to focus on "superbabies" and child prodigies rather than studying artistic and aesthetic development as a part of every child's experience (Howe, 1990; Szekely, 1981). This emphasis on the most extraordinary individuals has implied that the arts are mysterious, miraculous, and out of reach for the majority of people. Although it is undeniably interesting and instructive to study the lives of brilliantly creative and talented artists, we will ask and answer a different question in this chapter. Our question has been framed to address the larger issues confronting everyone who is responsible for young children's care and education. We ask, "What kinds of family characteristics and home environments support children's creative and artistic growth?" Weissbourd (1996) describes the minimum requirements for a home environment when he writes that all children

> should live in environments that provide some order and meet their basic physical and material needs. All children should have a continuous relationship with a consistently attentive and caring adult who treats them as special—not as just another inhabitant of this world—who is able to stimulate and engage, who provides appropriate responsibilities and challenges, who passes on important social and moral expectations. Some strong friendships and the affirmation and affection of community adults are often critical to children, especially those who are deprived of the consistent presence of a parent or guardian. All children should have freedom from exploitation and discrimination in their communities, some sense of justice in their world, and opportunities in school and in communities for constructive achievement. Many children also need special health, social, and educational services to deal with inherited and acquired ailments and disabilities. When children have these ingredients, they are likely to have trust in themselves and the world, inner vitality and resourcefulness, and the capacity in adulthood for zestful play and for gratifying work and love even if they suffer serious deprivations. (p. 8)

If these are the minimum ingredients for a positive home environment, then what types of environments are necessary to foster creativity?

As you read the following three brief descriptions of children's home environments, apply your understandings about creative home environments to three children's situations: Lynda's and her baby sister's experiences with folk arts, Mark's experiences with pop and rock music, and Sun's introduction to American arts education. Throughout your reading, keep two questions in mind:

1. What are the positive features of each home environment?
2. How could these families improve upon the arts experiences they are providing for the child or children?

Figure 4.1 Parents' Assets

Even though families have a limited understanding of school systems and base most of their ideas about early childhood education on their experiences as children, parents have many important things to offer.

1. Parents know their child in a way that no one else can; therefore, they can "round out" a teacher's understanding of a child.
2. Parents have a vested interest in seeing their child become educated; therefore, they are usually "on your side" if you will allow them to be.
3. Parents usually want to be informed, to be consulted, to be helpful; therefore, they can intensify the results of your teaching efforts if you help them to understand what you do and why.
4. Parents are the child's first teacher and have logged many hours observing teachers when they were students; therefore, they have firm ideas about good and bad teaching. One of your roles is to help them see that what you are doing is effective teaching that has their child's best interests at heart.
5. Parents are citizens who help to finance schools and whose offspring enable early childhood educators to have jobs; therefore, we need to treat them with all the courtesy and respect that a business person extends to a loyal customer.
6. Parents have special interests and hobbies, vocations and avocations, and they play a variety of community roles; therefore, parents possess knowledge, skills, and understandings that can be used to educate students and enrich the curriculum.

Source: Adapted from Sarason, S. (1995). *Parental involvement and the political principle: Why the existing governance structure of schools should be abolished.* San Francisco: Jossey-Bass.

- Five-year-old Lynda and her one-year-old sister April live in the Appalachian mountains with their family. The rest of the family includes their mother, father, maternal grandmother, teenage sister, and her six-month-old baby. The family does not own or want a television set, and most evenings they entertain themselves after supper with Papa's fiddle, Mama's dulcimer, and Grandma's autoharp. Lynda has a hand-carved dancing doll that she received as a Christmas gift. It is a little jointed figure attached to a stick that can be moved in time to the music. Because its feet tap on a small wooden platform, it creates a clicking sound similar to that created by rhythm sticks, but it can tap much more quickly and in more elaborate patterns. When the family shares music, Lynda strives to make her doll dance to the rhythm of the song while her little sister claps and bobs back and forth in response to the music.
- Kindergartner Mark's father abandoned the family last year. Shortly afterward, Mark's aunt and uncle separated. Now Mark lives with his twenty-two-year-old mother, his nineteen-year-old aunt, and his one-year-old cousin. Their home is filled with top-ten recordings, MTV, and T-shirts that advertise various musical groups. There is much excitement in the house when a new CD is purchased, and usually it is played loudly for days afterward. When Mark attends a Christmas party sponsored by the local VFW, he rips open his gift package and is thrilled to see a gold plastic toy guitar. Mark immediately begins to imitate the rock stars he has seen on television by dramatically playing imaginary riffs—all much to the amusement and delight of the adults.
- Seven-year-old Sun and her mother recently immigrated to the United States from China. Her father has been in graduate school for the past two years, and now that he has been employed as a faculty member, he has sent for

Families can support the arts by sharing their expertise and enthusiasm.

his family to join him. Sun remembers how much she hated learning the traditional dances in her home country from a teacher who was very demanding and critical even though her parents felt it was very important to master the routines and insisted that she practice at home. Sun wonders if her new teacher will be the same way and worries about whether the new dances will be too hard. Little does Sun know that in her elementary school, indeed almost everywhere in her new country, there are no dance programs at all in the public schools.

Clearly, Lynda, Mark, and Sun have very different cultural backgrounds and are being exposed to dramatically different home environments. Some would say that Sun is the only one who is having genuine arts experiences because she is learning classical music and dance through formal lessons. Others would say that Lynda's and April's informal experiences with folk music are just as valuable. And many would argue that the pop and rock that Mark hears are too common to qualify as art. There is no simple way to decide because people's views on these issues are, to a considerable extent, affected by their tastes, preferences, values, attitudes, interests, proficiencies, and background. One useful way of looking at these examples is to return to the characteristics of home environments that support creativity. From this perspective, the path becomes clearer. One thing that all of these home environments appear to be lacking, for example, has to do with variety and exposure to different musical styles. Lynda's and Mark's musical experiences, for instance, are focused almost exclusively on one specific type of music. In Sun's case, her new environment offers her few choices and fails to capitalize on her interests. As this chapter will help you understand, there are some guideposts along the road to creativity and artistry that can help families and other significant adults in children's lives to exert a more powerful, positive influence on the artistic and aesthetic development of young children.

The Child Artist at Work

Six-year-old Leslie and her mother are sitting at the kitchen table together chatting quietly and coloring pictures in a coloring book. When Leslie tires of connecting the dots and "coloring in the lines," she begins drawing pictures, asking her mother to show her how to draw a penguin and a puppy dog with a bow in its hair. Her mother does not realize it, but she is instructing her daughter in stereotypes. She shows Leslie how to make a bowling ball shape for a penguin, a dog from ovals, and a bow with two side-by-side triangles. In first grade, Leslie is learning to strive to copy the examples that adults provide, a lesson that her mother learned well when she was in school.

When we shared this example with experienced teachers, many of them protested with, "But I used to like to color," and some admitted, "I still like to color in coloring books." The first thing that needs to be examined is why copying and coloring pictures were associated with pleasure. We would argue that the attraction of these activities has more to do with having an adult's undivided attention and engaging in extended conversation than with the activities themselves. For both adults and children, coloring in books is monotonous and therefore keeps hands occupied, yet leaves the colorers free to think, talk, laugh, make plans, and give promises. We might just as well be cleaning strawberries or folding laundry because the arts and creativity are not being fostered. These experiences with stereotypes masquerading as "arts and crafts" communicate to children that their ideas aren't good enough and teach them to mistrust their own creativity. These activities are deliberately designed to "keep little hands busy." Some parents will no doubt protest saying, "But it's better than nothing!" Is it? Actually, we think "creating something out of nothing" is far more appropriate. Recycled paper, for instance, is more plentiful, less expensive, more environmentally friendly, and preferable from a creativity standpoint.

Suppose that, instead of coloring in the lines, Leslie and her mother decided to draw together on blank paper. In fact, this activity is exactly what arts experts would endorse. Golant (1992) suggests these ideas to parents:

- **Play the scribble game**—Try scribbling together, then look for shapes or objects in the scribbles, much as you would visualize pictures in cloud formations. Use a contrasting color to highlight whatever object you see; encourage your child to point out what he or she sees. There is no right or wrong answer, just fun and surprise at what your child will see and talk about.
- **Make up stories**—Use several of the objects that you discovered in your drawing and make up a story about them. Model talking aloud as you draw: "Hey! I see a little mouse right here in this corner, look. I wonder where he lives and what he's doing. Maybe he could follow this path. I wonder what he will find . . ."
- **The squiggle game**—Make a short, wavy twist or line, then use that line to suggest a drawing of something that is not the obvious, predictable response. Ask your child to make a squiggle, then turn it into something. If your child is able to make marks on paper, invite him or her to make a squiggle and then make it into something.

Notice how much more active and original these activities are than coloring in a book. The games call upon Leslie to use her imagination, interact more directly with her parent, play with ideas, and make discoveries. Ironically, the deceptively simple activity is often the more intellectually challenging one. This is one reason why children play with the wrappings and ignore the expensive, battery-operated toy, one reason why children return to basic materials like clay and water again and again, one reason why painting retains its child appeal throughout the early years. These basic pursuits that are a part of good programs for young children are more apt to make a lasting contribution to the young child's artistic and creative growth. In fact, "Research shows that when parents talk or sing or play with a young child they are doing something far more important than entertaining: they are providing basic stimulation that is essential to the development of the basic circuitry of the child's brain" (Weissbourd, 1996, p. 24). All over the world, young children sing, dance, draw, paint, dramatize, learn language, listen to stories, and make music. These are the natural activities of the child, and they are all unified by their relationship to play, cognitive development, and creative expression (Cane, 1983). As the Theory into Practice details, there are clear connections between communication through language and through the arts.

Theory into Practice

Research on Emergent Literacy and the Arts

Research exploring conditions for creative and artistic growth in young children is limited, particularly where the role of parents and families in aesthetic development is concerned. As mentioned earlier, much of the creative arts research about families focuses on case studies of child prodigies, and most studies of arts environments emphasize the classroom setting. There is, however, a large body of research on family characteristics and home environments that foster growth in literacy, and these data also form a foundation for understanding environments that support the arts. Clearly, children's responses to literature—as well as their original stories and drawings—are not only an integral part of emergent literacy but also part of creative and artistic expression (Gallas, 1991). Children do not differentiate among various means of expression until society begins to push them into separating learning into individual subjects or categories. To a very young child, for example, drawing and writing are one and the same thing: both are making marks on paper.

The arts can be conceptualized as a literacy, as a form of communication, and as a special language. Perhaps most importantly, emergent literacy research is pertinent to the arts because most of the research is based on direct, in-depth observation of children and families in natural settings, such as homes and classrooms that are developmentally appropriate (Morrow, 1995). For all of these reasons, we now make the connection between family and home variables that affect children's acquisition of literacy with print and their literacy in the arts.

In the same way that family support is regarded as essential for children's literacy development, the importance of family influences on children's responses to the arts is echoed in research. In both areas, there is a growing recognition of the significance of family involvement. As Rinaldi (1992) explains,

> The school is a system of communication, socialization, personalization, a system of interactions in which the three inseparable and integrated subjects of education—children, educators, parents—are primarily involved. To carry out its primary task, the school cannot worry about and be involved only in the children's welfare; it must also pay attention to the teachers' and the parents' welfare. The system of relationships is so highly integrated that the well-being or lack of well-being by one of the three protagonists is not merely correlated with that of the others, but it actually depends on them. This well-being is closely linked with the quantity and quality of awareness they have of the reciprocal rights, needs and pleasures and the occasions for meetings and get-togethers that form a natural part of a system of permanent relations.
>
> The participation of the families is an integral part of the educational experience. (pp. 8–9)

Yet, the role of family in creative arts development has been loosely defined in comparison to the field of literacy. While the role of the parent as a facilitator of children's growth in literacy is generally accepted and understood—most parents are aware that they should talk to their babies, read aloud to their children, and so forth—the role of the parent in creative arts development is less well defined. Many parents assume that there is little they can do, other than wait for some sign of talent to emerge and finance private lessons for the child, if they can afford them. Yet family roles and home characteristics are foundational to introducing, supporting, and extending both emergent literacy and aesthetic education in the life of the young child. Four themes that link literacy and the arts are:

1. Both emergent literacy and arts research emphasize the importance of role models. Creativity and artistic expression, like literacy, are learned primarily through interactions with role models (Auerbach, 1995). In order for children to become literate, they need family support for literacy activities, enthusiastic role models/readers, and opportunities to interact with pieces of print as the focal point. Likewise, in an "arts-friendly" home environment, children need family members who support the arts, enthusiastic consumers (not necessarily performers) of the arts, and opportunities for social interaction surrounding creative works and experiences.

Naturally, adult role models' confidence in their own abilities and personal literacy levels is a key factor in parental support of literacy development (Fitzgerald, Spiegel, & Cunningham, 1991). Parents with high levels of literacy are more likely to realize the importance of literacy events and experiences for their child whether for educational reasons, professional opportunities, or sheer enjoyment. Conversely, parents who function at lower literacy levels or who recall negative experiences with reading and composition in school may attribute less importance to children's literacy experiences. A parallel exists in the arts. Parents with less experience and expertise in the arts frequently place less emphasis on the value of those experiences for their children. On the other hand, parents who have experienced the arts recognize the value that they have for cognitive development, aesthetic growth, and emotional release; therefore, these parents are more likely to encourage, facilitate, and support these experiences for their offspring. Every child needs a person who will listen delightedly to her the first time that she coos in response to a song; someone who will sit down and pay attention when he begs, "Come and watch my puppet show!" and someone who will be genuinely appreciative when the child, splattered with paint and glue, holds up a paper sculpture while saying, "I made it for you." When such role models are present, young children can develop a healthy appreciation for, understanding of, and familiarity with artistic and aesthetic experiences.

2. Both emergent literacy and arts research stress the importance of the child's role as an active participant. One consistent finding in literacy research is the idea that children who have opportunities to hear stories, see print, and handle books prior to school entrance demonstrate more success as readers during their school years (Salinger, 1996). Both readers (and artists) are made, not born (Chambers, 1973). One way that people and environments shape children into readers and artists is through the active participation of apprenticeships. Apprenticeship is a time-honored way of inaugurating the child's entrance into the world of art, craft, and work. In the past, a child learned to grow crops, build cabinets, or tailor clothes by working alongside an expert as an apprentice. Today, many types of apprenticeship have been replaced by formal schooling. However, both children's language learning and their arts development can be seen as a social, cognitive, and aesthetic apprenticeship.

3. Both emergent literacy and arts research emphasize the self-expressive power of language and art. There isn't much point in acquiring language skills unless they are put to interesting and powerful uses (Smith, 1988). If children spend much of their time copying from the board or tracing letters, they will soon grow weary of writing. If, on the other hand, children use their newfound abilities to communicate and get a response, then the trouble it takes to master writing is worth the effort. The same holds true of the arts. Unless the arts are used as a medium for children's expression of their "inner existence," children will not glimpse the power of the arts. This power is revealed to children only if they have access to materials, time to explore them, and respectful encouragement from others as they investigate and experiment. Just having the teacher as an arts advocate is not enough. Teachers can stimulate interest, but parents must extend and continue the experiences in order to make the most of these experiences. Without nourishment from important adults, a child's interest and opportunity for artistic development may fade. This idea is underscored by other researchers who assert that parents essentially give their children "permission" to be artistically creative by directly influencing environment, providing stimulation, offering support, and supplying tools (Kegley & Siggers, 1989). "Playmaking, acting out ideas, drawing and sculpting, dancing and making music with instruments—these are natural and even essential means for people to gather and process information" (Carlisle, 1990, pp. 13–14).

4. Both emergent literacy and arts research give evidence that early experience exerts a powerful influence on later experience. Research indicates that the single most significant factor determining whether children are successful readers by grade two is whether

Adults do not need to be artists themselves in order to encourage young children's explorations of the arts.

they have heard stories read aloud before coming to school (Heath, 1983; Wells, 1986). Reading aloud to children provides opportunities for increased vocabulary, interactive speech, praise, and affirmation, and it builds a child's "sense of story." These early experiences increase a child's ability to engage in and respond to all kinds of literacy experiences and provide children with "tools" for pursuing reading on their own. Prior experience and familiarity are equally important in the arts.

"Schema" is the word that educators use to describe all of a person's existing knowledge and experiences. Schema has a direct effect on any new knowledge that is to be acquired (Pike, Compain, & Mumper, 1994). The most effective teaching and learning for young children, then, occur in settings where prior knowledge is acknowledged and capitalized upon. Likewise, research indicates that situations which have no relevance, connection, or interest for the learner are largely ignored in terms of learning (Smith, 1988). Studies of arts experiences indicate that involvement in early childhood arts experiences is definitely related to later participation in arts activities such as live theater, musical performances, and museum visits (Orend, 1987).

For all of these reasons, the home is a prime learning environment. Family influences and the home environment have an enduring effect on children's literacy growth that is echoed in research on the arts and aesthetics. Both in emergent literacy and in emergent artistry, there is a growing recognition of the many different and important roles that families play.

FAMILIES' ROLES IN THE ARTS

*W*hether a person is a parent, a teacher, or both, parents and teachers have increasingly complex and challenging roles to play in contemporary society. As you consider your interactions with parents, begin with these important understandings:

> Each family comes with its own set of values and beliefs. . . . It is important to appreciate and respect their values, goals, and concerns even when they are

different from your own. Start with the assumption that parents want what is best for their child. They have the lifelong responsibility of caring for their child and they have the right to make final decisions in all matters. (Rab & Wood, 1995, p. 117)

Billman and Sherman (1996) identify several roles that parents are expected to fulfill and juggle simultaneously, roles that we have adapted and applied to the arts:

Parents as nurturers.   Parents have full-time responsibility for their children, even if their children are in someone else's care at the moment. Gestwicki (1992) points out how pervasive that responsibility is when she refers to the "irrevocability" of parenting—the fact that once a person becomes a parent, there is no turning back. Parental responsibilities pertain to every hour of the day and extend into every facet of living.

When you teach you will no doubt encounter parents whose religious beliefs lead them to request that their child be excluded from art activities connected with Halloween, or parents who disapprove of a picture book from your classroom collection, or parents who will insist that dance will turn their son into a sissy. In these and other situations, strive to identify with the parent rather than judge. Remember that an angry parent is often a frightened parent who is deeply concerned about her or his child failing the system and becoming a misfit in society. It might also be the case that the parent who thinks the arts are a waste of time has childhood memories of feeling foolish or inept in the arts as a child. In order to nurture children's growth in the arts, you will need to respect the role that families play in nurturing creative and aesthetic growth because every child needs "an adult who considers that child's existence at least as important as his or her own and who has at least a rudimentary understanding of the child's needs. Children need an adult whom they admire and who has some capacity to mirror them, to reflect who they are" (Weissbourd, 1996, pp. 23–24). This nurturing role is especially important in the arts because the arts are so often deemphasized in schools.

Parents as participants in adult relationships and members of communities. Parenthood alters and redefines an adult's relationships with other adults. Parents with preschoolers often gravitate toward other parents with preschoolers because they have something in common—responsibility for a young child. Parents who support the arts call upon this circle of family members, friends, neighbors, and community members to enrich and enlarge the child's aesthetic experiences. It might be a brother in college who can get tickets and take the child to see a Russian dance troupe, a neighbor who baby-sits and will share picture books with the child, or perhaps a retired music teacher who gives piano lessons to elementary school children. By participating in these adult relationships, parents create networks of individuals who can enrich the child's growth in art.

Parents as individuals.   After a child is born, parents find it necessary to adapt and adjust their personal agendas to meet the overwhelming demands of a new baby. As the infant matures, the adults who are responsible for the baby's care are just as affected by the baby as the baby is by them. In other words, the interaction is reciprocal (Caulfield, 1995). After Katrina was born, her mother (who had always been too embarrassed to sing in front of anyone) purchased several lullaby tapes and began singing along with them in her car (Arnold, 1994; Music for Little People, 1995). When her baby was fussy and she was able to comfort her by singing, Katrina's mom was thrilled. If you asked this parent about singing, she would say that she had completely changed her outlook, thanks to her daughter. Instead of worrying about someone criticizing her singing, Katrina's mother regards her baby as her one truly appreciative audience. Katrina's mom has grown as an individual because she wanted to share the comforting mood of lullabies with her baby.

Parents as workers.   Yet another role that the majority of parents play is that of worker, often balancing the need to have productive work with concerns about entrusting their child to the care of others. Early childhood educators must understand that being a parent is a full-time job and many parents hold at least one other full-time job in addition to that of parent. As a result, parents "experience many emotions, including fatigue, frustration, isolation, guilt, and insecurity in their parenting abilities in addition to the rewards of joy, love, and pride in their children" (Billman & Sherman, 1996, p. 185). Although it is commonly assumed that poor parents do not work outside the home or that mothers who work do so for "the extras," recent statistics suggest that the poor in the United States are working and that even two paychecks frequently do not bring a family's income above the poverty line (Palokow, 1993; Sava, 1995). With 40 percent of America's young children living at or below the poverty line, both time and money can be at a premium (Allen, Brown, & Finlay, 1992). Outside-the-home arts activities that are scheduled at convenient times and can be enjoyed by the entire family without a major investment enable adults to do a better job of fulfilling their dual roles of worker and parent. When early childhood educators take the time to do such things as letting parents know that the ballet is performing at the local college, or alerting them to the fact that an award-winning nature show will be on television, or suggesting a picture book that is just perfect for their toddler, more families are empowered to share the arts together.

Parents as consumers.   Parents also have a role to fulfill with regard to managing finances, making purchasing decisions, and deciding which services to use. Where the arts are concerned, this role often takes the form of such questions to teachers as "Do you think we should try to get a secondhand piano for Lisa to play?" or, "What is your opinion about computer software that helps children to make pictures?" or, "I see that the high school is putting on the musical 'Oklahoma!' Do you think it is interesting enough for my four-year-old to sit through?" or, "What sort of toys would you buy for a two-year-old?" or, "What about art classes at the museum? Would they be worthwhile for Jamie?" When you try to stay informed about such things and pass that information along to the families, you can support parents in their efforts to be more intelligent consumers. One excellent resource that evaluates children's toys, books, records, and videos is a publication called *Parents' Choice*, a sort of "consumer reports" for parents. This organization also gives a seal of approval called the Parents' Choice Award to those materials that meet its standards of quality and have been well-received by families.

Parents as educators.   Howe (1990) contends that "the ways in which children develop in the early years are affected by the degree to which parents assume the role of teacher" (p. 99). Art educators are beginning to recognize that far too little attention has been given to the type and quality of art education that children receive in the home environment (Baker, 1990). It has often been said that parents are the child's first teachers, and this conviction applies to the arts and aesthetics as well (Hoffman, Kanter, Colbert, & Sims, 1991; Juan, 1985). An example of par-

Figure 4.2 **What Parents and Teachers Want**

✑ *What Parents Want*	✑ *What Teachers Want*
• Recognition of their roles and responsibilities as parents.	• Respect for their education, expertise, and experience.
• Support for their efforts on behalf of the child.	• Understanding that they are committed to individual children but responsible for a group.
• Confidence that teachers can motivate their child to learn.	• Support for what they are doing to enhance children's learning.
• Teachers who will take the time to listen to them.	• Parents' trust and confidence in them to behave ethically and responsibly.
• Information that keeps them apprised of their child's progress as well as potential problems.	• Appreciation for their efforts.
• Reassurance that teachers are really seeing their child as an individual and as a human being rather than as just another student.	• Consideration of their circumstances and the constraints under which they work.
• Consideration of their circumstances and constraints.	

Source: Adapted from Rab, V. Y., & Wood, K. I. (1995). *Child care and the ADA: A handbook for inclusive programs.* Baltimore: Brookes.

ents fulfilling their role as educators in ways that support the arts is "babyproofing" the house. While the child is an active toddler, the parents put away most of the things that would cause great upset if they were damaged rather than shouting "No!" every time the baby attempts to explore these objects. By giving the infant more freedom to actively investigate her world, parents are nurturing creativity and doing a better job of fulfilling their role as educators.

Part of being an effective teacher of young children is respecting these roles and working in ways that meet the family's needs as well as your own. One useful way of conceptualizing these needs is contained in Figure 4.2.

CHARACTERISTICS OF HOME ENVIRONMENTS THAT SUPPORT THE ARTS

*T*he home is unquestionably a powerful learning environment. Tizard and Hughes (1984) cite the following reasons to support this statement.

- The home environment generally includes a wide range of experiences available through day-to-day activities. This range of experiences encourages incidental learning—learning that occurs naturally as a product of a child's interaction with the environment (Palincsar & Klenk, 1992).
- The home environment provides opportunities for children to share experiences with parents or significant others.
- Home environments, unlike classroom settings, generally include a small number of children vying for adult attention.
- Meaningful activities that occur within the context of day-to-day life are a part of the home environment.
- The close emotional relationship between adult and child is a significant factor in the power of the home environment.

These factors can be capitalized on as parents identify ways to support their child's growth in the arts.

Early childhood programs that succeed in encouraging family support of the arts strive to keep three components in mind:

1. Assisting parents in interacting with their children through arts activities.
2. Increasing parental knowledge about and interest in arts materials and aesthetic activities.
3. Enriching and enlarging children's knowledge, skill, attitudes, and feelings about the arts.

To further clarify the messages that early childhood educators need to send to parents about creativity and the arts, refer to Figure 4.3, "How to Raise Creative Children" (Rich, 1992; Shallcross, 1981). As you read each recommendation, think about the types of home environments that lend the greatest support to young children's creative and artistic expression. Think also about how you would communicate these important messages to parents through your words and actions, a topic that we address in the next section.

Figure 4.3   How to Raise Creative Children

☙ **Allow them to investigate.** Provide children with a home that is safe. Then give them the freedom and time to explore and experiment. Expect a certain amount of mess and mishap to be part of every person's childhood. Try to designate an area for messy work and take clutter or noise in stride.

☙ **Let them pursue their own answers.** Tell children it's okay to make mistakes, and mean it. Let children try to find their own answers instead of simply telling them the answers, and encourage the child to "live the question" by working on it. Capitalize on the child's curiosity, interest, and motivation rather than imposing an adult perspective.

☙ **Give them support.** Build children's confidence that they can meet challenges and that their opinions and ideas are valued. Realize that what might seem like a silly question to an adult seems like a wonderful idea to a child: "What will happen if I bring this snowball indoors?" "How could I make a tent out of what is around the house?" Instead of criticizing when a child's ideas do not work out, help the child to figure out which parts might need rethinking, then encourage the child to give it another try.

☙ **Turn off the television set.** Skills required in order to watch television are very minimal. Children who are struggling in school are often the ones who watch television the most: they are "TV-induced illiterates" (Allington & Walmsley, 1995). Try something completely different like playing a game invented by the child. A toddler can toss a stuffed toy into a laundry basket, a preschooler can invent a game like Twister, and a school-age child can create a board game, for example.

☙ **Pose new challenges.** Ask questions that go beyond memorization and just the facts: "What might happen if . . ." "How could we . . ." Make comments that encourage your child to think: "What will you do now?" "I wonder why . . ." A young child's responses to questions and comments such as these are often surprising, entertaining, and charming even if they are not the "right" answers! Offer a large repertoire of challenging activities that encourage children to stretch their minds.

☙ **Provide role models of creative adults.** Demonstrate your own love of learning, respect for achievement, and enthusiasm for creative problem solving. Creativity is better caught than taught! Help children to connect with an ever-widening circle of other adults and older children who know how to gently guide children to doing their best.

☙ **Don't get carried away with formal learning experiences.** Make sure your schedule allows time for children to think, dream, contemplate, and invent. Avoid overscheduling of structured activities. A young child should not need to keep a calendar like a business executive! There will be plenty of time for that later on in life.

Sources: Adapted from Shallcross, D. (1981). *Teaching creative behavior.* Englewood Cliffs, NJ: Prentice Hall; and Rich, D. (1992). *Megaskills.* Boston: Houghton Mifflin.

ARTICULATING AN ARTS PHILOSOPHY

*M*any parents have serious doubts about their abilities and qualifications to nurture a child's growth in the arts. One of the most commonly noted hurdles that parents mention in supporting children's artistic development is the same one that teachers express: they may not be artists themselves, or they feel that their arts background is deficient. Actually, parents frequently "overestimate the degree of expertise that is required to give a child assistance with learning" (Howe, 1990, p. 226). In fact, high levels of skill may not be as important as interest and enthusiasm on the part of the parent. Feeney and Moravcik (1987) state an important truth: "It is not necessary to be an artist to help young children enjoy their creative process or help them to gain pleasure from the creations of others. It is necessary to believe that experiences with beauty, the arts, and nature are valuable parts of all of our lives" (p. 11).

Because parents frequently feel uneasy and insecure where the arts are concerned, they will sometimes turn to you as an early childhood professional for advice. If you are equally uncertain about the arts, you will not be of much help. If, on the other hand, you do the tough mental work that is required to put your knowledge, beliefs, attitudes, and values about art into words, you can be of tremendous help to parents. Some questions related to young children's artistic and aesthetic growth are fairly common, like the ones you are about to read. We hope that by giving you some models of the way to use a research base to formulate a response, you will feel more confident about articulating your arts philosophy and sharing it with families.

The Importance of a Relaxed, Informal Climate

Question: A grandmother picks up her three-year-old granddaughter at day care and says, "Sherri really seems to be graceful and interested in dance—yesterday she was practically floating around the room in one of my old nightgowns! What do you think about dance lessons. Is she too young?"

Research Base: Generally, people who have a firm commitment to the arts do not mention formal instruction first when they are questioned about the source of their interests and occupation. Instead, they are more inclined to mention a significant adult who was dedicated to the activity and introduced them to it (Smith, 1988). Encouraging a young child's interest in the arts

- is generally informal and relaxed.
- takes place in the company of loved ones.
- occurs while the child is not being evaluated. (Sloboda, 1990)

This context for creative endeavors is important because talent is the interaction of a child's environment with a child's innate ability. Homes and schools are all-important in providing those relaxed, informal environments that adult artists credit with starting them on a lifelong dedication to art. Homes and schools are equally important for those who never pursue a career in the arts but who nevertheless look to the arts for joy, solace, entertainment, and inspiration throughout a lifetime.

Some ways to tell if an arts program is really suitable for a child are contained in Figure 4.4. It is critical to remember that the role of parents in the process of arts development is not to overschedule or push children in many different directions,

Figure 4.4   Criteria for Evaluating Arts Programs for Children

Appropriate: The program is designed specifically for *young* children.
Inappropriate: The program is a downsized version of a program for adults.

Appropriate: The emphasis is on enjoyment, and activities have a playful quality.
Inappropriate: There is pressure to perform, and children feel anxious about their participation in these activities.

Appropriate: The child's efforts are celebrated as an inauguration into the activity.
Inappropriate: The child's efforts are viewed as accurate predictors of possible talent or future success in the activity as an adult.

Appropriate: The child is really taught the requisite skills in a supportive fashion (e.g., how to use a paintbrush, ways to communicate emotions through facial expression and gesture).
Inappropriate: Children's abilities are treated as innate and expected to manifest themselves in some and not in others.

Appropriate: The child actually handles the materials and does the activities.
Inappropriate: The child devotes much of the time to waiting and watching.

Appropriate: The program is designed so that all children can experience success.
Inappropriate: Some children become the stars, and the others feel like failures.

Appropriate: The activities respect each child's pace and style of learning and offer graduated challenges so that children's confidence can build.
Inappropriate: Every child moves at the same pace, and individual styles are not considered. There is one set standard for performance, and everyone is expected to achieve it.

Appropriate: The activities have a playful quality, and the social climate is relaxed and reassuring.
Inappropriate: The activities are lockstep, and the social climate is tense and competitive.

Appropriate: The instructor models enthusiasm, speaks warmly to children, and interacts with them in a supportive fashion.
Inappropriate: The instructor appears to be putting children through their paces, barks orders at them, and is harshly critical of mistakes.

but to recognize a measure of interest in the topic, provide a supportive environment for experimentation, and maintain an air of playfulness in the home.

Now reread the grandmother's question at the beginning of this section. How could you use the research base that you just read to formulate an answer? Here is one possible answer that makes both the underlying philosophy and the research that supports it clear: "You are right that Sherri really seems to be moved by and enjoy moving to music—I have noticed this interest too. But I also share your concern about getting too formal too soon. There are some excellent teachers who really know how to work with very young children and creative dance, but a perfectionist teacher who doesn't understand preschoolers could ruin Sherri's enjoyment, and that would be a terrible loss. Have you thought about perhaps sitting in on a class over at the college before you decide? I keep a set of guidelines on making this type of decision in my files that I'll be glad to share with you." (See Figure 4.4).

Notice how this answer was based on professional knowledge and was helpful. Try formulating your own research-based responses to the remaining questions, then share/compare/contrast them with the ones your instructor would give and the ones generated by other members of the class.

The Importance of High-Quality Materials

Question: The mother of a five-year-old child who is chronically ill says, "Jimmy has to spend so much of his time in waiting rooms, in the hospital, or in bed at home. I am always trying to find 'quiet activities' for him to do, and I had the idea of making a big tote bag, letting him decorate it, and keeping it well stocked so that he can take it with him, hang it on the arm of his wheelchair, play with it often, and use it for arts and crafts. Do you have some kind of list of materials that would be good to include?"

Research Base: Arts tools, materials, and equipment are important ingredients in arts experiences. According to Baker (1990), children who are exposed to high-quality arts experiences and materials experience an enhanced ability to function as knowledgeable adults. Learners can be sensitized to the aesthetic properties of objects through the manipulation of materials. "These skills will not transform children into artists," Broudy says, "but will instead give the child a sense of what the artist sees, hears, and imagines" (Broudy, 1979, p. 66). Access to arts materials is equally important to the development of the child because children are freer to create if they can independently access arts materials when they decide to use them (Baker, 1990; Stamp, 1994).

Supporting children's aesthetic sensibilities means that parents are right to provide fresh, beautiful materials for children's use in artistic activities whenever possible. A new set of markers in different hues, a fresh box of crayons, a homemade tutu, scraps of lovely fabric gathered from a tailor, or nicely grained bits of wood collected from a cabinet shop can all reignite children's enthusiasm. Figure 4.5 is a list of materials that are well suited to young children's artistic endeavors. Even

---

Figure 4.5   **Basic Art Materials**

A wide assortment of paper in various sizes, colors, and textures
Scissors (regular and pinking edges)
Paper punch
White glue, glue stick, and paste
Crayons and sharpener
Felt-tip markers—small, chisel tip, and fancy tips
Oil pastels (these look like crayons but are oil-based paints)
Tray of water colors and small brush
Colored chalks
Tempera paint—powder or gel
Brushes in various sizes (no. 12 is a good, basic size)
Containers for water (small plastic ones from yogurt or sour cream work well)
Sponges, paper towels, cotton swabs
Clear tape, masking tape
Stapler and staples
Wet clay and airtight containers
Vinyl floor tile squares (to use as platforms for clay or playdough modeling)
Florist's wire and pipe cleaners
Yarns and string
Paper bags (lunch size and grocery size) for puppet making
Tongue depressors, craft sticks, or Popsicle sticks
Paper and fabric scraps
Found objects (paint samples, wallpaper scraps, ribbons, lace, recycled toys)
Smocks (old shirts worn backward work well)
Magazines with beautiful pictures such as *International Design, Ranger Rick, Architectural Digest, Arizona Highways, National Geographic*
Natural objects such as shells, rocks, feathers, leaves
Heavy cardboard covered with heavy-duty foil (about 12 by 16 inches) or an old plastic tray to use as a work surface

Sources: Adapted from Beatty, J. J. (1996). *Skills for preschool teachers* (5th ed.). Englewood Cliffs, NJ: Merrill/Prentice Hall; and Cohen, E. P., & Gainer, R. S. (1995). *Art: Another language for learning.* Portsmouth, NH: Heinemann.

though high-quality arts materials are critical, neither teachers nor parents should be misled into believing that a new material is required each time the child wants to "do art." Young children learn best from repeated opportunities to work with materials. Having the chance to repeatedly explore an art material, its uses, and the satisfaction that it provides in an in-depth rather than fleeting fashion fosters the most effective type of learning for the young child (Clemens, 1991). Young children need access to materials, time to explore them, and respectful encouragement as they investigate and experiment. Now, using this information, how would you answer Jimmy's mother?

Immersion in Arts Experiences

Question: "My relatives think I'm crazy because I played music for my baby even while I was pregnant. Ever since we brought her home from the hospital, I have always played classical music in her room. Is this really as outlandish as my husband seems to think?"

Research Base: Adults have a role to play as arrangers of "arts-friendly" environments—contexts that immerse children in beauty from the earliest days of life. Contemporary children are deluged with sensory input, but much of it is of inferior quality and certainly not the best that various cultures have to offer. Under these conditions, children are convinced that they must have whatever is popular, gimmicky, and heavily advertised. Because these inferior toys, materials, books, and recordings seldom maintain children's interest, they have to be replaced frequently by the latest object of a media blitz. Children need exposure to high-quality listening experiences in music rather than simply hearing music in shopping malls, on radio jingles, or from a musical toy (Isenberg & Jalongo, 1997). Likewise, cartoon images of such characters as Bart Simpson or Garfield, which are so frequently presented to children, are far less nourishing than prints, paintings, and drawings by master artists (Baker, 1990). Children need to see works of the visual arts that cause them to look again, to wonder, to imagine. Someone might wonder aloud, "Paintings for a child?" but children need to experience the best that various cultures have to offer.

Children should experience immersion in the arts in the home environment through hearing high-quality recorded music at mealtimes or bedtimes. They should learn the social nature of watching a dramatic production together with members of their family. The communicative power of dance or visual art can be modeled in the home. Nurturing adults can encourage and support the arts efforts of children by encouraging drawing and painting, applauding singing and dancing. Finally, parents can immerse children in the arts by pursuing artistic interests on their own, in ways that children can see and understand, thus learning that the arts are useful, enjoyable, and worthwhile. Now, how would you answer the mother's question about whether it makes sense to play classical music for a baby?

We hope that these simulated experiences in putting your arts philosophy into words that are understandable and helpful to the significant adults in children's lives will enable you to approach your partnership with families more confidently. Another challenge that families and educators have to confront together is the elitism that endangers the arts in America. For more research support for the arts, see Murfee (1995) and the National Endowment for the Arts (1994).

MOVING BEYOND ELITISM IN THE ARTS

*A*rtistic development is a notoriously misunderstood area of human development (Perkins, 1984). Interest and ability in the creative arts are regarded by many as eccentric aspects of personality attributable to special inborn traits and possessed only by the "ablest" of the population. In the United States, the arts have traditionally been regarded as the province of only the most intelligent children. Kenny (1987) disputes the long-held belief that the arts are only for the "ablest," argues that all children have inherent creative talents, and contends that such talents can be identified at all levels of intelligence. Assuming that this is the case, many of the students who are now regarded as learning disabled might actually be "curriculum disabled" by programs that identify verbal and mathematical skills as the only abilities that matter. We can't help wondering how many of the children in our schools are frustrated in their attempts to develop their true talents. Perhaps such frustration helps to explain Pablo Picasso's observation that "every child is an artist. The problem is how to remain an artist once he grows up."

Early Identification of Talent

Research suggests that the creative arts are a primary vehicle for every young child's personal expression and that all children have pictures, stories, dances, or songs within them awaiting the opportunity for expression (Carlisle, 1990). Although it is common to proclaim that the arts are important in the United States, the nation does less than many other countries to demonstrate the belief that *all* children, regardless of demonstrated talent, should learn the language of the arts (Perrin, 1994). It is a strange contradiction that, despite our American democratic ideals, many Americans assume that only exceptionally talented children should pursue the arts, and, if they do, it should be done at their families' expense. Yet focusing exclusively on an "art star" and taking a "talent scout" approach is just as misguided, elitist, and inequitable as reserving reading instruction for only the "most talented readers" or science for those with National Merit Scholar potential.

Numerous studies of musicians with extraordinary talent support the contention that very few of these children had abilities that were identified early (Fox, 1990). Rather, they became extraordinary because they had the support of parents and teachers as their ability unfolded. Albert Einstein, one of the most celebrated creative geniuses of the century, once said, "I have no special gift. I am only passionately curious." An in-depth study of five modern-day prodigies concluded that talent isn't simply a gift, as is commonly assumed (Feldman, 1986). Rather, artistically gifted children live in a culture that makes a place for them and have parents who nurture and encourage. How many children are out there with great undiscovered artistic potential? It is a national disgrace that income level is frequently the great determinant of who will be born into the "right" circumstances to pursue an interest in the arts.

A large-scale research project led by Benjamin Bloom studied the lives of young persons with exceptional abilities in sports, music, and mathematics by interviewing the exceptional individuals, their parents, and their early teachers. The research team concluded that the one common characteristic of remarkably talented individuals was their early home lives. A child's special abilities nearly always emerged in the context of home activities that respected and supported the child's efforts to participate in and experiment with the arts (Howe, 1990).

In the budding artist's life, we can see an upward spiral—the child shows an interest, the family responds enthusiastically thus intensifying that interest, the child develops confidence and skill, the family recognizes and supports those talents, and the child becomes more talented. The next section describes features of this process in greater detail.

WAYS THAT FAMILIES CAN SUPPORT THE ARTS

Young children need guidance and exposure to a variety of experiences to develop artistically and aesthetically. The right environment and the right experiences will enable the young child's creativity to flourish. Particularly where young children are concerned, the right environment and experiences depend upon the adults. Six significant ways that parents support the arts are described in the following paragraphs, and each is illustrated with excerpts of interviews conducted with the parents of young children (Stamp, 1995).

1. **Parents can be co-enjoyers of informal arts activities.** Parents may model enthusiasm and interest in the arts by participating in projects or activities of their own. By doing so, they allow children to see that the arts, like spoken language, are useful, enjoyable, and worthwhile. Jim is one parent who does these things. With a demanding professional schedule, Jim often leaves home before his four children are awake and returns just before their bedtime, yet he is still able to communicate his passion for music. Jim enjoys playing the guitar and leaves the guitar in the family room so that it is available to play whenever he has a moment. His children have heard him play familiar songs, have watched him listen repeatedly to a recording to learn a new song, and have enjoyed singing along with Daddy when he plays. Jim's children recognize that the guitar is an important part of their father's life. Likewise, they see their father's respect for the instrument and know that it is to be handled carefully in order to continue to enjoy it. Through adult modeling, children receive powerful messages about the real worth of creative impulses, and these messages can foster the enthusiastic pursuit of creative endeavors within the family. It is enjoyment that invites and welcomes children into the world of the arts.

2. **Parents can resolve to compensate for their perceived limitations in the arts.** If parents themselves were deprived of arts experiences, they may be reluctant to try the arts experiences that are unfamiliar to them, and this reluctance, in turn, may adversely affect a child's opportunity or willingness to try something new. Yet by allowing children to see them in the role of a risk taker who is trying something new and working at something that takes effort and passion, children receive the message of dedication and devotion to the art, craft, and skill. Children also become very aware of the whole idea of artistic process and product.

Many parents feel that they missed out on aesthetic opportunities as young children and want to ensure that their children do not have a similar experience. Shay, a mother of three children, says that including the arts in the life of her children is especially important because "no one ever did that for me. My parents didn't think that I had any talent, so they didn't encourage me. I don't remember any materials other than crayons for art making, and my mother always seemed bothered by the mess if I cut out paper or tried to use glue. Finally, I just began to think of myself as someone who didn't `do' art. I feel sad about that now as I watch my kids and see what I really missed. I made up my mind that trying activities was something my children would do . . . no matter how messy. Not only do we do arts activities together . . . we clean up together." As this mother's description of her behavior illustrates, adults need not be artists themselves to bring the arts into children's lives. Moreover, it is possible to surmount deficiencies and gaps in adults' arts experiences as children rather than become resigned to a life bereft of art, just as this mother resolved to do.

   3. **Parents can follow the child's "arts agenda."** Sometimes families expect a child's artistry to burst forth like a flower in full bloom. Actually, play is the basis for identifying possible interests, motivations, and talents in the very young. Therefore, play must be encouraged and supported, and this effort is time-consuming for parents and other caregivers. In a world where adults are very busy, it is easy to overschedule children into a variety of activities in order to expose children to a variety of arts experiences. Families that have the money to finance these experiences can sometimes get carried away by trying to give their children all of the advantages that they had (or did not have) themselves as children. Parents frequently assume that formal lessons are the only or best way to support a child's special interest in the arts. It is also easy to overlook the fact that children's interests do not necessarily follow a clear, predictable unidirectional path simply because a parent purchased an instrument or arranged for some type of lesson.

   Valerie struggled with this issue when her daughter Ashley showed interest in music as a toddler. Ashley danced in response to musical sounds, sang early and on pitch, and was drawn to live and recorded musical performances. At church, Ashley was fascinated by the piano and organ. At the organist's suggestion, Ashley was allowed to "play" the organ for a few minutes every Sunday immediately after the service. As her fifth birthday approached, Ashley asked for a small electronic keyboard that she had seen in a catalog. After talking extensively with Ashley's father, Valerie decided to purchase the inexpensive keyboard. After several months of sustained interest, a spinet piano was rented for a three-month trial period, and Ashley was enrolled in a Saturday morning music activities class. Two years later, Ashley's interest and skill continued to develop through a weekly individual piano lesson. Her involvement in music has followed a logical developmental progression, never pushing her into more activities than she had demonstrated interest or ability for undertaking.

   In contrast, seven-year-old Keith, who is in Ashley's class at school, takes art, music, karate, and horseback riding lessons each week, and his family is kept busy just getting him to and from these structured activities. While Keith is economically privileged and fortunate to have access to professional instruction in all of these areas, he is left with no time to experiment, create, or reflect on his own ideas through play. Keith's interest in the piano has waned, and practice time has become a major point of contention. Because Keith's parents are making a monthly payment on the instrument, they are driven by their concern about the financial commitments they have made.

   It is important for parents to remember that children's arts interests and skills change over time. Therefore, it is probably better to start children with informal experiences with borrowed or rented equipment and follow the child's lead. This approach also makes arts experiences more accessible to families with less disposable income. Too often, families think that if they cannot afford the newest and

When families decide to provide special training in the arts for children, it is important to let the child's interests and developmental level serve as a guide.

most expensive equipment or materials, then nothing can be done in art. Yet many of our best-known entertainers began with inexpensive or used materials that were lovingly shared with the child.

4. Parents can create family traditions that celebrate the aesthetic. Rachel, a single mother of three, remembers that the arts were given a place of importance in her home. "Even though my mom was alone throughout our childhoods, she considered `culture' important. I know now that there was a really limited income, but both my brother and I had lessons and went to concerts. My mother was diligent about searching out opportunities for us. If she saw a concert advertised in the paper, we were there. I can remember taking the bus over to the concert hall very, very early one Saturday because my mother had heard that there would be free tickets for the first one hundred children. We stood on line with her. I can still see her trying to keep my brother and me neat as we waited for those tickets. We heard Tchaikovsky that day." Rachel stops and her eyes fill with tears as she remembers, ". . . and when I got my first stereo after I was out working, that was the first recording I bought."

When young children associate the arts with love and joy, the arts become part of an intergenerational tradition. Many families will need, as Rachel's mother did, to seek and find aesthetic experiences that do not strain the family budget. Celebrating beauty together might be as simple as going bird-watching, looking at the downtown light displays during Christmas, driving by a flower farm in the spring, taking a hiking trip through a National Forest, spending the day at the museum, or watching the sunset together. In fact, it is these arts traditions that draw families closer together.

5. Parents can arrange the environment to facilitate creative endeavors. Adults often object to the messiness, noise, or exuberance of arts activities. By setting aside an area for arts activities, parents and teachers alike can decrease their tension over this issue. Areas that will not cause too much upset if they get messy—a corner of the garage, a picnic table, a basement, or an attic—can become environments for messy activities if surfaces are protected by newspapers, an old bedsheet, or a recycled plastic tablecloth. To deal with noise as the objection to an arts activity, a special time or area can be reserved. When a baby is sleeping, a parent is studying, or the sound is simply too much for others in the home, a designated time or place is often the solution.

Children engaging in the playful activities that support artistic growth are often excited and boisterous. As a result, managing the child's behavior can sometimes become an issue. Parents may wonder if giving so much freedom will invite their children to be badly behaved, for instance. Research indicates that this is not the case (Amabile, 1989). Limits in behavior are different from limits to creativity and imagination. Achievement, independence, and personal time for thought and reflection have been shown to foster creativity in children. Allowing children to experience various cultures, ideas, and attitudes not only develops adaptability but also inspires creativity. Many families believe that the arts are "anything goes" when this is not the case. Learning the structure of care and courtesy has a significant place in the arts. Cleaning the paintbrushes thoroughly before putting them away today will assure that a painting done tomorrow is not marred by streaks of unwanted color; caring for the rhythm instruments and sharing them with friends will ensure much more playing enjoyment; and conserving paints, paper, and markers will afford many more opportunities to make pictures in the future.

To further illustrate different levels of environmental support for the arts in homes, contrast the experience of Kasha, a four-year-old girl, and Taylor, her classmate at preschool. Kasha's mother reports that all of the visual arts materials are within reach at home. "I just decided to devote a cabinet in the laundry area to the kids' art supplies. I realized how often they were asking for paint or paper and how often I was saying no because I had to fetch the items myself. I figured that we could give it a try." She laughs as she recalls an older neighbor's reaction. "She was horrified, and I think that she thought that I had lost my mind! But if they're going to learn to enjoy these things and be responsible about them, I have to give them a chance."

Taylor's experience with paints differs from Kasha's in that it is strictly limited to school. The easel is always her first choice during free play, and she speaks of a time last year when she was given a set of fingerpaints by a couple who had come to a picnic at her house. "My mom put them away for another day, and then when I'd ask for them she always said that I had on the wrong clothes or that we had to get ready to go somewhere. When my grandma came we finally got them out . . . but the colors were all dried up and yucky."

While Kasha builds skill and self-confidence through opportunities for self-expression, Taylor's curiosity and expertise in this area are being limited, even discouraged, by a well-meaning parent. By arranging the environment and making materials accessible to children, families support creativity and the arts.

6. Parents can demonstrate their appreciation for the child's art work. Prior to modern times few people cherished or preserved children's artistic products. Gardner's (1980) research included the examination of classical and Renaissance writings that disclosed only two examples of preserved artworks created by children. Think of the homes of young children that you know. Where do you see their art, and how is it displayed? Perhaps it is crowded onto a refrigerator door and practically obscured by other things. Maybe it is stuffed into an overflowing mail basket on the desk or thrown into a box stored under the child's bed. Conversely, maybe the child's fingerpainting is mailed to a family member, or a collage is put up on a bulletin board. Perhaps a paper sculpture is set in the middle of the dinner table for everyone to enjoy. The way that children's artwork is handled sends a message to the child. Adults sometimes fail to value children's arts experiences and artistic products. In too many classrooms, visual arts experiences encourage young children to dash something off on schedule and produce "throwaway art."

Edith shared her a story about her son's persistence in seeing to it that his works of the visual arts be appreciated and displayed. Edith smiled as she watched Tyler, her four-year-old son, kick a soccer ball around their small fenced backyard. Then she said, "Tyler wants to be the first professional soccer player who has paintings hanging in a real art museum," she says proudly. Edith described how her son continued to astonish her with questions about "real art." "He was always bringing home pictures from his preschool. Of course I thought they were wonderful, but apparently just looking at them and putting them on the refrigerator was not helping him to understand that. One day he came home and asked me for some tape. He disappeared with it and got awfully quiet. I figured I'd better investigate after about fifteen minutes. I found him in the living room putting pictures up in the window frame inside each pane. He told me, `Ma, this is how pictures should be . . . in a box thing, so that they get looked at for real.' I was amazed."

Edith's experience shows another way parents can support the arts. Note that she didn't need to be able to draw or be an arts expert, only to listen and respond in ways that validated Tyler's faith in himself. Because Edith understood the importance of displaying Tyler's work, she "bought a frame at a yard sale for twenty-five cents and framed a piece of his art that he called `A Field of Stuff.' I hung it on the wall in our kitchen. It's a great use of color and space, and everybody who comes in comments on it. I think Tyler feels like a `real' artist now." Edith recognizes that displaying her son's work in a particular way values and honors his efforts.

As these interviews and information have described, families lend support to children's artistic and aesthetic development in a variety of ways. But what about parents who don't do these things because they are preoccupied or convinced that the arts aren't worth the time, effort, and expense? One father expressed these ideas bluntly when he said, in reference to his five-year-old daughter, "Just teach her to use the computer—that's the only thing that ever got me anywhere in life. None of that other stuff they learn in school really matters. Who cares if you can slop paint on paper? What good will it do her to know some silly story? What difference will it make if she can sing or not?" Note that this father's comments are based on the erroneous assumption that his child is just like him and that she will follow in his footsteps. Note also that he assumes that the career he has in computer programming will continue to exist in abundance fifteen years from now when his daughter graduates from college even though computer programmers are in far less demand than previously and even though he was unemployed for more than a year. Note also that he is defensive about his background in the arts. We can just imagine him at a gala arts event, standing against the wall pretending to be bored or uninterested but really feeling nervous or inadequate and hoping to strike up a conversation with someone and move the topic of discussion to the one thing he feels comfortable talking about—computers.

As an early childhood educator you will no doubt encounter parents who have similar feelings even if they are not as outspoken. Interestingly, this father would be the first to admit that technology is moving rapidly, that he needs creative problem-solving skills in his daily work, and that being a five-year-old is dramatically different from being a thirty-five-year-old. When convincing parents about the value of the arts, you will often need to begin by identifying the "common ground," the issues on which you can agree rather than on the issues that divide. This father may never become an enthusiastic supporter of the arts for himself, but he can, at the very least, learn to allow his child the freedom to explore the entire range of her abilities.

COMMUNICATING THE VALUE OF THE ARTS TO FAMILIES

*P*arents need to be aware that the early childhood years are a "golden age of creativity, a time when every child sparkles with artistry" (Gardner, 1980, p. 86). The very "summit of artistry" is achieved by the end of the preschool years, according to Gardner. While the vast majority of American parents believe that the arts are important, they may simultaneously place greater emphasis on more "academic" subjects (American Council for the Arts, 1992; Perrin, 1994). Baker (1992) states:

> Even though parents appeared to be unclear about the role of art media and activities in their child's growth and development, over 90% of them believed art

to be an important subject in the schooling of their children. Supporting this belief was a conviction expressed by nearly 60% of the parents that not enough time is provided in school curricula for art instruction. Of even greater interest is the fact that no parent stated that too much time was given to the visual arts in pre- or public schools. (p. 8)

This mode of thinking dominates school experiences, creating an atmosphere in which a child's enthusiasm and joy for the artistic process may be lost. Sadly, the level of artistry that peaks during the preschool years resurfaces later in only a few children and adults. Creative behavior is greatly affected by attitudes, and adults can exert a powerful, positive influence on what the child feels, thinks, and acts upon in regard to the arts. That influence is even more powerful when families collaborate.

The best strategy that teachers can use to persuade parents of the value of the arts is to provide concrete examples for them. Even parents who are skeptical will often be won over by seeing their child singing happily, participating in a simple folk dance, or proudly standing next to a mural that was completed with a small group of peers. Many families also need to be reminded about what young children can be expected to do and helped to understand what is developmentally appropriate. Otherwise, everyone is disappointed. If family members are invited to see the class musical program, for instance, they may be expecting to see polished performers instead of preschoolers, most of whom cannot yet sing on pitch. If families are told that the videotape of the class play is available for loan, they may expect to see props, costumes, scenery, a stage, and a curtain instead of young children ad-libbing. By describing these arts experiences more precisely—for example, "Four-Year-Olds' Sing Nursery Tunes" or "Big Book Improv"—you can avoid misunderstandings. In all your communications with families, emphasize that arts activities should be regarded as basic experience for all young children simply because of the fact that all of the arts are interesting and enjoyable. Ms. Taylor sent a flyer home to parents of her three-year-old students at day care in an effort to communicate the value of creative activities to parents in a practical way (Figure 4.6).

Additional research indicates that the creative arts are well suited to the experience of the young child for at least four reasons, reasons that you can share with parents. First, artistic experiences foster sensory perception. Through visual art, music, dance, and drama, children are exposed to multiple opportunities to strengthen and refine visual, aural, and kinesthetic qualities that will serve lifelong learning. Second, the arts provide the opportunity to represent and symbolize childhood experiences in symbol systems other than letters and numbers. Third, the arts offer children a chance to experiment, create, and build—strengthening their ability to think, choose, and decide for themselves. Fourth, the arts expand the world for children—surpassing logical thought and promoting intuitive understanding. A lack of arts experiences may inhibit the child's ability to communicate spontaneously, respond affectively, and discern gradations of quality (Geoghegan, 1994). Therefore, the arts enable children to become more themselves instead of more like everyone else (Clemens, 1991).

American families are barraged by forces that undermine the arts and creativity. In a recent holiday season, for example, four heavily advertised toys were (1) fingerpaints that the child does not touch, (2) a machine that supplies small pictures to be made into stickers, (3) a book that reads itself, and (4) a toy that draws its own patterns! This passivity extends to family-oriented activities as well. Families frequently spend their "quality time" together staring at the latest feature-length

Figure 4.6   **A Day Care Flyer**

Dear Parents,

   Many of you have asked about the arts ideas that we use at day care. Here are a few tips for you and your child to share at home. Have fun!

- **Bubbles** can be an exciting experience for young children. By moving beyond the standard plastic bottle that is found in stores, the world of "creating" can be explored. Experiment with straws, spools, plastic soda holders, plastic berry baskets. For more of an outdoor adventure, use a hula hoop to build a bubble big enough to encase a child.

- **Collage** is another activity that you can share with your children. Torn or cut pieces of paper, newsprint, gift wrap, fabric, and ribbon can be used along with magazine pictures or discarded photographs. One half of a recycled gift box can make a frame for the collage.

- **Finger paints** provide an opportunity for conversation and artistic experimentation. Instead of commercial paints, which can be expensive and poorly textured, try using a base of liquid starch, in either a cookie sheet or tray, and then sprinkling powdered tempera over the starch. Here's a great recipe that we tried at school (see box). You can make it from items you probably have around the house.

- **Mud, clay, and sand** provide an opportunity for children to explore shape and texture while actively involved in forming different objects. In choosing clay, make sure that it is pliable enough for the child to work with. There are many different kinds of clay. Clay dug from the earth or potter's clay is wonderfully dense and can be molded with hands, but be aware that it will stain clothes and surfaces, so it is better to make clay and mudpies an outdoor activity and to keep a water hose handy. Sand is another interesting substance that children can mold into various shapes by combining it with water. To create a sandbox, get play sand at a nursery or masonry works. This sand is cleaner and softer than other types. You can use an old plastic dishpan for a small sandbox or the traditional size of sandbox. Whatever you do, be certain to cover the sand so that it is not infested with insects or visited by cats. Try making different patterns in the sand with a rubber spatula, a comb, or a piece of cardboard with a zigzag edge.

- **Natural items** such as leaves, branches, flowers, stones, feathers, shells, rocks, driftwood, or eggshells can be used for various types of constructions. Centerpieces for the table, arrangements for a shelf, or collages constructed from the natural items all provide opportunities for you to share in the creative process.

   Remember that valuing the process is the aim of shared artistic activities. Rather than asking what something is, try some of the following:

- I love the color you used . . .
- Tell me about how you made that shape . . .
- Can you show me how to do that with the clay?
- Where shall we put it so that everyone can enjoy it?

- **Bread sculpture.** Use defrosted frozen bread dough or unbaked bread dough from a bread machine to form a shape, bake it, and enjoy it with the family. Your child will delight in punching down the dough, rolling it into shapes, and decorating the finished product. We decided to make a snowman shape out of the bread dough we worked with at school, but let your child decide what he or she would like to create. Brushing the bread with melted butter or a beaten egg is another enjoyable way that a young child can participate in the baking project.

Enjoy!

Sincerely,

Millicent Taylor

Finger Paint

Makes about 3 cups of paint.

You'll Need:

1 envelope of plain gelatin (Knox) mixed with 1 cup of cold water

½ cup of liquid starch combined with ¾ cup of cold water

½ cup of mild soap flakes or granules (like Ivory Snow)

1 T. of food coloring *or* 1 T. of liquid tempera paint

What to Do:

1. Add two cups of hot water to the starch and cook slowly, stirring with a wooden spoon until the mixture comes to a boil and is thickened.
2. Remove the mixture from the heat and add the gelatin/water mixture.
3. Add the soap flakes and stir until completely dissolved.
4. Add food coloring or paint to make 3 cups of paint. You can divide the mixture into four portions to create a whole set of colors!
5. Store in a covered container. Clean, empty yogurt containers with tight-fitting lids work well (Perez, 1995).

cartoon or standing in line at a theme park so they can be amused for a couple of minutes. All of these commonplace activities erode children's creativity and play-fulness as well as undermine aesthetic sensibilities and artistry. Yet all of these families assume they are doing the right things for children because popular cul-ture presents them as such. As an early childhood educator and advocate for edu-cation, you stand for something better. You will have to gently remind families that the arts in general and your program specifically have much more to offer than any of these things, and you will have to do this without offending parents or making them feel defensive. As you work with families, keep in mind five essential points from Seymour Sarason (1995):

1. Remember that there is no justification for failing to listen to parents re-spectfully and take their concerns seriously.
2. Realize that if you are completely surprised by parental requests or demands, it means that you do not know the community well, that you neglected to communicate in ways that avoid misunderstandings before they occur, or that you allowed yourself to feel attacked rather than maintaining a steady focus on your work together with families on behalf of the child.
3. Respond to parents in ways that emphasize learning goals, state clearly what you are doing and why, and avoid taking criticism personally.
4. Expect that working with parents will be time-consuming, seem inefficient, and have rather unpredictable outcomes. You will need to learn when and how to compromise as well as learn the difference between compromise and "unprincipled caving in" (p. 80).
5. Realize that it is possible to have knowledge, skills, and experience as an early childhood educator yet be unable to deal effectively with parents be-cause of arrogance, inflexibility, a high need for control, biases that get in the way, or prejudicial attitudes against various groups.

CONCLUSION

*E*arly childhood educators have a special obligation to make every family aware of the power and value of the arts in children's lives. Because you are a teacher who comes into a child's life at an early, impressionable stage, you can exert an even greater influence on later experiences. Just as a proud parent who takes an eight-month-old baby for a checkup will expect to be told that the baby is growing rapidly and is tall for her age, parents will look to you to remark on the uniquenesses of their child so that they can glimpse the promise and potential there. Because the arts and aesthetic experiences are so inextricably linked with creativity, imagina-tion, and self-expression, they offer messages of hope and promise that will be overlooked when schools maintain a narrow focus on verbal and mathematical skills. As you interact with families, work to help them see that the arts are funda-mental to human experience. Work to counteract the harmful stereotype that the arts are "for" the idle rich. One way to communicate this message is by sharing stories that offer striking examples of the power of the arts in children's lives. Miller and Coen (1994) describe two such stories. They report that during a famine in Somalia, relief workers found entire villages' populations devastated by the lack of food. Yet, at the edge of many villages, thin, wasted, starving children met the relief workers and attempted to sing and dance their greetings and gratitude. One relief worker observed that the arts provided the only sustaining force in the nearly spent lives of these children.

In New York City, on the day that the World Trade Center was bombed, a group of kindergarten children was in the building on a field trip. When the explosion occurred, they were trapped in a dark, stalled elevator. Interviewed by the media after the rescue, their teacher was asked how she had managed to control the children's fear and panic. "We sang," she replied. Jane Alexander (1994), former chairwoman of the National Endowment for the Arts, explains why people turn to the arts in times of crisis and why the arts are so important to forging human relationships:

> You will carry the arts with you wherever you go. They will affect how you think and act and respond to others—children, family, friends, and acquaintances. I contend that the arts will make you better people, more compassionate citizens. . . . The arts demonstrate most clearly our connectedness, our common human nature. They speak to what unites us all under the skin, to the human spirit in all our pain and joy, our disenchantment and beguilement, our anger and our celebration. (p. B3)

The power to calm, to connect, to communicate: these are all available through the creative arts, and these are the messages that you as an early childhood educator must send to every family with which you work.

Learning about the Arts from Children

Parents Describe Their Children's Creative Behavior

The descriptions in this section were collected from personal interviews with parents about their children. Here were some of their answers to the question, "Could you give a specific example that illustrates your child's creativity?" After you read each anecdote, write a statement about how this parent's attitudes and behaviors appear to support the child's creativity.

Adam, Age 2

Adam's grandfather and uncle are both firemen, so he wants to be one too. Whenever he needs something to do, he gets out his firefighter jacket, puts his baseball cap on backward, hops up on a chair, and then drives to an imaginary fire. When he gets to the "fire," he uses a wooden spoon or rubber spatula as his fire hose and puts the fire out.

Sean, Age 4

Out of Lego blocks, Sean, with no patterns, makes vans with windows, backhoes that move, and helicopters with propellers that are able to turn. Another example is that last summer, Sean wanted a bow and arrow, but we said he couldn't have one. So he went up to the woods and got a branch and a piece of cord and made one. To make arrows, he got several branches and sharpened the ends of them with a stone.

Cheryl, Age 6

In school, my daughter was learning about birds molting. I had a hair on my sweater, and with a loving look on her face, Cheryl said, "Mommy, you're molting." I felt this was creative because she made an interesting connection.

Christopher, Age 6

One day Chris was eating alphabet cereal, and he came up with the idea of making a typewriter with the letters. He said at first he didn't know what to use to make the keys of, but then he decided to use little paper cups (the kind that hospitals put aspirins in). He glued the cups on a sturdy piece of cardboard, then pasted on the cereal letters.

Timmy, Age 6

Well, he likes to be different. One time he drew a holiday picture to send his aunt, and instead of just sending it to her in one piece, he cut it up like a puzzle. He said he wanted to make her work for her picture.

Dan, Age 6

Dan invented a language to write notes in school so that the teacher would be unable to decipher them. The written language was made out of symbols that Dan created. They looked almost like Chinese characters.

Meghan, Age 7

One day, Meghan took some paper and made it into a dollhouse. She folded it so it was actually a three-dimensional structure. She colored it and added windows and a door on it that opened and closed. Then she got some of my old catalogs and cut out pictures of people to use as family who lived in her house. She also cut out pictures of furniture to put inside the house.

Kelly, Age 8

Last Christmas, when Kelly was helping me make Christmas cookies, she insisted that we didn't use cookie cutters. She thought it would be more fun to design our own shapes. We ended up making an entire gingerbread family, a house for them to live in, and a car for them to drive—details and all!

Elaine, Age 8

Elaine had a teacher this year who taught them how to make books—real ones with cloth covers and the pages stitched together. Now Elaine has a book collection of stories she wrote and drew the pictures for. She gives books as presents, too.

Discussion Questions

- What can you infer about the attitudes and values expressed by the parents of each child?
- How might a different response undermine each child's creativity?
- Try to make the connection between these childhood traits and the personal characteristics needed for success on the job as an adult. How would you explain this connection to a parent who is less tolerant and supportive of the child who does not conform?
- As an early childhood educator, how could you use anecdotes like these to help parents recognize the importance of appreciating their child as a creative individual?

The Artist in You

Informal Ways That Families and Communities Can Support the Arts

The National Parent Teacher Association (1992) has been active in supporting the arts in schools. Their suggestions about ways for parents and teachers to collaborate and get more arts experiences into the curriculum include the following:

- Work to make the arts part of the school curriculum.
- Contribute materials that can be used in children's art.
- Maintain an ongoing student art exhibit.
- Share a videotape of students' art activities at a parents' meeting.
- Work with the school to invite community artists and art professionals to the school.
- Organize a field trip to visit an artist's studio, a museum, an exhibit, or an arts event.
- Begin an artist-in-residence program.
- Share your enthusiasm and knowledge of the arts with children.
- Arrange special-interest classes in the arts after school.

Here are some specific examples of successful arts activities that we have seen:

- A student teacher's roommate who is from Germany performed one of his traditional dances, complete with Tyrolean outfit. The five- and six-year-olds were taught a short sequence of steps so that they could try the dance for themselves.
- A retired nurse and grandmother who volunteers at the hospital and sings to comfort the infants in the nursery also volunteered to visit the infants in a child care center. She shared all of her wisdom with the staff as well as entertaining the babies with her sweet, clear voice. Later, she donated an audio cassette tape of her best lullabies to the center.
- A mother who is an interior decorator came to class and shared her portfolio. Afterward, the children brainstormed a list of the purposes of a portfolio and the materials included in one. They noted that she included "what she does," "what she works hard at," "stuff she's proud of," and "her best work." These experiences gave the children insights about developing their own portfolios.
- An aunt who creates downtown department store dis-

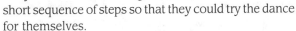

plays brought in large photographs of some of her work. Later, the preschoolers went window shopping at the mall and looked for some of the elements that she had explained, such as theme or motif, balance, and color.

- A chef who creates ice sculptures demonstrated how he works. Each third grader had a chance to help chip off some of the rough edges at the beginning and see the sculpture take shape. The finished product was stored in the freezer so the children could enjoy it longer.
- Grandparents who participate in a community theater group came and performed a scene from a play for the children. Afterward, the kindergartners performed their play for the grandparents and everyone had refreshments.
- A father who is a landscaper made slides from his fa-

vorite landscape books and talked about the basic principles of design. Afterward, the third graders worked in groups to plan their "dream backyard."

- The drum and bugle corps from the middle school performed for second graders, then corresponded with the children about their musical interests.

Discussion Questions

- If someone invited you to share the arts with children, what would you feel comfortable doing?
- How would you go about determining family and community resources that could be used in support of the arts?
- What other ideas do you have for collaborating with families and the community at large to enrich arts opportunities for young children?

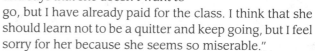

Situations and Solutions

Coping with Conflict

Situation 1

The three-year-olds in your nursery school have been experimenting with mixing colors. A parent looks at what his child produced and comments, "That's very nice." Then he turns to you and says, "When are they going to start making things that look like something? My neighbor's kid goes to ABC School, and he is already coloring pictures."

Situation 2

A parent says angrily, "I just found out last night that they had to bring in an old shirt for a paint smock today. Can't you give me a little more warning when Shelley needs something for school? I am a working single mother, and I was running around at midnight last night trying to find a shirt for her to bring."

Situation 3

A mother says, "I was always uncoordinated, and Sheila seemed to be the same way, so I enrolled her in a ballet class. Now she cries and says that she doesn't want to go, but I have already paid for the class. I think that she should learn not to be a quitter and keep going, but I feel sorry for her because she seems so miserable."

Situation 4

A grandmother says, "My daughter bought Stevie paint, and he decided to sit on my bed and paint something on my new bedspread. I told him, 'No more paints for you!' and now my daughter says I am overreacting. Don't you think it's important for children to respect other people's property?"

Integrating the Arts

Toys and Playthings

What is it that virtually all young children own, enjoy, and are interested in knowing more about? What sort of project could children undertake that would deal with basic concepts, such as colors, shapes, classification, and seriation, as well as more challenging concepts like analysis, application, and evaluation? What could chil-

dren study that would also build children's knowledge of other cultures in a concrete way? These are the questions that Angelina asks herself as she thinks about a project for the two- to five-year-olds in her class. She decides to follow the children's lead and observe their activities for inspiration. When three-year-old Jason walks in the door, he immediately reaches inside the pocket of his parka and pulls out a small, plastic wheeled toy. "They give it to you free with a Happy Meal," he explains. Lisa Jean, a five-year-old, arrives with a child-sized rag doll that she wants to share at circle time. "Aunt Sue made it for me," she announces proudly. "It has my clothes on it from when I was little." As Angelina scans the room, she sees children playing with plastic farm animals, unit blocks, puzzles and other manipulatives, a toy cash register, a child-size kitchen unit, a baby doll with a high chair and cradle, and many other toys. When they meet as a large group on the carpet, Angelina says, "I want you to tell me about toys. First, what is a toy? How is a toy different from other things like a pencil or a chair?" Some of their answers are "It's for fun"; "Toys are for kids"; "But sometimes grown-ups have toys: my mom calls Daddy's boat a toy"; "You need them to play with"; "But they cost money." Next, Angelina asks, "Why do children like toys so much?" Brian says, "'Cause they give you something fun to do." Lindy says, "When other kids come to your house you can use them." Jeff remarks, "I have trucks to play in the dirt with." Her last question is "Why do children sometimes fight about toys?" And children give answers like "Because you had it first, but they want it"; "It's mine"; "There's one toy but more kids"; and "They don't share." Angelina writes all of their responses on a chart and asks if they would be interested in learning something more about toys, and the answer is a resounding "Yes!"

That evening, Angelina starts rounding up some of her old toys and others that her son has outgrown. She brings in a stuffed dog toy that her parents gave her for her birthday. She explains that she wanted a real puppy, but her parents said no because they lived in an apartment in the city. They got her the stuffed toy instead. "I was so mad that I didn't get a real dog that I started swinging the toy around by its head really hard and the head ripped off. Then I started to cry because I thought my mom and dad would be mad that I ruined my brand new toy," she explains while removing the toy dog collar. "You can see the black thread here where my mother sewed it back on," she explains. "My mom didn't yell, she just told me to be more careful with my toys. Did any of you ever break a toy?" After the children share numerous examples of toys that are out of service or were repaired, Angelina reaches into her bag and takes out a small burgundy-colored box about the size of a gift box for jewelry. "This is a toy that my grandmother had when she was a little girl back in Italy. Let me show you how it works. I can tell you that there is a surprise at the end." The children carefully take off lid after lid of successively smaller boxes until they reach one that is about 2 by 3

inches. Inside is a tiny family made out of lead: a father, mother, child, and baby. "Do we have any toys in this room that are something like this—a toy that starts out with something big and keeps getting smaller? Let's look on our toy shelf." Angelina walks over and invites a child to select something. Mercedes chooses a set of wooden boxes that fit one inside another and range in size from large to small. The children agree that the toy from their classroom is like the old-fashioned toy in that the "boxes keep getting littler." Jacob has an idea. He takes a set of small wooden people from the doll house and puts them inside the smallest of the boxes saying, "Now it's *really* like your grammy's toy." Russ points out that "you have to open the old toy, but this one, you don't." "Good thinking, Russ," Angelina responds. "Some things are different, some things are the same about the toys. Does anyone see any other differences?" The children point out the size, the materials used, the colors, and the amount of wear. Then Angelina takes out a set of nesting dolls made of papier-mâché and painted in primary colors. "This is a toy from Russia. Let's take it apart and see how it works." The children work to put the dolls together and line them up in a row. "How is this toy like my grandmother's toy? How is it different? Can someone show us how they usually play with this toy? Why would children like it?" After this introduction, the children become more curious about toys. Angelina has several goals in mind. She intends for the children to

- understand that toys are tools for play.
- realize that toys are part of each person's cultural and ethnic heritage.
- see themselves and others as people who can construct as well as play with toys.
- understand that a person can become emotionally attached to a toy and treasure it.
- recognize that toys cost money and that some children own very few toys.

Before beginning this study of toys, Angelina communicated with families about the theme and enlisted the support of many family and community members. Here is a summary of what Angelina and the children did during their investigation into toys:

1. What Is a Toy?

- When the children arrive, Angelina has gathered a wide variety of toys and put them in the center of the floor; then they work to categorize them. The groupings they decide upon are toys for making things (e.g., various types of construction toys and blocks), toys for riding (e.g., tricycle, wagon), and toys to make believe with (e.g., dolls, puppets, housekeeping area).
- A poster-size collage of toys is constructed out of pictures cut from catalogs and magazines. One half of

the poster is called "Toys at School"; the other half is "Toys at Home."

- Over the span of a week, Angelina interviews each child to get her or his ideas about what a toy is and why children like to play with them. She types their responses on the computer, prints them out in 25-point print, puts the children's names with the comments that they shared, and makes them into a bulletin board.

2. What Makes a Toy Special?

- Children bring the toys that they usually sleep with to the center. On that day, the rule is that nobody has to share a toy because it is each child's most treasured possession! Angelina reads *Goodnight Moon* (Brown, 1934), *Ten, Nine, Eight* (Bang, 1988), *Guess How Much I Love You* (McBratney, 1995), and *Max's Bedtime* (Wells, 1985) while the children rest with their toys.
- Each child's photograph is taken, and each child dictates some comments or a story about the toy. These become part of a bulletin board display called "Toys We Love."
- A simple graph that shows the favorite toy of each member of the class is constructed by putting a card with each child's name next to the toy that he or she likes best.
- Angelina uses Tom Paxton's (1984) well-known children's song "The Marvelous Toy" as a guided listening activity. She invites them to close their eyes, listen, and try to picture what the toy he is talking about might look like. Then all the children get a turn to describe what they pictured in their mind's eye.

3. How Are Toys Made? Who Can Make a Toy?

- A mother demonstrates the elaborately dressed dolls she makes and sells at craft shows. The toys are cloth rabbits that have bows, ribbons, lace, and frilly dresses on. Then the mother leaves behind a box of scraps for the children to use in their collages and on the puppets some of them are making.
- The children make their own giant version of the nesting toy by collecting boxes of various sizes from the office and putting a teddy bear family inside. They visit several other classrooms in the center to demonstrate their toy for the other students.
- Grandparents who make and sell wooden toys bring their scroll saw and show the children how they make a wooden puzzle, then donate one to the class.
- A teacher who has visited several countries in Africa brings toys she has collected including a complete set of African animals carved from wood. The children compare the plastic animals that they play with to the wooden ones that African children play with. Some are the same (lion, elephant) while others are different (warthog, rhinoceros), and the children classify them into three sets: animals in both sets, animals in

the American set only, animals in the African set only. The teacher also shares an example of the detailed wheeled vehicles constructed by Tanzanian children out of metal and wire scraps that they find, such as tin cans, and demonstrates a *mbira,* or thumb piano, a simple instrument that the children in Africa taught her how to play.

- Donna's aunt brings her portable sewing machine to school, and the children help to plan, design, and stuff a giant soft toy mascot for the class. The teacher shares three stories about toys that are misplaced or argued over: *David and Dog,* by Shirley Hughes (1978), *Are You There, Bear?* by Ron Maris (1984), and Elizabeth Winthrop's (1977) *That's Mine!*

4. How Do Children Get Toys?

- The dramatic play area is turned into a toy store complete with cash register, play money, price tags, posters announcing sales, shopping bags, shopping carts, a toy wooden car that children can drive to the store, and a parking lot with a meter. Angelina leads the children in a discussion about some children having many toys while others do not.
- A guest speaker from the Toys for Tots program talks to the children about the work that they do.
- A father and mother who own an antique business bring numerous examples of toys that are very old and talk with the children about why a person keeps a toy even as a grown-up and then gives it to a child. The children see numerous examples of old toys from other lands as well as toys from the United States.

Included among the toys are a mechanical bank, metal toy soldiers, a doll with a china head, and the original Tinkertoys. The children compare these items with their battery-operated toys, plastic action figures, contemporary baby dolls, and the Tinkertoys in the classroom. They also listen to the Ozark folk tune *Mommy, Buy Me a China Doll* (Zemach, 1966).

The dramatic play area is turned into a toy shop. Children create a sign, a window display, and a shelf full of toys. They use a cash register, play money, paper bags, and a catalog of toys with order blanks to make their purchases.

Discussion Questions

- What would Angelina's toy study have been like without the support of families and community members?
- Do you think that Angelina achieved her goals? What would you have done differently?
- If your professor in an early childhood methods course required you to develop a unit on imagination, how could you adapt this toy theme to meet that requirement? If you had to write a unit on basic concepts of economics for young children, how might you adapt this toy theme to those goals?

Individual and Group Projects for Teachers

Take-Home Kits and Packets

By making some of your arts materials portable, you can get more materials that will spark creativity into children's homes. Try some of the projects described in this section, and plan to have children work with you to invent more packets after they have seen several examples.

The Writing Suitcase

Find an old backpack, luggage carry-on, briefcase, or child's suitcase. Equip it with writing supplies—lined paper, construction paper, pencils, sharpener, colored pencils, crayons, markers, and small stapler with staples. Children take turns borrowing the suitcase for a week, then bring in the writing that they produced to share.

Birthday Box

A special box that contains such things as a tape of birthday songs, a game to be played at a party, children's books about birthday celebrations, birthday cards created by all of the children, a birthday letter from the teacher, party hats, balloons, and so forth can be sent home on the child's birthday.

Take-Home Mascot

A stuffed toy is identified as the class mascot, and children take turns taking the mascot home along with his journal. With the parents' help, the child is supposed to write briefly about the toy's experiences while visiting the home.

Storytelling Audiocassettes

Children read and record their original stories on cassette tapes, then the tapes are loaned out along with typed copies of the stories.

Prop Boxes

Children make simple props for various types of play—a magic wand, a crown, some wings—that can fit into a cardboard box and be borrowed to stimulate dramatic play. Anyone who borrows the box is supposed to contribute to it in some way.

Plastic Bag Pouches

The teacher can use gallon-size plastic storage bags (or boxes with lids, or baskets) and equip them with the materials that children need to make a book, sing a song, and so forth. Commercially available record and cassette tape sets (often available for free from book clubs if you order regularly) can also be circulated.

Videocassettes of Performances

After children dramatize a scene or do a special project, copies of the videotape can be circulated to the parents so that they can see the performance even if they were unable to attend.

REFERENCES

Alexander, J. (1994, June 15). The artist and society. *Chronicle of Higher Education, 40*(41), B3.

Allen, M., Brown, P., & Finlay, B. (1992). *Helping children by strengthening families*. Washington, DC: Children's Defense Fund.

Allington, R. L., & Walmsley, S. A. (1995). *No quick fix: Rethinking literacy programs in America's elementary schools*. New York: Teachers College Press/International Reading Association.

Amabile, T. (1989). *Growing up creative: Nurturing a lifetime of creativity*. New York: Crown.

American Council for the Arts. (1992, March). Americans believe arts are an essential part of education. Press release on *Americans and the arts, VI*. National public opinion survey on the arts, Washington, DC, March 19, 1–2.

Auerbach, R. (1995). Which way for family literacy: Intervention or empowerment? In L. Morrow (Ed.), *Family literacy: Connections in schools and communities* (pp. 11–27). New Brunswick, NJ: International Reading Association.

Baker, D. W. (1990). The visual arts in early childhood education. *Design for Arts in Education, 91*(6), 21–25.

Baker, D. W. (1992). *Toward a sensible education: Inquiring into the role of the visual arts in early childhood education*. Paper presented at the Conference on Making Meaning Through Art (Urbana, IL, September, 1992). ERIC Document Reproduction Service No. 356080.

Beaty, J. J. (1996). *Skills for preschool teachers* (5th ed.). Englewood Cliffs, NJ: Merrill/Prentice Hall.

Billman, J., & Sherman, J. A. (1996). *Observation and participation in early childhood settings*. Boston: Allyn & Bacon.

Broudy, H. S. (1979). How basic is aesthetic education? Or is art the fourth R? In S. Dobbs (Ed.), *Arts education and back to basics* (pp. 56–66). Reston, VA: National Art Education Association.

Cane, F. (1983). *The artist in each of us*. Craftsbury Commons, VT: Art Therapy Productions.

Carlisle, B. (1990). *The making of a grass blade: A practical guide to promoting the arts in education*. Battle Creek, MI: Kellogg Foundation.

Caulfield, R. (1995). Reciprocity between infants and caregivers. *Early Childhood Education Journal, 23*(1), 3–8.

Chambers, A. (1973). *Introducing books to children*. Boston: Horn Book.

Clemens, S. G. (1991). Art in the classroom: Making every day special. *Young Children, 46*(2), 4–11.

Cohen, E. P., & Gainer, R. S. (1995). *Art: Another language for learning*. Portsmouth, NH: Heinemann.

Feeney, S., & Moravcik, E. (1987). A thing of beauty: Aesthetic development in young children. *Young Children, 42*(6), 7–15.

Feldman, D. H. (1986). *Nature's gambit*. New York: Basic Books.

Fitzgerald, J., Spiegel, D. L., & Cunningham, J. W. (1991). The relationship between parental literacy level and perceptions of emergent literacy. *Journal of Reading Behavior, 23*(2), 191–123.

Fox, D. B. (1990). Music TIME and music times two: The Eastman infant toddler music program. In B. Andress (Ed.), *Promising practices* (pp. 13–24). Reston, VA: Music Educators National Conference.

Gallas, K. (1991). Arts as epistemology: Enabling children to know what they know. *Harvard Educational Review, 61*(1), 19–31.

Gardner, H. (1980). *Artful scribbles: The significance of children's drawings*. New York: Basic Books.

Geoghegan, W. (1994). Re-placing the arts in education. *Phi Delta Kappan, 75*(6), 456–458.

Gestwicki, C. (1992). *Home, school and community relations: A guide to working with parents*. Albany, NY: Delmar.

Golant, S. K. (1992). Encourage your young child's creativity through play. *PTA Today, 18*(2), 10–12.

Heath, S. B. (1983). *Ways with words: Language, life, and work in communities and classrooms*. Cambridge: Cambridge University Press.

Hoffman, S., Kanter, L., Colbert, C., & Sims, W. (1991). Nurturing the expressive arts. *Childhood Education, 68*(1), 23–26.

Howe, M. J. A. (1990). *The origins of exceptional abilities*. Oxford: Basil Blackwell.

Isenberg, J. P., & Jalongo, M. R. (1997). *Creative expression and play in early childhood* (2nd ed.). Englewood Cliffs, NJ: Merrill/Prentice Hall.

Juan, S. (1985). The Yoji Gakuen—The Suzuki philosophy in the preschool. *Childhood Education, 62*(1), 38–39.

Kegley, J. F., & Siggers, W. W. (1989). The creative child in an orderly environment: The parents' challenge. *Gifted Child Today, 12*(4), 2–5.

Kenny, A. (1987). Counseling the gifted, creative, and talented. *Gifted Child Today, 10*(1), 33–38.

Miller, A., & Coen, D. (1994). The case for music in the schools. *Phi Delta Kappan, 75*(6), 459–461.

Morrow, L. M. (Ed.). (1995). Family literacy: New perspectives, new practices. *Family literacy: Connections in schools and communities* (pp. 5–10). New Brunswick, NJ: International Reading Association.

Murfee, E. (1995). *Eloquent evidence: Arts at the core of learning*. Washington, DC: National Assembly of State Arts Agencies.

National Endowment for the Arts (1994). *Schools, communities, and the arts: A research compendium*. Washington, DC: National Arts Education Network.

National Parent Teacher Association. (1992). Let's be smart and include art. *PTA Today, 18*(2), 7–9.

Orend, R. J. (1987). *Socialization and the arts*. Washington, DC: National Educational Association.

Palincsar, A. S., & Klenk, L. (1992). Fostering literacy learning in supportive contexts. *Journal of Learning Disabilities, 25*(4), 211–225, 229.

Palokow, V. (1993). *Lives on the edge: Single mothers and their children in the other America*. Chicago: University of Chicago Press.

Perez, J. (1995). Toddler time: A positive place. *First Teacher, 16*(5), 8–9.

Perkins, D. N. (1984). Creativity by design. *Educational Leadership, 42*(1), 18-25.

Perrin, S. (1994). Education in the arts is education for life. *Phi Delta Kappan, 75*(6), 452–453.

Pike, K., Compain, R., & Mumper, J. (1994). *New connections: An integrated approach to literacy*. New York: HarperCollins.

Rab, V. Y., & Wood, K. I. (1995). *Child care and the ADA: A handbook for inclusive programs*. Baltimore: Brookes.

Rich, D. (1992). *Megaskills*. Boston: Houghton Mifflin.

Rinaldi, C. (1992, July). *Social constructivism in Reggio Emilia, Italy: Presentation prepared for the Images of the child: An International exchange*. Newton, MA: Mt. Ida College.

Sadler, J. E. (1969). *Comenius*. London: Collier-Macmillan.

Salinger, T. S. (1996). *Literacy for young children* (2nd ed.). Englewood Cliffs, NJ: Merrill/Prentice Hall.

Sarason, S. (1995). *Parental involvement and the political principle: Why the existing governance structure of schools should be abolished*. San Francisco: Jossey-Bass.

Sava, S. G. (1995). Teaching the "new poor." *Principal, 75*, 64.

Shallcross, D. (1981). *Teaching creative behavior*. Englewood Cliffs, NJ: Prentice Hall.

Sloboda, J. (1990). Music as language. In F. Wilson and F. Roehmann (Eds.), *Music and child development: Proceedings of the 1987 Denver Conference* (pp. 28–43). St. Louis: MMB Music.

Smith, F. (1988). *Joining the literacy club*. Portsmouth, NH: Heinemann.

Stamp, L. N. (1995). A descriptive study of the creative arts. (Doctoral dissertation, Indiana University of Pennsylvania, 1994). *Dissertation Abstracts International, 55,* 3739A.

Szekely, G. (1981). The artist and the child: A model program for the artistically gifted. *Gifted Child Quarterly, 25*(2), 67–72.

Tello, J. (1995). The children we teach. *Early Childhood Today, 10*(3), 38.

Tizard, B., & Hughes, M. (1984). *Young children learning: Talking and thinking at home and at school*. London: Fontana.

Weissbourd, R. (1996). *The vulnerable child: What really hurts America's children and what we can do about it*. New York: Addison-Wesley.

Wells, G. (1986). *The meaning makers: Children learning lan-*

guage and using language to learn. Portsmouth, NH: Heinemann.

Children's Books and Recordings

Arnold, L. (1994). *Lullaby land*. Hollywood, CA: A&M Records.

Bang, M. (1988). *Ten, nine, eight.* New York: Greenwillow.

Brown, M. W. (1934). *Goodnight moon*. New York: Harper.

Hughes, S. (1978). *David and dog.* Englewood Cliffs, NJ: Prentice Hall.

Maris, R. (1984). *Are you there, bear?* New York: Greenwillow.

McBratney, S. (1995). *Guess how much I love you*. Boston: Candlewick.

Music for Little People. (1995). *Lullaby: A collection*. Redway, CA: Author.

Paxton, T. (1984). The marvelous toy On *The marvelous toy and other gallimaufry*. Cherry Lane Records. Distributed by Linden Tree, Los Altos, CA.

Wells, R. (1985). *Max's bedtime*. New York: Dial.

Winthrop, E. (1977). *That's mine!* New York: Holiday House.

Zemach, H. (1966). *Mommy, buy me a china doll*. New York: Follett.

I would suggest we begin by asking ourselves two questions framed by curriculum theorist James B. MacDonald: What does it mean to be human? How shall we live together? Focusing on such questions would allow us to go beyond the limits of vocational preparation, cultural literacy, and even higher-order thinking skills as the primary goals for education and allow us to think about what matters most in our lives and those of children. It would also allow us to see that, regardless of subject, how we teach is also what we are teaching—about self, others, and the world we share.

—Susan Stinson (1992, p. 27)

Teachers' Roles in Supporting Artistic Growth

FIVE

Chapter Reflections

❧ What can you do to capitalize upon young children's active imaginations and creative strengths as you teach?

❧ How does the classroom environment—physical, social, and emotional—affect the development of children's artistic potential?

❧ Which teaching practices in art, dance, music, story, and drama stimulate the child's creative thinking?

DEVELOPING AN ARTS ENVIRONMENT IN THE CLASSROOM

*A*sk any teacher if she or he is creative, and you are likely to elicit a wide range of responses. A group of classroom teachers who were reflecting upon their own creative abilities made these comments about their arts backgrounds and creativity:

Brian: My teaching-of-music class was a traumatic experience. I consider myself to be tone deaf, but I was expected to learn to read music, play the piano, and teach a song to thirty-five of my peers—all while being graded by a concert pianist.

Angela: My idea of art is an Elvis painting on velvet. How am I supposed to put more art into my kindergarten curriculum when I don't know a thing about it?

Mary: I always close my door when I dance with the children so no one can see my overweight body in motion—it's not very pretty.

Paulo: I just don't see myself as being particularly creative. When I am in one of my teaching methods courses, I am amazed by all of the ideas that seem to come so easily to other students. I have found that I am most creative when I can bounce ideas off of others.

These four teachers expressed misgivings about their talents in the arts, but their doubts do not mean that they lack creativity. Truly creative teachers know how to establish the conditions and provide the opportunities for their *students* to be creative. As a first step, teachers need to forgive themselves for lacking performance skills in the arts that other adults would envy. When you work with young children, it is helpful to keep the level of arts skill that is really necessary in perspective.

If you lack confidence in your musical ability like Brian, remember that most early childhood songs have simple melodies and require a vocal range of about five notes. Even if you never learn to play a musical instrument, you can sing along with recorded music and learn to use it more effectively (Jalongo, 1996). Remember also that young children are beginners in the arts and not harsh critics. As a result, they will accept your efforts even if you are a beginner yourself. If, like Mary, you lack confidence in your ability to lead children in creative movement, attend a conference and concentrate on the sessions that offer practical suggestions and active participation in creative movement. No one will expect you to have five years of private lessons in various types of dance. Most of the teachers there will be just like you—trying to learn and improve. Perhaps you lack confidence in your arts background like Angela. One possible solution is to seek high-quality resources. These "teacher idea books" are usually written by and for teachers and are designed to let you profit from the backgrounds of others. In art, for example, Janet Amann's (1993) *Theme Teaching with Great Visual Resources: How to Involve and Educate Students Using Large, High-Quality, Low-Cost Art Reproductions* offers a "crash course" in great art from around the world arranged by themes like oceans, clothing, and ancient art.

People who are experts in aesthetic education have a saying that every teacher should take to heart: "There is nothing worth doing that isn't worth doing badly at first." So even if, like Angela, you don't feel particularly well versed in the arts, you can build your background and share those new enthusiasms with the young children in your classes. Often, as Paulo has discovered, working with other people helps to "get the creative juices flowing." Even if you regard yourself as less creative than your classmates or colleagues, you can contribute to the creative enterprise in some capacity. You may, for instance, have excellent organizational skills that are essential for implementing a good idea. Over time, as you work with others in a supportive group setting, you will find yourself becoming more confident, relaxed, and creative.

What makes one teacher more successful in facilitating children's creative and artistic growth? Evidently, attitude has much to do with it; in other words, creative teachers see themselves as being creative. This self-image does not mean that everyone is equally creative, however. According to Rogerian theory, one person becomes more creative than the next because he or she has learned to play with ideas, elements, and concepts; to be open to experience and receptive to ideas; and to rely more on self-evaluation than the evaluations of others (Rogers, 1954). Over and over again, experts in the arts who work with teachers make the following points: Teachers who are the most effective in providing high-quality arts experiences for young children

Teachers can support the arts and aesthetics by providing an ample supply of interesting materials.

- know how to share their enthusiasm for the arts and aesthetics.
- continue to be avid learners in the arts.
- focus on developing children's creativity.
- strive to become more creative themselves.

As we have seen, classroom environments that are high in interest and low in risk are the most conducive to fostering creative expression from children and their teachers. To get an idea of how that generalization translates into practice, consider what Alice de Entremont (1990), an executive who works with people who create new technologies, has to say about fostering creativity in her employees:

> There are two things about dealing with creative people. One is acknowledging their creativity, exploring it with them, getting them to commit to doing something other than just talking about it, and the other is helping them, because it's a hard process and they can get discouraged, and then you want to be there to talk with them about the latest problem and make them able to go back to it. . . . They need those little helps when they've lost confidence in what they're doing, and they need to hear from somebody else that they are on track. . . . it is like holding up a mirror, so they can see what they have achieved and that's more important than the actual advice you give. . . . I could lose some of my smartest people if they got bored. (pp. 182–183)

The relationships between a workplace environment that supports the invention of new technology and a classroom that supports creative expression are striking. Educators also need to create that workshop atmosphere, to tread that line between *laissez-faire* and interference, to serve as that reflective mirror, and to realize that boredom and busywork are sure ways to stifle children's creativity—as well as their own. To illustrate the effects of the classroom environment on young children's behavior, reflect upon eight-year-old Jonathan's experience in the next section.

The Child Artist at Work

Why is second grade so much better for Jonathan than first grade was? When he was in first grade, there were many mornings that he cried about going to school and many afternoons when his mother was called at work to bring him home because he had a stomachache. Ask Jon's single parent mother about it, and she will say,

> It was a terrible year for both of us. At first I thought my son was just having difficulty adjusting from kindergarten to the demands of first grade. It seemed like the teacher was really pushing the children hard, but this is difficult for me to judge, since I am not a teacher. Jon kept bringing home piles of papers. He seemed tired and worried. Then the weekend would come, and just about the time he'd relax and act like a kid again, it would be Monday morning. It broke my heart to overhear Jon's prayers one night when he said, 'God, please make it Saturday again so I don't have to go to school tomorrow.' The teacher told me that Jon daydreamed too much and didn't finish his work. I visited his classroom several times and talked with him about it afterward. He said that he just didn't like school and that his teacher yelled a lot. I wanted to move him out of there, but there really were no other options. On my salary, a private school is out of the question. So we just struggled through together. This year, everything has changed, and I am so thankful. When I asked my son why he thinks second grade is so different, he said, 'I like my teacher. She doesn't just tell us stuff, we get to do things.' After visiting Jon's second grade classroom, I see what he means. When you go in there, it's like Santa's elves right before Christmas—everyone enthused and working hard and everyone involved in all kinds of interesting learning activities. In a way, it's hard to believe that life can be so different in the very same school building one door down the hallway.

As Jon's experience illustrates, educators exert a powerful influence on children's creative and artistic growth. The Theory into Practice for this chapter will familiarize you with the work of Teresa Amabile, a contemporary psychologist who has studied creativity extensively.

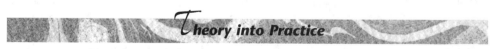

heory into Practice

Teresa Amabile on the Teacher's Role in Creativity

Teresa Amabile's (1989) investigations of children's creative behavior have led to several conclusions that have great significance for early childhood educators. As a first step in understanding Amabile's (1989) contributions to our understandings of children's creativity, teachers need to know her definition of creativity. She contends that the word "creativity" refers to ideas, behaviors, and products that are both appropriate and novel. In other words, it is not enough for thoughts, actions, or works of art to be original, although originality is one facet of creative work. Creative works must also be appropriate, meaning that the idea, behavior, or product is useful to the one who created it—in this case, the child—and regarded as useful by others as well. Because there is a certain amount of risk associated with producing something new that also meets the criterion of appropriateness, children need to learn certain "survival skills" that enable them to realize their full creative potential. In order to keep creativity alive throughout their lives, children need to learn

- to become self-disciplined about work.
- to persevere, even when frustrated.
- to assert their independence.
- to tolerate ambiguity—the absence of clear-cut answers.

- to resist conformity to society's stereotypes.
- to delay gratification and rewards.
- to become sufficiently self-disciplined to do excellent work.
- to take risks and welcome new challenges (Amabile, 1989).

The question for teachers is, What sort of school and classroom environment supports the development of these traits in young children? As you read each of Amabile's (1989) criteria for environments that support creative expression and aesthetic education, try to relate her ideas to specific classrooms or activities that you have experienced as a student, as a teacher, or as an observer in schools.

1. *Time limits are removed.* Adhering to a rigid schedule interferes with the creative process because there is no time for experimentation or refinement of an idea. Take, for example, the process of writing a story. No professional writer would ever be expected to come up with a great idea, write it, and submit it for evaluation in thirty or forty minutes. Yet some teachers expect this accomplishment from children on a regular basis. Modern methods of teaching written composition respect the creative process in children by giving them time to revisit and revise their work over time (Graves, 1983). This "process approach to writing" also gives children a free choice of topic, something that makes the writing more likely to hold the child's interest as he or she returns to it again and again. The same principle of a relaxed, flexible schedule applies to all types of creative problem solving—fashioning a shape out of clay, experimenting to create the best soap bubble mixture, or inventing a melody in music. In every case, children are permitted to make judgments about their use of time. This approach means that children are given real choices and the freedom to act upon those choices.

2. *Intrinsic motivation is emphasized.* One thing that characterizes creativity is the "labor of love" aspect. At their creative best, children are motivated mainly from within (intrinsically) rather than from without (extrinsically) by such things as prizes, stickers, and so forth. Consider for a moment the lives of some artists you have read or heard about. Often, they remained unrecognized for long periods of time and failed to achieve financial success during their lifetimes. We have all heard of artists who lived in poverty or who were scorned by their contemporaries. Today these artists would see their paintings or sculptures auctioned for millions of dollars, hear their musical compositions performed frequently in modern concert halls, find their books in nearly every library, or see that their performances on film are now considered to be classics. Delayed recognition is just one reason why it is important to downplay tangible rewards as the measure of excellence in creativity (Miller, 1994). Sometimes an idea, behavior, or product is so innovative that the society isn't quite "ready" for it yet, and sometimes those who bestow the awards are wrong about which works of art will withstand the test of time.

For all these reasons, children need to develop their own inner standards for evaluation rather than becoming totally dependent upon others for evaluation and rewards. To illustrate this point, reflect upon what happens when a third grade teacher announces that there will be a book jacket contest. The teacher and the librarian will be judges, and there will be first, second, and third prizes for the children who create the most attractive book covers. Prizes awarded will include stuffed toys of storybook characters, ribbons, and bookmarks. Now consider the responses of four different children: Claudia, Jason, Aimee, and Rashid. Claudia has just discovered oil pastels and would like to use them, but since she is unfamiliar with the medium, she decides to play it safe and use markers instead. Jason doesn't think he has the slightest chance of winning, so he does a hasty pencil drawing. Aimee gets very excited about the prizes, so her mother decides to cheat a little bit by giving her an idea for the cover. Rashid wants to win so badly that he decides to trace pictures from books and then color them in rather than drawing his own. In each of these cases, the goals of fostering children's creative expression and building literary appreciation have been perverted by the introduction of external rewards. For this reason, Amabile (1989) advocates acknowledging children's successes, but suggests that any awards or prizes be given as *unexpected* "bonuses" after the work is finished. That way, children can be uninhibited in doing their best work because they will not be preoccupied with the rewards.

3. *Praise is used judiciously, and self-evaluation is encouraged.* When adults are striving to build children's artistic ways of knowing, they encourage children to develop skill in self-evaluation. Part of learning to be creative is being able to determine the value of your own ideas and to persist in spite of adversity. Any teacher who really wants to develop creativity is careful with praise. It does children a disservice to gush over everything they do in the name of the arts. Children can tell that the praise is insincere if every child hears, "Oh that's wonderful!" all the time. A better strategy is to show interest in children's work through nonevaluative comments ("I see you are experimenting with mixing the colors with white to make them paler and softer, Xavier") or questions ("What will you do now to get your mobile to balance, Trudy?").

As you work with young children, respond to what children have accomplished and encourage them to keep trying rather than judging their work as good, satisfactory, or needing improvement. Teachers can encourage self-evaluation by saying, for example, "Let's look at the videotape of our first puppet play and the one that we did this week. Which one would you choose to show on parents' night? Why?" Cast children in the role of making the assessments and deciding what modifications might be necessary for improvement.

4. *Adults provide a balance of challenge and support.* When children are encountering new experiences, they need sensitive, caring, and enthusiastic guides to lead the way. Take, for example, looking at prints of paintings together. Unlike looking at drawings of cartoon characters that are already familiar to children, the teacher's goals would be to encourage children to really look, not just for the purpose of instant recognition, but to look beneath the surface to the underlying meaning. Other goals might include expanding children's vocabulary of art, building children's confidence in their responses or interpretations, and encouraging them to respond not only with thoughts but also with feelings.

How, then, does this creative process apply to young children's experiences in the arts? The arts process begins with thoughtful observation, personal meaning, and the exercise of choice. Suppose a second grade teacher says, "We have been studying our feelings or emotions. Today I want you to look in the mirror and make your best happy, angry, sad, frustrated, or confused face. After each person has had a turn, we will talk about how artwork can show an emotion—the colors you may choose for your painting, the way that you might work with the clay, or the things that you could make from the materials at our beautiful junk table." What kind of responses would you expect to get? One child painted "a thunderstorm" for angry. Another painted his Christmas gift—a puppy—for happy. Notice that in each instance, the child thought deeply about the topic and selected a form that truly communicated the emotion he or she was trying to portray. The next step in the arts process is to explore relationships between the artist, materials, and ideas. Thus the child who painted his puppy might decide to show a Christmas tree in the background or tackle the challenge of showing the puppy licking his face. Maybe he will choose to draw the pet care items that were part of the present—a brush, a collar, a leash, and a food bowl. Whatever the young artist decides, it will be based upon the fundamental arts questions "What do I want to express?" and "What are the best ways of expressing that?" Observing relationships is relatively straightforward when children are drawing representationally, but much less so when their work is nonrepresentational. Usually adults find it more difficult to "see" the art in scribbles. The thing to remember when responding to representational art is that the child is exploring—experimenting with materials, trying out new processes, and enjoying the task itself (the process) rather than focusing, as adults frequently do, on getting it done (the product).

But whether the child is scribbling or not, time limits need to be removed to increase the child's independence and intrinsic motivation. When children make choices about art, they frequently do so through trial and error. Sometimes, children begin with the materials and allow them to suggest possibilities. During the study of emotions, for example, one

Figure 5.1 **Ways of Responding to Children's Creative Work**

- **Present several alternatives**—Rather than turning art into an "assignment," provide children with choices, not only of how the finished product will look, but also of the process they will use to get there.

- **Treat child artists and their work with respect**—Let children know that their work is valued by displaying it proudly, helping them to transport it home safely, and finding something positive to say about their work.

- **Emphasize feelings and responses**—Rather than treating art as an assembly task or an exercise in following directions, encourage children to explore emotions through the arts.

- **Intervene when children seem stalled or frustrated**—Ask questions that will help children to take a different approach or perspective rather than falling into a rut or quitting in frustration. Encourage children to persist when tasks are challenging rather than becoming discouraged if the way to proceed is not clear or obvious.

- **Help children to sort out what is essential from what is unnecessary**—Teach them the skills of emphasizing what is most important in their creative products, and help them to understand that many times "less is more" and aesthetic experiences are improved by the elimination of extraneous details.

- **Recognize children's efforts, but do not accept slapdash work**—Guide children in doing their best, and give recognition to their achievements, not as a highly competitive contest, but as a "bonus" after the work has been produced. When it is clear that children did not make a real effort to explore the materials or produce their best work, try to find out why and give them another chance to excel.

Source: Adapted from Cohen, E. P., & Gainer, R. S. (1995). *Art: Another language for learning* (3rd ed.). Portsmouth, NH: Heinemann.

child chose a small box from the beautiful junk table, made a small figure by cutting one finger off an old glove, stuffing it with cotton, and drawing a face on it with a marker. Then she made a small coverlet from a piece of felt. She said the doll was feeling the way she feels when she is tucked into her bed at night by her parent. In this case, the opportunity to explore and experiment in a supportive yet challenging environment led to an interesting idea, a creative process, and a product that the child experienced as whole, complete, and satisfying. Because her teacher understands the creative process, this child and the others in the class were able to create meaningful forms of their own, original design. Contrast this example with that of a teacher down the hallway who duplicated a booklet that she has used for the past five years called "Our Feelings Book." Each page has a picture for the children to color and a sentence for them to trace over. Based upon what you have been reading in this book thus far, this second activity and others like it are *not* recommended even though they may be very common in schools. Figure 5.1 offers sound advice for early childhood educators as they strive to support children's creative expression and artistic growth.

MODELING ENTHUSIASM FOR THE ARTS

*O*ver and over again as we work with teachers, we hear statements like these: "I can't carry a tune. How could I ever sing with children?" "I can't draw a straight line, and I know nothing about art. I think that is why art in my classroom is pretty much easels and clay." In each of these common protestations, the message is the same: "I am not a performing artist; therefore, I cannot make much of a contribution to young children's growth in art." Yet this objection is entirely wrongheaded. In the first place, teachers do not need to be performing artists in order to share

When time limits are removed, intrinsic motivation is emphasized, and self-evaluation is encouraged, young children's creativity can flourish.

enthusiasm for art and craft, music and movement, play and enactment. The foundation for arts experiences in early childhood is threefold—process, enjoyment, and participation. To the extent that teachers can create environments for the exploration of arts processes and media, encourage children to associate enjoyment with the arts, and foster fuller participation in the arts, all teachers are capable of providing better arts experiences for all young children. Remember, you will be in a classroom with children, not at an audition in front of judges or in a recital hall in front of critics. As educators of the very young, we don't need to sing or dance *for* children, we sing or dance *with* them; we don't draw or paint or construct *for* children by giving them a teacher-made sample to imitate, we create the conditions that allow children to do these things for themselves. Thus, contrary to widely held opinion, being an effective teacher of the arts in early childhood is not dependent upon being a talented performer in the arts (Gharavi, 1993; Greenberg, 1979).

To further reinforce this point, consider the experience of professional musician Rene Upitis (1991), who decided as an adult to communicate with her former elementary school teacher, the teacher she credited with inspiring her to pursue a professional career in music. Much to Upitis's surprise, her former teacher had no formal background in music. In fact, this teacher had volunteered to teach the music class because no other teacher wanted to! The teacher's approach was to communicate enthusiasm for music, to give the children opportunities to make music, and to facilitate and encourage them in their efforts. Upitis was astonished to discover that her most admired music teacher did not play any instrument and knew little about musical theory or notation. The same holds true in our classrooms—children need to be invited into the world of art and aesthetics by gentle, supportive, enthusiastic guides.

Thus one essential role for teachers is that of a fellow arts enthusiast, a co-enjoyer. Being a co-enjoyer does not require exceptional talent. In fact, talent can sometimes get in the way. Two teachers recalled, for example, how they had attended a session on music for young children at an international conference. Their goal as nonmusicians themselves was to learn some new things that they could share with their students. Much to their embarrassment, they discovered that the two music professors from London who were directing the workshop expected them to begin by playing the xylophone, composing a tune, and singing their own names to the tune in front of the entire group. The next task was to invent an original musical composition with a partner and perform it on the xylophone for the audience! When it came to the last portion of the workshop, an experiment with a partner about harmony, both teachers took the opportunity to quietly slip out the back door.

It was clear that those who already knew music found the workshop delightful while those who were inexperienced generally felt inept. Because the workshop presenters did not offer choices and insisted that everyone "have a go" (give it a try), many members of the audience had their confidence undermined rather than built. Because full freedom to work at one's own level was denied, members of the group were quickly identified as either "haves" or "have nots"—those with prior musical training or those without it. Children in a classroom would no doubt experience some of the same emotions and frustrations if these structured activities were required of every child. Thus the teacher who is sensitive to this problem, the one who can identify with a child who lacks confidence in his or her own creativity or artistry, may be able to compensate for lack of talent with a supportive attitude.

Without a doubt, fostering children's growth in the arts and aesthetics demands that you become an enthusiastic role model. From your example children learn that the arts are pleasurable; that aesthetic education connects mind, body, and spirit; that the arts enrich our lives in countless ways. You don't need experience on the stage to facilitate children's enactments; you can learn the techniques of creative drama. You don't have to draw; you can borrow prints of the world's greatest paintings and learn to discuss them with children. You don't have to dance; you can provide encouragement, supply props, offer suggestions, and give encouragement.

Of course, it would be wonderful if every teacher could be supremely talented in each area of the arts, but few of us can claim impressive achievements in even one area. Furthermore, even those who do possess performance skills in the arts are not necessarily talented in sharing them with children in ways that foster children's growth as musicians, actors, dancers, or storytellers. A parent who was a concert violinist, for example, volunteered to bring her violin and share it with the children. First, she performed an elaborate musical piece. Then she passed around the violin and bow so that the children could examine it. The children had seen her play very dramatically, plucking strings and striking the instrument with the bow. Since none of them had ever seen a violin before, they assumed this was how the instrument was played and followed her example. The mother had not shown the children how to handle the violin, nor had she stressed the importance of handling it carefully. She soon became uncomfortable because the children were handling the violin roughly and took the bow away. Next she resorted to holding the violin while the children looked at it, and finally she put the violin back in its case. To be successful, aesthetic education for young children ought to focus on children's responses and emphasize what they can learn and do in the arts. It would have been preferable, for example, to let each child gently touch the strings and then perform a song for them.

Whenever you share arts experiences with children, remember your role as co-enjoyer. If the experience is frustrating for you, as this violinist's was, then it is probably frustrating for the children as well. Contrast the concert violinist with David, a student teacher who shared a story accompanied by song with the children. He memorized the classic story of *Bread and Jam for Frances* (Hoban, 1964). In this book the main character is a little badger named Frances who refuses to eat anything but bread and jam. Her parents go along with her dietary preferences until even Frances gets sick of the same menu for every meal every day. In the book, Frances sings a little song to herself about bread and jam. David made up a melody for the song, taught it to the children, and invited them to sing along each time it was repeated in the story. Even though David is less talented musically than the violinist, he has done more to motivate and encourage. He has also focused on his particular group of children, their developmental levels, and how *they* are likely to respond rather than becoming absorbed in his own performance. Another excellent resource for arts experiences is children's literature. Figure 5.2 contains more suggested arts experiences that begin with a picture book.

ENCOURAGING DISCUSSIONS ABOUT ART PROCESSES AND PRODUCTS

*H*ave you ever visited an art museum and noticed how reticent and cautious most people become? Because few of us have experience talking about art, we often fear that we will sound foolish to others who know more. So, rather than venturing an opinion, we keep silent. One of the goals of early experiences with the arts is to break that silence. Eaton (1992) uses an analogy to explain why developing a vocabulary of art is important:

> We describe a tree, for example, in vocabulary familiar to us; we use words like "branch," "leaf," and "trunk." Imagine what it would be like if we were not familiar with trees or tree vocabulary and suddenly were asked to talk about them. The more extensive one's vocabulary, the better able one is to produce a description that is truly "descriptive," that is, one that gives detailed information. But, of course, an extensive vocabulary only gives information to hearers who share that vocabulary. Someone who knows the terms for various shapes of leaves will learn a lot from a description that utilizes them. But information will not be exchanged if the hearer is ignorant of the meanings of the special words. And lacking words for leaf-shapes, we are likely to overlook details of the leaves themselves.
>
> One is confronted with a circle into which it seems impossible to break. On the one hand, you have to be familiar with something before you can talk about it; on the other hand, you have to know how to talk about it before you can become familiar with it. . . . Experts who are also good teachers know where to begin with novices so that they can break into the circle. (p. 161)

A good example of helping children to "break into the circle" is the use of concrete images that enable children to connect with the words and descriptions of an art form. If children are trying to perform a puppet play, teachers can use the same vocabulary that artists use but use the vocabulary in context—talking about stage, props, curtain, scenery, and so forth.

Another way that teachers build a vocabulary of art is asking good questions. Experts in the arts have concluded that there are ten basic questions about a work of art and that nearly all questions are variations on or elaborations of these gen-

Figure 5.2   **Arts Experiences That Begin with a Picture Book**

Amazing Grace (Hoffman, 1991)

Story Synopsis: Grace is an aspiring actress who wants to play the role of Peter Pan in the class play. With her nontraditional family's support and encouragement, Grace develops her confidence and skill and plays the starring role.

Story and Enactment	*Music and Movement*	*Art and Craft*
What do you like to pretend? Act out another fantasy story such as *Barn Dance:* (B. Martin & Archambault, 1986).	Listen to Mary Martin's "I'm Flying" (1992) from Peter Pan.	Create simple puppets to tell Grace's story.

Other Activities: Watch the video of Peter Pan, and create a comparison chart that contrasts the video with the movie.

Roxaboxen (Mclerran, 1991)

Story Synopsis: A group of children create an entire imaginary city by using ordinary boxes and cartons. They enjoy the process as much as the product, and when the work is done, it is truly impressive.

Story and Enactment	*Music and Movement*	*Art and Craft*
Use blocks to enact the scene where the children get the idea of building a city.	Learn a work song to sing while constructing: "Whistle While You Work."	Collect boxes and decorate them like buildings; examine several books about architectural design.

Other Activities: Watch the video of Pat Hutchin's *Changes, Changes* where toys come to life and build out of blocks.

The Maestro Plays (B. Martin, 1995)

Story Synopsis: Bright circus colors, cartoon-style drawings, and creative arrangements of various styles of lettering are used to describe the dramatic directorial style of the main character as he leads an orchestra through a wide range of emotionally gripping music.

Story and Enactment	*Music and Movement*	*Art and Craft*
Direct a rhythm band using a baton.	Play your instruments "glowingly," "beseechingly" as in the book.	Study the design of a book, and create a book of your own that uses different lettering styles to convey emotion.

Other Activities: Watch a film of a conductor directing an orchestra.

The Snowman (Briggs, 1978)

Story Synopsis: In this charming wordless book and accompanying academy award-winning video, a young child and a snowman who comes to life enjoy playing, flying, and visiting the north pole together.

Story and Enactment	*Music and Movement*	*Art and Craft*
Read two other stories about dreams, *Free Fall* (Wiesner, 1988) and *Baby Wants the Moon* (Murdocca, 1995). Create a dream picture.	After watching the video, invite children to listen to several classical pieces of music, move in response to the music, and select a story to tell with the music as background.	Create another type of snow creature out of paper or construct a snow sculpture outdoors.

Other Activities: Create a group story mural about a work of art that comes to life after watching a video of *Harold's Fairy Tale* by Crockett Johnson.

Source: Portions of this chart were contributed by Divonna Mohr Stebbick.

eral questions (Levi, 1970; Smith, 1992). Both the basic questions about art and specific examples of them are contained in Figure 5.3.

Building a vocabulary of art means more than learning some new terminology. It also means that teachers become more skilled at discussing children's work with them. Suppose a toddler smears blue and green finger paint onto a piece of wet, shiny paper. When the child is finished, how will you respond? If you say, "What is it?" your question implies that the child's work has to look like something. "What is wrong with that?" you might ask. First of all, the very young have a different agenda

---

Figure 5.3 **Questions about a Work of Art**

1. *Who made it?*

   Situation: Looking at a UNICEF calendar of children's artwork.

   Question: "Do you think these drawings were made by adults or children? What are you seeing right now that can give you a clue?"

2. *How was it made?*

   Situation: Looking at a large metal sculpture.

   Question: "Does anyone know how pieces of metal are joined together?"

3. *When was it made?*

   Situation: Looking at an ancient piece of sculpture.

   Question: "If you look at this carefully, you will notice that some of the pieces are broken off. Do you think this sculpture is new or old? Why?"

4. *For whom was it made?*

   Situation: Looking at a wooden toy.

   Question: "One of my neighbors makes toys out of wood like the ones I brought today for you to play with. Who do you think he makes the toys for?"

5. *What is the message or meaning, if any?*

   Situation: Looking at a heritage quilt.

   Question: "Do you know anyone who makes clothes by sewing them instead of buying them already made at the store? The owner of this quilt said that her great-grandmother made it from scraps of fabric that were left over from the sewing she did for her family. Why would their grandmother do all this work to make a quilt?"

6. *What is its style?*

   Situation: Looking at the art in picture-book illustrations.

   Question: "On this table, we have several books written and illustrated by the same person. These three are by Rosemary Wells, these by Keith Baker, these by Jerry Pinkney, and these by Diane Goode. What can you say that explains what each artist's work is like? How are these drawings by Rosemary Wells alike? How are they different from all the others?"

7. *What is the quality of experience it affords?*

   Situation: After viewing a film.

   Question: "You all know the book, *Frog Goes to Dinner* by Mercer Mayer (1974). Which did you like better, the movie or the book?"

8. *What was its place in the culture in which it was made?*

   Situation: Watching a Navajo sand painter at work from the video on the sense of sight by Diane Ackerman from the PBS series "Mystery of the Senses."

   Question: "Were you surprised to see that someone could paint with sand? Why are these sand paintings made?"

9. *What is its place in the culture or society of today?*

   Situation: Visit to an art museum.

   Question: "How do you decide which of your art projects or paintings to keep and which ones to throw away? One of the people we will be meeting has a special job taking care of these paintings. The paintings need to be cleaned, and sometimes they need to be fixed. Can you think of some reasons why people think these paintings are important enough to keep?"

10. *What peculiar problems does it present to understanding and appreciation?*

    Situation: Looking at an art print that uses pointillism.

    Question: "Some of you were wondering why this picture looks so different close up than it does from a distance. If you look very closely, you will see that the picture is made up of hundreds of dots. Did any of you ever experiment with dots as a way to make pictures? When you work at the computer to make a picture, the computer actually makes the dots for you. Use this magnifying glass to look at one of the pictures you made last week. Now look at this piece of a newspaper. You can see that the print is made of dots too."

when they use art materials. They are not rushing to produce a product; they are experimenting and exploring the medium. The object of their attention might be the gliding sensation of the palms of their hands as they slide them on the wet, slippery paper. It might be the discovery that red and yellow swirled together make orange. It could be the revelation that different portions of their hands—a fingertip, a fist, or palms down, fingers spread out—all affect the marks on the page.

Teachers are usually advised to say something like "Tell me about your picture." This is an improvement, but after children are older and have begun creating art that looks like whatever it represents, this comment implies that the child's art isn't communicating. A child who is fashioning a dinosaur out of clay and hears "Tell me about what you are making" might feel disappointed that another person cannot clearly recognize that his or her clay creation is a *Tyrannosaurus rex*. Whenever you discuss children's art with them, it is usually better to respond rather than evaluate. Too often, teachers rush to an assessment of the child's work, saying things like "That's really good!" or "Wow! I don't think I could draw a rabbit that well." Some suggested responses that avoid this trap of passing judgment on the child's work for her or him are (Cecil and Lauritzen, 1994):

"How did you get the idea for this?"
"This makes me feel . . ."
"This reminds me of . . ."
"Your _____ [story, painting, dance, song, etc.] was interesting to me because . . ."
"Will you choose this one for your best-work folder? How did you decide?"
"I'd like to know about how you . . ."

Or, instead of posing a question, you can comment, affirm, or recap what the child does or says:

"That's the first time that you covered the whole page with paint."
"Just look at all that green!"
"I heard you experimenting with the instruments."
"Now you feel ready to share your story."

Notice that in every case the response provides for individualized, specific responses rather than general comments. To further illustrate, read this conversation between Ms. Hanks and Greg, a four-year-old in her class.

Ms. Hanks: I see dots everywhere, Greg.
Greg: Them's ants.
Ms. Hanks: I see. Tell me more about your ants.
Greg: See, these bigger dots is ones that eat grease. The little ones is the ones that like sugar. Now I'm gonna draw their houses so you can see inside the anthills like in that book. [The child is referring to *Ant Cities* (Dorros, 1987).]
Ms. Hanks: I'm looking forward to seeing those anthills, Greg. Did you get your idea from watching our ant farm?
Greg: Yeah, from watching them.

Of course, it is important to engage children in conversation about works of art created by other people as well as about their own.

Teachers can extend their own and children's vocabulary of art by discussing different properties of works of art. One recommended structure for these discussions follows the acronym FRETS (Eaton, 1992).

F stands for the *formal* properties, such as shape, color, and the way space is handled. After looking at the big book version of John Steptoe's (1987) *Mufaro's Beautiful Daughters: An African Tale*, for instance, the teacher might ask, "Why do you think the artist, John Steptoe, used two whole pages for this picture of the jungle instead of just one?"

R stands for the *representational* properties, the things or ideas that are being portrayed. For example, as children watch a film of the famous mime Marcel Marceau, they are trying to guess what his gestures represent, trying to infer the things or ideas he has in mind.

E equals the *expressive* properties, the response it evokes from the audience. After watching a video of "The Dance of the Sugarplum Fairies" from *The Nutcracker* ballet, the teacher might ask, "How did watching this make you feel inside?"

T refers to the *technical* properties, the techniques used by the maker and the way all these properties interrelate. Suppose that a teacher used a print of the well-known painting by Auguste Renoir called *Girl with a Watering Can.*
Children could be asked such questions as

- "What can you tell me about this girl?"
- "Where do you think she is?"
- "How do you think she feels?"
- "Here is a photograph of my daughter in our garden. What is the same about these two pictures?   What is different?"

S refers to the *symbolic* properties, the attitudes and feelings that are expressed indirectly through the work of art. Symbolism is distinct from representation in that it is more abstract and calls for making inferences, for "reading between the lines" rather than literal interpretations. As children look at a print of "A Peaceable Kingdom," the teacher might say, "As you look at this painting, animals that usually chase one another or fight with one another are all together. What do you think the artist might be trying to say?" By using this FRETS framework (Eaton, 1992), you can develop questions to guide a discussion of virtually any art form.

MOTIVATING AND ENCOURAGING THE CHILD ARTIST

*T*he same teachers who would never think that making paper available qualifies as teaching writing or that making books available qualifies as reading instruction often feel that simply by making materials available, they are teaching the arts. Why? In some instances, it is because there is a tendency to believe that art is all feeling and not thinking, all intuition and no technique, yet such beliefs are clearly not true. Children need supportive demonstrations of many tasks that adults take for granted, such as how to paint with a brush or how to clap along with the music. Often, skills need to be presented at various levels, from low to high, to accommodate individual children. Think about an ability that many beginning teachers take for granted, cutting paper. There are actually many different levels to this ability, each requiring a more sophisticated level of fine motor control. These levels include

Tearing paper
Tearing paper into strips
Short cuts or "nibbles" with scissors
Long, straight cuts with scissors
Cutting curves or gradually rounded shapes
Cutting sharp angles or curves, such as squares or circles
Cutting interior spaces, such as cutting out the eyes on a mask
Cutting up to a point and stopping, such as cutting "fringe" or making a "door"

Young children do not "automatically" progress through these stages in technique. In order to make steady progress, they need guidance from adults who accept and understand their roles as motivators and encouragers.

Imagine walking down the corridor of a school and looking in on several different early childhood classrooms. What do these environments communicate about children and the arts? In a preschool class, the teacher has arranged letter cards on the floor, and the children are moving slowly in a circle while they sing a song about the alphabet. Down the hall in first grade, the teacher reminds children that their picture is to look just like the model she has presented, a square structure with a triangle roof and a rectangular door and windows. In second grade, the children are cutting dinosaur shapes from clay using cookie cutters.

Now while it could be argued that none of these activities does irreparable psychological harm, it is also clear that none of the activities qualifies as art and, as a result, not one of these common activities is doing the child much good where aesthetic education is concerned. In the first case of marching around the alphabet, the message is that music is for skill and drill, not for enjoyment. In the case of making houses from shapes, the message is that visual art is merely an exercise in following directions. And, in the instance of using cookie cutters, the message is that children's creations are inferior to those produced by adults, that children cannot be trusted to produce something of quality. True, each activity described here has some loose connection with the arts, but none of them really contributes to the child's artistic growth. In every case, we are looking at busywork, not education in the arts and aesthetics. What can teachers do, generally speaking, not only to support children's creativity but also to show children that they value the arts?

In order to transform a routine activity into a creative one, teachers would first need to consider how developmentally appropriate it is to expect children to do the activity in the first place. Most children begin to produce representational art (art that "looks like" whatever it depicts) around age five. Forcing a scribbler to produce representational art earlier by doing the drawing for her or him is misguided, at best. The recommended way of building a child's growth in the arts and aesthetics is to present open-ended challenges that are mutually agreed upon by the children and the teachers.

Take as an example the "art" activity of directing the child to place his or her hand palm down on a piece of paper with the fingers spread out, then tracing an outline of the hand, and then directing the children to make that shape into a turkey. Every November, these hand turkeys can be seen decorating the walls of some classrooms at every early childhood level from toddlers to third graders. There is nothing inherently wrong with creating a representation of a turkey, assuming that the child is at the stage of representational art. But if you really want to stimulate children's creative thinking, we would propose this as a challenge, not as an exercise in tracing and following directions. If representing a turkey is the challenge agreed upon by children and their teacher, you would need instead to give children a variety of opportunities to really look at turkeys in various photographs, drawings, and, if possible, on film or in real life. It would be better to give children choices about how to represent their ideas about turkeys. Will they choose cray-

---

Figure 5.4   **Ten Creative Activities to Try**

1. Inside/outside collage. Begin by developing the concept of a collage—a collection of things that communicates a message. Show the children several picture books that use collage, such as Ezra Jack Keats' (1964) *Whistle for Willie.* If you happen to own a small curio, keepsake, or display box, bring it in to show children the items you've selected and tell why. Explain to the children that you will be making an inside/outside collage box. Inside the box, have children glue pictures and objects that represent the things they do in school. On the outside of the box, children can glue pictures and objects that represent their lives out of school (Alter-Muri, 1994).

2. Felt dolls. Children can make simple dolls by rolling a small square of felt into a cylinder, then tying yarn or using pipe cleaners to create a neck, waist, and hands. Children can draw facial features with markers and glue on yarn for hair (Alter-Muri, 1994). Other scraps of fabric can be used to create clothing. By inserting their index fingers in the bottom of the cylinder, children can use these dolls as finger puppets for storytelling. Allow children to choose a favorite story with three or four characters and make a set of felt dolls for the story during the week, then share their story and dolls with a friend.

3. Create a rebus song. Make a favorite children's song into a poster-sized version that you can use as a song chart to read and sing, such as "On Top of Spaghetti." Illustrate with drawings or pictures cut out from magazines. Sing the song together. Go through a song book with the children, and decide which songs you will make into charts next.

4. Props while you listen. Begin with a large piece of clay and a box of other materials for making simple props. Tell the children that you will be sharing a familiar story such as "The Three Billy Goats Gruff." Ask the children to volunteer to make the props you'll need. They can mold their piece of clay into one of the characters or combine some of the materials (such as clay and Popsicle sticks) into a key piece of scenery (like the bridge). Leave the model set up so that children can retell the story again and again using the props they've made.

5. Instant puppets. Bend metal coat hangers into a diamond shape or circular shape for the children. Bend the hanger portion into a loop/holder for them also. Then give children pieces of old, clean panty hose to stretch over the hanger and create a puppet/mask. Invite children to decorate as they wish to represent familiar or imaginary story characters. Have the children wrap the loop with yarn or tie fabric around it to represent the character.

6. Storytelling. Memorize a good story by borrowing a tape of a professional storyteller, by recording your reading of a good story from a collection of stories for young children, or by memorizing a story told in verse. Listen to the tape whenever you have time, such as in your car on the way back and forth to work. Try telling rather than reading the story using flannel board figures or paper figures that are put up with tape or magnets. Make the figures available for children to use in their own storytelling.

7. Tape basket. Make a set of tapes of different kinds of music available for children to listen to when they arrive in the morning, as they get ready to leave, or during a quiet time using headphones. Consider including waltzes, polkas, symphonies, opera, show tunes, zydeco, marching bands, movie themes, choirs, barbershop quartets, etc. Use the public library, friends, and family as resources for a variety of musical styles.

8. Creative movement. Choose picture books with an arts theme, then ask children to respond to the book in their own way. Ann Jonas's (1989) *Color Dance,* in which children dance with lengths of sheer fabric, is a good choice.

9. Favorite toy. Ask all the children to describe their favorite toy—what it is, what it is called, why it is their favorite, how they use it during play. Bring in your favorite toy from childhood and discuss it with the children. Explain why it was your favorite and the different ways that you played with it. Invite parents, grandparents, or other family members to do likewise and share their favorite toys with the children.

10. Recycled materials mobile. This activity is best suited to primary grade children. Develop the concept of a mobile—a piece of art that is hung up (suspended from the ceiling), that is balanced so that it hangs straight, and that moves gently. Children will need to work on this challenge by suspending their mobiles from a clothesline or string; otherwise their work will hang awkwardly instead of being balanced. Encourage them to use yarn, string, sticks, straws, and different kinds of weights such as buttons, bottle caps, and other recycled materials to balance the mobile. When the children's work is done, hang their mobiles from the ceiling.

ons, paints, collage, grocery bags stuffed with paper, stockings stuffed with polyester fiber fill, or boxes glued together and decorated? How will the feathers be represented?

When this challenge was posed to a group of first graders, one six-year-old child "stole a few" feathers from his mother's duster. Another decided to use curls of recycled ribbon. Yet another cut "fringey paper" and glued it on. As children sought creative ways of meeting the challenge of representing feathers and other physical characteristics of turkeys, they used a variety of problem-solving strategies. As a result, they were learning that the artist is a master of symbols and that art relies more upon images than on words. Ten activities that support young children's creative growth are described in Figure 5.4.

SUPPLYING APPROPRIATE MATERIALS FOR YOUNG CHILDREN

$\mathcal{T}$oo often, early childhood teachers seek more and more unusual arts materials. They fear that the children will become bored with art activities if they encounter the same basic materials day after day. Although it is necessary to provide a range of materials and to introduce new materials or uses for the materials periodically, we need to keep in mind that many professional artists use exactly the same materials year after year throughout an entire lifetime—clay in the case of a potter, wood in the case of a furniture designer, marble in the case of a sculptor. It isn't simply working with unusual material that leads to creativity. Rather, it is the case that new *experiences* lead to new ideas, and having new ideas leads to interesting and different uses of the materials (Seefeldt, 1995).

A new teacher who worked with a group of two- and three-year-olds learned the mistakes inherent in seeking out exotic materials. She had heard about using shaving cream on a table as a "creative activity" and decided to use it. One child rubbed her eye while using the shaving cream and started to cry. Another, thinking that it was whipped cream, put his fingers into his mouth and began to spit it out. When she stopped the activity, she sent several children to the sink to wash up. She was too preoccupied with the two children who were upset to notice that, back at the sink, mounds of bubbles were overflowing the basin and plopping onto the floor. Years later, she still calls this her "disaster lesson."

Teachers need to model enthusiasm, demonstrate skills, and gently guide children's artistic responses.

This example leads to another reason why the quest for more and more unusual materials is misguided. Usually, they are not authentic art materials—when did you ever see a shaving cream, macaroni, or puffed rice creation by an adult? Because these materials are not designed to last, they are not used by adults. Using them with young children sends the message that materials beneath an adult's consideration are acceptable for a young child. This warning does not mean that found or collected materials cannot be used, only that teachers should be cautious about getting carried away. Recycled materials, used judiciously, can enrich available classroom resources for stimulating creative thinking (Drew, 1995). Figure 5.5 offers suggestions for obtaining recycled materials and using them appropriately.

Figure 5.5 **Appropriate Uses for Recycled Materials**

↝ *Goals*

- To help children think creatively—"Let's see what we can make!"
- To encourage children to work together—"Oh, no! We can't let it fall!"
- To get children involved in perceiving and inventing patterns—"First red, then blue, then yellow, now green again."
- To build children's problem-solving skills—"If I do this, I think it might . . ."
- To allow children to explore ideas—"I wonder what would happen if . . ."
- To support creating and inventing—"Teacher, look at what I made!"

↝ *Sources*

Ask **families** to collect decorating items (wallpaper, fabric, floor tile, paint chips, framing materials; craft and hobby items (yarn, wood scraps, lace, buttons); kitchen items (plastic containers, egg cartons, paper towel tubes, plastic milk gallon caps, detergent bottles); machines and machine parts (old telephones, alarm clocks, typewriters, computer parts). Gather materials from **businesses** too—restaurants (bags, straws, cups, bowls, trays, spoons, corks, boxes, ice cream cartons, pizza boxes, plastic containers); building supply and home centers (lumber, sawdust, wood curls, nails, wire, wallpaper books, linoleum tiles, plastic pipe pieces, carpet samples, ceramic tile pieces); cleaners and tailors (buttons, hangers, large spools, fabric scraps); camera stores and frame shops (usable expired film, plastic film cylinders, matboard pieces, frame scraps); plastic injection molders, die cutters, or packaging companies (plastic scraps and punch-outs in a wide variety of colors and shapes, gaskets, washers, sponge-type foam, and styrofoam); newspaper or printer (card stock, newsprint, fancy papers of many types); and grocery, drug, or department store (boxes, divided cartons, corrugated paper, countertop displays, floor displays).

↝ *Storage Suggestions*

1. Create a central storage "warehouse" for materials.
2. Label the storage bins, and involve children in sorting materials.
3. Provide small plastic baskets for children to transport materials from the storage area to the work area.
4. Develop a collection schedule so that materials arrive at predetermined times.
5. Make families aware of materials you need, then put labeled containers next to the door for collecting donated materials.

Source: Adapted from Drew, W. F. (1995). Recycled materials: Tools for creative thinking. *Scholastic Early Childhood Today, 9*(5), 36–43.

The important point to remember is that creativity is, by definition, an ability to make something new out of the available and familiar.

STIMULATING CHILDREN'S REFLECTIVE THINKING

*R*eflective thinking is active, persistent, careful consideration of ideas (Dewey, 1933). When we encourage children to reflect, we are asking them to "avoid behaving purely according to impulse, tradition, and authority" and to deliberate instead with "open-mindedness, wholeheartedness, and intellectual responsibility" (Cruickshank, 1987, pp. 3, 8).

In the arts, as with any type of teaching, asking questions, offering comments, and presenting new challenges are an integral part of the reflective thinking and learning process. If the foremost early childhood arts experts visited our class-rooms, we would notice something very interesting. Those who are skilled in the early childhood arts neither drag children through activities nor disengage themselves from the activity. Rather, they present the children with interesting challenges and ask open-ended questions like these:

- How will your dance show the metamorphosis from caterpillar to chrysalis to butterfly?
- What kind of props or costumes will you make for your play?
- Can you use these pieces of fabric in the house you are building from the hollow blocks?
- You feel that the weaving you made from yarn with your group is very special. What do you want your sign to say?
- Can you show me and explain to me how your invention works?
- How can you make your music sound excited with your instruments?
- You liked the surprise at the end of the story. Let's see if we can write a group story that ends with a surprise.
- How could we make our own movie about our kindergarten class?
- Now let's hear you invent a verse for "Skip to My Lou."

As these sample questions and challenges suggest, the arts process is concerned primarily with solving problems and meeting challenges. Notice that in these challenges, several conditions are met. Figure 5.6 is a summary of the characteristics of good challenges.

Posing challenges does not mean, however, that teachers are totally uninvolved in the process.

> When children evidence restlessness or boredom, they may be sending signals that they are ready for a higher level of stimulation. They need ideas and suggestions. Teachers must be alert and ready for this important moment. We are opposed to the idea of never giving information or ideas until children ask for them. If they do not know what alternatives exist in life, or in art, how can they know what to ask for? Intervention or suggestions, strategically used, can often be of enormous help. (Cohen & Gainer, 1995, p. xvi)

Good teaching calls upon educators to provide gradual challenge and continuous support. You do not want children to be frustrated, nor do you want them to think

Figure 5.6   **Characteristics of Effective Challenges**

Effective challenges

- are relevant to the learner—appropriate, interesting, and understandable.
- meet the needs of children at different levels of development because the challenges have multiple answers (rather than one right answer).
- support children as they use the processes of exploring, selecting, combining, and refining.
- are framed by teachers and students, with teachers structuring or limiting as necessary.
- give the students something practical to do that engages thoughts and feelings, mind and body.
- lead to further learning and more challenges.

Source: Felton, H., & Stoessiger, R. (1987, September). Quality learning: The role of process in art and mathematics. *National Association for Drama in Education*, pp. 14–21.

that the work is too easy to merit their attention. Striking that balance is what differentiates the excellent teacher from the ordinary one.

PROVIDING HIGH-QUALITY ARTS EXPERIENCES

*A*ll of the preceding teacher roles—stimulating children's reflective thinking, supplying appropriate materials, motivating and encouraging the child artist, encouraging discussions about art processes and products, and modeling enthusiasm for the arts—have explored the teaching philosophy of art and appropriate teaching strategies. In order to teach well, you will also need to articulate what you hope to achieve. That kind of clarity is what program goals give you. These goals may range from general (for the entire program or unit) to specific (goals for a particular lesson).

For example, the overall program goals of an arts program developed for Florida's at-risk children were as follows (State of Florida Department of State, 1990):

- To provide opportunities for young children to develop socially, emotionally, mentally, and physically.
- To promote development of self-concept, self-esteem, and self-discipline through arts activities, as well as develop an understanding and a sense of cooperative relationships with others.
- To help children communicate ideas and express feelings through participating in arts activities.
- To provide the opportunities for children to enjoy and appreciate their own creative expressions, as well as those of others.
- To provide learning events that are child centered, that emphasize active involvement, and that lead to independent work habits.
- To provide a learning environment that encourages language development, vocabulary and concept building, and creative thinking through participation in the arts and arts activities.

Notice how these general goals explain what your program is all about. They can be shared with various publics—parents, other teachers, school administrators from other districts, or members of an evaluation team. By taking the time to clearly state goals, those in the program develop shared understandings and common purposes.

Suppose that your goal was to get across the idea of different artistic styles. Now think about specific goals, such as the goal for a lesson that you plan to teach. One of the widely available resources for high-quality works of the visual arts in early childhood classrooms is picture books. Four picture-book illustrators with very distinctive and recognizable styles are Eric Carle (1969, 1977), Helen Cowcher (1988, 1990), Steven Kellogg (1979, 1986), and Faith Ringgold (1991, 1994). You might begin with just two authors by saying, "I have four books here. See if you can decide which pair of books were done by the same artist." After the children have sorted the books, you can ask, "How did you decide which two books were by the same artist?" Next, you can add two more artists and follow the same procedure until all of the books are matched to an author. When children use likenesses and differences to justify their sortings, explain to them that the way that a particular artist draws is referred to as *style*. After several such activities, children will develop the concept of style, and you can introduce even more challenging questions, such as these:

1. Are these books illustrated in the same style? If not, describe the differences.
2. Is the choice of style an accident, or did the artist use it on purpose?
3. If you think that the artist chose this style on purpose, why did the artist choose this style? What messages and feelings do the illustrations communicate?
4. How did the style of these illustrations "match" or go along with the story?
5. Could a different style of illustration be used with this story? Would it match the story just as well? Why or why not? (adapted from Eaton, 1992)

As this example illustrates, the teacher's role in providing high-quality arts experiences is much more active than many teachers imagine. Notice also that the discussion of style was based on concrete experiences, things that children could observe directly. From these examples, you should begin to see that the creativity, the arts, and aesthetic education are neither haphazard for children nor *laissez-faire* for teachers. Rather, they are an interesting blend of freedom and structure, of spontaneity and careful planning. As teachers in the arts, we need to remember that "experience has shown that teachers who fail to plan are really in essence planning to fail" (Gallahue, 1993, p. 192).

METAPHORS FOR THE TEACHER'S ROLE IN THE ARTS

*W*hat metaphor, symbol, or image would you use to characterize your role as a teacher? According to recent studies, many teachers subscribe to the "horticultural metaphor," which casts them in the role of "gardeners" who have the task of preparing the environment for growth. The horticultural metaphor extends even further because the child, like the seed, is considered capable of taking root only if the right conditions exist (Cortazzi, 1990). This "informal learning" orientation is more strongly associated with art, music, drama, dance, and creative writing than with other areas of the curriculum. When teachers subscribe to this metaphor, they often describe the children's growth as completely spontaneous, uneven (coming in spurts), and basically unrelated to anything that they as teachers have done (Cortazzi, 1990). Learning, particularly learning in the arts, is evidently perceived by teachers as pure serendipity—a happy accident—rather than the result of careful planning and thoughtful preparation.

This attitude raises an interesting paradox. On the one hand, we have teachers whose concept of creative activities is totally spontaneous. Yet, as we have seen, there is also a tendency to go to the other extreme and present children with mindless, ready-made products and projects to trace, color, cut out, or assemble. One view is all process; the other is all product. Both are wrong. As this chapter has described, the teacher has an important, multifaceted role to play in children's artistic and aesthetic growth. When teachers take the "stand back and let them grow" approach and do not work with the children to develop their aesthetic sensibilities, children's progress can remain stalled at the sensory stage. On the other hand, when teachers try to rush and push toddlers into producing work that is more characteristic of preschoolers or push preschoolers into work that looks more like

Figure 5.7   **Guidelines for Arts Educators**

ᔈ   *A Dozen Dos for Art*

1. Make time and materials for art experiences available every day.
2. Encourage children to use their own imaginations and ideas in this artwork. Do so through your attention to their work and your personal comments. Allow children to find individual solutions to lesson objectives.
3. Guide children to be observant of their surroundings. Help them to use their awareness to create their own artwork.
4. Provide a variety of materials with which children can experiment. The quality of materials is important to the success of the experience. (For example: Paint should be thick, creamy, and rich in color; clay should be soft and pliable.)
5. Experiment yourself with the materials provided for the children.

6. To increase observation skills and expand imagination, relate lessons to a theme that can be discussed by the group.
7. Encourage children to stretch vocabulary by using descriptive words when discussing art.
8. Provide visual materials (both real objects and fine art reproductions) and opportunities to talk about them.
9. Identify items in a picture as a way of focusing attention. Dramatic play responses to pictures are also helpful.
10. Guide children to enjoy the process as well as complete the art projects that they begin.
11. Help children to respect and care for art materials by teaching them to clean up and use storage properly.
12. Exhibit artwork created by all of the children, not only the "talented" children.

ᔈ   *A Dozen Dos for Music*

1. Use music informally throughout the day; transition times such as cleanup, snack, lineup, and center times are good opportunities.
2. Encourage spontaneous experiences with music by singing a song whenever it feels natural, by joining in singing with a child, by dancing with a child who is listening to a recording, by playing an instrument to accompany a child's activities, and by making instruments available to children for their independent use.
3. Sing songs that appeal to the children's interests every day—children learn to sing by singing!
4. Memorize the songs you'll sing in order to maintain eye contact with the children.
5. Use an autoharp to provide support to your singing.
6. Select songs that you like—your enjoyment will be conveyed to the children.
7. Discuss the meanings of unfamiliar words in a song to help children expand their vocabularies.
8. Clarify word meanings by allowing children to dramatize songs they sing.
9. Make classroom instruments available—a few at a

time—for experimentation. Provide an instrument cart, center, or corner. Teach children to respect and care for musical instruments.
10. Use instruments to enhance songs and/or stories. It is neither necessary nor desirable for every child in the group to play an instrument at the same time.
11. Provide a listening center with a variety of tapes, a tape player, and headsets so children can listen independently. Develop children's awareness of their feelings about music and their feelings aroused by music, by eliciting and listening to their responses.
12. Develop children's awareness of great music by playing recorded music at various times during the day, such as rest time or at the start of the school day. Selections must be short, aesthetically suitable, and of a quality that will arouse the interest and stimulate listening skill development in children. Works of a variety of composers such as Grieg, Grofé, Gilbert and Sullivan, Saint-Saëns, Debussy, Mussorgsky, Stravinsky, Rossini, Joplin, Gershwin, and many others may be effectively used.

ᔈ   *A Dozen Dos for Drama and Story*

1. Provide a dramatic play center in the classroom.
2. Offer a variety of props such as kitchen utensils, flowers, and a telephone that children may use freely during dramatic play; change these periodically to promote extended play.
3. Encourage children to develop their own dramatic play ideas by allowing time for them to play independently without teacher direction. Encourage children to create prop boxes to accompany stories and themes.

4. Develop a classroom library of age-appropriate books to provide ideas for play creations.
5. Develop your own dramatic reading ability. Read with expression and emotion to encourage the children to do likewise.
6. Discuss meanings of words, feelings, and actions of storybook characters so that children will expand their understandings.

continued

Figure 5.7 **Guidelines for Arts Educators, continued**

7. Encourage children to "try on" voices and actions of storybook characters.
8. Offer a collection of puppets (both commercial and child-made) for puppet play creation.
9. Encourage children to add sound effects to their dramatic play by providing a variety of percussion instruments such as a drum, a tambourine, and rhythm sticks.

10. Increase children's self-confidence through acceptance of their creative efforts.
11. Provide time for children to share their performances with each other. Encourage their creativity by accepting and building on their ideas.
12. Provide opportunities for children to view "live" theater, productions by professional groups as well as by older children.

A Dozen Dos for Dance

1. For the children's safety, have them wear flat shoes with nonslip soles and comfortable clothes.
2. Provide an uncluttered space that has no distractions and is large enough for freedom of movement.
3. Use all styles of music to stimulate creative expression.
4. Use instruments, music, or verbal sounds to initiate or accompany movements.
5. Increase the children's self-confidence through acceptance of their dance and creative movement.
6. Remember that creative movement is self-expression and expect students' responses to vary.
7. Encourage the children to look at each other's

creative attempts without too much discussion on the part of either the student or the teacher.
8. Allow children to volunteer to share their movement ideas and avoid requiring them to perform.
9. Provide opportunities to repeat favorite movement concepts.
10. Change activities frequently during the experience in order to maintain interest and attention.
11. Remember that even though creative movement activities are designed for the group, each individual's actions may be different.
12. Utilize community resources and the media to give children the opportunity to see dance at its finest.

Source: State of Florida Department of State. (1990). *Children and the arts: A sourcebook of arts experiences for Florida's pre-kindergarten early intervention programs.* Gainesville, FL: Author. ERIC Document Reproduction Service No. ED330454.

that usually produced by children in the primary grades, this pressure can undermine children's confidence.

Based on the most recent research into children's aesthetic and artistic growth, the solution is to find a balance point, a process/product blend. Thomas Edison once remarked that genius was one percent inspiration and ninety-nine percent perspiration. A similar argument could be made for the arts. The arts are thinking seriously, solving problems creatively, and working skillfully with symbols as much as they are inspiration. The arts are not all technique, and they are certainly not all imitation. Rather, the arts and aesthetics are ways of knowing and types of know-how that enable our students to interpret and invent other types of symbols. These symbols involve dynamic interactions between and among the children, the adults, the arts medium, the cultural context, and various works of art. Figure 5.7 offers suggestions for the teacher's role in art, music, drama and story, and dance.

CONCLUSION

The ways in which you define your role in bringing aesthetic experiences to children and leading children to the arts have far-reaching consequences. Teachers influence children's creativity and artistic growth by modeling enthusiasm for the arts, encouraging discussion about arts processes and products, motivating and encouraging the child artist, supplying appropriate materials, stimulating children's reflective thinking, and providing high-quality arts experiences. As you work with young children, strive to maintain a balance between challenge and support, between process and product. As you consider your role as teacher, remember above all, as Albert Einstein once remarked, "It is the supreme art of teachers to awaken joy in creative expression and knowledge."

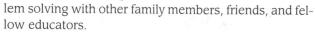

Learning about the Arts from Children

The Imagination of Meghan, Matty, and Lauren

As anyone can tell you, young children have active imaginations. But what, exactly, does this statement mean? What contributions does imagination make to children's lives? In the stories that follow, you will meet three young children as seen through the eyes of their parents. As you read, think about the material that you have read in this chapter. What evidence do you see, for example, of ideas, behaviors, and products that not only are original, but also serve the child's purposes?

Meghan's Story

Dan is a former marine sergeant who has decided to return to college, earn his elementary teaching certificate, and become a classroom teacher. One of the influences on his decision to become a teacher was his experience as a parent of two preschoolers. Dan had this story to tell about his daughter Meghan, who is now in first grade. It seems that some of the mothers at Meghan's school made little "tooth fairy pillows" for the children to take home so that they could put their baby teeth inside the little pillows and await the money from the tooth fairy. Meghan lost one of her front teeth, maybe a little earlier than necessary, in order to begin this exchange with the tooth fairy. But that night before going to sleep, she was having second thoughts. In a way, she wanted to keep her tooth.

The first night, after much deliberation, she decided not to put the tooth under the pillow, but she was worried that the tooth fairy would take the tooth anyway if she left it in the room. Her father assured her that the tooth fairy was not prone to petty thievery and suggested that she put the tooth away in a drawer. Now Meghan worried that the tooth fairy would see her tooth inside the drawer, but her father reassured her that the tooth fairy does not have X-ray vision.

She didn't mention the tooth the next day, but the following morning Meghan said at breakfast, "It looks like my trick on the tooth fairy didn't work." When Dan went and looked under his daughter's pillow, he found a small drawing of her tooth that had been colored and cut out. About this incident, Dan said, "She's looking for a loophole in the tooth fairy deal?! I'm thinking, future lawyer." Dan could hardly wait to share this story about his daughter's creative problem solving with other family members, friends, and fellow educators.

Matty's Story

Four-year-old Matty has a favorite stuffed toy that he takes along with him almost everywhere—a stuffed dog named Colby. Like many treasured objects of young children, Colby has seen better days. His once plush fur is now pilled and pulled out in places. When an acquaintance sees Matty in the store and remarks, "It looks like you've had Colby for a long time," Matty replies, "Yes, a really long time—ever since I was born!" Then, when the adult says, "Good-bye, Matty. Good-bye, Colby," the four-year-old picks up the toy's paw, makes it wave, and says in a squeaky voice, "Good-bye."

Then Matty does a pantomime and asks the adults to guess what it is about. He pretends to put on some sort of headgear, sits up straight as if in a seat, moves his hands about as if handling switches, a throttle, and so on, and then makes a loud, rushing noise. "You want to be an astronaut and take off in a rocket ship," Matty's mother says.

"I knew what it was," Matty's mother explains, "because that is the theme for the day—astronauts. He saw them on the news this morning and it became part of his play."

Lauren's Story

A friend invited me and a school psychologist to lunch one day to share his concerns about Lauren, his three-year-old daughter. It seems that she had created an imaginary friend named Mousie, and every time they would go somewhere in the car, the child would walk to the side of the family car, open the gas tank door, and tuck her invisible friend inside while talking aloud to it. I assured my friend that this behavior was normal, that studies suggest that approximately three-fourths of the three- to eight-year-olds create imaginary friends, and that he should enjoy this opportunity to witness his child's fantasy play. Still unconvinced, my friend turned to the psychologist and sought his opinion.

The psychologist began by asking, "What is it about this that bothers you?"

"It just seems so strange, talking aloud to something that isn't there. When other people see her in the driveway, they might think she is acting strangely."

"Well then," the psychologist replied, "Why don't you just let Mousie ride in the car with you?"

We laughed, and over the next few months, my friend relaxed about the imaginary friend and even began to enjoy sharing the latest behavior he had observed in his young daughter. I share this story as a reminder and a starting point because even early childhood educators sometimes forget that, just as logical thought is the hallmark of adulthood, imagination and fantasy are the great assets of childhood.

Discussion Questions

- What is the apparent role of imagination and fantasy in children's lives?
- How did the acceptance and support of adults influence the behavior of these children? If children had not had this support, how might their behavior have differed?
- What relationships exist between the imagination of childhood and later forms of creative expression?
- When these children become adults, how could their active imaginations be an asset?

The Artist in You

Alice Reexamines Her Assumptions about Art

Alice is a nontraditional college student. She already has three years of teaching experience in a private preschool but has returned to the university to earn her early childhood teacher certification so that she can teach in the public school preschool program in her area. As she begins to study the arts and aesthetics in early childhood, she also begins to reassess what she has done previously in the classroom. As you read her student teaching journal entry, consider the following questions:

- Why might a teacher equate "cute" activities with art?
- What is the teacher's role in guiding young children's growth in aesthetics?
- How can teachers move beyond the "creative" activities that they copy for children to assemble?
- What will you do in your classroom to assure that children are protected from doing busy work in the name of art?

Alice's Story

"When I first began teaching young children, I realized that I had an enviable skill—I could draw. Nothing fancy, you understand, just simple sketches that were recognizable so that nobody had to ask that question so often put to children, 'What is it?' As a result of the encouragement of other teachers, I not only put this modest ability to work in creating visual aids for lessons, but I also began to draw—or so I mistakenly thought—*for* children. I sketched puppet patterns, pictures to color, and games designed to help children learn basic skills such as colors, numbers, shapes, and letters. I hardly questioned that this was a service I could perform for children, one that many of my teaching associates were unable to provide. When Todd, a five-year-old in my class, scrutinized a calendar from the local bank that was illustrated with cameo-style paintings of each president and asked, 'Did you draw this?' I was really flattered.

"Parents and my principal were equally impressed. When the PTA obtained some recycled building materials, such as a piece of a cement pipe to be used as our playground's tunnel, I stayed after school and painted bright cartoon characters that I sketched freehand while looking at pictures from a book. As a result of incidents like these, I was reputed to be a creative teacher. With practice and praise, my confidence grew, and I invented my own visual aids, bulletin boards, and activities for the children to do. Yet despite the approval I then enjoyed, I have come to see those early activities as inappropriate and have begun to question just how creative a teacher I am.

"My first inkling that I needed to rethink my approach came when a teacher from England visited my classroom. He asked me why more of the children's work wasn't displayed and wondered aloud at the use of teacher-made decorations. He bluntly stated that, in his view, it was the children's classroom and they should have major responsibility for its beauty. A second experience that caused me to reconsider was a folk music workshop in which the presenter encouraged us, the nonmusician participants, to find ways of enjoying music with the children rather than attempting to perform for them. Gradually, after many such experiences, I began to reformulate my ideas about creative activities. I realize now that creative teaching is not something you do for or in front of children, but how you encourage *them* to respond in their own ways through the arts."

Discussion Questions

- Alice responded constructively to the criticisms of her classroom visitor. Would you have responded similarly? Why or why not?
- Should Alice abandon her image of herself as a maker and doer, or are there some more-appropriate uses of her talents?

- What are some of the ways that a teacher can acquire a reputation for being creative other than doing work *for* children?
- How did Alice use her reflections on experience to re-think her teaching? Where do you think her new ideas might lead her?
- What can you as a teacher do to assure that you keep developing as a professional rather than getting "stalled" at one stage?

Situations and Solutions

Thinking and Teaching More Creatively

Situation 1

Lately you have been wondering if some children are really paying attention during story time. You want to assess children's listening comprehension and their knowledge of story structures. How could you use masks, puppets, toys, or flannel board characters to determine whether children are understanding a story and responding to it?

Situation 2

Office supplies and instructional materials were delivered to the school recently, and there are many different sizes of boxes that need to be disposed of. How can you use these cardboard cartons as a resource for children's creative expression?

Situation 3

Children's interest in the block area seems to be waning. Mostly, they are laying blocks flat to make "roads" or simply building towers. How can you rekindle interest and enthusiasm? What new challenges can you pose?

What materials could you add to stimulate children's imaginations? What experiences could you give to children that would make their constructions more elaborate?

Situation 4

Music in your classroom is just a few traditional, well-known action songs—"Eency Weency Spider," "The Hokey Pokey," and the like. Research suggests that children's musical preferences are formed by about age seven. What can you do to expand children's repertoires and introduce them to a variety of musical styles?

Situation 5

You are on a very limited budget but want children to have an extensive supply of materials for creative expression. What are some strategies that you can use to give children greater choice of materials, even when funds are limited?

Integrating the Arts

Jyotsna Pattnaik's Indian Folk Arts Class for Children

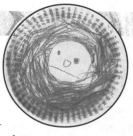

The scene is a college campus where fourteen children ages four through eight have enrolled in a summer class entitled "Multicultural Literacy through Art: An East Indian Experience." Ms. Jyotsna Pattnaik will be sharing the traditional dances, crafts, painting, and festivals of East India with these young children throughout the week.

Dance

Dance instruction begins by practicing different facial expressions and gestures that are used to express emo-

tion. The class participates in interpretive movements ranging from very literal (rowing, yawning, climbing) to more abstract interpretations (flickering stars, symbols of friendship). Next, the teacher models the enactment of a short scenario that combines many of the movements and facial expressions already explored. Here is the story she tells and enacts:

> The king and his friends were riding horses through the woods. Bows and arrows on their backs, they

went deep into the forest to hunt. The king saw a deer and chased it, but he lost sight of the deer, got separated from his friends, and lost his way. He was scared to be all alone in the deep forest. Now he is desperately searching for his friends and intently listening for the sound of their horses' hooves or their footsteps. But he hears other noises in the forest as well and occasionally jumps at the unfamiliar sounds.

Afterward the children write their own sentences and dance them out. Tanya, a second grader, beautifully expressed the movement of a butterfly as it goes from flower to flower gathering nectar. Joe, a third grader, expressed the smooth ebb and flow of the tides in a calm sea as well as the crashing waves of a turbulent sea.

The children had an experience with a more structured dance called Dandia. Girls wrapped a colorful scarf around their waists and shoulders; boys wore scarves around their heads. The goal was for the dancers to coordinate their footsteps and the sticks in their hands in time to the rhythm of the music. Practice for the Dandia folk dance moves from the simple to the complex. Instruction begins with individual movements in a circle that imitate the opening and closing of a flower. Next, children work with a partner to coordinate their movements with those of their partners. Finally, the dancers work in a circle and learn to change partners while moving in the circle.

The children learned that the beauty in an Indian dance lies in the masterful coordination of hands, feet, and eyes. A Sanskrit sloka was chanted and explained to the children:

Where the hand goes, the glance follows,
Where the glances lead, the mind follows,
Where the mind goes, the mood follows,
Where the mood goes, there is real flavor born.

Painting and Paper Cutting

Another aspect of Indian art that the children learned about was the decoration of floors, walls, and yards. Indians use colored rice grains, colored rice powder, flower petals, liquid rice paste, and other colored liquids to decorate for important social or religious occasions. It is considered a sign of welcome to God and guests who visit the house. After examining several examples of typical designs, the children created their own floor decorations. One child drew a dinosaur and expressed his wish to invite a dinosaur to his home. Paper cutting is also frequently used to decorate houses. Common motifs are banana trees, coconuts, and an elephant with its trunk upraised—all emblems to communicate piety. After the children examined many examples of Indian paper cutting, they created their own designs.

Architecture

Indian architecture includes both the Hindu and Muslim influences. Children heard the story of the sun temple while they looked at pictures of it. This temple is designed like a chariot of the sun god and contains many sculptures. They also examined pictures of the Taj Mahal and heard the story about the king who had built it in the memory of his beloved wife Mumtaz Begum. The king was imprisoned by his own son in later life. His only wish was to have a window in his prison that would allow him to gaze upon the monument. Afterward, the children used paper and crayons, playdough, building blocks, and cardboard boxes to create models of the architecture they had studied. During the construction, children contrasted the Hindu and Muslim styles, wrote captions and titles for their constructions, and used a variety of materials to replicate what they had seen. One child, for example, noticed that the walls inside the monuments had writing on them, so she glued pieces of her writing to the walls of her cardboard-box monument. Children were caught up in the stories surrounding this architecture as well. One student drew a picture of the king in prison who was gazing upon the Taj Mahal while tears rolled down his cheeks.

Festivals

While in the Indian arts class, the children learned about a festival that honors the relationship between brothers and sisters. The rakhi, a scarf decorated with trinkets, feathers, beads, ribbons, and so forth, is created by sisters and tied on the wrists of their brothers. The brothers reciprocate by giving presents to their sisters. Children had many questions about this custom, including these:

- "Is it just for children, or do adults participate also?" (Answer: "Yes, you are still brothers and sisters no matter how old you are.")
- "How will you tie on the rakhi if you are not at the same place that day?" (Answer: "In that case, you mail it.")
- "What happens if you do not have a brother?" (Answer: "Cousins and other male members of the community are considered to be brothers also.")

During the class, children made rakhis, tied them on each other's wrists, ate Indian sweets, and listened to the authentic music of the festival.

Discussion Questions

- How did learning about East Indian arts enable children to appreciate the culture?
- What did you notice about children's responses to the activities?
- How is this alike or different from other multicultural activities you have used, seen, or heard about?

Individual and Group Projects for Teachers
Using Prop Boxes to Encourage Enactment

What Is a Prop Box?

A prop box is a collection of materials designed to promote more imaginative dramatic play. Each prop box should be clearly marked and easily accessible to the children. The contents of each box should be presented to the children, and the use of these materials should be modeled for them and practiced in a large group before children are expected to use them independently. Children can create new props and add to the existing boxes, or they can create entire prop boxes on their own. The idea is to give them some materials that will support their efforts to enact favorite stories, songs, poems, roles, and situations.

Traditional Tales

Example: Begin with *The Little Red Hen* (Domanska, 1973; Galdone, 1973). Props include a set of garden tools, a seed packet, masks or ears and noses for each of the characters, a plastic model of bread.

Film

Example: Watch Rosemary Wells' (1975) *Morris's Disappearing Bag: A Christmas Story*. Props include some pieces from a science kit, a makeup kit, and a hockey set. Make a disappearing bag by sewing two old sheets together into a huge sack.

Story Songs

Example: Sing "Down on Grandpa's Farm" (Sharon, Lois, & Bram, 1994). Props include a farm set with a black dog, a white sheep, a brown cow, and a pink pig.

Occupations

Example: Firefighter. Props include a plastic hat, a length of hose, a carton decorated by the children to look like a fire engine (with shoulder straps attached so the child can step inside and wear the engine).

New Places

Example: Safari. Props include an explorer's hat, replicas of African animals, a piece of blue cloth for a watering hole, posters of African wildlife, a backpack.

REFERENCES

Alter-Muri, S. (1994). Art eases the process of attachment and separation. *Day Care and Early Education, 22*(1), 4–6.

Amabile, T. (1989). *Growing up creative: Nurturing a lifetime of creativity*. New York: Crown.

Amann, J. (1993). *Theme teaching with great visual resources: How to involve and educate students using large, high-quality, low-cost art reproductions*. Rosemont, NJ: Modern Learning Press.

Cecil, N. L., & Lauritzen, P. (1994). *Literacy and the arts for the integrated classroom: Alternative ways of knowing*. New York: Longman.

Cohen, E. P., & Gainer, R. S. (1995). *Art: Another language for learning* (3rd ed.). Portsmouth, NH: Heinemann.

Cortazzi, M. (1990). *Primary teaching: How it is—A narrative account*. London: David Fulton.

Cruickshank, D. (1987). *Reflective teaching: The preparation of students of teaching*. Reston, VA: Association of Teacher Educators.

de Entremont, A. (1990). In M. C. Bateson, *Composing a life* (pp. 182–183). New York: Plume.

Dewey, J. (1933). *How we think: A restatement of the relation of thinking to the educative process*. Boston: D. C. Heath.

Drew, W. F. (1995). Recycled materials: Tools for creative thinking. *Scholastic Early Childhood Today, 9*(5), 36–43.

Eaton, M. M. (1992). Teaching through puzzles in the arts. In B. Reimer & R. A. Smith (Eds.), *The arts, education, and aesthetic knowing* (pp. 151–168). Chicago: University of Chicago Press.

Felton, H., & Stoessiger, R. (1987, September). Quality learning: The role of process in art and mathematics. *National Association for Drama in Education*, pp. 14–21.

Gallahue, D. L. (1993). *Developmental physical education for today's children*. Daybook, IA: Brown & Benchmark.

Gharavi, G. J. (1993). Music skills for preschool teachers: Needs and solutions. *Arts Education Policy Review, 94*(3), 27–30.

Graves, D. H. (1983). *Writing: Teachers and children at work*. Portsmouth, NH: Heinemann.

Greenberg, M. (1979). *Your children need music*. Englewood Cliffs, NJ: Prentice-Hall.

Jalongo, M. R. (1996). Using recorded music with young children: A guide for nonmusicians. *Young Children 51*(5), 6–14.

Levi, A. W. (1970). *The humanities today*. Bloomington: Indiana University Press.

Miller, E. (1994). Letting talent flow: How schools can promote learning for the sheer love of it. *Harvard Education Letter, 10*(2), 1–3, 8.

Rogers, C. (1954). Towards a theory of creativity. *ETC: A Review of General Semantics, 11*, 249–260.

Seefeldt, C. (1995). Art—Serious work. *Young Children, 50*(3), 39–45.

Smith, R. A. (1992). Toward percipience: A humanities curriculum for arts education. In B. Reimer & R.A. Smith (Eds.), *The arts, education, and aesthetic knowing* (pp. 51–69). Chicago: University of Chicago Press.

State of Florida Department of State. (1990). *Children and the arts: Experiences for pre-kindergarten early intervention programs.* Gainesville, FL: Author. ERIC Document Reproduction Service No. ED330454.

Stinson, S. W. (1992). Reflections on student experience in dance education. *Design for Arts in Education, 93*(5), 21–27.

Upitis, R. (1991). *This too is music.* Portsmouth, NH: Heinemann.

Children's Books

Briggs, R. (1978). *The snowman.* New York: Random House.

Carle, E. (1969). *The very hungry caterpillar.* New York: Harper Collins/World.

Carle, E. (1977). *The grouchy ladybug.* New York: Cromwell.

Cowcher, H. (1988). *Rainforest.* New York: Farrar, Straus, & Giroux.

Cowcher, H. (1990). *Antarctica.* New York: Farrar, Straus, & Giroux.

Domanska, J. (1973). *The little red hen.* New York: Macmillan.

Dorros, A. (1987). *Ant cities.* New York: Cromwell.

Galdone, P. (1973). *The little red hen.* New York: Scholastic.

Hoban, R. (1964). *Bread and jam for Frances.* New York: Harper.

Hoffman, M. (1991). *Amazing Grace.* New York: Dial.

Jonas, A. (1989). *Color dance.* New York: Greenwillow.

Keats, E. J. (1964). *Whistle for Willie.* New York: Viking.

Kellogg, S. (1979). *Pinkerton, behave!* New York: Dial.

Kellogg, S. (1986). *Best friends.* New York: Dial.

Martin, B. (1995). *The maestro plays.* New York: Holt.

Martin, B., & Archambault, J. (1986). *Barn dance!* New York: Holt.

Martin, M. (1992). I'm flying. *A child's celebration of showtunes.* Redway, CA: Music for Little People.

Mayer, M. (1974). *Frog goes to dinner.* New York: Dial.

Mclerran, A. (1991). *Roxaboxen.* New York: Lothrop, Lee, & Shephard.

Murdocca, S. (1995). *Baby wants the moon.* New York: Lothrop, Lee, & Shephard.

Ringgold, F. (1991). *Tar beach.* New York: Scholastic.

Ringgold, F. (1994). *Aunt Harriet's underground railroad.* New York: Crown.

Sharon, Lois, & Bram (1994). Grandpa's farm. On *All the fun you can sing.* Toronto: Elephant Records.

Steptoe, J. (1987). *Mufaro's beautiful daughters: An African tale.* New York: Lothrop, Lee, & Shephard.

Wiesner, D. (1988). *Free fall.* New York: Lothrop, Lee, & Shephard.

Wells, R. (1975). *Morris's disappearing bag: A Christmas story.* New York: Dial.

*T*he arts have never achieved the superstatus of mathematics, science, social studies and English. People do not connect the arts to what they consider the purpose of education—to get a job, to get into college, to do well in life. . . . We have something unique to offer. We do facilitate communication within and across cultures. And we teach a different kind of perception and understanding that you really can't get any other way. If you don't have the arts, you don't have a complete education.

—Charles Fowler (1994, p. 8)

The Integrated Arts Curriculum

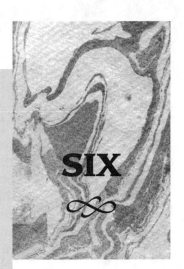

SIX

Chapter Reflections

~ What is a high-quality early childhood curriculum, and where do the arts fit in?

~ What theoretical support exists for aesthetic education in the early years?

~ How can the arts be successfully integrated into the total early child-hood curriculum?

~ How can teachers plan and implement a curriculum that provides rich opportunities in the arts?

CHILD-CENTERED, DEVELOPMENTALLY APPROPRIATE CURRICULUM

*T*he word "curriculum" comes from the Latin word *currere*. It literally means a path or road. When we speak of curriculum for young children, we are referring to the path that we have chosen as educators. Will the journey that we take with children be a purposeful one that empowers the learner? Will it capitalize on the interests of students, extend what children already know, build on classroom events, provide a time for sharing, encourage children to invent their own ways of responding, and create an arts environment (Burke & Short, 1988)? Providing a high-quality curriculum, literally choosing the right path, is one critical element of effective teaching. American educators have been debating curricular questions for decades.

In the early twentieth century, John Dewey discussed what was then a revolutionary educational idea—a child-centered curriculum (Cuffaro, 1995). A child-centered curriculum meant that instead of forcing children to conform to adults' predetermined curriculum plans, the curriculum would be tailored to each child's needs. Nearly eighty years later, we are just beginning widespread efforts to put the concept of a child-centered curriculum into practice. As you reflect upon curriculum for the very young, keep in mind that "early childhood education is not an exercise or a schedule or a machine. It is young children exploring their world with sensory thoroughness, experimenting with people and places and materials, encouraged by a teacher who respects and uses their ideas and ways of learning to help them discover what has meaning for them in our society" (Law, Moffit, Moore, Overfield, & Starks, 1966, p. 12).

Developmentally appropriate practice supports children as they meet new challenges by applying problem-solving strategies.

Curriculum is not abstract and removed from the day-to-day operations of the classroom. Rather, curriculum is central to everything that children learn and experience in school, intentional and otherwise. If you doubt that this statement is true, consider what children learn from three different teachers' curricular approaches to poetry. The first teacher ignores poetry; the second reserves it for a one-week unit every school year; and the third models enthusiasm for poetry through expressive poetry sharing, then invites his students to follow his example and share poems that they enjoy every day. Clearly, as each teacher makes these curricular choices, the consequences for the students' appreciation of poetry are far-reaching. In every choice we make as educators, we decide whether children will get an education that is inferior, similar, or superior to the one that we experienced as children ourselves. "Curriculum expresses the desire to establish a world for children that is richer, larger, more colorful and more accessible than the one we have known" (Grumet, 1988, p. xvii). The two teachers who did little with poetry probably experienced the same disregard for poetry from their teachers when they were in school, and they have done nothing to improve the curriculum for the students in their classes. The third teacher knows that, generally speaking, poetry has been memorized, overlooked, or limited to whatever happens to appear in the reading book. He wants to offer more to his students. It isn't enough for children to be aware of poetry, as important as that awareness is. This teacher wants his students to explore poetry, delve into it, and appreciate it throughout their lives.

Yet whenever changes to the curriculum are proposed, objections are invariably raised. Adults who experienced success with the traditional curriculum are frequently the foremost critics and will remark, "That's what they did when *I* was in school, and *I* turned out okay." But the point is that "okay" is not good enough. As a society, we need to seek exemplary curricula, not ordinary curricula, if our democratic ideal of education for all is to be fully realized.

One important concept in early childhood education is developmentally appropriate practice (Bredekamp & Rosegrant, 1992; Kostelnik, 1992, 1993; Kostelnik, Soderman, & Whiren, 1993; Raines, in press). As you read the following definition of developmentally appropriate practice, notice how consistent it is with Dewey's notion of a child-centered curriculum.

> Developmentally appropriate practice refers to applying child development knowledge in making thoughtful and appropriate decisions about early childhood program practices. Everything that has been learned through research and formulated into theory about how children develop and learn at various ages and stages is used to create learning environments that match their abilities and needs. This means that developmentally appropriate practice is based only on what is presently known and understood about children. It is not based on what adults wish children were like, or hope they will be like, or even surmise they might be like. (Gestwicki, 1995, p. 5)

As this definition explains, a teacher's knowledge of how children grow and develop is the foundation for developmentally appropriate practice. Figure 6.1 is a summary of the developmental principles that early childhood educators use to guide their professional practice, principles that we have applied specifically to education in the arts. In "The Child Artist at Work," you will meet two kindergarten teachers who are collaborating to transform their stale curriculum to one that is more child-centered and developmentally appropriate.

The Child Artist at Work

Mr. Belsky and Ms. McCullough are experienced teachers who work in a public school kindergarten program. Recently they attended a teacher in-service education session on developmentally appropriate practice. The professor who presented the session strongly endorsed more active, learner-centered approaches to teaching. As they carpooled back home after the meeting, the two teachers shared some

---

Figure 6.1 Developmental Principles Applied to the Arts

- There is a predictable sequence in aesthetic development.
- Artistic development at one stage lays the base for later development.
- There are optimal periods in children's aesthetic development.
- Development results from the interaction of biological factors (maturation) and environmental factors (learning).
- Development proceeds as an interrelated whole, with all aspects (physical, cognitive, emotional, social) influencing the others.
- Each individual develops aesthetic abilities according to a particular timetable and pace.
- Development in the arts proceeds from simple to complex, from general to specific.

Source: Adapted from Gestwicki, C. (1995). *Developmentally appropriate practice: Curriculum and development in early education.* Albany, NY: Delmar.

dissatisfaction with the way they had been teaching. During the previous five years, they had taught the same old units—fall, all about me, friends, dinosaurs, community helpers, dental health, the food pyramid, and living things. The presenter suggested that they try some innovative themes that integrate all of the subject areas and include important learning concepts with lasting value. Some of the themes she suggested were celebrations, cooperation, patterns, transformations, collections, music makers, just imagine, and buildings/construction. Additionally, the presenter emphasized the importance of integrating the arts with these themes.

Mr. Belsky and Ms. McCullough found that *Book Bridges* (Moore & Hampton, 1991), *Themes Teachers Use* (Kostelnik et al., 1996), and *A Child Goes Forth* (Taylor, 1994) were excellent sources for more original themes. They decided to try a theme on patterns that has three major goals: awareness of patterns, exploration of patterns, and creative expression through patterns. The concepts that they sought to develop included the following:

- We perceive patterns when we detect similarities, regularities, and repetition.
- Patterns can communicate a message, such as a road sign, tracks in the snow, or a table set for dinner.
- There are observable patterns in nature, such as a spider's web, the changing seasons, or the life cycle of a frog.

Figure 6.2 **A Kindergarten Theme on Patterns**

ᣭ *Basic Concepts*

- We perceive patterns when we detect similarities, repetition, and regularities.
- There are patterns in nature, such as seasons or life cycles.
- People can create patterns by using various materials such as beads, yarn, wood, and so forth.
- Some objects are designed specifically for the purpose of reproducing patterns (stamps, looms, etc.).
- Dance is a physical pattern.
- Music is a pattern of sound.
- Art is a visual pattern.

ᣭ *Day One: Recognizing Patterns*

What is a pattern?

- Introduction—demonstration using cut-out paper dolls.
- Pattern match with wallpaper samples.
- Stringing beads using picture cards.
- Creating pictures with Color Forms.
- Parquetry blocks.

ᣭ *Day Two: Exploring Patterns*

Look all around you to discover patterns!

- Introduction—play in a rhythm band using cue cards of patterns.
- Go on a pattern walk.
- Look for patterns in the clothing people are wearing.
- Investigate protective coloration.

ᣭ *Day Three: Interpreting Patterns*

What can patterns tell us?

- Introduction—reading signs that use pictures.
- Play with attribute blocks.
- Match patterns of animal tracks to the animals that made them.

ᣭ *Day Four: Creating Patterns*

We can make patterns!

- Introduction—using rubber stamps to make patterns.
- Make our own version of a song with a pattern such as "Today Is Monday."
- Make stamp pads from pieces of sponge and tempera paint; print with styrofoam, erasers, or other objects.
- Make people patterns using our bodies—thumbprints, handprints, and so on.

ᣭ *Day Five: Celebrating Patterns*

What have we learned about patterns?

- Examine works of graphic art by various artists.
- Use the computer to generate patterns.
- Sing "Two by Two" by Sweet Honey in the Rock (1989), and invent dance patterns.

- There are patterns created by human beings, such as a kente cloth, a hand-knit sweater, or silk-screened T-shirts.
- Some objects are designed to produce patterns, such as a loom, a stamp, or computer software.
- Music is a pattern of sound.
- Dance is a pattern of movement and gesture.
- Art is a visual pattern.

To further articulate their patterns theme, the two kindergarten teachers thought in terms of a weeklong plan and created a diagram or web of ideas. Their curriculum planning web is contained in Figure 6.2. As the kindergarten teachers' web reveals, the arts can and should be part of a child-centered curriculum. Aesthetic education is not an afterthought, it is a basic foundation for developmentally appropriate practice.

Theory into Practice

Howard Gardner's Theory of Multiple Intelligences

Howard Gardner's (1993, 1995) theory of multiple intelligences is making inroads into education. Gardner contends that American schools have focused almost exclusively on verbal/linguistic and logical/mathematical forms of intelligence. He challenges schools to educate other distinct forms of human intelligence, including musical/rhythmic intelligence, visual/spatial intelligence, bodily/kinesthetic intelligence, intrapersonal intelligence, and interpersonal intelligence. Figure 6.3 explains each of these seven types of intelligence.

Instead of asking the old intelligence test question, "How smart is this child?" multiple intelligences theory poses the question "In what ways is this child intelligent?" Note that in the first instance the purpose is to sort and compare, with some children labeled as bright, others as dull. In the second instance, where "seven kinds of smart" are proposed, the purpose is to maximize each child's potential. This is a useful and dramatic difference in

---

Figure 6.3 The Seven Intelligences

Verbal/Linguistic

Sensitivity to the sounds and meanings of words and to the different functions of language.

Logical/Mathematical

Capacity to discern numerical patterns and use logical reasoning.

Visual/Spatial

Capacity to interpret and manipulate forms and shapes.

Bodily/Kinesthetic

Ability to control one's body movements and handle objects skillfully.

Musical/Rhythmic

Ability to produce and appreciate rhythm, pitch, and timbre.

Interpersonal/Relational

Capacity to discern the moods, temperaments, motivations, and desires of others.

Intrapersonal/Self-Knowledge

Having detailed, accurate self-knowledge and access to one's own feelings.

Source: Gardner, H. (1993). *Frames of mind: The theory of multiple intelligences* (10th anniv. ed.). New York: Basic Books.

educators' orientation. How might this theory be translated into practice? Fortunately, Gardner's ideas have been so powerful that many educators have applied it to their curriculum, notably Armstrong (1994) and Chapman (1993).

One early childhood educator who demonstrated her understanding of multiple-intelligence theory by applying it to her work with very young children is Robin, a Native American who has been working with infants and toddlers in child care since junior high school. Now that Robin is attending community college classes, she has decided to pursue her commitment to young children by obtaining a two-year associate's degree. One of the classes that she is required to take is child development, and in that class, her major assignment is to investigate a learning theory in greater depth. Robin is fascinated by Gardner's theory of multiple intelligences, and she decides to show how her ideas can be applied to curriculum planning for the preschoolers she will be working with during her practicum on

---

Figure 6.4 **Application of a Native American Theme to Multiple-Intelligence Theory**

ॐ *Verbal/Linguistic*

- A storyteller visits and shares the story of Kokopelli, the southwestern trickster.
- Children listen to *Navajo ABC: A Dine' Alphabet Book* (Tapahonso & Shick, 1995).

ॐ *Bodily/Kinesthetic*

- Children observe a weaver, and each child takes a turn at putting in a stitch.
- Each child takes a turn at beating on a ceremonial drum and feeling the vibrations.

ॐ *Logical/Mathematical*

- Children sort a collection of pictures of Native Americans (Inuit, Lakota Sioux, and Navajo) into the correct tribes by looking at their homes, clothing, and environments.
- Children examine numerous examples of pottery decorated with traditional Navajo motifs and arrange them from largest to smallest.

ॐ *Musical/Rhythmic*

- Children watch the Grey Eagles' (1994) video of Native American Dances, then move their bodies to a tape of Native American music.
- Children learn and recite a Navajo chant in unison.
- Children sing "Circle Around" (Tickle Tune Typhoon, 1983), a Native American song.

ॐ *Visual/Spatial*

- Children play a teacher-constructed matching game made from picture notecards produced by children (obtained from the Heard Museum in Phoenix, Arizona).
- Children examine three blankets made by Navajo tribe members and compare the patterns and colors.

ॐ *Interpersonal/Relational*

- Children participate in the local Native American Arts and Crafts Show.
- A Navajo artist who makes storytelling dolls (clay figures in which an adult is covered by children anxious to listen to a story) visits the class. He shares the story behind these figures and the tribe's reverence for story.

ॐ *Intrapersonal/Self-Knowledge*

- Children take turns sharing the experience that made the greatest impression on them during the theme study.
- Children reflect upon the ways that their favorite stories influence them.

ॐ **See page 183 for additional resources.**

the Navajo reservation. Figure 6.4 describes the curricular brainstorming that Robin did as she worked on her Native American culture theme using multiple intelligences as a theoretical foundation.

CURRICULAR PRINCIPLES

*A*ll of these influences on early childhood curriculum—multiple-intelligence theory, developmentally appropriate practice, and child-centered curriculum—can be directly applied to aesthetic education for young children. A high-quality, arts-based curriculum has the following features:

1. The arts are regarded as fundamental to the total curriculum rather than superfluous.
2. Linkages between the arts and other curricular areas are emphasized, and subjects are not isolated into separate blocks of time.
3. Barriers between the fine arts and popular arts are broken down so that children can see the aesthetic elements in their daily lives.
4. Art is valued as a distinctive way of learning that connects sensing, knowing, and feeling.
5. Children are generally given time, choices, materials, and a low-risk environment so that they can invent and discover rather than simply performing assigned tasks.
6. Special learning projects, centers, and outdoor play are standard features of the curriculum.
7. The curriculum is not completely predetermined by the curriculum guide, teacher's manual, or teacher. Children have input into the curriculum; their interests, motivations, and curiosities exert an influence on what happens at school.
8. The emphasis is on process and self-evaluation by children rather than products and tangible rewards dispensed by teachers.

As you work to implement an arts-based curriculum, you will need to focus on five components: (1) understanding how children learn, (2) formulating a philosophy, (3) preparing the physical environment, (4) integrating the curriculum, (5) organizing the curriculum, and (6) matching methods to goals.

HOW CHILDREN LEARN

*I*n her review of the early childhood research, leading early childhood expert Lilian Katz (1988) identified four types of learning: (1) knowledge, (2) skills, (3) dispositions, and (4) feelings.

Knowledge and Skills in the Arts

The first type of learning is knowledge. **Knowledge** is information children get through their senses, from direct or vicarious experience. Consider, for instance, how children develop the concept of rhythm. At the prenatal stage, the rhythmic sounds of the mother's heartbeat and respiration are imprinted upon the baby. This first experience with rhythm is soon extended to other experiences with rhythm—

the motion of a rocking chair, the sound of lullabies, the ticking of a clock, the words of a nursery rhyme recited aloud. Over time, the child amasses experience and processes information to construct a personal understanding of rhythm. As this example illustrates, knowledge begins with sensory input and grows into understanding.

Skills are the second type of learning. Skills are more than "knowing about"; they have to do with "knowing how." **Skills** are abilities or techniques that build on and apply knowledge. They are developed through practice. Clearly, the arts are fundamentally connected with techniques as children learn many different ways of creating new forms—drawing, painting, sculpting, dancing, singing, dramatizing, composing stories, constructing objects, and making music. Returning to the earlier example of rhythm in music, an example of a skill would be learning to clap "in time" to the music or to play in a rhythm band.

Although knowledge and skill are considered to be "the basics" in learning, they are not enough. Every year, thousands of parents enroll their children in classes that teach them about some aspect of the arts and enable children to acquire certain knowledge and skills. Children go to the dance studio, take music lessons, participate in creative writing classes, and study arts and crafts. If the goal of these activities is the early identification of artistic genius and the child does not appear to be extraordinarily gifted, parents often view these experiences as a waste of money. If, however, the goal of these activities is to provide breadth and depth to learning throughout life, then all of those arts experiences that parents provide are well worth the investment. Why? Because aesthetic education goes beyond basic knowledge and skills to affect the third and fourth levels of learning: dispositions and feelings.

Dispositions and Feelings in the Arts

The third category of learning is dispositions. **Dispositions** are inclinations or "habits of mind" such as curiosity or flexibility. A disposition is an orientation to the world that was learned from role models. When an interested, enthusiastic adult shares Vivaldi's *The Four Seasons* and calls a child's attention to how the musical piece captures the moods of winter, spring, summer, and fall, that musical selection becomes deeply imbued with meaning for the child. After many such experiences, the child would be disposed to listen more carefully to music and to pay attention to the mood it creates or the story it tells. The child might become fascinated with other musical selections that tell a story, perhaps Vladimir Vagin's (1995) picture book version of *The Nutcracker Ballet* or Prokofiev's *Peter and the Wolf* accompanied by Ian Beck's (1995) picture book. In other words, a disposition or habit of mind has been formed as a result of working with enthusiastic role models. Dispositions are a major goal of aesthetic education and arts experiences. We want children to be more observant, to appreciate the artwork of others, to persist at a task even when difficult, to explore possibilities, to play with ideas, and so forth. All of these things are more than knowledge, even more than skills. They are dispositions.

The fourth and final type of learning is feelings. **Feelings** are the emotions associated with the learning experience. When it comes to learning about feelings, the arts have no equal in any area of the curriculum. They are the best way we human beings have of giving form to the imaginative inner workings of our minds. Returning to the earlier example of developing a concept of rhythm, that concept

Figure 6.5   Four Types of Learning Promoted through the Arts

Knowledge about the arts *is developed by*

- sensory experiences and the exploration of materials.
- meeting real, live artists and watching them at work.
- thoughtful examination and discussion of works of art.

Skills in the arts *are developed by*

- experimenting with arts materials, tools, and processes in a low-risk environment.
- gentle guidance from others who have already acquired the skills.
- a certain amount of trial and error: making mistakes and learning from them.

Dispositions toward the arts *are developed by*

- interaction with role models—more competent peers, teachers, and professional artists.
- experiencing the arts alongside enthusiastic arts advocates.

Feelings about the arts *are developed by*

- a sense of belonging to a community and being supported by the group.
- opportunities to respond to works of art created by others.
- the sense of efficacy that results when a child's artistic efforts evoke a positive response from others.

would be incomplete even if the child had knowledge about rhythm, had the skills to make rhythmic sounds, and had the disposition to explore rhythms in the environment. Ultimately, a concept of rhythm enables you to "feel the beat"; it makes you want to get up and dance or tap out a drumbeat on the dashboard of the car. Real learning takes place when all four types of learning are combined—not only knowledge and skills, but also dispositions and feelings. Figure 6.5 is an overview of the four types of learning and how they are developed through the arts. As Howard Gardner (1989) asserts, if the arts "provide access to the major ways of knowing and understanding experience which our culture has developed, then the arts must be part of the curriculum" (p. 6).

FORMULATING A PHILOSOPHY

When teachers hear the word "philosophy," they often assume that it has little to do with the real world of teaching. Actually, your philosophy is the very heart of your teaching because your philosophy is what you understand, believe, and value. These things have a profound and undeniable effect on your behavior. When Martin, a sophomore majoring in early childhood education, was told that he would have to write a philosophy statement for his professional portfolio, he "didn't know where to start." After his instructor for the course, "Creative Activities for Young Children," provided him with a set of questions and discussed them in class, Martin began the hard work of putting his personal teaching philosophy into words.

The instructor began by stating, "A conceptual philosophy is your philosophical and theoretical orientation to the role of teacher. It includes the answers to fundamental questions that guide your decision making. The first question to ask yourself is 'What do I believe about how children learn?' Create a statement, a web of ideas, or a list of your beliefs about how children learn. When you see someone else who looks like he or she is finished, go over and share your ideas with that person." After the students participated in this activity, Martin's instructor shared the following list of ideas that Cohen (1995) used to answer the question "How do young children learn?"

- By laughing
- By playing
- By meditating
- By forming
- By modeling
- By communing
- By exploring various ways of knowing

Next, the instructor added these questions to guide students in formulating their philosophy statements:

- What aspirations do I have for children's creative and artistic growth now and in the future?
- How can aesthetic education meet young children's developmental levels, celebrate their individual differences, and respect their cultural diversity?
- What kind of classroom environment, teaching methods, and learning experiences will enable me to support children's creative and artistic growth?
- How will I educate others about the importance of the arts and aesthetics in children's lives?

Articulating a philosophy will clarify values, establish long-range, growth-oriented priorities for children, and put the entire program into perspective (Peterson, 1987). Often, teachers will rush to choose an activity—a "What do I do Monday?" approach—rather than thinking deeply about why they are making these choices. Whether it is explicit (stated) or implicit (expressed by your actions), your personal teaching philosophy is evident to others.

PREPARING THE PHYSICAL ENVIRONMENT

One of Maria Montessori's great contributions to early childhood education was the concept of the prepared environment. The prepared environment means that much of the work we do in working with young children occurs behind the scenes as we identify goals, select materials, and arrange the classroom in ways that support children's active learning. Generally speaking, preparing the physical environment involves attention to the things discussed in the following paragraphs.

Selection has to do with making choices about what is worth purchasing or procuring. In most programs, budgetary restrictions make it important to consider the value of various materials and to come up with creative alternatives to expensive resources. You may find, for example, that a retired grandparent is willing to construct a puppet stage if you supply the instructions, whereas a puppet stage ordered from a catalog would break the budget. Many early childhood educators expand the selection of art materials by asking for donated materials or using recycled materials. In new programs, teachers may find themselves very involved in making purchasing decisions, while teachers in existing programs are frequently expected to "make do" with what is already available. Whatever choices you have to make about art materials, try to select things that will have lasting value. It is better to have paints available regularly, for instance, than to buy glitter pens or scented markers that won't last beyond a couple of uses.

Access has to do with the range and supply of materials available to children. In some classrooms you will visit, all materials are out every day, and supplies are often in a state of disarray. Children's interest is more likely to be maintained, however, when some materials are rotated in order to give the feeling of "new" toys, materials, or equipment. There are some toys, supplies, and equipment that you want children to access easily, while other materials are restricted to use under your supervision (e.g., hammers and saws) or reserved for your use (e.g., teacher resource books).

Storage and display have to do with where materials will be kept when they are not in use and the prominent places where completed work will be put on display. In an early childhood classroom, there are many different storage solutions—a coat tree for dress-up clothes, a plastic shoe rack to stand up hand puppets, a wooden rack for horizontal stacking of puzzles, a set of labeled boxes for dramatic play props, or a divided salad-server dish for art materials such as se-

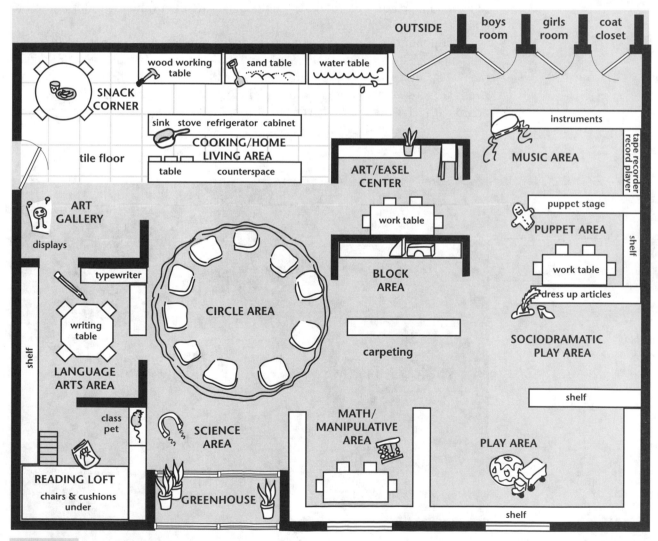

Figure 6.6 Preschool Classroom Floor Plan
Designed by Natalie K. Conrad.

quins, buttons, bits of yarn, scraps of felt. Methods of displaying children's work might include a clothesline to display paintings, a refrigerator box with a wrapping-paper background to display photographs of various projects, a shelf draped with fabric for clay creations, or pieces of yarn hung from the ceiling with paper clips attached for displaying drawings (Figure 6.6).

Centers and pathways have to do with the large-scale arrangement or floor plan of the classroom. Children need to be able to scan the room and see what is available, so it is important to keep the child's eye level in mind when using partitions, dividers, or storage cabinets to define an area or center. It is generally recommended that large-muscle activities, such as blocks or woodworking, be arranged near one another and that the art area be close by the sink. You will also need to consider pathways and how children will get from one area to the next. Problems with other children running through a house area, for example, can sometimes be eliminated by using some shelves to create low barriers. You will also want to have a large group area for activities done with the total group, such as meeting a visiting musician and listening to her play an instrument. Every classroom should also provide more quiet, secluded spots to read, listen, rest, and reflect. Some pillows or bean bag chairs make the environment softer and more comfortable and homelike.

Independence has to do with arranging the physical environment so that children share responsibility for the care and maintenance of materials and equipment. You may want to use signs, labels, and drawings to show children what needs to be done without constant reminding. Some good examples are a pegboard with all of the musical instruments outlined next to the appropriate hook so

Young children's attention can be sustained when they are given the freedom to initiate and direct their own activities.

that children can clean up the music laboratory with little prompting or supply shelves labeled with laminated photographs cut out from catalogs so that even nonreaders can see where toys and materials belong.

To see how these ideas are put into practice, you will be meeting three teachers who are in the process of articulating their philosophies, setting the stage for learning, and advancing their curricular goals, all through careful attention to the physical environment. The first is Chris, who works with three infants in a child care center; the second is Leilani, who teaches a class of three-year-olds in the Head Start program; and the third is Brian, who teaches in a pre–first grade program designed for children who experienced difficulty in kindergarten.

Chris has this to say about working with infants: "This isn't just baby-sitting where all I do is feed them when they are hungry or change them when they need it. Babies learn through their senses, so my program is organized around sensory stimulation, mainly sight, sound, and touch." The three cribs in Chris's small room are arranged in a cluster so that she can take just a step or two in any direction and reach each baby. She has a comfortable rocking chair nearby. In terms of auditory stimulation, Chris has a portable cassette/CD player and a collection of recordings—sounds recorded inside the womb, earth sounds (e.g., rain, the forest, whales), lullabies from around the world, and other types of music. Based on her observations, she has concluded that the babies respond particularly well to the soothing sounds of New Age music. Chris also sings to the babies and can tell you each infant's favorite songs, rhymes, and chants.

She knows the research about infants' visual preferences that suggests that a baby's favorite thing to look at is the human face, so she has constructed mobiles from snapshots of family members supplied by the families and pictures of faces cut from magazines. Chris changes these mobiles periodically and also uses commercially available musical mobiles of nursery rhyme characters and animals as well. She also uses a small ceramic Christmas tree with blinking lights, a music box carousel, and other wind-up musical toys for visual stimulation.

To stimulate the infants' sense of touch, Chris has experimented with many different things. Bradley, a three-month-old, still appears to prefer being wrapped snugly, just as he was in the hospital. Alaina, who is five months old, likes being propped up in an infant seat that is lined with a soft blanket. Josie, a seven-month-old, is interested in trying to move about. Chris has a piece of sheepskin that she spreads out on the floor so that Josie can practice rolling over, raising her head and chest, sitting with support, and attempting to get into a crawling position. Chris has all of the infant stimulation materials and baby care supplies labeled and organized so that she can instantly locate what she needs to calm a fussy baby or play with an infant who is wide awake.

Leilani describes her Head Start class for three-year-olds as "a learning environment where children can learn independence, confidence, competence, and collaboration." In planning the physical environment, Leilani takes advantage of the fact that children in Hawaii can do many activities outdoors. As you examine Leilani's indoor and outdoor plan in Figure 6.7, think about how you might make better use of the outdoors in your program, even if it can only be used when weather permits.

Note that Leilani has carefully analyzed how many things there are for children to actually do. In an introductory course in early childhood education, Leilani learned about simple, complex, and super units (Jones, 1977; Feeney, Christensen, & Moravcik, 1996). A simple unit is basically used by one child at a time, for example,

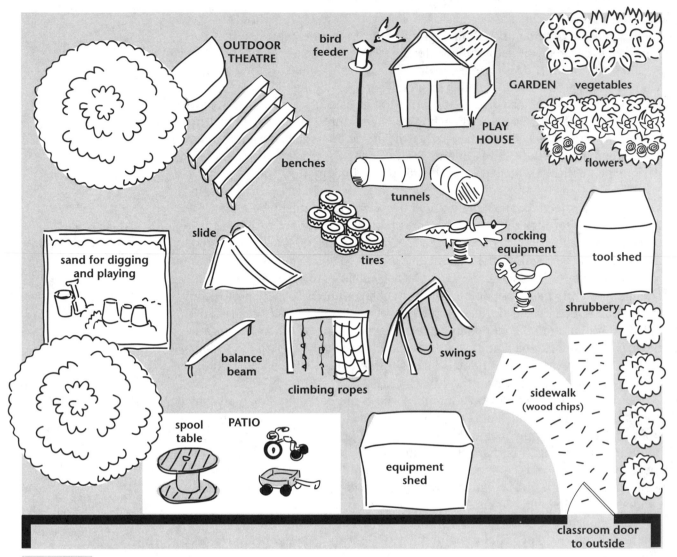

***Figure 6.7*   Outdoor Play Area**
Designed by Natalie K. Conrad.

a puzzle, a tricycle, or an easel. A complex unit typically combines simple units to accommodate more children—for example, sand and toys, blocks with wooden people, animals, and vehicles. Super materials are like sponges that can absorb the attention of many children at once—for example, sand with toys *and* water; a dramatic play area with dress-up clothes, props, and dolls.

Brian knows that the six-year-olds in his class are the students who are already labeled as struggling in school, particularly in reading and writing. Rather than keeping the children in kindergarten for another year, the school district has created another grade level between kindergarten and first grade. Although Brian would prefer to see multiage, ungraded classrooms for young children, he has accepted the job, welcomes the challenge, and hopes eventually to change the system to be, as he puts it, "more child-friendly." About his philosophy, he says, "My first goal is to work with families and children to overcome the self-doubt and stigma associated with placement in this class. Even though it is called pre–first grade, most of the adults in the community think of it as 'flunking' kindergarten. I need to show the other teachers that these children are not rejects. Everyone—the children themselves, their families, and my colleagues—will need to be persuaded that these children can learn. Everything that we do in this classroom is designed to help children break through these barriers, especially barriers to literacy." Brian has decided to make literacy the focal point, as the floor plan of his classroom in Figure 6.8 depicts.

Brian's, Leilani's, and Chris's teaching philosophies and efforts to plan the physical environment have given you some ideas about what you can do to arrange your classroom with active learning and an arts-enriched curriculum in mind. After you have articulated your philosophy and prepared the environment, you will need to plan the curriculum.

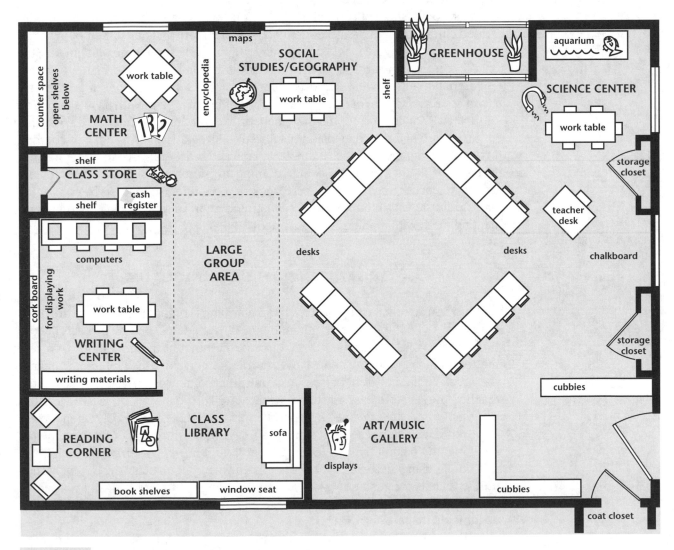

Figure 6.8 **Primary Grades Classroom Floor Plan**
Designed by Natalie K. Conrad.

INTEGRATING THE CURRICULUM

*A*s an initial step in curriculum planning, teachers need to accept their roles as decision makers. The reality of the classroom is that even though teachers are required to address a certain body of content in their instruction, exactly *how* they will do so is left largely up to them. One way to make your curriculum more meaningful for children and more efficient for you is called integration (Drake, 1993). When educators speak of integrating the curriculum, they are generally referring to several ways of breaking down barriers to more flexible, child-centered, developmentally appropriate teaching.

The three main barriers to be addressed through integration are schedule, selection, and content. If the curriculum is integrated, a teacher's daily schedule is not broken down into small segments of time and does not adhere to a strict schedule (e.g., 20 minutes for free play, 20 minutes for circle time, etc.). Rather, the schedule provides for large, flexible blocks of time that enable children to explore, experiment, and undertake larger projects.

A second aspect of curricular integration has to do with freedom. In an integrated curriculum, children exercise choice and initiate and direct their own activities. Rather than everyone doing the same thing at the same time and limiting the arts to certain times of day, the classroom is organized around centers so that children can pursue what interests them at various times throughout the day. Instead of an art lesson, for example, there might be an art cart with a wide selection of materials for collage, for making puppets, for creating costumes, and so forth.

The third and final dimension of curricular integration has to do with content. Instead of planning activities that isolate content, teachers strive to integrate subject matter. Rather than practicing counting by simply reciting out loud, for example, a teacher might use a picture book of a counting song, thereby combining art and music with math, or use an illustrated chart of a fingerplay, thereby connecting math with reading and enactment.

ORGANIZING THE CURRICULUM

*O*f course, another aspect of curriculum planning is organization. There are three main ways of organizing curriculum: by units, by themes, and by projects. These three approaches differ primarily in terms of the amount of integration of subject matter and the amount of control over curriculum given to the children. Units are the most traditional of the three. In a unit, the content is predetermined by the teacher, often before ever meeting the learners. The goal of a unit is to cover subject matter and skills deemed appropriate for children. For example, when a class is working with clay, a sequence of skills might be learning to pound the clay flat, pinching and poking the clay to shape it, rolling it into a ball, creating long coils, and finally, using these basic shapes to form a variety of objects. The old-fashioned unit is usually the result of one teacher's thinking. Units are typically written as class assignments during undergraduate days; as a result, they tend to be lengthy documents that are seldom changed and can become stale rather quickly.

The focus of a theme is concepts and teaching for understanding rather than just knowledge and skills. A good example is the theme on patterns in "The Child Artist at Work" in this chapter. Rather than emphasizing the acquisition of discrete skills, the goal was for children to come away with a thorough understanding of a meaningful concept. The theme included many firsthand experiences and hands-on learning activities and offered the children more choices about what they would do. The theme also gives learners more input into the curriculum than the unit. Note that rather than having a single-subject-area focus, the theme integrates areas of the curriculum in meaningful ways. True theme teaching is most effective when teachers incorporate the following principles into the planning and implementation of their themes (Kostelnik et al., 1991):

1. Themes should relate to children's real-life experiences and build on what they know.
2. Each theme should represent a concept for children to discover more about. The emphasis in a theme is on helping children build major concepts rather than expecting them to memorize isolated bits of information.
3. Every theme should be supported by a body of content that has been adequately researched by the teacher(s).
4. All themes should integrate content learning (new terminology, basic facts, and underlying principles) with process (hands-on) learning.
5. Theme-related activities should represent a variety of curricular areas. Imaginative play and aesthetics are considered to be just as basic as subject areas such as literacy, mathematics, and social studies.
6. In a teaching theme, the same content should be offered more than once and incorporated into different kinds of activities.
7. The theme should allow for integration of several subject areas in the program.
8. Each theme should be expandable or revisable according to children's demonstrated interests and understandings.

Unlike units, themes tend to take on more flexible formats. Often an abbreviated chart format is used to provide an overview of a theme, like the concert theme depicted in Figure 6.9.

Of all the curriculum planning options available to teachers, projects give children the most power over the curriculum. The essence of a project is that it is child-initiated (generated by the children's play and interests) and child-directed, meaning that the evolution of the project is determined by the children. How long a project lasts, the different directions that it takes, and when it is abandoned for an entirely new project are determined by the children. In other words, a project is an in-depth study of something that is suggested, planned, monitored, and evaluated by the learners. In a project, the teacher's role is that of a facilitator. You have already read about two projects, Sue Ann's garden center and Ms. Lemley's movie theater project, in Chapter 1. Projects often have the characteristic of being prompted by some unanticipated event that piques the children's curiosity, such as seeing the plants at the garden center or seeing the theater under renovation. One critical feature of projects is that they need to be something that children can experience directly (Hartman & Eckerty, 1995). Consequently, a study of the polar regions might be a unit or theme, but not a project—unless children happen to live in a polar region.

Chenfeld (1996) gives an interesting account of a project that ensued at a child care center when one of the parents donated a boat for the children's playground. In preparation for the arrival of the boat, the adults and children dug an 8-by-20-foot hole to set the boat in. But as they waited for the boat to be delivered, the hole itself became a project. Children dug in it, buried treasures, looked for artifacts, studied insects, wrote stories, and sang work songs—all about the hole in the ground.

Figure 6.9 **Theme Chart on Concerts**

⟫ *Basic Concepts*

- A concert is a live musical performance in front of an audience.
- Concerts can take place indoors or outdoors.
- Members of the audience are expected to listen and are sometimes asked to participate.

⟫ *Circle Time*

Set up chairs for audience, and watch several children's concert videos—*Raffi on Broadway* (Raffi, 1994), *For the Family* (Jenkins, 1994), and *Peter, Paul, and Mommy, Too* (Peter, Paul, and Mary, 1994).

⟫ *Listening Center*

Provide various choices of concert performances to listen to, such as *Manhattan Transfer Meets Tubby the Tuba* (Manhattan Transfer, 1994) and *Doc Watson Sings Songs for Little Pickers* (Watson, 1990).

⟫ *Block Area*

Equip the area with people, cars, and unit blocks so that children can build a concert scene.

⟫ *Art Center*

Get the children involved in constructing props such as a conductor's baton, a music stand, microphones, tickets, signs advertising the concert, and a concert program.

⟫ *Library Corner*

Provide various books about concerts such as *The Orchestra* (Bruna, 1984), *Mama Don't Allow* (Hurd, 1984), *Emmett Otter's Jug-Band Christmas* (Hoban, 1971), *The Pelican Chorus* (Lear, 1995).

⟫ *Dramatic Play Area*

Use the props and other materials in the room to enact a summer concert and picnic lunch next to the gazebo (Bunce, 1995).

After a hard rain, the hole became mud, and a new array of activities emerged. Then, following a California earthquake, a tree fell across the hole. For weeks, the hole, the mud, and the tree maintained the children's interest. As this example illustrates, children are very much the leaders in a project. Figure 6.10 summarizes the distinctions between and among units, themes, and projects.

Whether using a unit, theme, or project approach, teachers need to consider whether the content has value for young children. Some questions to guide you in this process include these:

1. *The "So what?" question:* Why investigate this topic at this time with this group of children? What real value will it add to their lives?
2. *The authentic learning question:* What contributions will this topic make to children's overall development? How does it educate the "whole child"?
3. *The developmentally appropriate question:* What are the requisite knowledge and skills? How much background knowledge would have to be built in order for children to experience success with this investigation? Is each child working to his or her strengths and gaining competence?
4. *The substance question:* What new vocabulary, ideas, abilities, and insights will be acquired as a result of these activities?

To illustrate what happens when these issues are ignored, consider one teacher's lesson on Native Americans for four-year-olds. Ms. Chambers began by showing the children some pictographs that were in a teacher idea book. Pictographs are simple drawings used to communicate ideas, such as wavy lines for water or a circle with lines radiating from it for the sun. She told the children that Native Americans used the pictographs to decorate their tipis, an assertion that is actually incor-

Figure 6.10 **Units, Themes, and Projects: A Comparison**

	Unit	*Theme*	*Project*
Definition	A collection of lessons usually focused on a single subject area; attainment of knowledge and skills is specified in advance by the teacher.	Hands-on learning experiences organized around a central focus that integrate subject matter and help children to develop concepts and deeper understandings.	An in-depth study of an actual object, event, or experience initiated and directed by the children's interests, curiosities, and motivations.
Goal	To cover content deemed important by adults.	To integrate subject matter in meaningful ways.	To empower students as curriculum planners.
Teacher's role	To plan, direct, and evaluate.	To plan activities, to guide and monitor children's concept development.	To facilitate the children's play and follow their interests.
Child's role	To master the requisite knowledge and skills.	To apply concepts learned and think critically.	To participate in curriculum building, implement ideas, and self-evaluate.
Primary means of evaluation	End-of-unit tests.	Child's understanding of concepts as reflected by responses to activities.	Children's enthusiasm for learning and their problem-solving processes throughout the life of the project.

rect. These markings were used to record a story, not simply to decorate. Furthermore, only the Plains Indians lived in tipis. In fact, the Native Americans who lived in this class's region of the country called their homes hogans, and some live in hogan-style homes rather than conventional housing today.

Then Ms. Chambers distributed a ditto of a tipi that she found in a book of seasonal activities and told the children to color it, decorate it with pictographs, and cut it out. Only one child drew pictographs because the rest were not drawing representationally (drawing pictures) yet. Only three of the children could cut out the circular shape, and none of them could independently cut out the tabs that were supposed to be used to make the flat circle into a cone shape. The teacher and the aide were frantically cutting for them and using tape to fix the tipis that children had tried to cut out. After the tipis were completed, several children placed them on their heads while the teacher chided them, saying, "Now, you know that isn't a hat. What is it? [no answers from the children] It's a home. It's a shelter. Does anyone remember what it is called? It's a tuh, tuh, tuh . . . [still no response from the children] It's a tipi." Clearly, the tiny party hat shapes were not understood in this way by four-year-olds! Because this teacher didn't stop to think about her lesson from a child's point of view, she failed miserably in meeting her goals. Her students were confused and left feeling inept. Should anyone be surprised if a child from this class is asked, "What did you learn in school today?" and that child remains silent? Although it is undeniably important for children to know about and respect other cultures, nothing that they did in school promoted knowledge or fostered respect. How much better it would have been to invite members of the local tribe to share their cultural heritage, just as Robin did in her project based on Howard Gardner's multiple-intelligence theory.

When you contrast these two approaches to curriculum planning—Robin's and Ms. Chambers's—you begin to glimpse the difference between a high-quality curriculum and a "canned" curriculum. Early literacy expert Anne Haas Dyson (1986) uses the metaphor of a dance to describe effective teaching and curriculum planning when she writes: "Teaching is not the doing of 'activities'—it is a . . . dynamic interactive dance; teachers and children interact to create activities; to create curricula as they work to reach their respective goals" (p. 135).

The final aspect of curriculum, matching teaching methods to instructional goals, further elaborates on aspects of quality.

MATCHING METHODS TO GOALS

*P*edagogy refers to methods of teaching children and the specific strategies that teachers select to support learning goals. Effective teachers are flexible when choosing teaching/learning strategies that are appropriate for a particular situation. Effective teachers are also perceptive about when to use, adapt, or switch strategies to meet individual learners' needs. Kostelnik et al. (1991) summarize the major methods that are available to teachers as they strive to promote children's learning. These methods include the following:

- *Firsthand experiences* that bring the world into the classroom or take the classroom outside into the world—for example, giving children the opportunity to gather and study wildflowers, then make them into arrangements or create a still life.
- *Simulations* that imitate a real-world experience such as creating a photographer's studio as a play center or making a house out of a refrigerator box.
- *Demonstrations* that give children opportunities to observe how something is done, then attempt the task—for example, asking a candle maker to visit and allowing the children to dip candles.
- *Questions and discussions* that give children an opportunity to relate ideas to their own experiences, to express ideas, to modify ideas, to interact with peers and adults, and to practice listening and speaking skills. For example, the teacher could lead the children in "Show and Ask" where one child shares an ordinary object, the others pose questions about the object, and the first child answers.
- *Response activities* that allow children to respond to what they have heard, seen, experienced, discussed, and studied, such as using creative dramatics to enact a familiar folktale.

CONCLUSION

*A*lthough most educators would agree that the arts are important, the curriculum we see in schools often contradicts their words. In John Goodlad's (1992) research in elementary schools, he gathered evidence that the arts were generally neglected in American schools. He made the following observations:

- Time devoted to the arts in elementary schools varied considerably—from 2.1 to 4.7 hours per week on the average.

- Use of instructional time was often inefficient, thus wasting valuable time that could have been devoted to the arts.
- Programs were generally deprived of resources, particularly highly qualified teachers.
- The arts were virtually absent in some schools, aside from a few visual arts projects included with other topics.

Addressing the issues raised by this research demands that teachers work to change and improve curriculum to make it more arts-enriched. Christopher and Vallentutti (1990) make this need clear when they write,

> Too often the role of the arts in the curriculum is viewed either as a diversion—a way to relax children before they settle down for the important business of academics—or as enrichment to liven up an otherwise pedestrian curriculum. Because of these attitudes, the arts are often considered a frill and are the first thing cut when fiscal problems arise. Our position is that arts deserve full and equal status with other curriculum areas. They should be studied independently and recognized for the contributions they make to the quality of life. The arts objectify, clarify, and document feelings, moods, and ideas. Each art medium is a special language for expressing and appreciating these feelings, moods, and ideas. The fine and performing arts should hold a central place in the curriculum. (p. 7)

When young children engage in personally meaningful activities such as inventing their own picture books, they learn the arts and the three Rs simultaneously.

The Association for Supervision and Curriculum Development is the most prominent organization in the United States dedicated to the development of curriculum. In its most recent publications, ASCD has called for flexible curricula that meet the needs of diverse groups of students (Cole, 1995). More specifically, ASCD has called for curricula that

- emphasize problem solving, reasoning, conceptualization, and analysis.
- are developmentally appropriate.
- are grounded in authentic experiences meaningful to learners.
- result in redefined bodies of knowledge that are integrated, connected, and supported by standards.
- result in performance standards that support these curricula and drive assessment.

As you read these criteria for curriculum, it is clear that each and every one of these goals is supported by the arts. In fact, it is hard to imagine any curriculum like the one outlined by ASCD that fails to recognize aesthetic education as a basic foundation for curriculum.

Learning about the Arts from Children

Jeffrey Brewster on Creating Books with Children

Jeffrey Brewster is an early childhood educator who works in a learning support program in Brussels, Belgium. Children come to the resource room for 45 minutes a day to get additional support in learning to read and write in French, a language of Belgium, as well as in English, the second language taught in the school. Unlike many teachers who try to improve children's reading and writing, Jeffrey does not resort to drill on low-level skills. Rather, he emphasizes creativity and the arts and, in doing so, capitalizes on the interests, curiosities, and motivations of the children. One of the most popular projects with six- and seven-year-olds is making their own books. This is offered to children in a permanent center where they have access to many different materials. The instructions for making various types of books are on illustrated posters, and a wide variety of published books with interesting formats are on display. Jeffrey has identified seven important reasons for including bookmaking in his program:

1. Children are intrinsically motivated to record stories, experiences, observations, wishes, and dreams in book form so that they can share them with others.
2. Bookmaking is a natural way to integrate two powerful modes of communication, the linguistic and the visual.
3. Bookmaking involves the use of many fine motor skills as well as opportunities for creative problem solving.
4. Bookmaking is a way to record meaningful experiences and create a lasting object that can be revisited.
5. Books provide tangible evidence that sustained effort, careful crafting, and subtle differences can make a world of difference.
6. Bookmaking provides opportunities not only for private expression but also for public sharing.
7. Collaborative bookmaking, whether with a partner, a small group, or an entire class, provides opportunities for children to contribute to something larger than self and to celebrate community efforts (Brewster, in press).

Jeffrey begins with several simple book formats that children in the primary grades can manage. Some of these formats include

- books cut in a shape or outline of something.
- books that are folded accordion style.
- stapled or sewn books.
- books in oversized format or "big books."
- books with simple moving parts, such as lift-the-flap books.

As the children worked on their books, Jeffrey Brewster recorded the following observations:

> Rachel, who was inspired by Tana Hoban's (1971) lift-the-flap book *Look Again!,* said, "I know what kind of book I'm going to make today! Its gotta be one of those with hidden pictures with just a little bit of the picture showing and lots of really good clues so that people try to guess what it is." Rachel has decided to stitch the binding with yarn and an oversized, blunt needle "because it's so strong and this book will probably get a lot of looking at by the kids in my class 'cause they like this guessing part."

> Ori, who recently participated in a class trip to collect frog spawn, bring it back to class, and watch it mature, said, "Not me. Mine's gonna be one of those long zig-zaggy ones 'cause that'll be the best kind for my book about how tadpoles grow into frogs." Later, Ori thinks over some other possibilities for this story-at-a-glance accordion book format: "After I finish this tadpole book I'm probably gonna make one about how caterpillars turn into butterflies or about how a baby chick grows inside the shell. Maybe I'm gonna make a whole set of books where one day it's like this, the next day there's a change, the next day there's a bigger change, and more and more changes!"

> Myles, who has decided that books make good gifts, said, "I want to make a book for a present for my little brother's class. They're studying about the forest. I think a big book'll be best 'cause they're little kids in preschool and they like big pictures and only a couple of words."

Discussion Questions

- What can you infer about Jeffrey Brewster's teaching philosophy based on this example?
- How does the bookmaking project meet children's individual needs?
- Suppose that another teacher, a parent, or an administrator criticized the bookmaking project and argued that it would be better to drill children on their letter sounds and sight words. What evidence would you use, both from Jeffrey's classroom and from this chapter in general, to support bookmaking as a better way of developing skills in literacy?
- Review the seven intelligences that Howard Gardner has identified (Figure 6.3). Describe how the bookmaking project addresses each type of intelligence and integrates the curriculum.

The Artist in You

Shandelle's Sculpture Study

Shandelle is an early childhood major who is enrolled in a methods course, "Aesthetic Experiences for Young Children." Her assignment is to develop a teaching theme that makes the arts a focal point. In class, the instructor showed a video of Italian children from the city of Reggio Emilia (1990) in which the children made an in-depth study of a lion sculpture that evolved into a project. The children were completely absorbed in examining the piece of sculpture closely and responding to it through their conversations and artwork. After watching and discussing the film in her college class, Shandelle was reminded that she passes by a large piece of sculpture every day on her way to the school where she is completing her junior-level student teaching experience. Why not take a walking field trip with the children to see this huge sculpture, "The Spirit of Detroit"? The sculpture, which is made of dark metal, depicts a huge, powerful figure, seated with his legs crossed and arms extended, palms up.

But first, Shandelle knows that she needs to build her background knowledge of sculpture. She locates a book that is particularly helpful in informing her about the basic concepts underlying sculpture, Andrew Pekarik's (1992) *Sculpture behind the Scenes*. Then she watches a film at the library that models how to talk with children about art by showing an experienced children's museum guide at work: *Barry's Scrapbook: A Window into Art* (Polisar, 1994). With these resources to guide her, Shandelle feels much more confident about stating the learning concepts that she wants her kindergarten students to acquire.

Concepts to Be Developed about Sculpture

- To sculpt means to shape into a form.
- Sculptors are people who mold, shape, and join together materials to create forms that express feelings as well as ideas.
- Sculptures are formed using a wide variety of materials—wax, wood, metal, stone, found objects and pieces of objects, and fabric—which are cut, molded, carved, or arranged into sculptures.
- Each type of sculpture uses tools that match the material being formed by the sculptor.
- A statue is a three-dimensional representation—usually of a person, animal, or mythical being—that is produced by sculpting, modeling, or casting.
- Appreciating sculpture is as much a tactile experience as a visual one.

Here are some of the questions that Shandelle generated to use on their trip:

- When you look at this statue, what do you think? What kind of being is represented?
- Stand next to the statue. How big are you compared to it?
- This sculpture is called "The Spirit of Detroit." A spirit is something you can't really see but you know is there, like your feelings when you are sad or happy. What is the sculptor trying to show us about the feelings people have about Detroit, our city?

These are some of the things Shandelle plans to say after the children return from their excursion.

Here is a photograph of the Spirit of Detroit sculpture that we visited. How is looking at the photograph different from going to see it for real?

Now let's look at some pictures of other sculptures. Remember that if we could go and see each one for real, we would be able to walk around it, look at it from every angle, touch it, see how big it is, and examine the details more closely. [Look at pictures from Pekarik's (1992) *Sculpture behind the Scenes*.]

I have also brought some small sculptures for you to see. This one is a duck decoy carved by a local artist. This one is a Chinese goddess. This one is a small metal sculpture made by one of my friends from college. And this is a statue I got when I was in Mexico. As you look at each one, try to answer these questions:

- What materials were used? [wood, jade, ceramic]
- What tools do you think the artist used?
- Why do you think that the artist chose these materials for this sculpture?
- Why would people want these objects in their homes?
- What other sculptures have you seen?

As they pursued the sculpture theme further, Shandelle borrowed books with color photographs of sculpture from the library and put them on display, set up several centers where children could experiment with different modeling materials (such as clay dug from the earth, sawdust clay, and cooked cornstarch clay), and invited a person who makes headstones and monuments to come and demonstrate sculpting tools and techniques on a small piece of marble.

Discussion Questions

- What strategies did Shandelle use to build her knowledge base and overall appreciation for sculpture?

- Do you think that what Shandelle has planned will enable her students to acquire the concepts that she identified?
- Review "Matching Methods to Goals," page 176. Which strategies did Shandelle use? Did she make good choices in matching her teaching methods to her learning goals?

- If you were in class with Shandelle and were asked to peer evaluate her theme, what would you say are the strengths of her plans? What suggestions do you have for expanding upon or improving her plans?

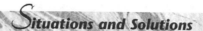

*S*ituations and Solutions

Planning and Organizing the Classroom Arts Environment

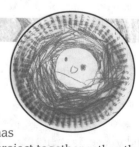

Situation 1

Belinda is student teaching in a public preschool program for four-year-olds. One of her first responsibilities is to plan an art activity for the children. The classroom teacher tries to help Belinda by saying, "I have a bunch of idea books here on the shelf. You can copy any of the patterns you like. Something with chicks or eggs might be nice, since Easter is a couple of weeks away." How could Belinda respond tactfully, yet still show that she understands aesthetic experiences and the arts' rightful place in the curriculum?

Situation 2

Ms. Denise and Ms. Tammi teach in a building that first was a high school, then was a middle school, and now is an elementary school. They want to make painting at easels and modeling with clay permanent centers, but their classroom does not have a sink, and the entire floor is carpeted. How can they adapt to the constraints of their new environment without compromising their goals for the young children in their classes?

Situation 3

Carlene has visited her first grade classroom several times to get it set up before the children arrive. The more she has thought about it, the more she is convinced that she would like to organize her room in learning centers. The room was originally arranged in straight rows, but she has sketched a floor plan that would include an art cen-

ter with drawing materials, paints and easel, clay and modeling materials, and resources for collage construction. Another first grade teacher drops by and remarks, "You must be an artist or something. I leave all of that sort of thing to the art teacher. They have a special art class once a week, you know." How can Carlene respond in a way that shows her commitment to children's art, yet does not alienate her new colleague?

Situation 4

As a former exchange student to Sweden, Sean has had experience with adventure playgrounds. An adventure playground actually looks more like a junkyard than anything else. It typically has pieces of wood, earth, stone, old tires, tools, and any other interesting materials teachers can procure. Based on his experiences, both as a child and in the Swedish preschool, Sean knows that although these adventure playgrounds may not be pleasing to the adult's eye, children look upon them as incredibly exciting play spaces. Sean wants to implement what he has learned, but the other teachers are skeptical. They worry that children might be hurt if they use real tools and fear that such a messy looking area will create a negative public impression of the child care facility. Should Sean try to persuade the other teachers of the value of a play area that encourages creative problem solving? How might he begin to make his point?

*I*ntegrating the Arts

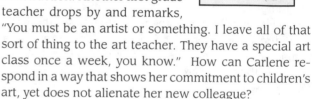

Song Picture Books:
A First Grade Teacher, the Music Teacher, and the Art Teacher Collaborate

Ms. Richards teaches first grade in an elementary school where children have just 30 minutes per week to work with the art teacher and 30 minutes to work with the music teacher. This year they have a new principal who has encouraged them to plan a project together rather than

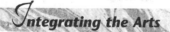

working in isolation. Over the years, Ms. Richards has been using song picture books—books that contain illustrated versions of song lyrics—to support children's growth in reading. Song picture books offer several advantages, including these:

- They build on familiarity. Children already know the words of the song, making it easier for them to attempt to read it.
- They provide repetition, rhyme, and predictable patterns (such as numbers, days of the week). Children can use the predictable features of the text to figure out what comes next.
- They offer opportunities for creative expression. After teachers have shared many published song picture books, children can work individually or in groups to invent song picture books in various sizes, shapes, and styles.
- They integrate subject matter. All of the language arts—listening, speaking, reading, writing—as well as the arts—art and craft, music and movement, story and enactment—can be addressed through song picture books (Ribblett & Jalongo, in press).

After discussing these advantages of song picture books, the three teachers agree that this will be an excellent collaborative venture. Ms. Richards will be responsible for sharing many examples of song picture books with the children. Mr. Barron, the music teacher, will teach children several new songs that lend themselves to song picture book representations and help the children to do an audiotaped recording session of the class singing the lyrics for each song picture book that children plan to create. Ms. Lipinsky will guide the children in moving from making rough sketches of their song picture books in booklets to the final, hardbound version. She will also guide the children in selecting the art materials best suited to the mood and style of their story/ song. Then Ms. Richards will be responsible for creating a classroom lending library.

Discussion Questions

- Why do you think the principal suggested that these teachers collaborate?
- What advantages does this collaboration represent over each teacher doing a project on her or his own?
- What messages, both implicit and explicit, will children get from participating in this project?
- Try to generate some other collaboratively planned curriculum ideas for younger and older children. Share your ideas with the group.
- How did the inclusion of the arts enhance the overall quality of the learning experience?

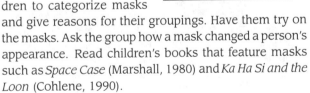

Individual and Group Projects for Teachers

Creating Curriculum Webs and Maps

One shorthand way of planning curriculum is to use a web. A web is a map, chart, or diagram of interconnected concepts, experiences, and activities with a central focus. That central focus can be a topic—for example, a concept like contrast or symmetry. The focus could also be on a particular author or artist such as Rembrandt or Maurice Sendak. Read the following map on masks, a theme that grew out of the kindergarten children's interest in Halloween costumes. These were the concepts the teacher wanted to develop:

- Masks represent a face or a portion of a face and obscure the wearer's face.
- Masks enable us to take on someone or something else's identity and disguise our own.
- Masks portray emotions and characters, not just the physical features.
- Masks can be used just for fun (e.g., Mardi Gras), to tell a story (e.g., Kabuki theater masks), or for rituals (e.g., African tribal masks).

Looking at Masks

Have children collect and bring in various masks. How are they alike? How are they different? Invite children to categorize masks and give reasons for their groupings. Have them try on the masks. Ask the group how a mask changed a person's appearance. Read children's books that feature masks such as *Space Case* (Marshall, 1980) and *Ka Ha Si and the Loon* (Cohlene, 1990).

Defining Masks

People used to call masks false faces. False means not true or real. What is a mask? Why do we use them?

Multicultural Perspectives on Masks

Look at pictures of Native American masks (Griffin-Pierce, 1995), Mexican masks used for the Day of the Dead, sixteenth-century costume ball masks, and Egyptian full-head masks. Watch excerpts from the *Mystery of the Senses: Seeing* video with Diane Ackerman (Green Umbrella, 1995) to see a display of many different types of masks.

Constructing Masks

How are masks made? Visit a theatrical products company or look in a catalog. Invite the owner of a costume shop to the school. Make Native American masks such as the Hopi Corn Man, a bird mask, or the Aztec Fire God (Smith & Hazen, 1989).

REFERENCES

Armstrong, T. (1994). *Multiple intelligences in the classroom.* Alexandria, VA: Association for Supervision and Curriculum Development.

Bredekamp, S., & Rosegrant, T. (Eds.). (1992). *Reaching potentials: Appropriate curriculum and assessment from birth through age eight.* Washington, DC: National Association for the Education of Young Children.

Brewster, J. (in press). Teaching young children to make books. *Early Childhood Education Journal.*

Bunce, B. (1995). *Building a language-focused curriculum for the preschool classroom* (Vol. 2 is a planning guide). Baltimore: Brookes.

Burke, C., & Short, K. (1988). Creating curriculums which foster thinking. In J. Harste (Ed.), *Critical thinking.* Urbana, IL: National Council of Teachers of English.

Chapman, C. (1993). *If the shoe fits . . . How to develop multiple intelligences in the classroom.* Palatine, IL: IRI/Skylight.

Chenfeld, M.B. (1996). The whole truth about hole language. Oops! I mean the whole truth about whole language. Can you dig it? *Early Childhood Education Journal, 23*(3), 175–177.

Christopher, F., & Vallentutti, P. J. (1990). Developing children's creative thinking through the arts. Bloomington, IN: Phi Delta Kappa. (Fastback No. 303)

Cohen, M. D. (1995). Reconstruction alternatives: Opening the curriculum. In W. Ayers (Ed.), *To become a teacher: Making a difference in children's lives* (pp. 89–98). New York: Teachers College Press.

Cole, R. W. (Ed.). (1995). *Educating everybody's children: Diverse teaching strategies for diverse learners.* Alexandria, VA: Association for Supervision and Curriculum Development.

Cuffaro, H. K. (1995). *Experimenting with the world: John Dewey and the early childhood classroom.* New York: Teachers College Press.

Drake, S. M. (1993). *Planning the integrated curriculum: The call to adventure.* Alexandria, VA: Association for Supervision and Curriculum Development.

Dyson, A. H. (1986). Staying free to dance with children: The dangers of sanctifying activities in the language arts curriculum. *English Education, 18,* 135–146.

Feeney, S., Christensen, D., & Moravcik, E. (1996). *Who am I in the lives of children?* Englewood Cliffs, NJ: Merrill/Prentice Hall.

Fowler, C. (1994, January). Quoted in J. O'Neil, Looking at art through new eyes: Visual arts programs pushed to reach new goals, new students. *ASCD Curriculum Update,* 1–8.

Gardner, H. (1989). Zero based arts education: An introduction to ARTS Propel. *Studies in Art Education, 30*(2), 71–83.

Gardner, H. (1993). *Frames of mind: The theory of multiple intelligences* (10th anniv. ed.). New York: Basic Books.

Gardner, H. (1995). Reflections on multiple intelligences: Myths and messages. *Phi Delta Kappan, 77*(3), 200–209.

Gestwicki, C. (1995). *Developmentally appropriate practice: Curriculum and development in early education.* Albany, NY: Delmar.

Goodlad, J. (1992). Toward a place in the curriculum for the arts. In B. Reimer & R. A. Smith (Eds.), *The arts, education, and aesthetic knowing* (pp. 192–212). Chicago: University of Chicago Press.

Griffin-Pierce, T. (1995). *Encyclopedia of Native America.* New York: Viking.

Grumet, M. (1988). *Bitter milk: Women and teaching.* Amherst: University of Massachusetts.

Hartman, J., & Eckerty, C. (1995). Projects in the early years. *Childhood Education, 71*(3), 141–147.

Jones, E. (1977). *Dimensions of teaching/learning environments: Handbook for teachers.* Pasadena, CA: Pacific Oaks.

Katz, L. G. (1988). *Early childhood education: What research tells us.* Bloomington, IN: Phi Delta Kappa.

Kostelnik, M. (1992). Myths associated with developmentally appropriate programs. *Young Children 45*(4), 17–23.

Kostelnik, M. J. (1993, March). Recognizing the essentials of developmentally appropriate practice. *Child Care Information Exchange,* 73–77.

Kostelnik, M. J., Soderman, A., & Whiren, A. (1993). *Developmentally appropriate programs in early childhood education.* New York: Macmillan.

Kostelnik, M. J., et al. (1991). *Teaching young children using themes.* Glenview, IL: GoodYear Books.

Kostelnik, M. J., et al. (1996). *Themes teachers use.* Glenview, IL: GoodYear Books.

Law, N., Moffit, M., Moore, E., Overfield, R., & Starks, E. (1966). *Basic propositions for early childhood education.* Washington, DC: Association for Childhood Education International.

Moore, T. J., & Hampton, A. B. (1991). *Book bridges: Story-inspired activities for children three through eight.* Englewood, CO: Teacher Ideas Press.

Pekarik, A. (1992). *Sculpture behind the scenes.* New York: Hyperion.

Peterson, K. (1987). *Building curriculum for young children: Deciding on content.* (ERIC Document Reproduction Service No. ED 297 886).

Raines, S. C. (in press). Developmental appropriateness: Curriculum revisited and challenged. In J. P. Isenberg & M. R. Jalongo (Eds.), *Early childhood trends and issues: Challenges, controversies, and insights.* New York: Teachers College Press.

Ribblett, D., & Jalongo, M. R. (in press). Using song picture books to support emergent literacy. *Early Childhood Education.*

Smith, A. G., & Hazen, J. (1989). *Cut and make North American Indian masks in full color.* New York: Dover.

Taylor, B. (1994). *A child goes forth.* New York: Macmillan.

Children's Books and Recordings

Beck, I. (1995). *Peter and the wolf.* New York: Simon & Schuster/Atheneum.

Bruna, D. (1984). *The orchestra.* Los Angeles: Price/Stern/Sloan.

Cohlene, P. (1990). *Ka Ha Si and the loon.* Vero Beach, FL: Rourke.

Flournoy, V., & Flournoy, V. (1995). *Celie and the harvest fiddler.* New York: Morrow.

Frank, V., & Jaffe, D. (1996). *Masks from countries around the world.* San Diego, CA: Harcourt Brace.

Hoban, R. (1971). *Emmett Otter's jug-band Christmas.* New York: Parents.

Hoban, T. (1971). *Look again!* New York: Macmillan.

Hurd, T. (1984). *Mama don't allow.* New York: Harper.

Lear, E. (1995). *The pelican chorus.* New York: Harper/Collins. (Illustrated by F. Marcellino)

Marshall, E. (1980). *Space case.* New York: Dial.

Penner, F. (1989). *Collections.* Hollywood, CA: A & M Records.

Sweet Honey in the Rock. (1989). "Two by two." On *All for Freedom.* Redway, CA: Music for Little People.

Tapahonso, L., & Schick, E. (1995). *Navajo ABC: A Dine' Alphabet Book.* New York: Simon & Schuster.

Tickle Tune Typhoon. (1983). *Circle around.* Seattle: Tickle Tune Typhoon.

Vagin, V. (1995). *The nutcracker ballet.* New York: Scholastic.

Watson, D. (1990). *Doc Watson sings songs for little pickers.* Waterbury, VT: Alacazam.

Videos

City of Reggio Emilia, Italy [Producer]. (1990). *To make a portrait of a lion.* Distributed in U.S. by the Early Childhood Educational Exchange.

Green Umbrella Ltd. (1995). *NOVA: Mystery of the senses: Seeing.* Washington, DC: WETA. Videotape.

The Grey Eagles. (1994). *Native American Indian Dances.* Available from Educational Record Center: 1–800–438–1637.

Jenkins, E. (1994). *For the family.* Available from Educational Record Center: 1–800–438–1637.

Manhattan Transfer. (1994). *Manhattan Transfer meets Tubby the Tuba.* Available from Educational Record Center: 1–800–438–1637.

Peter, Paul, and Mary. (1994). *Peter, Paul, and Mommy, Too.* Available from Educational Record Center: 1–800–438–1637.

Polisar, B. L. (1994). *Barry's scrapbook: A window into art.* Towson, MD: American Library Association Video. Available from ALA Video: 1–800–441–TAPE

Raffi (1994). *Raffi on Broadway: A family concert.* Available from Educational Record Center: 1–800–438–1637.

Additional Resources on Native North Americans

Begay. S. (1995). *Navajo: Visions and voices across the mesa.* New York: Scholastic.

Blood, C. L., & Link, M. (1984). *The goat in the rug.* New York: Aladdin.

Bruchac, J. (1993). *The first strawberries: A Cherokee story.* New York: Dial.

Carlson, L. (1994) *More than moccasins: A kid's activity guide to traditional North American Indian life.* Chicago: Chicago Review Press.

Detroit Institute of Art & Penney, D. W. (1996). *Art of the American Indian frontier: A portfolio.* Detroit: New Press.

Goble, P. (1978). *The girl who loved wild horses.* New York: Bradbury.

Goble, P. (1984). *Buffalo woman.* New York: Bradbury.

Goldin, B. D. (1996). *Coyote and the fire stick: A Pacific Northwest Indian tale.* San Diego, CA: Harcourt Brace.

Hakim, J. (1993). *The first Americans.* New York: Oxford University Press.

Hoyt-Goldsmith, D. (1991). *Pueblo storyteller.* New York: Holiday House.

Hoyt-Goldsmith, D. (1993). *Cherokee summer.* New York: Holiday House.

Lepthien, E. U. (1985). *The Cherokee.* New York: Childrens Press.

Living Arts Seminars (1992). *Meet the masterpieces: Strategies, activities, and posters for understanding great works of art.* New York: Scholastic Professional Books.

Martin, R. (1992). *The rough-face girl.* New York: Putnam.

Murdoch, D. (1995). *North American Indian.* New York: Knopf.

Pennington, D. (1994). *Itse Selu: Cherokee harvest festival.* New York: Charlesbridge.

Petersen, D. (1991). *Sequoyah: Father of the Cherokee alphabet.* New York: Childrens Press.

Ross, G. (1995). *How turtle's back was cracked: A traditional Cherokee tale.* New York: Dial.

San Souci, R. D. (1994). *Sootface: An Ojibwa Cinderella.* New York: Doubleday/Delacorte.

Sewall, M. (1990). *People of the breaking day.* New York: Atheneum.

Steltzer, B. (1995). *Building an igloo.* New York: Holt.

Stott, J. C. (1995). *Native Americans in children's literature.* Phoenix, AZ: Oryx.

Swetzell, R. (1992). *Children of clay: A family of pueblo potters.* New York: Lerner.

Thomson, P. (1995). *Navajo sheepherder.* New York: Cobblehill.

Van Laan, N. (1995). *In a circle long ago: A treasure of native lore from North America.* New York: Knopf.

See also the *Native Dwellings Series* by Bonnie Shemie (Tundra Press) and the *New True Book* series (Childrens Press), *Native Artists of North America* by Reavis Moore (John Muir) and a set of 14 color slides of *Native American Art* (set number 838) published by Sandak (1–800–343–2806).

The *determination of judgments of value continues to confound educators. It may not be the most profound question on the planet earth to ask if something is good, but it is certainly one of the most perplexing. It lies at the heart of evaluation practices. Its partner is, How does one know? Given that these are the two questions evaluators struggle with in all professions—from those who judge art, music, film, literature, drama, and design to those who judge livestock at county fairs—teachers are in very good company.*

—Selma Wassermann (1989, p. 210)

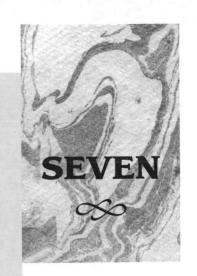

Assessment Issues in the Arts and Aesthetics

SEVEN

Chapter Reflections

- ☞ What recollections do you have about tests and grades during childhood?
- ☞ Why does assessment in the arts and aesthetics pose a particular challenge?
- ☞ How do the arts support the trend toward performance-based assessment?
- ☞ What strategies can you use to assess young children's growth in the arts?

WHAT IS ASSESSMENT?

$\mathcal{W}$hen most people hear the word "assessment" they immediately think of things such as tests and grades in school, competitions or rankings in sports, or evaluations of job performance. In fact, many educators have argued that one major reason why the arts do not have a prominent place in American schools is that they do not lend themselves to quick and easy numerical rankings or group-administered paper-and-pencil tasks. Educator and arts advocate Elliot Eisner (1992) points out the fallacies in thinking that numbers alone can answer important educational questions when he writes:

> To describe a human being in numbers alone is to say *some* important things about that person's features. It is also to neglect those features that do not lend themselves to quantitative description, and the features neglected may be precisely those considered most important for particular purposes. If I want to purchase a pair of shoes for a friend, knowing my friend's size is important, but it is also important to understand what kind of shoes my friend is likely to desire. . . .

> There is also the assumption that comparisons among 50 states serving 47 million students attending 11,000 schools overseen by 1,600 school boards can be meaningful. We seem to believe that somehow . . . a telling comparative picture of the significant consequences of schooling can be revealed. I do not believe that this is likely and I know for certain that we are not currently in a position to even approximate such an aspiration. (p. 3)

This point of view is consistent with a quotation that Albert Einstein reputedly had posted on his office wall: "Not everything that counts can be counted and not everything that can be counted counts" (Herman, Aschbacher, & Winters, 1992). Obviously, appropriate assessment of student growth and learning, particularly in the arts and aesthetics, requires much more than numbers. The National Association for the Education of Young Children defines assessment as the "continual process of observing and recording and otherwise documenting the work that children do and how they do it, as a basis for a variety of educational decisions that affect the child" (Bredekamp & Rosegrant, 1992, p. 21).

Significantly, the word "assessment," which we so often associate with evaluating, measuring, and judging, comes from the Latin verb *assidere* which means to sit beside (Herman, Aschbacher, & Winters, 1992). This view of "sitting beside" the children as they acquire skills, exhibit growth, and achieve learning is ideally suited to the arts, and, in fact, many of the recommended strategies for authentic assessment in all subject areas of the curriculum have been borrowed from the arts. You will, for example, often hear the words "performing" and "arts" used together because the arts and aesthetic education are difficult to evaluate in any way that is apart from doing, sharing, and responding—in a word, performance. Suppose that you wanted to know if a child understands the musical concept of dynamics—the loudness or softness of musical sounds. Even though this is a relatively simple task, it would be hard to devise a multiple-choice test that would adequately assess the child's understanding of the concept. You can, however, get a reasonably good idea of whether or not children understand dynamics if you ask them to perform a task. You might give a child a drum and say, "Can you tap your drum softly and make a quiet sound?" "Now show me how you would make a loud sound with your drum."

The more complex the learning, the less likely it is that paper-and-pencil tasks will assess the child's true abilities. This statement is particularly true of young children because they are totally unsophisticated as test takers. They do not understand the significance of tests or the basic procedures used to respond, and, if very young, they cannot perform the physical actions required to respond, such as controlling the pencil well enough to circle the correct response. Even when young children are capable of complying with standardized testing procedures, the instruments themselves are too flawed and limited to be of much value. A third grader's creativity would be better assessed by his ability to plan and present a puppet show than by the common, artificial creativity test tasks of converting various lines and shapes into drawings or trying to think of as many uses as possible for an object, like a plastic cup.

Responses are even more difficult to measure than skills or abilities. The field of reading offers a good example of the difficulties inherent in measuring responses. Experts know many things about readers' eye movements while reading, the formation of various letter sounds (phonics), and common errors children make when decoding words. But very little is known about why a particular child loves a particular book above all others or the processes involved in formulating an individual response. Because the arts are rooted in responses, they pose a particular challenge in assessment. If you are interested in responses, such as the power of various lullabies to calm a fussy baby, no conventional test will do. Of all the assessment options available to educators, performance assessment is uniquely well suited to evaluating complex tasks (Stiggins, 1995). Performance assessment in the arts implies that

- students are active participants rather than passive subjects.
- evaluation and guidance occur simultaneously and continuously.
- processes as well as products are evaluated.
- development and learning are celebrated.
- multiple indicators and sources of evidence are collected over time.
- results of the assessment are used to plan instruction, improve classroom practice, and optimize children's learning.
- the assessment process is collaborative among parents, teachers, children, and other professionals as needed (Black & Puckett, 1996; Isenberg & Jalongo, 1997; Tierney, 1991).

There are some ways to tell whether an arts and aesthetics program is using performance assessment. In these programs, you would certainly see the following:

Careful, reflective observation is one of the teacher's best assessment tools. What can you infer about the original dance and costumes these girls have created?

1. Young children using their knowledge to reason aesthetically.
2. Young children arriving at multiple solutions to challenging arts activities.
3. Young children developing proficiencies in the arts and aesthetics that they did not previously possess.
4. Young children demonstrating significant skills in the arts.

Teachers will know that they are providing quality experiences in the arts and aesthetics when they see children . . .

using their knowledge to reason aesthetically.

arriving at multiple solutions to challenging arts activities.

developing proficiencies in the arts and aesthetics that they did not previously possess.

demonstrating significant skills in the arts.

learning to apply those skills to create artistic and aesthetically pleasing products.

learning to evaluate their own aesthetic and artistic works.

Figure 7.1   **Photo Essay of Performance Indicators**

5. Young children learning to apply those skills to create artistic and aesthetically pleasing products.
6. Young children learning to evaluate their own aesthetic and artistic works.

The photo essay in Figure 7.1 depicts these performance indicators for early childhood programs in the arts and aesthetics. As you read Sam's story in "The Child Artist at Work," think about how each one of these purposes is being supported by his teacher's actions in the classroom.

The Child Artist at Work

Sara, a day care center director, described how Sam, a child in her class, wanted desperately to dance to the theme music from the Disney movie *The Lion King*.

Although Sam was less physically coordinated than some of his five-year-old class-mates, he had wonderful ideas for choreographing various "moves" that he had seen on dance programs, such as spinning, leaping, swaying his arms overhead rhythmically, and sliding forward on his knees at the grand finale. By having Sam talk about and demonstrate his choreography on videotape, Sara was able to trace his growth as a choreographer of creative movement.

During an individual conference, Sara encouraged Sam to self-evaluate several of the tapes from the project. "How do you feel about your dance?" she asked Sam after they had viewed the tapes together.

"I got better," he beamed. "At first I couldn't really do the dance, I could only see it in my head, but I can sure dance it on the last one!"

"What would you do if you were starting all over again to make that dance?" the teacher inquired.

Sam paused and then responded with a grin, "I'd get better dancing shoes at the beginning!"

Sam's shoes were not the only thing that had improved as he developed his dance. It was clear from the tape that his coordination and balance had increased notably during the dance production, and the videotapes of the dance were useful in documenting his growth. Additionally, Sara was able to share Sam's dance experiences with his parents by sending home a videotape with a brief note that pointed out signs of Sam's progress.

Experiences like this one show how assessment of children's artistic and aesthetic development is not merely possible and but also a natural outgrowth of child-centered teaching. In your role as an early childhood educator, much of the assessment that you will do in the arts and aesthetics is informal, holistic, and observational. Most performance assessments in early childhood are integrated into daily practice, based on positive social interactions, and designed to foster young children's skill in self-evaluation. As you read the Theory into Practice, you will note how performance assessment complements the natural way that the human brain works.

Theory into Practice

Research on the Human Brain

Support for aesthetic education and performance assessment in the arts comes from a large body of research on the human brain and its functioning (Gardner, 1995). Historically, there has been a tendency to treat the arts as if they were limited to the affective (feeling) realm when in fact, the arts are every bit as much cognitive (thinking) as they are affective (Hargreaves & Gardner, 1992). What do we now understand about how the human mind works and ways in which the arts support cognitive functioning? We know that the mind does the following things:

The mind seeks the patterns in complexity (Bruer, 1994). The human brain is programmed to instantly recognize patterns and interpret them. Because these patterns generally make information storage and retrieval more efficient, the patterns our brains perceive tend to be remembered longer and accessed more readily than random information. This is one reason why we can remember song lyrics long after we have forgotten other things that our brains cannot impose such a clear pattern upon, such as isolated historical facts. For example, one type of pattern for which the human mind has a special affinity is narrative or story (Jalongo & Isenberg, 1995). Studies show that human beings have a natural tendency to organize information by cases or episodes—into stories—because this is one major way that the brain imposes a pattern or structure on complex experiences.

The mind functions on many levels simultaneously (Neve et al., 1991). As you are reading this sentence, for example, your mind might be simultaneously deciphering each word, trying to make sense of the entire chapter, reminding you that you have a test tomorrow, alerting you that your stomach feels empty, and so forth. Because the arts engage the mind of the child on a wide array of tasks simultaneously, they support the mind's natural style of operating on several different levels at the same time.

The mind is capable of both breadth and depth (Carnine & Carnine, 1990). The human mind can function flexibly both as a telescope (e.g., "seeing the forest") or as a microscope (e.g., "seeing the individual trees"). Once again, the arts are compatible with both ways of processing information. By their very nature, the arts teach children that the smallest details can be significant, yet remind them to step back periodically and look at something in its entirety. This broad view enables the artist, whether child or adult, to determine the overall quality and effect of an artistic product or performance. For example, at the same time that Sam learned more about holistic features of dance, like order and proportion, he also learned that subtle differences in gesture, like the curve of his fingers or the angle of his head, matter too. That is how the arts teach both range and depth.

The mind has an affinity for real problems, examples, and contacts that can be put to actual, productive uses (Kline, 1995). Research indicates that situations which have no relevance, connection, or interest for the learner are largely ignored in terms of learning (Smith, 1989). This is one reason why hands-on, active learning is recommended. Because the arts foster intuitive thinking, a grasp of useful patterns, aesthetic activities, and nonverbal abilities, the arts are entirely consistent with the brain's "natural" style of functioning (Boyer, 1988; Brandt, 1988; Wolf, 1988).

UNDERSTANDING ASSESSMENT

*I*n the faculty lounge, two third grade teachers are discussing their concerns about the upcoming musical aptitude tests. Because the school district has limited resources, some children will be permitted to play instruments while others will not—all based on a single test score. After children hear about the test, they begin making comments like "I hope I get to learn to play the drums like my brother" or "My mom and dad said if I do good, they might get me a guitar for Christmas" or "My aunt plays the piano at the Baptist church. Will I get to play the piano?" These teachers know that not one of the specific musical interests that these children expressed will be part of the program because everyone who is accepted into the program will learn to play a plastic flute. The teachers know that the test results will be used to sort and classify the children. They also know that not all of the children's strengths will be measured by the low-level tasks on the test, such as simple pitch matching and readiness to read musical notation. Additionally, the teachers are aware that the children's abilities in other areas of the arts have not been adequately assessed. There is no way that Conrad's well-planned, unique collage or Mira's lively original song can be measured by an assessment by conventional tests. Sadly, both teachers realize that many children will be disappointed by the musical aptitude test. They feel that it is unfair to deprive the students of musical opportunities based on such a tiny sample of behavior.

Lilian Katz (1993), a contemporary early childhood leader, states: "The younger the child being tested, the more errors are made; therefore the younger the child, the more likely false labels are applied to them; the longer children live with a label, the more difficult it is to escape from it" (unpaged). "If education is supposed to be about helping every kid to reach his potential," one teacher argues, "then how can we justify a system that deliberately deprives large numbers of children of instruction in music?"

These teachers face a very real problem. The expressive arts are often approached in the American educational system as matters of the heart rather than of the intellect (Engel, 1983); therefore, the arts are given low priority and seldom get their fair share of two essential resources: money and time. Under these conditions, the intellectual value of the arts is discounted, and the arts languish rather than flourish in schools in the United States. As William Teale (1994) explains:

> We say the arts matter, and we seem to be doing something about it. But as I look at . . . what is actually going on in schools, I can't help being skeptical about how much schooling really believes in the importance of the arts. . . . I think the proof of the pudding is not in the tasting but in the testing. And what most schools test for bears little resemblance to the arts. So, even though we may have essential elements, or national standards, or requirements that such and such an amount of instructional time each week be spent on the arts, teachers soon learn what really counts. And what counts is not how much a student's artistic sensitivities have grown, or how much more she knows about or enjoys music than she used to, or the changes in a child's response to the visual arts. What counts most in schools today is how well the child can read, write, and compute. (p. 8)

To illustrate this point, consider the fact that two major documents issued by the U.S. government failed to make any mention of the arts (Department of Education, 1991; Executive Office of the President, 1990). John Goodlad (1992) explains the irony of this situation when he writes:

> The rhetoric of school reform during the 1980s offered little hope for a surge in the place of the arts in the K–12 curriculum during the 1990s. The national education goals emerging out of the education summit called by President George Bush in the fall of 1989 gave high priority to mathematics and the natural sciences: Our schools are to lead the world in these fields by the year 2000. There is no mention of the arts.
>
> It is difficult to imagine a real debate arising out of the following resolution: Be it resolved that a child born today will enjoy a richer life in adulthood because of his or her early education in the arts rather than mathematics . . . we need not choose; we can have both. . . . School curricula mirror a society's values. Look into that mirror and we do not see the arts. Ironically, however, one of the indices included in the never-ending polls and surveys to determine America's most livable cities is the richness of cultural life as measured by their support of symphonies, dance companies, art galleries, theaters, and the like. (p. 192)

Not until publication of the National Standards for the Arts in America did this valuable aspect of children's educational experience take a place among the "most important" areas of academic development. Figure 7.2 summarizes the arts standards that apply to young children. In order to survive and thrive as a vital part of the curriculum, the arts must not only become fully integrated into the total curriculum but also tackle the tough issue of how to document growth and progress. Clearly, the assessment situation in America needs to be restructured, and many leading educational organizations such as the National Association for the Education of Young Children, the Association for Childhood Education International, and the Association for Supervision and Curriculum Development are calling for reforms. Generally speaking, most tests are highly structured and product oriented, and do not assess growth in the expressive arts adequately. If the arts and aesthetic experiences are to have their rightful place in the curriculum, then assessment measures must be developed and implemented that will serve to inte-

Figure 7.2 National Standards for Arts Education in Brief

☙ *Dance*

- Demonstrating skills in creative dance.
- Understanding principles, processes, and structures of choreography.
- Understanding dance as a way to create and communicate meaning.
- Applying and demonstrating critical and creative thinking skills in dance.

☙ *Theater*

- Role playing, play making, and dramatizing.
- Visualizing, arranging, and directing classroom dramatizations.
- Interpreting classroom drama and dramatization in theater, film, television, and electronic media productions.

☙ *Music*

- Singing a variety of songs alone and in groups.
- Performing on instruments, alone and with others, a varied repertoire of music.
- Improvising melodies and composing music.
- Reading and notating music.
- Listening to, analyzing, and describing music.

☙ *Visual Arts*

- Understanding and applying art media, techniques, and processes.
- Using knowledge about the purposes and processes of art.
- Choosing and evaluating art content, form, and creative expression.

☙ *General Standards*

- Reflecting upon and assessing the characteristics and merits of own work and the work of others in dance, theater, music, and the visual arts.
- Recognizing the role of dance, theater, music, and the visual arts in life.
- Demonstrating an understanding of the historical and cultural purposes of dance, theater, music, and the visual arts.
- Making connections not only among the areas of the arts but also with other disciplines.

Source: Adapted from Music Educators National Conference. (1995). *National standards for arts education: What every young American should know.* Reston, VA: Author.

grate the arts with other areas of the curriculum. As an initial step in understanding assessment, you will need to examine the basic principles of performance assessment in the arts.

PRINCIPLES OF PERFORMANCE ASSESSMENT IN THE ARTS

*J*t is a widely held assumption that facts and figures can "speak for themselves," yet "all of our research, all of our information about children, is embedded in political, cultural, and social class contexts that give data meaning" (Bowman, 1995, p. 33). In other words, numbers alone tell you something, but they do not tell you very much when they are taken out of a social context. Something that seems entirely objective, such as a height of 5 feet, 11 inches, can mean something very different in a different social context. A person who is nearly six feet tall would be a virtual giant among pygmies but well below average if he were a forward in the National

Basketball Association. Efforts to measure creativity are also affected by the context. What is visionary or creative under one set of political, cultural, and social class circumstances would cause a person to be labeled as a criminal, heretic, or mentally ill in another context. Even when the context remains the same, individual differences affect assessment. As an educator of young children, you are obligated to give every child a chance to shine, not to sort and label. In all of your attempts to measure children's creative growth, there is one glittering, overarching goal that can serve as a guide in aesthetic education. Ideally, the culmination of all of our efforts to provide education in the arts and aesthetics would be that "students understand that people respond to beauty and can be expressive in the arts. They explore the rich variety of artistic expression, learning about the various works of art, recognizing the benefits of making art, and knowing some of the ways in which visual and performing arts have evolved in different societies" (Boyer, 1995, p. 94).

Whenever educators undertake performance assessment in the arts, they need to arrive at consensus and share a vision of the knowledge, skills, attitudes, and proficiencies that they seek to develop in the children they teach. The following classroom scenario offers an example of a teacher who successfully translates this vision and goals into classroom practice.

A Classroom Scenario: Mr. Giambetti's Circus Theme

Mr. Giambetti teaches five- and six-year-olds in a multiage classroom, and the circus theme he planned with the children offers a good example of appropriate assessment practices. After posters announcing the arrival of the circus went up all over town, the children were excited and curious about the circus. Although Mr. Giambetti would have liked to take every child to see the circus, the cost was prohibitive. As an alternative, he decided to "bring the circus to the children" through a simulation. After work, he visited the public library to borrow books, records, and videos. He chose *Carnival of the Animals* by Saint-Saëns and calliope music for the recordings. Mr. Giambetti felt confident that a video he had previewed by a group called Cirque de Soleil (1992) would spark a whole new level of creativity. This troupe of versatile performers showed the children that it is possible to have a circus with people rather than trained animals. Then the entire class began collecting circus paraphernalia—balloons, crepe paper, old costumes, hypoallergenic face paint, photographs gathered from magazines, and so forth. The children freely chose circus roles that they wanted to play in their classroom circus production. For weeks the room was filled with activity. The art area was dominated by large pieces of paper and cardboard that the children were making into posters. Dennis wanted to sell the popcorn and was using invented spelling to create a sign advertising his wares. Twila used a large cardboard box to make a "funny clown car" similar to the one she saw on a televised circus performance. Bobby decided to be the strong man and made a set of barbells from a cardboard tube and two black balloons. Yuko painted a small, sturdy box with bright colors to be "that thing the lion sits on." Images of the big top, trapeze artists, and the ringmaster emerged at the easels. At the art table, animal masks began to appear as children determined whether to be a lion or a bear or an elephant. Some children practiced their writing and paper-cutting skills to produce tickets for the show.

Throughout all of these activities, Mr. Giambetti functioned as a facilitator. He asked Twila questions and offered helpful suggestions as she figured out how to make a clown car from a cardboard box. After experimenting with several designs, she decided on suspender-type strings that would enable her to stand inside the box and move with it. When Bobby tried to create barbells, Mr. G. encouraged him to problem-solve ways to attach his balloons to the cardboard tube. Bobby quickly figured out that the inflated portions below the knots of balloons don't mix with staples and was surprised and thrilled to discover that stapling the uninflated end of the balloon *did* work. Mr. Giambetti also noticed that Yuko understood how to mix colors. She selected the bright primary colors of red, yellow, and blue tradition-ally used at the circus to paint her props, then mixed these colors to get orange and green.

As the big day approached, a curious parent with a child in third grade passed by Mr. Giambetti's kindergarten/first grade class and asked, "What play will you be doing?"

"Oh . . . well, I suspect whatever play the children act that day," Mr. Giambetti replied.

Mr. Giambetti understands that children need opportunities to enact drama from their own imaginations rather than from scripts and adult direction. When family members of the children from Mr. Giambetti's class come to see the children's performance, what they will witness is not a theatrical performance, but dramatic play with a circus theme. There will be no script, no stage-whis-pered lines that children have forgotten, no pressure to make the circus conform to an adult's preconceived plan. Rather, it will be a child-directed and engineered activity that the children have grown from the experience of planning, preparing, and enacting.

During the weeks of the circus project, Mr. Giambetti had helped the children to collect samples of drawings and writings about their work. Models of masks, sketches of costumes, lists of animals, and examples of signs were collected and filed in the children's portfolios. Mr. Giambetti had set the families' expectations ahead of time by letting them know that what they would see was entirely the children's work. On the day of the play, children and parents were seen sitting in clusters around the room, sharing in the process, not just the performance. Caitlin's father examined her drawings of the circus tent, and her paintings using stripes, and finally escorted his daughter to the sheet hung from the ceiling which this day was the big top. C. J.'s grandmother was introduced to her grandson, now dressed as a lion. "See Grammy," he said, "this is why I asked you how to make curls at the beauty shop." Judging from the curled strips of paper that surrounded his paper-plate mask, C. J. had applied what he learned about making curls!

Before the children began, Mr. Giambetti reminded the family members of the purpose by saying, "What you are about to see has been completely planned by these five-year-olds, not by me. You will see their original ideas in action and hear it in their own words. Remember, they aren't charging admission; they are learning to work together and to communicate their ideas to others." Under these condi-tions, a prop that is accidentally dropped does not cause embarrassment for the child or the family. There are no tryouts or bit parts, no children who become stars while others fade into the background. Instead, the family members enjoy the op-portunity to see every child in action.

The circus theme illustrates several key principles of performance assessment in the arts: the importance of recognizing talent in every child, the value of active involvement in relevant tasks, and the need to incorporate both formative and summative evaluation.

Recognize the Talent in Every Child

Talent is usually defined as superior ability that is partly natural and partly acquired. Using that definition, all young children are talented because they are, taken as a group, naturally superior to adults in playfulness, imagination, and lack of inhibition. This is one reason why, throughout this book, we argue that the arts are for every child. Most experts view talent as clusters or constellations of abilities and characteristics in three areas: creativity, motivation, and skills (Baum, Owen, & Oreck, 1993). It is the interplay of these three categories of abilities that will ultimately determine talent. There are artists who are very skilled and motivated yet lack creativity, such as those who can reproduce a famous artist's painting. There are those who are very creative and skillful yet lack the motivation to capitalize on these strengths. And, there are many people who are creative and motivated but do not achieve sufficient skill to express that creativity or put that motivation to good use. Figure 7.3 shows how creativity, motivation, and skills affect the development of musical talent. As you look at the chart, think about the many different ways that you can support children's talents.

Of course, some children will have more natural or acquired proficiency in areas of the arts than other children, and these differences are to be expected. But being "better at" something is not the same as being "better than" someone else. This is an important and useful distinction. What is learned from performance assessment in the arts should be used to develop talent in every child, not simply to validate preexisting talent in those children who have already had the chance to develop it. Assessment should directly benefit children and their teachers by enriching the learning experience, improving the instructional process, and informing the teacher about the direction and nature of future experiences. As educators, we do children lasting harm when we lead them to believe that they are without assets in some area of the arts. Walter Mathieu (1991) is a concert musician who frequently volunteers to work with adults who claim to be tone deaf and completely unmusical. Based upon these experiences, he explains why we must be so careful about rushing to evaluate a child's singing:

> When we sing, the heart is alive in the larynx, and that narrow channel is highly sensitive to aggression. It takes only a small blow to cause big damage. Some

Figure 7.3 Dimensions of Musical Talent

෫෭ *Motivation*

Enthusiasm—perseverance—ability to focus

෫෭ *Creativity*

Expressiveness—movement qualities—composition—improvisation

෫෭ *Skills*

Physical control—rhythm—coordination—agility

Perception of sound—spatial awareness—observation and recall

Source: Adapted from Baum, S. M., Owen, S. V., & Oreck, B. (1993). *Talent beyond words. Identification of potential talent in dance and music in elementary school.* Paper presented at the annual meeting of the American Educational Research Association, Atlanta, GA.

> unconscious little meanness, an offhand dig, might seem to a child like a slap on the heart, and the heart has a long memory for pain. . . . Pretty soon we have a kid who can't sing and who feels partially ostracized. Then we have a grown-up, capable if not extraordinary in every way, who can't sing. (p. 128)

It is bad enough that American children are arts-deprived because of the paltry resources generally allocated to the arts. There is no need to add insult to injury by testing them and perpetuating an inferiority complex about their abilities in the expressive arts. As you work with young children, try to keep in mind that lack of talent is frequently an absence of opportunity in another guise (Eisner, 1981).

Emphasize Meaningful Tasks

Think about your life as a child in school and how many times you said (or said to yourself), Why do we have to learn this, anyway? When will I ever use this in real life? Why are you teaching it, teacher? Why is it important? As the Theory into Practice section of this chapter described, recent research on the human brain suggests that the perceived relevance, significance, and usefulness of a task influences curiosity, interest, motivation, and enthusiasm. The very heart of performance assessment is documentation of student growth through "real-world" skills and tasks. The items and behaviors assessed should have some sort of *practical* significance and some useful application to children's lives (Katz, 1993). The world in which students will live and work as adults will seldom require coloring in a bubble with a number two pencil on a computer-scored answer sheet or choosing the best answer from a list of possibilities. Investigations into aesthetics and the arts are far more intriguing because art "responds to questions such as: 'Why do musical instruments make different sounds?' 'What's a poem?' 'Why does the artist paint that way?' 'Is it all right to color outside the lines?' Students discover that art is a profoundly significant human experience woven through history and across cultures. They begin to understand how art shapes our lives" (Boyer, 1995, p. 95). Effective problem-solving, communication, and collaboration skills will be required in the real world, and it is in this area that the arts excel.

Combine Formative and Summative Evaluation

Consider this travel analogy: A traveler plans a trip from Washington, D.C., to New York City and sets off on the journey, but travels due west. If the traveler's progress is being monitored, a correction in course can be made, the trip can be salvaged, and the traveler can arrive at the desired destination. If, however, the traveler's error in course is not measured until the *end* of the trip, the entire enterprise turns out to be a mistake. Too often, our approach to teaching and learning is like this analogy. The assessment terminology for these two types of assessment are formative ("along-the-way" assessment) and summative ("wait-until-the-end" assessment). If educators rely solely on a summative evaluation, students frequently reach the wrong "learning destination." Fortunately, this mistake is avoidable. By combining summative evaluation with its complementary counterpart, formative evaluation, educational programs can offer continual opportunities for teachers and students to monitor growth, document progress, and propose new possibilities during instruction. Formative assessment not only allows but also encourages the sort of midcourse adjustments that enable all children to learn. By assisting children in changing strategy or technique, teachers can learn a great deal about children's problem solving and their abilities to apply new knowledge.

An expert on assessment in the arts explains how he and his colleagues approach the task of evaluation in the arts as follows:

> We would try to assess both the particular understandings of artworks that students acquire through instruction and also how their interpretive abilities in general develop. This would require a multiplicity of kinds of data—about students' backgrounds, about artworks and art traditions, about instructional approaches, about kinds and levels of understandings—collected over a period of time. In other words, assessment itself would have to be heavily interpretive, and for this reason would probably be used as much for diagnostic as for summative purposes. . . . Second, and closely related to the first aim, we need to investigate *the process* of artistic development alongside its *products.* This is reflected in the distinction between *formative and summative* assessment; both are equally important, and observational studies are [also] needed. (Parsons, 1992, pp. 89–90)

When you consider not only the finished product but also the process used to get there, you are combining formative with summative evaluation.

Redefine Control and Structure

One of the greatest deterrents to arts activities in classrooms is the teachers' fear about loss of control over the children's behavior. This worry that children will "get out of hand" is amplified because the arts are rightly associated with emotional intensity and high spirits. Some teachers have such a need for neatness that they put away the easels in favor of crayons and paper; they place such a premium on quiet that they rarely use the rhythm instruments; and they are so afraid that the children may act silly that they seldom use creative drama. Ironically, the less frequently these materials are used and the less children are coached in appropriate ways to participate, the more likely it is that the mess, noise, and misbehavior will occur! When children are given so little freedom, they often overreact; when they are given so little coaching in how to participate in the arts, they are more apt to respond inappropriately.

Young children need to literally be "walked through" procedures. A teacher who wants work at the easels to run smoothly, for instance, could *show* the children the steps, then invite them to take turns enacting them. Another way to make the procedure clear is by creating a picture poster of the basic rules like the one in Figure 7.4.

In order to keep a rhythm band in service yet control the noise level, a teacher can limit the number of children permitted to use the instruments or limit the use of the music center to specific times. Even very young children can be kept informed about these limits by creating a simple sign that reads STOP or OPEN on one side and GO or CLOSED on the other. Likewise, maintaining order during a creative dramatics activity can be facilitated by anticipating disruptions before they happen. One common cause of dispute when children are dramatizing is bumping into one another, so simply asking children to stand, arms outstretched, before beginning and spreading out so that they are not interfering with anyone else's space can prevent arguments later on. Similarly, if a child seems to be wandering around the room aimlessly when there are several choices of activities, there is nothing wrong with reminding the child of the available options or even inviting

Figure 7.4 **Picture Poster of Center Procedures**

the child to participate in an activity he or she has been watching from a distance. Structure and control need not become oppressive and lead to passivity from the children. They can be made explicit through careful planning and clear procedures that facilitate purposeful activity from the children.

Encourage Self-Evaluation

Encourage students to evaluate their own work through such questions as "How do you feel about _____?" or "Can you pinpoint what went wrong?" or "Could you maybe do this in a different way?" or "What outcome would you like better?" Many children have been conditioned to rely solely on an adult's opinion to determine how they feel about their own work. A way to steer children away from this dependence is to gently encourage them to discuss what they like about their own work before you state an opinion. Ask them about what they plan to do next or how they might do the same thing differently next time. Urge children to make judgments about the works they produce as well:

"Which of your wood sculptures is your favorite?"

"Are you satisfied with your mobile now?"

"Will you change the ending of your play?"

"Which of your dances will you do for the class?"

This goal of building skills in students' self-evaluation has to be communicated to parents as well. Be certain to convey the message to parents that assessment in the arts emphasizes "What did you learn?" rather than "How did you do in comparison to the other children?"

PERFORMANCE-BASED ASSESSMENT STRATEGIES

*I*n order to implement a performance-based assessment successfully, you will need to become conversant with specific strategies that are used for assessment purposes. As a start, recognize that any attempt to implement performance-based assessment must

- be founded on appropriate evaluation.
- arise from and serve clear purposes.
- emanate from and reflect clear and appropriate achievement targets.
- rely on a proper assessment method, given the purpose of the target.
- sample student achievement appropriately.
- control for all relevant sources of bias and distortion (Stiggins, 1995, p. 240).

Sue Wortham (1997) provides an overview of assessment strategies that are available to early childhood educators when she writes,

> There are numerous strategies for assessment that are considered appropriate for young children. For many decades, early childhood educators have used observation, checklists, rating scales, work samples, and teacher-designed assessments. . . . These strategies are still part of the repertoire available to teachers; moreover, they contribute to the current emphasis upon assessments that are contextual to the child's learning experiences. Two terms that are used to describe this type of assessment are authentic assessment and performance assessment. . . . [In performance assessment] the child demonstrates understanding through performing an activity. The assessment activity is meaningful in that it is connected to the real world. Performance-based assessments are particularly useful with young children because developmental progress can be measured as well as learning. (pp. 14–15)

This girl's surprise and delight at the effect of blended chalk is the sort of anecdote that should be recorded.

As you have seen, formal assessment tools such as paper-and-pencil standardized tests have provided inadequate descriptions of children's growth in the expressive arts. Therefore, informal assessment tools like the ones just described are generally more useful. These informal means of evaluation typically rely upon observations of the child's behavior, encourage interaction between child and teacher or between child and peers, and emphasize analysis of the child's creative works (Goodman, Goodman, & Hood, 1989). More specifically, some of the strategies for conducting performance-based assessments in early childhood classrooms include games and simulations, conferences and interviews, anecdotal records and other observations, and student work samples, both in progress and as finished products (Ariasian, 1994; Porter & Cleland, 1995).

Assessment via Games and Simulations

Three-year-olds Jessie and Cole are working together on a matching game. Eight recycled snack-food cans covered with contact paper have been filled with four different substances: dried beans, bolts, coins, and sand. The children are trying to find the pairs of sounds. After shaking the cans, Jessie determines that "this one is real quiet."

"Not this one," Cole announces while demonstrating the sounds produced by a can with a handful of bolts inside.

"Here's the twin one!" Jessie claims triumphantly after shaking several more.

Cole places the matching sound cylinders side by side on two red circles on a prepared mat. There are colorful pairs of circles for each set of twin sounds, Ms. Bowling notes that the children are working steadily with the sound cylinders; she jots down a record of Jessie and Cole's partnership. Dated cards bearing the information will go into their portfolios.

A simple way to assess an infant's responses to music is to watch for movement, such as moving arms and legs in response to a lively song, or to listen for vocalizations in response to music. An infant that is six to nine months old will often make cooing sounds in response to a song that he or she likes, for instance. With preschool children, musical development in singing can be assessed by playing an echo game. The child attempts to sing a line from a song on pitch immediately after hearing the teacher sing it. In this way, even nonmusician teachers can get a sense of how the child's singing voice is developing. Figure 7.5 describes some additional games that can be used to assess children's progress in the arts.

Simulations are another way to evaluate progress. Mr. Giambetti's circus theme described in this chapter is a good example of a simulation. The children could not actually attend the circus as a group, so they created a version of it right in their classroom, and, in the process, Mr. Giambetti was able to assess their growth in the arts.

Assessment via Anecdotal Records and Observations

"Look, Ms. Hall!" Dustin called as he raced across the playground. "A feather . . . it's pretty, huh?" Dustin's teacher was delighted that this usually shy preschooler had approached her with his treasure. Hoping to engage Dustin in an extended conversation, Ms. Hall asked if the feather had come from a fish, but Dustin shook his head as he proceeded to explain the physical characteristics of fish. His teacher then suggested that perhaps the feather was from a cat, and Dustin giggled as he explained the incongruities between cats and feathers. Ms. Hall then said, "Hmmm. Then this feather must have come from . . ." and Dustin responded emphatically, "A chief's hat!" as he raced away to show the feather to his friends. Ms. Hall was surprised and delighted by Dustin's imaginative, original response and briefly recorded the anecdote on a 3-by-5 card so that she could share it later with Dustin's parents. Anecdotal records are informal, nontechnical descriptions of episodes prepared by the teacher to document growth. The anecdotal record of Dustin's "feather" episode was dated and placed in the accordion file that Ms. Hall maintains for each of her students. Figure 7.6 contains an anecdote of Dustin's experience as well as two other examples of anecdotal records in the arts. Note that it includes the time, setting, people, and events in abbreviated form.

Of course, teachers' observations need not always be written as anecdotes. They can also take other forms and use tools other than written notes. When Tracy's classroom teacher watched her at play in the dramatic play area, she heard Tracy say, "Brrnngg, brrnngg . . . oh, hello. Yes, I can come and pick you up. Where are you? Well, sit down, and if you have to throw up again, try not to get it on your dress." Hanging the receiver back on the wall phone, three-year-old Tracy picked up her handbag and put on a hat from the dress-up trunk. "That was my daughter, Sleeping Beauty! Some old witch gave her an apple, and now her tummy don't feel good at all!" From this episode, Tracy's teacher was able to identify and record actions that are new to Tracy's play routine. What seems at first to be an ordinary episode in a child's play actually reveals much more information. Tracy's behavior suggests that she is progressing in her development through expressive arts in three significant ways.

First, the three-year-old is integrating a familiar story, "Sleeping Beauty," into her play for the first time. Second, Tracy is engaging in "what if/as if" thinking or imaginative thought (Weininger, 1988). She pictures in her mind's eye what would happen if a fairy-tale character came to life, assumes the parental role, and then treats Sleeping Beauty as if she were a sick child. Finally, Tracy relates the problem to her playmates after the telephone conversation. Teacher-constructed play logs like the one in Figure 7.7 enable teachers to jot down a few words about children's play behavior. This form can be used later to make comparisons as each child grows and changes in play patterns, themes, and roles.

Video and audio tapes may also serve as a valuable assessment tool during dramatic play. A permission form should be provided to parents prior to any recording of their child's work or play on tape, and only those children whose parents grant permission should be taped for later reference and review. A teacher may view or listen to the tapes after the fact to get a glimpse of the child's world. The various actors in a dramatic play production can be identified as can the initiator of the play, the writer, and director. In this way, the teacher can identify children who create play scenes, such as Tracy; those who join in, such as her classmates; or children who choose to continue an independent or original play script.

Young children are capable of making decisions about their own performance based on standards of quality.

Assessment via Conferences and Interviews

Four-year-old Rainie has been singing a song about painting to the tune of "Jingle Bells" for days. His teacher listens, then says, "I heard you singing about painting and really liked hearing your song. Where did it come from?" After Rainie explains that he made it up, his teacher says, "Would you like to write it down so you can keep it?" Rainie nods his head enthusiastically. Then the teacher goes on, "Here's an idea! Maybe you could write it on big paper and then teach it to us." Rainie and his teacher sit down together, and she takes dictation on a piece of lined chart paper while Rainie sings the lyrics of his improvisational song. When teachers take the time to ask children questions that are specifically related to the child's work or to a unit of study, the exchange is referred to as a conference or an interview. In a writing conference with second or third graders, the teacher might ask such questions as these:

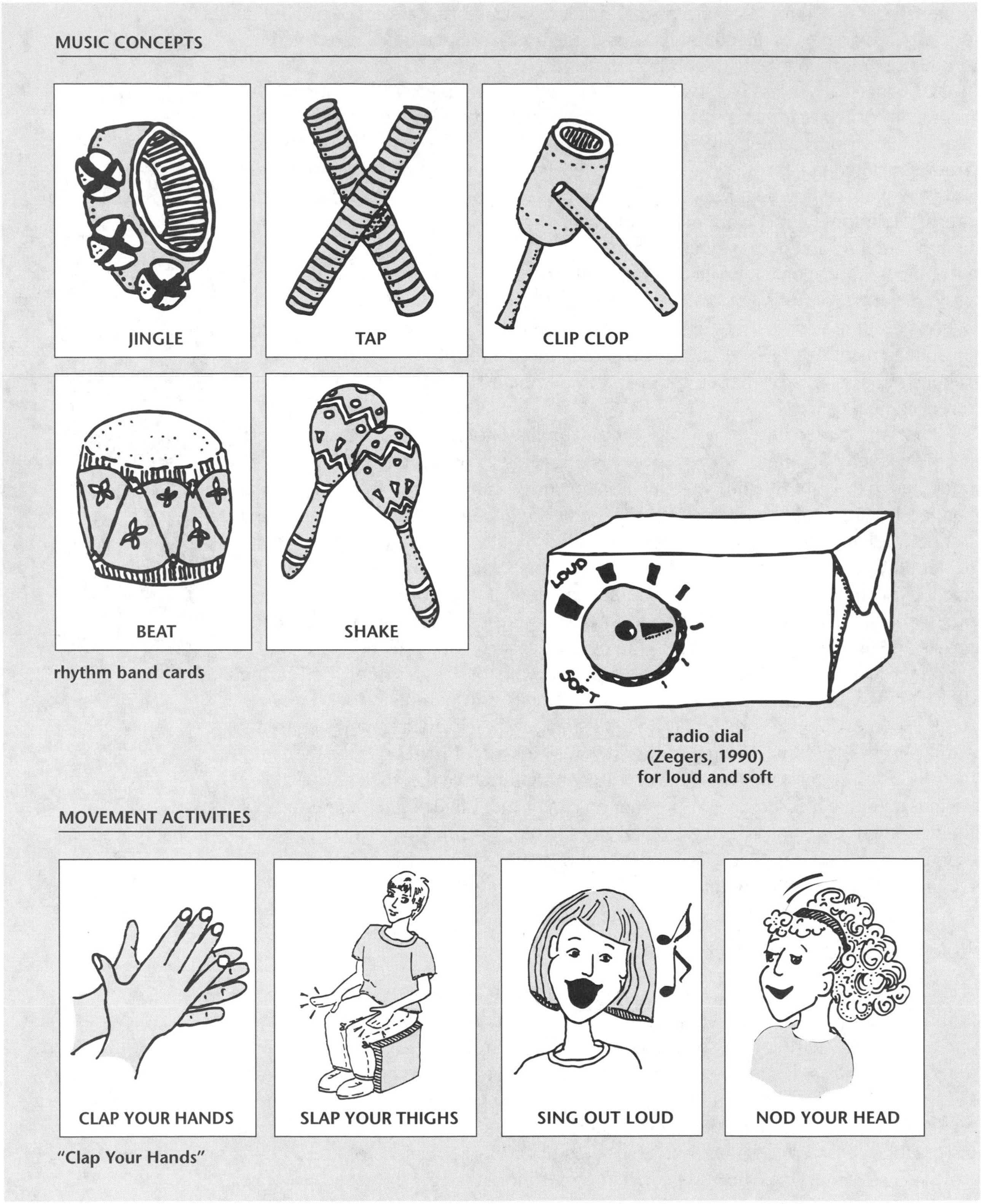
MUSIC CONCEPTS
JINGLE
TAP
CLIP CLOP
BEAT
SHAKE
rhythm band cards
LOUD
SOFT
radio dial
(Zegers, 1990)
for loud and soft
MOVEMENT ACTIVITIES
CLAP YOUR HANDS
SLAP YOUR THIGHS
SING OUT LOUD
NOD YOUR HEAD
"Clap Your Hands"

Figure 7.5 **Using Visual Aids as Assessment Tools**

VISUAL ARTS

masterpiece match

bead-shape/
color-pattern
cards

DRAMA

STALK LIKE A LION   ACT LIKE A QUEEN   SOAR LIKE AN EAGLE   GLIDE LIKE A SKATER

role cards

mood dice

Figure 7.5 **Using Visual Aids as Assessment Tools, continued**

Figure 7.6 **Sample Anecdotal Records**

> *Date: 12/11/96*
> *Time: 10:00*
> *Setting: playground*
> *D. found a feather outside. When I asked him about it (did it come from a fish? a cat?) he answered, "a chief's hat!" and raced off to show it to some of the other ch.*

> *Date: 4/3/96*
> *Time: 9:15*
> *Setting: circle time*
> *K., who recently immigrated to the U.S., joined in a group sing-along for the 1st time today. He clapped/sang with enthus., and several ch. remarked on it. K. delighted to be one of the group!*

> *Date: 6/3/96*
> *Time: 11:30*
> *Setting: free play*
> *J. (just turned 2) rocked a baby doll and sang:*
> *"Rock baby, baby, baby,*
> *Baby tweetop,*
> *Baby fall, fallee baby."*

"How is the writing going?"

"Is there anything that is giving you trouble?"

"What are you most pleased about in your writing?"

"What did you do that improved this piece of writing?"

When children are engaged in a long-term project, teachers will sometimes interview children in small groups to assess their progress. During these project conferences, students and teachers converse about current creative endeavors. If, for example, a small group of children is working on a mural, the teacher might say,

"Tell me about how you made this mural."

"What was your biggest problem?"

"How did you solve it?"

"Are there any problems that still need to be solved?"

"Tell me about how you worked together on this."

Responses to informal interviews with children are another way to assess growth. Before beginning a theme on dance, the teacher might ask each child,

"What does it mean to dance?"

"What is a dancer?"

"Are you a dancer?"

Figure 7.7 **Teacher-Constructed Play Log**

C. K. (2)

9/11 enacts baby care rituals

10/1 plays the role of the baby in older girls' family play by getting inside the wooden cradle and covering up with a blanket

10/4 cooperates with being pushed around in the wooden buggy

10/5 refuses the role of baby

L. M. (3)

9/15 pretends to be a lost puppy who finds a home (based on a favorite book)

9/20 participates in a veterinary play center by bringing in a stuffed toy that was "runned over by a car"

10/2 creates a leash for a stuffed toy out of ribbon, takes dog for a walk

10/6 uses larger and smaller stuffed toys as puppies and mother dogs

---

J. R. (2)

9/5 wears the red firefighter or yellow hard hat all day

10/1 plays with wheeled vehicles (dump truck, bulldozer, etc.) in sand

11/7 watches the other children on the climber and tries to do what they do; sometimes needs help

11/9 begins to look to J. J. for help and (occasional) translation. J. J. is adept at finding roles for J. R. to play

---

M. A. (5)

9/3 fascinated by royalty and high fantasy play, often based on fairy tales

9/9 makes a magic wand and crown to use as props

10/1 works with two other students for several days to transform a large cardboard box into a castle

10/5 begins restaurant play based on recent experiences; makes a menu

---

J. J. (4)

9/6 hero/superhero play on television-based themes (Rescue 911, Power Rangers)

10/5 often initiates chasing games (boys vs. girls, good guys/bad guys)

11/2 engages others in play based on the Thomas the Train videos

11/14 undertakes complex block constructions (farm, house, gas station)

"Can you show me how you dance?"

After the theme is completed, the teacher might ask the same four questions in order to document the child's growth in understanding. In each of these examples, the goal is to promote interaction between teachers and students.

Assessment of Works in Progress and Completed Works

Ashley's mother related the story of her preschool daughter's creative endeavor. "She planned it all herself," her mother said proudly. "She made a drawing one afternoon and brought it to me as I was setting the table. At first, I wasn't really paying attention, but as I listened to her I figured out that she wanted to make a doll when Ashley told me that she didn't want her drawing to be 'just a picture.'" Ashley's mother suggested cutting out the drawing, thinking that a paper doll would satisfy her daughter. "No" she had announced firmly, "this isn't what I mean." Realizing that Ashley was struggling with expressing an idea, her mother took time to help with the creative process. "What would you need to make this not just a picture?" her mother had asked. "Fabric and glue," Ashley had said, "and something like a ball to make the head." Opening a book, Ashley's mother found a picture of a rag doll. "That's her!" declared Ashley touching the page, "but she has to be squooishier than this paper."

Clearly, Ashley has engaged in the four classic phases of the creative process: preparation (getting resources assembled), incubation (mulling over ideas), illumination (a flash of insight about how to proceed), and verification (arriving at a satisfying conclusion) (Wallas, 1925). By documenting the process of doll making, Ashley's teacher can examine and analyze her creative development. A project portfolio for Ashley's creation might include such items as

- a photocopy of Ashley's original drawing.
- a sketch of the doll.
- a list of materials.
- pictures of the doll-making process.
- photographs of the intended or alternative product.
- notes regarding Ashley's ideas along the way.
- an analysis of the finished product and what Ashley would do differently "next time."

A paper-and-pencil test could not begin to describe the skills involved in this project or the degree of creative thinking displayed by this child. Through the process of analysis, both formative and summative evaluation are possible.

Now that you have seen some of the specific strategies used to conduct performance assessment, we will focus on the primary method of compiling the information gathered through these strategies, the portfolio.

CHILDREN'S ARTS PORTFOLIOS

Several years ago, the art building of a university was destroyed by fire. As the art majors whose work was stored inside stood out on the sidewalk, many of them were in tears. "What happened?" a passerby asked, "Has someone been hurt?"

"Yes," one student answered solemnly, "An irreplaceable part of our lives is gone. Our art portfolios were in there."

These students who were grieving the loss of their portfolios help to illustrate why collections of work are so important to performance evaluation in the arts. Some of the most common questions about portfolios and their use in the performance assessment of young children are discussed in the following paragraphs.

- *What is a portfolio?* Whether an artist is a child or a professional, the materials in the portfolio can

    tell us who the artist is.
    identify the goals the artist has selected.
    document the work the artist has done.
    chronicle the processes the artist has used to accomplish these goals/works.
    suggest what the artist aspires to do in the future (Hansen, 1992, p. 73).

    The word "portfolio" comes from the Latin verb *portare*, meaning to carry, and the Latin noun *foglio*, meaning sheets or leaves of paper. *Portfolios* are cases for holding papers, prints, drawings, maps, or musical scores that are carried from place to place (Chiseri-Strater, 1992, p. 61). "For artists, the most concrete definition of a portfolio is a case or binder in which loose papers, paintings, drawings, photographs, and the like are kept. Artists collect their work with an eye on gaining entry into art schools, gallery shows, or jobs" (Seger, 1992, p. 117). Similarly, children maintain an arts portfolio to highlight their growth, share it with others, and advance to higher levels of proficiency.

- *Why use arts portfolios with young children?* A child's arts portfolio is a diverse collection of work that provides a biographical look at how interests, attitudes, skills, and understandings change over time (Gelfer & Perkins, 1996). Just as an artist's portfolio displays samples of various kinds of work, children's portfolios can demonstrate various areas of artistic endeavor and growth. The picture painted last September will help us to evaluate the child's growth in dexterity, color use, and perception when compared to the picture created at the end of May. The tape recording of singing during October will allow comparison in pitch discrimination next spring. Many artistic, aesthetic, and developmental aspects of the child can be documented, traced, and preserved through the portfolio.

- *What does a child's arts portfolio look like?* Portfolios offer teachers and students the unique opportunity to design and shape procedures that are best suited to their individual and classroom needs. Portfolios may be maintained in single file folders, in expandable accordion files, in milk crates, or in various other types of containers. Figure 7.8 illustrates some of these options in portfolio storage.

- *What items are included in the child's arts portfolio?* A portfolio is not simply a haphazard collection of the child's work. Rather, it is a carefully selected and maintained collection of work that is arranged to highlight growth and document progress. Materials that are included in the portfolio should be matched to general program goals as well as project, theme, unit, and lesson goals. Figure 7.9 suggests some ways of gathering data using different media and offers examples of materials that might be included in a young child's portfolio.

Because very young children are just learning about themselves, most portfolios for young children also combine the child's work with the teacher's observational notes.

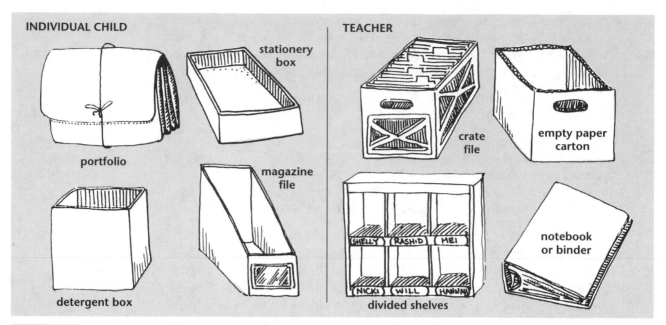

Figure 7.8 **Portfolio Storage Ideas**

The Role of Children's Portfolios in Authentic Assessment

Portfolios encourage student involvement and reflection, and expand traditional achievement measures. Unlike a traditional test, in which students have something done "to them," portfolios invite students as participants. The system of educational winners and losers is greatly decreased in the portfolio assessment process as students become actively involved in critique, choosing work, and identifying

Figure 7.9 **Portfolio Contents and Media Used to Record Them**

✣ *Photographs*

Create a photo essay using magazine pictures (see Appendix G).
Document a class project using photographs.
Construct a model of something.
Group mural.
Class collage.

✣ *Videotapes*

Dramatize a story or a scene from a book.
Choreograph a dance or singing game
Perform a puppet play.

✣ *Written Work*

Invent a text for a wordless book.
Maintain a reading or listening log.
Create a discography.

✣ *Audiotape*

Read an original story aloud.
Retell a familiar story in own words.

✣ *Drawings, Sketches, and Charts*

Plan a model.
Illustrate a favorite song as a chart or book.
Make a storyboard.
Make a class pictograph.

✣ *Combinations*

Make a class scrapbook that shows the life cycle of a major project.
Maintain an illustrated journal.
Perform a rap, chant, song, or poem.
Invent a song, type the lyrics, and illustrate it.

their own areas of strength and growth. Portfolios are particularly valuable in allowing teachers to examine students' development in risk taking, creative thinking, and self-evaluation (Paulson, Paulson, & Meyer, 1991).

Portfolios can serve as a particularly helpful assessment tool when teachers are trained and committed to using them with young children. As children gain independence and skill in cooperative work with classmates, they can also assume a great deal of the responsibility involved in weekly or monthly "weeding out" sessions, in which some work is chosen as the best example of "right now" and other work is sent home for the child to enjoy with the family.

Portfolios reach their full potential as assessment tools when they are used as tools for self-reflection by students. At a recent showing of children's art, portfolio work was displayed from children in grades K–3. Each piece was accompanied by a small card bearing a short narrative by the artist. One second grader's card read, "I think that this art in my portfolio will affect me even after I'm big, because I've learned that there's no wrong way to imagine."

Professional, Project, and Program Portfolios

So far, this chapter has focused on the assessment of progress in the arts and aesthetics made by individual children. It is equally important for educators to use portfolios to assess their personal and professional growth, to chronicle the progress of a class- or schoolwide project, or to evaluate the overall arts program (Porter & Cleland, 1995; Rogers & Danielson, 1996).

Early childhood educators can also maintain a professional portfolio that chronicles their growth as teachers of the arts and aesthetics. Before you begin teaching, you should assemble a professional portfolio that includes such things as your philosophy statement, outstanding lessons that you designed, a photo essay of a highly successful theme or project that you did with children, selected samples of children's work in response to these activities, and a brief list of professional readings that have had a great impact on you as a teacher. Your professional portfolio must be concise and carefully organized so that you can locate materials quickly. If it is, you can use your portfolio in an interview situation to showcase the work that you have done and demonstrate your competence as a teacher. Your professional portfolio is *not* a scrapbook! Few potential employers will allocate more than five minutes to an interview, and it is up to you to use your portfolio as support for the statements that you make in response to questions. If, for example, an administrator asks "What experiences have you had with thematic teaching?" you can say, "I was assigned a Head Start classroom for seven weeks during my junior year, and I developed and taught a theme on celebrations. [Then flip quickly to the right section of your portfolio.] Here are some photographs with captions that show the highlights of the theme. As you can see, it integrated all the subject areas."

Portfolios can also showcase the progress of a particular project that is done with the entire class or school. One school that we visited in Geneva, Switzerland, was having a new wing added, and the children were intrigued by the process of construction. All the teachers agreed that the construction offered a unique learning opportunity, and all the classes worked together to develop a portfolio that chronicled the building's progress from the architect's first visit to the grand opening gala.

Figure 7.10   Program Evaluation Questions

- Does the children's work show any conceptual growth as the program progresses?
- Have they experienced work in new media? Has their range of performance expanded?
- Have they developed some technical facility in any or all of these new media?
- Has their knowledge of art vocabulary increased?
- Is there any indication that they have learned to see more perceptively?
- Do they work more imaginatively than before?
- Is there any indication that they approach art more enthusiastically?
- Have they learned that evaluating their own work and that of others is part of the art process?

Source: Cohen, E. P., & Gainer, R. S. (1995). *Art: Another language for learning.* Portsmouth, NH: Heinemann.

Of course, you will also want to assess the overall quality of your arts program. One excellent way to begin is to use a set of standards or criteria (Cohen & Gainer, 1995). Figure 7.10 includes a series of questions that you can use to "take stock" of your program as well as to make judgments about the appropriateness of other arts programs that you may encounter. To summarize, you can use the portfolio strategy to chart the progress of an entire program, a special arts project, an individual child's development, or your personal and professional growth as a teacher of the arts.

CONCLUSION

*E*ducators must begin to consider arts assessment as a vehicle for providing additional information about children's strengths and areas of interest. The image of "sitting beside" the child is worth remembering as you conduct performance evaluations. When assessment provides children with guidance, information, and alternatives, they are given the chance to develop more than a set of academic skills. They are given the tools of imagination. Conductor Murray Sidlin (1978) expressed the unique contributions of the performing arts to our lives this way: "When words are no longer adequate, when our passion is greater than we are able to express in a usual manner, people turn to art. Some people go to the canvas and paint; some stand up and dance. But we all go beyond our normal means of communicating and *this* is the common experience for the people on this planet."

When early childhood educators implement performance assessment in their classrooms, they are giving every child an opportunity to be heard. Providing many opportunities for creative self-expression gives all young children a chance to communicate in ways that educate the whole child.

Learning about the Arts from Children

Profile of Jon: "I'm Two Thirteens Tall!"

Jon Persio is five years and ten months of age. He is a new student in Mr. Gamble's kindergarten class, having just moved with his family to the community. Lisa, a junior-level early childhood major, is completing a field assignment where she is working both as an observer and as a participant conducting observations of children's play. She has decided to focus on Jon. Excerpts from Lisa's observation log are reported in the following paragraphs. As you read through these anecdotal records, consider the following questions:

- What assessment strategies were used to study and interact with Jon?
- What information did the alternative assessment provide that might have been missed in one observation or a rating scale?
- How does Jon's play integrate the subject areas and contribute to Jon's development in all areas—physical, cognitive, social, emotional, and aesthetic?

Day 1

During his first week of class, Jon has chosen the construction area most frequently during free play. His structures use multiple shapes and sizes of blocks. At various times during the construction process, Jon asked for block shapes through statements and questions like "I need that moon-shaped one" or "Can I have the pointy one?" I asked Jon if he could find any other "moon-shaped" items in our classroom. He looked around, but shook his head no, even though there are two crescent-shaped tables close by.

Day 3

I noticed this week that Jon displays little interest in number concepts. During manipulative activities in the math center, Jon was distracted several times. He began to slide the blocks and tiles around the tabletop, stacked his tiles to make a tower, and asked his classmates for all their black tiles.

Day 5

Jon wanted to play in the construction area today, but was unable to do so because there were already four children building. (We have a rule that no more than four children can be at a center at any one time.) "Come to the art table and make some plans for what you'll build when it's your turn." I showed him an architect's drawing to try to entice him. He spent much of his time looking over his shoulder at the construction area but did draw a picture that he stored in his cubby. Jon asked, "Can I play yet?" three times in fourteen minutes.

Day 7

Jon volunteered to show his drawing today. He pointed out each feature of the airport to me with explanations like "This is where all the people go in" and "The suitcases will come out of this little door." I then asked Jon, "Would you like to have your drawing in the construction area with you?" He nodded his head and took the drawing over to the area, asking Kayla to help him hold it.

We taped Jon's drawing to the wall beside the construction area, and he and Toby began to stack blocks for the main part of the structure. I sat down with them and asked, "Which of these are bigger? Do you have any blocks that are not square?" Jon sorted the blocks in his bucket according to shape and called them "squares, circles, pointy ones, and tangles."

Day 8

When the teacher announced the five-minute preparation for clean-up time, Jon came over and said, "I want to keep my airport." I asked Jon how we could let others know that. "Just make a sign . . . *Don't Touch This Airport.*" Together we created the sign, and Jon taped it on his structure.

Day 9

Jon has continued to show little interest in math concepts, but today while he was building with David, they decided to build towers using rectangles only. This was Jon's suggestion, and he seemed very pleased to help David identify all the appropriate blocks by shape. They began stacking, and David stood up to compare his height to the stack of blocks. "I'm eleven tall," he reported.

Jon stared at him and asked, "How did you know that?"

David knelt down and from the bottom of the block tower counted the eleven blocks. "Now you try it," he encouraged.

Jon stood by the tower, but found that it only came to his shoulder.

"You're bigger," David suggested, seeming pleased now to be the teacher.

"Can I get more blocks?" Jon asked.

"Sure," David replied, while handing his friend one block.

Once again, Jon just stood there, hesitating to make a move.

"You have to check again," urged David.

Jon checked again, noting that he was still bigger than the tower. He reached for one more block and then compared his height once again.

"Perfect!" shouted David. "Now do I count?" asked Jon.

"Sure . . . from the bottom."

Jon counted haltingly but needed no prompts to get to thirteen. He then turned to his original block tower and pulled it over against David's. Using a few more blocks he made the second tower as tall as the first, then proudly turned to David and announced, "I'm two thirteens tall!"

Discussion Questions

- If Jon's teacher had used a paper-and-pencil test as the only means of evaluating his growth in mathematics, how could this limitation have affected Jon's view of himself as a learner?
- As you have read elsewhere in this book, Russian theorist Vygotsky proposed a social learning theory in which interaction with adults and more competent peers supports children's growth. In what ways did Jon's experience lend support to this theoretical perspective?

The Artist in You

Nathan "Teaches against the Grain"

Nathan is student teaching in a third grade classroom. As the holiday season approaches, he is increasingly uncomfortable with the "art" displays that he sees placed on bulletin boards and in the hallway. "Most of it is copying, not creating," Nathan explains to his student teaching supervisor from the college. As you read about Nathan's situation, consider how you might respond in a similar situation. Discuss the issue with your classmates after you have formulated a personal response.

Nathan expresses his feelings: "I just don't feel right about making a pattern, putting it on display at the front of the room, and handing out construction paper and patterns or templates for children to trace. That's just not an arts experience to me. But . . . this seems to be the norm, I mean, no one else seems troubled by it. Maybe I'm just being naive and idealistic."

Consider the following:

- What about Nathan's criticism of the activity? What aesthetic value do these "standard" school activities have for children?
- Suppose that you were Nathan's friend, and you were trying to coach him on what to say to others. State some reasons why it is ill-advised for a teacher to have every child make a "cute" holiday decoration. Support your opinions with material from this book.

- What is your personal response to Nathan's predicament? What advice would you offer, and what does it indicate about your view of the arts and aesthetic experiences?

Nathan talks more with his supervisor: "Maybe I could offer an alternative activity or an additional option for a more creative project after the decoration project is finished."

His supervisor asks what Nathan's cooperating teacher will say.

Nathan responds, "Well . . . she always says that I have to try out my ideas to see how they work. Maybe I can set up an alternative activity as a center for free time after their assignments are complete."

Discussion Questions

- What ideas do you have for alternatives to using patterns, templates, and models for children to copy?
- What about Nathan's confidence in his ideas? his own creativity? If Nathan feels certain that his teacher will not object, why is he being so cautious?

*S*ituations and Solutions

Avoiding the Talent Scout Mentality

Situation 1

A three-year-old who has thoroughly enjoyed working with wood scraps, white glue, and paint to make sculptures of various types seems to have lost interest rather suddenly. When you ask her about it, she says, "My mom said she doesn't want any more of that junk around the house."

Situation 2

You and the children have worked very hard to develop portfolios of each student's work. As you are meeting with Giselle's parents and sharing her portfolio, Giselle's father says, "Look, that's all very nice, but we want to know how Giselle is doing compared to the other kids. Does she have some special talent we should be working on?" How would you respond?

Situation 3

A new colleague who is a dance instructor for elementary school students volunteers to teach the second graders some dances, but you observe that she treats it like a contest or a recital instead of as something for the children to enjoy. You overhear her yelling at the students and making comparisons ("Louise, has been taking dance lessons. The rest of you have a lot to learn, so eyes up here. Look at what Louise can do.") Afterward, your colleague says, "Whew! I never saw so many uncoordinated kids in my life!" How would you respond in a way that would not alienate your colleague, yet defend every child's right to participate in dance?

Situation 4

A frustrated classroom teacher says at a workshop, "Observation seems to be a cop-out! Anyone can have chaos and portfolios in their classroom and justify it by calling it alternative assessment. When I give a *real* test, I know who has learned what." Based on what you have learned about performance assessment, what counterarguments could you offer?

*I*ntegrating the Arts

What Is an Artist?

Tracy, Lisa, and Ricardo are three college students who are working together on an assignment for their creative activities class. Because they do not know their grade level assignments for student teaching yet, their instructor is not requiring them to have their theme fully planned at this point. Rather, she is expecting them to identify resources and do some group brainstorming so that they will be ready to develop the theme later on during their field experience. When the three students convene for their first planning session, Ricardo brings along a book that includes a well-developed theme about art and artists. The group agrees that this is a versatile and appropriate topic, one that they can envision teaching to three- to eight-year-olds. The general concepts to be developed through the theme are the following:

1. Art is a deliberate expression of feelings, mood, or a message created by a person for his or her own enjoyment and the enjoyment of others.
2. An artist is a person who creates art.
3. Anyone can be an artist; artists may be grown-ups or children, men or women, boys or girls.
4. Art is both the process (the way something is made) and the product (what is made).
5. Art is created all over the world, in all cultures, and in special ways that express ideas about that culture.
6. Art is experienced by people in various ways; many forms of art can be seen, touched, heard, smelled, or even tasted (Kostelnik, 1996).

Tracy, Lisa, and Ricardo have decided to use the following strategies to gather resources for their theme "What Is an Artist?"

Children's Literature Develop a bibliography of children's picture books to use as resources throughout the unit using reference tools such as *A to Zoo: Subject Access to Children's Picture Books* (Lima & Lima, 1989) and *The Potential of Picture Books: From Visual Literacy to Aesthetic Understanding* (Kiefer, 1995). Consult recent issues of the periodicals *Booklist, Booklinks,* and *School Library Journal* to identify award-winning picture books about the arts.

Computer Software   Compile an annotated list of software that is used in art such as *Kindercomp* by Queue, *Kidpix* by Broderbund, *Color Me* by Mindscape, *Delta Drawing* by Power Industries, and *Magic Crayon* by C&C Software.

Professional Readings   Complete a computer search of the current periodicals on the topic of teaching children about art. Review several books about teaching art to children. Visit the curriculum center to examine several curriculum guides for the arts in early childhood. Use the directory of associations, and write to several of them to gather materials about the arts. Contact the state department of education to obtain guidelines for early childhood programs and arts education. Develop a bibliography.

Visual Aids   Borrow prints of famous paintings from the library. Instead of telling children the painting's title, play the game "Let's Name It" in which children look at a painting and decide upon a title for it.

Nonprint Media   Review films, videos, and filmstrips that give children a glimpse of how artists work. Check into the Weston Woods Studios videos that show picture-book artists at work.

Teaching Resources   Go to the computer center and explore the ArtsEdNet on the World Wide Web (www.artsednet.getty.edu/.) to obtain examples of teachers' ideas for art activities in classrooms.

Guest Speakers   Visit the crafts show at the mall to find out about local artists and identify two or three who would be willing to make a presentation to the children. Contact art education majors who might be willing to help.

Here is the bibliography of arts resources that the three students initially compiled:

Art Elements: Color, Shape, Line, Texture, and Arrangement

Amoss, B. (1996). *The Cajun gingerbread boy.* New York: Hyperion.

Auch, M. J. (1992). *The Easter egg farm.* New York: Holiday House.

Carle, E. (1972). *The secret birthday message.* New York: HarperCollins.

Carle, E. (1992). *Draw me a star.* New York: Philomel.

Charles, E. (1975). *Calico cat looks around.* New York: Childrens Press.

Chocolate, D. (1996). *Kente colors.* New York: Walker.

Crews, D. (1980). *Truck.* New York: Greenwillow.

Dewey, A. (1995). *Naming colors.* New York: HarperCollins.

DiSalvo-Ryan, D. (1995). *City green.* New York: Morrow.

Dodds, D. A. (1994). *The shape of things.* Cambridge, MA: Candlewick.

Ehlert, L. (1989). *Color zoo.* New York: HarperCollins.

Ehlert, L. (1990). *Color farm.* New York: HarperCollins.

Ehlert, L. (1992). *Red leaf, yellow leaf.* San Diego: Harcourt Brace Jovanovich.

Emberley, E. (1988). *The wing on a flea.* Boston: Little, Brown.

Falwell, C. (1992). *Shape space.* New York: Clarion.

Feldman, J. (1991). *Shapes in nature.* New York: Childrens Press.

Fisher, L. E. (1987). *Look around!* New York: Viking.

Friskey, M. (1973). *Three sides and the round one.* New York: Childrens Press.

Gardner, B. (1984). *The look again . . . and again, and again, and again book.* New York: Lothrop.

Heller, R. (1995). *Color.* New York: Putnam.

Hill, E. (1994). *Spot's big book of colors, shapes, and numbers/El libre grande de Spot colores, formas, y numeros.* New York: Putnam.

Hindley, J. (1994). *The wheeling and whirling-around book.* Cambridge, MA: Candlewick.

Hoban, T. (1978). *Is it red? is it yellow? is it blue?* New York: Greenwillow.

Hoban, T. (1984). *Is it rough? Is it smooth? Is it shiny?* New York: Greenwillow.

Hoban, T. (1986) *Shapes, shapes, shapes.* New York: Greenwillow.

Jackson, E. (1995). *Brown cow, green grass, yellow mellow sun.* New York: Hyperion.

Jonas, A. (1989). *Color dance.* New York: Greenwillow.

Lionni, L. (1950). *Little blue and little yellow.* New York: Aston-Honor.

MacKinnon, D., & Sieveking, A. (1995). *What color?* New York: Dial.

MacKinnon, D., & Sieveking, A. (1995). *What shape?* New York: Dial.

Magnus, E. (1992). *Around me.* New York: Lothrop, Lee, & Shephard.

Marshall, J. (1996). *Look once, look twice.* New York: Ticknor & Fields.

Reid, M. S. (1990). *The button box.* New York: Dutton.

Reiss, J. J. (1982). *Shapes.* New York: Simon & Schuster.

Serfozo, M. (1996). *There's a square.* New York: Scholastic.

Turner, G. (1991). *Shapes.* New York: Penguin.

Wells, R. (1995). *Night sounds, morning colors.* New York: Dial. (Soft paintings)

Yenawine, P. (1991). *Colors.* New York: Delacorte.

Yenawine, P. (1991). *Line.* New York: Delacorte.

Yenawine, P. (1991). *Shapes.* New York: Delacorte.

Music, Musicians, and Instruments

Czernecki, S., & Rhodes, T. (1993). *The singing snake.* New York: Hyperion.

Hausherr, R. (1992). *What instrument is this?* New York: Scholastic.

Isadora, R. (1979). *Ben's trumpet.* New York: Greenwillow.

Lloyd, M. (1995). *Zin! zin! zin! A violin.* New York: Simon and Schuster.

Medearis, A. S. (1994). *The singing man.* New York: Holiday House.

Melmed, L. K. (1994). *The first song ever sung.* New York: Lothrop, Lee, & Shepard.

Musical instruments. (1994). New York: Scholastic.

Schroeder, A. (1989). *Ragtime trumpie.* Boston: Little, Brown.

Schroeder, A. (1996). *Satchmo's blues.* New York: Doubleday.

Sutcliff, R. (1993). *The minstrel and the dragon pup.* Cambridge, MA: Candlewick.

Thiele, B., & Weiss, G. D. (1995). *What a wonderful world.* New York: Sundance.

Tornqvist, R., & Tornqvist, M. (1993). *The old musician.* New York: Farrar, Straus, and Giroux.

Zalben, J. B. (1996). *Miss Violet's shining day.* Honesdale, PA: Boyds Mills Press.

Lives of Artists

Alderson, B. (1994). *Ezra Jack Keats: Artist and picture-book maker.* New York: Pelican.

Anholt, L. (1994). *Camille and the sunflowers: A story about Vincent Van Gogh.* Hauppauge, NY: Barron's.

Bjork, C. (1985). *Linnea in Monet's garden.* New York: R&S.

Brown, L. K., & Brown, M. (1986). *Visiting the art museum.* New York: Dutton.

Christelow, E. (1995). *What do authors do?* New York: Clarion.

Cohen, M. (1980). *No good in art.* New York: Greenwillow.

de Paola, T. (1988). *The art lesson.* New York: Putnam.

de Paola, T. (1989). *The art lesson.* New York: Putnam. (Scholastic Big Book)

Dunrea, O. (1995). *The painter who loved chickens.* New York: Farrar, Straus, and Giroux.

Everett, G. (1992). *Li'l sis and Uncle Willie: A story based on the life and paintings of William H. Johnson.* New York: Rizzoli.

Fleischman, S. (1996). *The abracadabra kid: A writer's life.* New York: Greenwillow.

Hart, T. (1993) *Famous children: Leonardo da Vinci.* Hauppauge, NY: Barron's.

Hart, T. (1993). *Famous children: Michelangelo.* Hauppauge, NY: Barron's.

Hart, T. (1993). *Famous children: Toulouse-Lautrec.* Hauppauge, NY: Barron's.

La Pierre, Y. (1994). *Native American rock art.* Charlottesville, VA: Thomasson-Grant.

Lyons, M. E. (1993). *Stitching stars: The story quilts of Harriet Powers.* New York: Scribner.

Markun, P.M. (1993). *The little painter of Sabana Grande.* New York: Bradbury.

Mason, A. (1994). *Cezanne.* Hauppauge, NY: Barron's.

Mason, A. (1994). *Monet.* Hauppauge, NY: Barron's.

Raboff, E. (1987). *Leonardo da Vinci.* New York: Knopf.

Raboff, E. (1987). *Rembrandt.* New York: Knopf.

Raboff, E. (1988). *Henri Matisse.* New York: Knopf.

Stanley, D. (1996). *Leonardo da Vinci.* New York: Morrow.

Stevens, J. (1996). *From pictures to words.* New York: Holiday.

Van Allsburg, C. (1995). *Bad day at River Bend.* Boston: Houghton Mifflin.

Venezia, M. (1988). *Vincent Van Gogh.* New York: Childrens Press.

Venezia, M. (1989). *Da Vinci.* New York: Childrens Press.

Venezia, M. (1990). *Mary Cassatt.* New York: Childrens Press.

Venezia, M. (1991). *Francisco Goya.* New York: Childrens Press.

Venezia, M. (1992). *Pieter Bruegel.* New York: Childrens Press.

Venezia, M. (1993). *Georgia O'Keeffe.* New York: Childrens Press.

Venezia, M. (1993). *Monet.* New York: Childrens Press.

Venezia, M. (1993). *Salvador Dali.* New York: Childrens Press.

Venezia, M. (1994). *Diego Rivera.* New York: Childrens Press.

Winter, J. (1991). *Diego.* New York: Knopf.

Winter, J. (1996). *Josefina.* New York: Harcourt.

Wolkstein, D. (1992). *Little mouse's painting.* New York: Morrow.

Zhensun, Z., & Low, A. (1991). *A young painter: The life and paintings of Wang Yani, China's extraordinary young artist.* New York: Scholastic.

Performing the Arts

Auch, M. J. (1993). *Peeping beauty.* New York: Holiday House. (Ballet.)

Auch, M. J. (1995). *Hen lake.* New York: Holiday.

Brett, J. (1991). *Berlioz the bear.* New York: Putnam.

Carlson, N. (1982). *Harriet's recital.* Minneapolis, MN: Carolrhoda.

Catalano, D. (1992). *Wolf plays alone.* New York: Philomel.

Deetlefs, R. (1995). *Tabu and the dancing elephants.* New York: Dutton.

Esbensen, B. J. (1995). *Dance with me.* New York: HarperCollins.

Gray, L. M. (1995). *My mama had a dancing heart.* New York: Orchard.

Gregory, C. (1990). *Cynthia Gregory dances Swan Lake.* New York: Simon & Schuster.

Isadora, R. (1993). *Lili at ballet.* New York: Putnam.

Kraus, R. (1990). *Musical Max.* New York: Simon & Schuster.

Marshall, J. (1993). *Fox on stage.* New York: Dial.

Martin, R., Jr. (1994). *The maestro plays.* New York: Henry Holt.

Moon, N. (1995). *Lucy's picture.* New York: Dial.

Pinkney, B. (1994). *Max found two sticks.* New York: Simon & Schuster.

Raschka, C. (1992). *Charlie Parker played bebop.* New York: Orchard.

Spinelli, E. (1993). *Boy, can he dance.* New York: Four Winds.

Thomassie, T. (1996). *Mimi's tutu.* New York: Scholastic.

Tryon, L. (1992). *Albert's play.* New York: Atheneum.

How Things Are Made

Ancona, G. (1994). *The pinata maker/El pinatero.* New York: Harcourt.

de Paola, T. (1977). *Charlie needs a cloak.* Weston, CT: Weston Woods Studios.

Flournoy, V. (1985). *The patchwork quilt.* New York: Dial.

Gibbons, G. (1987). *The pottery place.* New York: Harcourt.

Kuskin, K. (1994). *Patchwork island.* New York: HarperCollins.

Paul, A. W. (1991). *Eight hands round: A patchwork alphabet.* New York: HarperCollins.

Scholastic. (1994). *How things work.* New York: Scholastic First Encyclopedia.

Turner, A. (1994). *Sewing quilts.* New York: Simon and Schuster.

Waddell, M., & Milne, T. A. (1992). *The toymaker.* Cambridge, MA: Candlewick.

Sources of Art Reproductions

First Discovery Art Books by Claude Delafosse (*Portraits, Landscapes, Animals, Paintings*). New York: Scholastic.

Blizzard, G. S. (1993). *Come look with me: World of play.* Charlottesville, VA: Thomasson-Grant.

Greenberg, J., & Jordan. S. (1995). *The American eye: Eleven artists of the twentieth century.* New York: Delacorte.

Micklethwait, L. (1992). *I spy: An alphabet in art.* New York: Greenwillow.

UNICEF (1996). *Art games.* New York: Author. (Uses designs from greeting cards to play Concentration, Go Fish, and other games.)

Resources for Teachers

Barchers, S. (1993). *Readers theatre for beginning readers.* Englewood, CO: Teacher Ideas Press.

First Teacher. (1995). *Open-ended art: Explorations.* Wilmington, NC: Author.

Mallan, K. (1992). *Children as storytellers.* Portsmouth, NH: Heinemann.

Olshansky, B. (1992). *Children as authors, children as illustrators: The whole story.* Portsmouth, NH: Heinemann. (Video.)

Panzer, N. (1995). *Celebrate America in poetry and art.* New York: Hyperion.

Raboff, E. (1988). *Art for children.* New York: Harper & Row.

Turner, J. B., & Schiff, R. S. (1995). *Let's make music: An interactive musical trip around the world.* New York: Hal Leonard.

Weikart, P. (1987). *Round the circle.* Ypsilanti, MI: High Scope Press.

Individual and Group Projects for Teachers

Guidelines for Portfolio Assessment in the Arts

Elise Vasquez, a twenty-eight-year-old kindergarten teacher, recalls her initial forays into portfolio arts assessment. "I wanted to do what was best for the children, but I found myself going crazy with trying to catalog all their work. I think that in the effort to do alternative assessment 'right,' I missed the whole point of involving the children and empowering them as partners in their progress. I also needed to establish a more systematic way of guiding and assisting children in the selection of work for their portfolios." As Elise started a second year of teaching using alternative assessment, she examined a variety of assessment techniques that she planned to include in her classroom practice. Then she created four valuable ground rules for herself based on her previous struggles to institute performance assessment in her classroom.

Guideline 1: The Portfolio Must Include Observation Tools That Are Realistic for Managing a Whole Classroom.

Elise wanted to observe her students at work and play, but she needed to find observation tools that provided information on individual children in a "user-friendly" way. Elise chose checklists as one such tool. These checklists were posted on the walls of her classroom, close to every activity center, so that in the course of a day's activity Elise could chart her observations in the area that children had chosen and the activities in which they had engaged. "I found checklists to be an enormous help. Prior to the checklists, I had tried to scribble notes to myself about every child's activity, and I found myself very frustrated. The checklist provides an accurate profile, is reasonable for my class size, and provides a weekly record of children's choices and activity levels."

Notice that the checklist allows a quick notation system for each child, each school day, and individual levels of involvement in the activity. The checklists can be filed, and a profile of each child's participation readily drawn from a relatively simple instrument. Such a checklist might look like Figure 7.11.

Guideline 2: Involve the Children More Thoroughly in the Process of Assessment.

Elise's students were introduced to arts journals as a way of engaging them in more reflective and cooperative thinking about their own progress and that of their classmates. Though the journals were more time-consuming than the checklists, Elise reports that the results were well worth the effort. The children were encouraged to write and draw about their feelings related to their art, music, drama, and dance experiences in the classroom. These entries ranged from simple sketches of smiling faces to well-structured sentences and paragraphs explaining various pieces of work. The journals were stored in Ms. Vasquez's classroom on a central shelf, from which they were periodically collected and examined. "These journals allowed me to chronicle children's growth in reflection and expression. Looking at the first entries compared to the last few for each child is amazing. They have learned to critique their own work, explain ideas, and plan future projects."

Elise Vasquez also introduced her students to arts conferences. Preassigned clusters of children met on a rotating basis to look at, talk about, and evaluate various artistic projects and products. By using this technique, Elise was able to keep records of children's interests, frustrations, and expressive abilities regarding their work. Elise began to hear praise and support offered for the ideas of others, as well as noticing children asking questions about their classmates' techniques and styles. Through the notes from these conferences, Elise was able to extract valuable information regarding each child's progress in planning, reflecting on, and discussing his or her individual work. This information was easily accessible at parent conference time and also when it was time to send grade reports. "Twenty minutes a day is a small investment for such important returns," Elise states, "Not only are the children gaining skills in fine arts, but they are also gaining skills in communication, social interaction, critical thinking, and self-expression. They have surprised me with their ability to take on responsibility and follow through."

Guideline 3: Make Assessment Tasks Manageable in Terms of Time and Storage.

With all of the data that Ms. Vasquez was able to collect, a manageable and realistic way to organize the materials for assessment seemed unlikely. Elise smiles as she recalls her first attempt at portfolio assessment. "Each child had an accordion file. It took work on my part not to do everything for them, though. We talked from the first day about storing all our paintings, papers, and projects in the file. Then, Fridays were devoted during conference times to choosing the work that would stay in the portfolio at school or be shared at home. This system really helped the children to begin to choose for themselves." Ms. Vasquez also notes growth in the children's ability to critique

Figure 7.11 **Teacher-Constructed Art Participation Chart**

Coding system:

I—initiated activity   P—participated with encouragement   O—observed the activity

	David	Casey	Steve	Emilio	Shamir	Liz	Amy	Brian
Finger painting	P	P	P	O	I	P	I	O
Collage	P	P	P	I	I	I	I	O
Printmaking	I	I	I	I		I	I	P
String painting	I							O
Rubbings	I	I	I	P	I	I	I	I
Splatter paint	P	P	I	O	I	P	P	P

and encourage the work of their classmates. "Our conference groups really supported their members. Children would confer about pieces of work and encourage each other to take the work home or keep it in their portfolios." The accordion files were dubbed Process Portfolios, with work added and removed each week. From those, the children chose their favorite pieces each grading period. "It took time to acquaint the children with the concept of conferencing and choosing. Initially I guided these selections a little more than I do now," says Elise. "The selections from the Process Portfolio went into Project Portfolios where the 'favorite of the favorite' was displayed."

Guideline 4: Use Portfolios as Communication Tools with Students and Parents.

According to Elise, "All the data that the portfolios contain allow me to share with children and their parents a record of their work and play habits." Parents appreciate the fact that they have a chance to see their child's work from week to week, and that they are invited to comment in writing on the projects and products on which their child is working." Ms. Vasquez laughs as she recalls a parent meeting at which one mother thanked her for sending home only a few pieces of work each week. "Another parent shared the fact that the child had asked

for a portfolio at home. Every few weeks the projects from school are examined. Some pieces are kept while others are set aside to be sent to grandparents or friends as gifts or greetings." One family in this year's class shares work that is taken out of the home portfolio with a local nursing home. "I believe that the students are beginning to see the arts as a part of everyone's life and as a way of sharing themselves and their joy."

Project portfolios in Ms. Vasquez's classroom are contained in large binders with rings and pockets for storing work in a variety of formats. There is a section in each portfolio for photographs of three-dimensional works, a section for audiotapes of musical endeavors, a videotape of children's drama or dance creations, and many examples of visual art from watercolor to collage. One large bookcase located in the corner of the room serves as the portfolio center.

Discussion Questions

- What have you learned from this teacher's experiences with portfolios?
- Have you had any experiences in creating and maintaining a portfolio yourself? in using portfolios with children?
- Now that you know more about assessment strategies in the arts, what strategies do you plan to use?

REFERENCES

Ariasian, P. W. (1994). *Classroom assessment* (2nd ed.). New York: McGraw-Hill.

Baum, S. M., Owen, S. V., & Oreck, B. (1993, April). *Talent beyond words: Identification of potential talent in dance and music in elementary school.* Paper presented at the annual meeting of the American Educational Research Association, Atlanta, GA.

Black, J. K., & Puckett, M. B. (1996). *The young child: Development from prebirth through age eight* (2nd ed.). Englewood Cliffs, NJ: Merrill/Prentice Hall.

Bowman, B. T. (1995). The professional development challenge: Supporting young children and families. *Young Children, 51*(1), 30–34.

Boyer, E. L. (1988). It's not "either or," it's both. *Educational Leadership, 45*(4), 3.

Boyer, E.L. (1995). *The basic school: A community for learning.* New York: Carnegie Foundation for the Advancement of Teaching.

Brandt, R. (1988). On assessment in the arts: A conversation with Howard. *Educational Leadership, 45*(4), 30–34.

Bredekamp, S., & Rosegrant, T. (Eds.). (1992). *Reaching potentials: Appropriate curriculum an assessment for young children* (pp. 9–27). Washington, DC: National Association for the Education of Young Children.

Bruer, J. T. (1994). The mind's journey from novice to expert. *American Educator, 17*(2), 6–15, 38–46.

Caine, R. N., & Caine, G. (1991). *Teaching and the human brain.* Alexandria, VA: Association for Supervision and Curriculum Development.

Carbo, M. (1995). Educating everybody's children. In R. W. Cole (Ed.). *Educating everybody's children: Diverse teaching strategies for diverse learners: What research and practice say about improving achievement.* Alexandria, VA: Association for Supervision and Curriculum Development.

Carnine, D. (1990). New research on the brain: Implications for instruction. *Phi Delta Kappan, 71*(5), 372–377.

Chiseri-Strater, E. (1992). College sophomores reopen the closed portfolio. In D. H. Graves & B. S. Sunstein (Eds.), *Portfolio portraits* (pp. 61–72). Portsmouth, NH: Heinemann.

Cohen, E. P., & Gainer, R. S. (1995). *Art: Another language for learning.* Portsmouth, NH: Heinemann.

Department of Education. (1991). *America 2000: An education strategy.* Washington, DC: Author.

Eisner, E. W. (1981). The role of the arts in cognition and curriculum. *Phi Delta Kappan, 63*(1), 48–52.

Eisner, E. W. (1992). The reality of reform. *English Leadership Quarterly 14*(3), 2–5.

Engel, M. (1983). Art and the mind. *Art Education, 36*(2) , 6–8.

Executive Office of the President. (1990). *National goals for education.* Washington, DC: Author.

Gardner, H. (1993). *Frames of mind: The theory of multiple intelligences* (10th anniv. ed.). New York: Basic Books.

Gardner, H. (1995). Reflections on multiple intelligences: Myths & messages. *Phi Delta Kappan 77*(3), 200–203, 206–209.

Gelfer, J. I., & Perkins, P. G. (1996). A model for portfolio assessment in early childhood education programs. *Early Childhood Education Journal, 24*(1), 5–10.

Goodlad, J. I. (1992). Toward a place in the curriculum for the arts. In B. Reimer & R. A. Smith (Eds.), *The arts, education, and aesthetic knowing* (pp. 192–212). Chicago: University of Chicago Press.

Goodman, K. S., Goodman, Y. M., & Hood, W. J. (1989). *The whole language evaluation book.* Portsmouth, NH: Heinemann.

Hansen, J. (1992). Teachers evaluate their own literacy. In D. H. Graves & B. S. Sunstein (Eds.), *Portfolio portraits* (pp. 73–82). Portsmouth, NH: Heinemann.

Hargreaves, D. J., & Galton, M. J. (1992). Aesthetic learning: Psychological theory and educational practice. In B. Reimer & R. A. Smith (Eds.), *The arts, education and aesthetic knowing* (pp. 124–150). Chicago: University of Chicago Press.

Herman, J. L., Aschbacher, P. R., & Winters, L. (1992). *A practical guide to alternative assessment.* Alexandria, VA: Association for Supervision and Curriculum Development.

Isenberg, J. P., & Jalongo, M. R. (1997). *Creative expression and play in early childhood* (2nd ed.). Englewood Cliffs, NJ: Merrill/Prentice Hall.

Jalongo, M. R., & Isenberg, J. P. (1995). *Teachers' stories: From personal narrative to professional insight.* San Francisco: Jossey-Bass.

Katz, L.G. (1993). *A developmental approach to the education of young children: Basic principles.* Paper presented at the summer Institute on the Project Approach, International School of Brussels.

Kiefer, B. Z. (1995). *The potential of picturebooks: From visual literacy to aesthetic understanding.* Englewood Cliffs, NJ: Merrill.

Kline, L. W. (1995). A baker's dozen: Effective instructional strategies. In R. W. Cole (Ed.), *Educating everybody's children: Diverse teaching strategies for diverse learners* (pp. 21–41). Alexandria, VA: Association for Supervision and Curriculum Instruction.

Kostelnik, M. J. (Ed.). (1996). *Themes teachers use.* Glenview, IL: GoodYear Books.

Lima, C. W., & Lima, J. A. (1989). *A to Zoo: Subject access to children's picture books* (3rd ed.). New York: Bowker.

Mathieu, W. A. (1991). *The listening book: Discovering your own music.* Boston: Shambhala.

Music Educators National Conference. (1995). *National standards for arts education: What every young American should know.* Reston, VA: Author.

Neve, C. D., Hart, L. A., & Thomas, E. C. (1986). Huge learning jumps show potency of brain-based instruction. *Phi Delta Kappan, 68*(2), 143–148.

Parsons, M. J. (1992). Cognition as interpretation in art education. In B. Reimer & R. A. Smith (Eds.), *The arts, education, and aesthetic knowing* (pp. 70–90). Chicago: University of Chicago Press.

Paulson, F. L., Paulson, P. K., & Meyer, C. A. (1991). What makes a portfolio a portfolio? *Educational Leadership, 48*(5), 60–63.

Porter, C., & Cleland, J. (1995). *The portfolio as a learning strategy.* Portsmouth, NH: Boyton/Cook.

Rogers, S. E., & Danielson, K. E. (1996). *Teacher portfolios: Literacy, art, facts, and themes.* Portsmouth, NH: Heinemann.

Seger, F. D. (1992). Portfolio definitions: Toward a shared notion. In D. H. Graves & B. S. Sunstein (Eds.), *Portfolio portraits* (pp. 114–124). Portsmouth, NH: Heinemann.

Sidlin, M. (1978, June). *Someone's priority.* Speech given at the Aspen Conference on the Gifted, Aspen, CO, June 1978.

Smith, F. (1989). Overselling literacy. *Phi Delta Kappan, 74*(5), 354–359.

Stamp, L. N. (1994). A descriptive study of influences on preschool children's development of the creative arts. *Dissertation abstracts 55*(12), 3739A.

Stiggins, R. J. (1995). Assessment literacy for the 21st century. *Phi Delta Kappan, 77*(3), 238–245.

Teale, W. (1988). Developmentally appropriate assessment of reading and writing in the early childhood classroom. *Elementary School Journal, 89,* 135–146.

Teale, W. H. (1994). Dear readers. *Language Arts, 71*(1), 8–9.

Tierney, R. J. (1991). *Portfolio assessment in the reading writing classroom.* Norwood, MA: Christopher Gordon.

Wallas, G. (1925). *Our social heritage.* Salem, NH: Ayer.

Wassermann, S. (1989). Reflections on measuring thinking, while listening to Mozart's *Jupiter* symphony. *Phi Delta Kappan, 70*(5), 365–370.

Weininger, O. (1988). "What if" and "as if" imagination and pretend play in early childhood. In K. Egan & D. Nadaner (Eds.), *Imagination and education* (pp. 141–149). New York: Teachers College Press.

Wolf, D.P. (1988). Opening up assessment, *Educational Leadership, 45*(4), 24–29.

Wortham, S. (1997). Reporting young children's progress: A review of the issues. In J. P. Isenberg & M. R. Jalongo (Eds.), *Major trends and issues in early childhood education: Challenges, controversies, and insights* (pp. 104–122). New York: Teachers College Press.

Wright, F.L. (1957). *A testament.* New York. Horizon Press.

Zegers, D. C. (1990). *Discover music: A guide for teaching musical concepts.* (mimeographed copy).

*A*rts education for young children is not only about explorations in making art, important though this sensory experience is. In their art making activities children can experience with their hands some of the processes that are involved when an artist makes a piece of art. Without some participation in these processes, children may remain unresponsive to art and their potential faculties remain latent. It is not a question of who is going to be a professional artist, but rather a matter of bringing out the artist in all of us.

—Ann Veale (1992, p. 6)

Awakening the Artist Within

EIGHT

Chapter Reflections

- ✌ In what ways does contemporary society give a mixed message about the arts?
- ✌ What are your thoughts on the future of the arts in America?
- ✌ What can you do to involve the community in arts education?
- ✌ How do the arts and aesthetics contribute to developing the artist within us all?

THE ARTS IN A TECHNOLOGICAL SOCIETY

According to futurist John Naisbitt (1992), American society is ready to begin embracing the arts and restoring them to a more honored place in society. As one indicator of a major trend toward respect for the arts, he points out that Americans already devote more of their leisure time to arts events than to sporting events. In the twenty-first century, he predicts that

- as we are continually barraged by new technologies that unsettle our lives, we will attempt to restore our balance through a global renaissance in the arts.
- as we become a world community, we will gain a heightened awareness of the arts' role in enabling us to examine what is fundamentally human.
- as the nations of the world become more homogeneous, we will value the arts for their ability to define our cultural identities and values (Naisbitt, 1992).

Evidently, children are already convinced of the value of the arts. In a recent survey conducted by the magazine *Zillions,* children were asked to rank their favorite subjects in school. Art was rated first, with nearly three-quarters—71 percent of all the children surveyed—placing art among their favorite subjects. Music came in second with 49 percent of children choosing it as their favorite subject. English, on the other hand, was a favorite subject of just 28 percent of the children. What is it about aesthetic experiences that make them so appealing to children?

Part of learning to be artistic is sharing materials and responding appropriately to criticism.

Perhaps these subjects are so intrinsically appealing because "Children can't fail art—and the arts won't fail our children" (Cortines, 1994, p. 10).

Despite the arts' popularity with children, our technological society communicates many mixed messages about the arts. As a result, confusion and contradictions abound. In a technological society, there is a naive faith that advances in technology will solve our problems. But, if technology is the answer, what was the question? Usually, the question is whether or not a task can be accomplished more quickly and conveniently. Yet speed and convenience do not assure quality; in fact, a focus on expedience often undermines quality. A business can install voice mail so that everyone who calls hears a recording, waits to choose one of several options, and stays on hold listening to prerecorded music, but that process does little to satisfy a customer with a problem. Additionally, many of the highly touted advantages of new technologies are never realized. Before personal computers and powerful word-processing systems were widely available, many experts predicted that we would have virtually "paperless" offices when clearly, even in the most high-tech offices, computer files have to be backed up by paper documents. As Csikszentmihalyi and Schiefele (1992) contend, there is a tacit assumption that knowledge in the natural sciences and mathematics is somehow more "basic," more essential to human survival than other forms of knowledge. They identify several reasons why society may need to rethink this assumption:

> The first reason is that the technical progress made possible by intensive research in physics and the other sciences is at least as threatening for man's future as it is beneficial. At the very least, it seems desirable to slow down the development and production of energy-consuming goods and to direct human creativity increasingly to other fields of meaningful activity and productions. Second, the increasing automatization of production, the decreasing amount of working time, and the increasing average age of the population pose problems about the use of free time. . . . Our analysis suggests that creating, responding to, or learning about art have more relevance for people's everyday life experience and their existential struggles than do the natural and technical sciences. If one wants to find a suitable way of *living* or to understand how another person feels, mathematical equations, physical laws, or sophisticated computer programs won't provide much help. It may be argued that psychological knowledge will bring helpful advice. While this is certainly true for some well-defined problems, psychological knowledge cannot solve many basic existential problems with which we have to struggle. (p. 192)

A technological mentality is evident in education too. Many educators are on an endless and futile quest for the educational panacea. They think that if they can just find the one, true, perfect method, then all of their problems will be solved. Day after day, we are barraged by messages telling us that this or that hardware or software will give us a life of ease, yet our lives become increasingly complex and, at times, overwhelming as we struggle to take care of the things that we already have and dream about what we will acquire next. Ironically, many Americans are so caught up in acquiring the latest gadgetry that they don't even recognize their dilemma. That dilemma becomes more apparent when teachers and caregivers reflect upon the confusion that is evident in their actions and behaviors. Early childhood educators, for example, may

- believe that aesthetic education is essential, yet have difficulty articulating their philosophy.
- say that the arts are basic for children, yet neglect the arts in favor of the three Rs.

- agree that there is an artist within every child, yet approach art experiences as if they were a talent contest.
- understand the importance of the arts, yet fail to communicate that importance to parents.
- credit the arts with enriching life and being fundamental to human experience, yet see them as impractical and a "frill."

Yet as you have seen throughout this book, the arts are fundamental. You can never become a creative teacher unless you make a deliberate, concerted effort to bring the arts into your classroom. Ann Waymire's observation of a music specialist offers a good example of awakening the artist within each child.

The Child Artist at Work

Ann Waymire is a college student who is observing the music class of third graders. The music teacher's major goals are to involve the children in German folk dances and build their appreciation for other cultures. Figure 8.1 summarizes Ann's observational notes. In her summary of the observation, Ann writes:

> The children were mesmerized by the music teacher. She was as festive as the music and the children could not help but get swept up in all of the excitement. She has all of the children work together and problem solve as much as possible, starting off with asking them to arrange themselves in the star pattern on the board. When she began speaking German, the children started to brainstorm what she was trying to tell them. It was like a game of charades. The children

---

Setting: The music room
Time: 11:30 am–12:00 pm
Activity: The children were participating in German folk dances.

Observer: Ann Waymire
Site: George Mason University

Teacher's Activity

The music teacher began the class by having the students arrange themselves in the shape of a star which she had drawn on the board. German folk music was playing in the background. She began reading directions for the dance in German very slowly. She asked what they thought some of the words meant, such as Kinder = children. She went over the vocabulary to make sure they understood what they were going to do. The children began to dance in their groups following the counts that she was giving in German. As the music started getting faster, so did her counting. She was very enthusiastic about the lesson and danced around the room singing the songs and counting in German.

Group's Response

The children were quick to organize themselves according to the pattern on the board. They were a bit surprised to have the directions given in German but as the music teacher went through the words one by one they realized they could figure out most of them. The children began to pick up on her counting in German and began to join in with her by the end of the class. They enjoyed the dancing and kept up pretty well as the music got faster. They were laughing and having a fun time while staying on task. It was incredible to see how they hung on every word she said.

Specific Behaviors

As a whole the children were on task for the entire class. The teacher had the children moving or singing from the moment they walked in the door. I heard positive remarks such as: "Hey I can understand German!", "This is cool!" "I can count to ten in German!", and "I'm getting tired, but this is fun." At times a few of the children looked a bit confused because the pace of the class was quick, but it did not take them long to get back on track again.

Figure 8.1   Music Observation—Third Grade

were so excited. I admire this teacher and the way that she continually encourages the children to gain new understandings and meet new challenges in the arts. She builds their confidence and enhances their enthusiasm toward the lesson and the dance. I do not think that I would have changed anything in this lesson. The children were very engaged and followed her every minute of the class. It looked like so much fun that I wanted to join in!

Theory into Practice

The Psychology of Optimal Experience

Think of something that you enjoy, something that makes you happy. At first, you might think of something that is relaxing or pleasurable like watching television, making love, hanging out with friends, or taking a drive. But if you reflect more deeply on this question, you will probably identify something that you do even though it is challenging, requires skill, and does not depend upon some sort of external reward (Csikszentmihalyi & Csikszentmihalyi, 1988). Some examples of these activities include white-water rafting, playing basketball, composing music, writing poetry, and engaging in a stimulating conversation. Csikszentmihalyi (1990) and his associates have been conducting research at various sites around the world to try and understand these optimal experiences. In an optimal experience, we would find people

- becoming so completely absorbed in what they are doing that they become unself-conscious.
- pursuing an activity for its own sake rather than out of expectation of rewards.
- continuing to seek higher and higher levels of proficiency without prompting from others.
- getting better at the task, doing it more, and getting even better, thus creating a positive upward spiral.

People in this research on optimal experiences so often reported feeling "carried away" by their experience as if drawn into a current that the experience was referred to as "flow." They were completely captivated by the experience and the joy of learning by doing. Figure 8.2 characterizes optimal experience and contrasts it with other experiences. Ultimately, leading children to optimal experiences is one important function of learning and schools. If schools focus exclusively on accumulating information, they fall far short of the mark. It is widely understood that young children are naturally curious, enthusiastic, imaginative, and uninhibited. Unless some of those traits remain when they complete school, schools have failed children. It is the "deeper mission" of schooling to make certain that children continue to be interested and motivated to learn more about themselves and the world (Sarason, 1995). In other words, our ultimate goal in education is to create lifelong learners who will seek gratification through optimal experiences rather than by diminishing or injuring others. In his book, *Power and Influence,* Rollo May (1972) contends that "deeds of violence are performed largely by those who are trying to establish their self-esteem, to defend their self-image, and

Figure 8.2 **Optimal Experience**

↑ High challenge + ↑ High skill =	FLOW
↑ High challenge + ↓ Low skill =	FRUSTRATION
↓ Low challenge + ↑ High skill =	BOREDOM

to demonstrate that they, too, are significant" (p. 23). When you reflect upon conflict and violence in this way, the arts become even more fundamental in education. Stubbs (1992) contends, for example, that "every unkind or harmful act committed on the planet has been done by someone who felt powerless in some way, and the stronger the feeling of powerlessness, the greater the unkindness or harm in the act" (p. 74). When you use the arts to give young children optimal experiences, you are doing more than teaching techniques. You are giving all children an outlet for self-expression and a sense of their own power.

Sarason (1995) asked hundreds of adults to describe their experiences in schools. The great majority of them did not characterize their overall school experiences in positive ways. When they were asked specifically to describe a positive experience, however, the thing that was most frequently mentioned was the special commitment and interest of a particular teacher. Over and over again, former students describe teachers who treated them as individuals, who gave of their time, who went out of their way to help, and who appreciated them for their uniquenesses rather than treating them as one of the crowd as the most important school experience (Bluestein, 1995). Once again, this is an area where the arts can help. By their very nature, arts experiences promote self-expression and give teachers a way of seeing each child as an individual.

COMMUNITY-BASED ARTS EDUCATION

Henry Giroux (1992) contends that in order to restructure schools, we will need to reflect upon three things and the interactions among them: power, knowledge, and culture. When a stronger sense of community exists both inside and outside the classroom, all members share in power, contribute to knowledge, and hold others' cultures in high esteem. The process of building a sense of community begins with a clear and vital mission and a shared sense of purpose (Boyer, 1995). The arts are frequently at the heart of that mission and purpose, as the following scenario describes.

Scenario: A Playground Project

When a group of student teachers first visited their school in an urban setting, they saw a playground that was surrounded by a seven-foot chain-link fence, walls covered with obscenities, trash strewn around, and equipment in poor repair. Some of the things that they saw were real hazards—broken beer bottles, used hypodermics, plastic bags that once held drugs. As a first step, they rallied the community around the goal of a safe, interesting, and aesthetically appealing place for children to play. When families passed by and saw that the teachers and some student volunteers had stayed after school to paint over the obscenities on the school wall, they knew that the teachers were serious about improving the playground. Gradually, the playground became a schoolwide project. The first step was a Saturday clean-up, paint-up, fix-up. With the help of children and their families, the student teachers cleaned the play area, gave the equipment a fresh coat of paint, and repaired or removed broken equipment. Afterward, there was a covered-dish meal in the school cafeteria.

Next, two university professors with experience in designing playgrounds with recycled materials visited the site, were interviewed by the children, and made suggestions on ways to create durable equipment on a very limited budget. The ideas that they shared through colored slides of their work sparked children's creativity. The kindergartners were interviewed about their play preferences by the fifth graders. The second graders wrote suggestions for the new suggestion box. The third graders made scale models of the new playground, and the sixth graders researched the topic of playgrounds.

Because the student teachers had taken photographs and maintained a portfolio of the project's progress, they were able to get some recognition for their efforts in the local newspaper when "before" and "after" photos were published. Shortly after the photographs appeared, a local business donated $1,000 to the project, and the PTA, $200. These student teachers had galvanized the community around a shared goal, and, as a result, the dream of a better place for children to play became a reality. With the new equipment in place, the old equipment repaired, and the area maintained by inspection teams of children, a new and attractive playground was formed. As a result of participating in the process, children learned basic principles of design, economics, research, cooperation, and caring for the environment.

This scenario illustrates the characteristics of a real community. In a true community all members

- share a mission and have a clear purpose.
- come to know and appreciate one another.
- feel cared about and therefore comfortable in revealing themselves to others.
- reach out, connect, and lend their support to the goal.
- feel confident that justice will prevail when decisions are made.
- find and participate in occasions for celebration (Boyer, 1995; Sapon-Shevin, 1995).

As the playground example illustrated, community-based art education has significance for the child as a person, the curriculum, and the community. Figure 8.3

Figure 8.3 **Features of Community-Based Art**

ᴈ⁊ *Child as a Person*

- begins with the student's knowledge and curiosity.
- is relevant and contemporary.
- is accessible and encompasses children at risk.
- nurtures self-identity and self-esteem.

ᴈ⁊ *Curriculum and Learning Experiences*

- acknowledge concerns about safety.
- are inexpensive.
- are multisensory.
- are natural and easy.
- are interdisciplinary.
- enhance the transferability of learning.

ᴈ⁊ *Community*

- reveals hidden dimensions of the community.
- builds community cohesion.
- builds closer relationships between the home and community.
- contributes to advocacy on behalf of the arts.

Source: Adapted from London, P. (1994). *Step outside: Community-based art education.* Portsmouth, NH: Heinemann.

provides an overview of London's (1994) conceptualization of community-based art education. By involving the community in creating "usable art"—in this case, a play area—these teachers made a significant contribution to the goals of arts education in their urban setting.

OVERARCHING GOALS OF AESTHETIC AND ARTS EDUCATION

*W*hat can we as early childhood educators hope to achieve by offering programs for young children that are thoroughly steeped in the arts? There are at least three important outcomes: perceptivity and imagination, interpretation and appreciation, and commitment to craft.

Perceptivity and Imagination

Watch a toddler as she studies the effect of water mixed with sand at the seashore. Every fiber of her being is absorbed by the experience. She steps in the wet sand, sits down in it, squishes it through her fingers, buries her legs under it, and shapes the wet sand into various forms. The toddler cries when it is time to leave. She even manages to bring some of the beach home with her because after she gets changed, there is at least a cupful of wet sand still trapped in the creases of her swimsuit. This is an example of the heightened perceptivity that begins with sensory experiences and leads to aesthetic experiences. It is "wide awakeness," a type of full attention and thoughtful reflection that is an important by-product of education in the arts. Maxine Greene (1978) explains it this way: "Only the performing and especially the working self is highly interested in life and, hence, wide awake. It lives within its acts and its attention and is exclusively directed to carrying its project into effect, to executing its plan. The attention is an active, not a passive one. Passive attention is the opposite to full awareness" (Greene, 1978, p. 163).

In order to observe this full awareness, you need only to look at young children's intense concentration as they examine flowers, study ants on an anthill, or pore over the pages of a picture book for details. Fully perceived sensory input of this kind is necessary to enrich imagination. Young children's artwork is clearly affected by their sensory impressions and their imaginations. If you listen and watch, you will see these connections made possible through the arts. A thirty-month-old might be scribbling with a fat crayon as she thinks about the new classroom pet, a long-haired guinea pig. A four-year-old who hears a story about bears might be seen with friends trying to figure out how to make a "cave" out of available materials so that they can enact a confrontation with a hibernating bear. A first grader might be drawing and writing an original story about a dinosaur inside an egg, inspired by a puppet she saw at the library. "Imagination is fed by perception and perception by sensibility and sensibility by artistic cultivation. With refined sensibility, the scope of perception is enlarged. With enlarged perception, the resources that feed our imaginative life are increased" (Eisner, 1991a, p. 15). Art is sensory experience, full awareness, and active imagination expressed in a concrete form.

Interpretation and Appreciation

Perhaps you have heard the familiar statement that something is "subject to interpretation," meaning that it cannot be immediately understood in the same way by those who experience it. What, exactly, is interpretation, and how does it relate to the arts? Imagine this scene: A teacher is sharing prints of modern art with her preschool class. She begins by saying, "I have several copies of paintings here. As we look at each one, I want you to tell me what you see, what you think, and how the picture makes you feel." The children have many comments to make. They remark on the colors, the shapes, the texture, the line, and the arrangement using their own words. Jason says that the colors in one of Paul Klee's paintings "look like they are friendly." Risa thinks that Picasso's "Three Musicians" looks like "the people are mixed up."

Whereas many adults can be heard to say that they do not like modern art because they "don't know what it means," these young children are growing in confidence about their ability to interpret art, even art that does not clearly "look like something." One reason why adults might have difficulty interpreting modern art is that they feel pressured to come up with the correct answer about what it means.

Children, on the other hand, are inclined to look for their own answers. Part of experiencing the arts is being able to take these naive impressions from childhood and build them into interpretation. If young children do not have repeated exposure to high-quality works of art, they will choose whatever is heavily advertised or simply familiar. Then their ability to make fine-grained distinctions about the relative merits of art objects, aesthetic experiences, and artistic performances atrophies with disuse. As Veale (1992) points out, "We all need to be aroused to the possibilities of a medium or genre before understanding can develop. It is only through gradual and repeated exposure to visual ideas and visual objects that the verbal and artistic vocabulary can develop. We probably all can recall some instances where we gradually came to like a piece of music, or the work of certain artists to which we had not responded at first sight or hearing." The reward for our efforts is "the gradual development of a connoisseurship" (p. 6). In other words, after many experiences in responding to art, children gain confidence in interpreting it and appreciate its contributions to their lives.

Young children are not born with knowledge of what is good, true, beautiful, and valuable in human beings and in society. This is something that they learn, and the arts are one of the best ways to teach it to them.

Commitment to Craft

"When we think of our own early childhoods—happy or unhappy, chaotic or relaxed—or perhaps even more powerful, the imagined childhoods we might have had or wished for our children, what images surface: what places, experiences with people, moments of pure pleasure, or wonder?" (Greenman, 1994, p. 64). Close your eyes and reflect on your early school experiences. What scenes and spaces come to mind? Is it an endless succession of paper and workbooks that threatened to engulf your desk? Is a wonderful teacher/facilitator who enabled you to work on many interesting projects?

Whatever your personal view of early childhood is, be aware that it remains with you and may affect your actions even now. Be aware that if most of your work in school consisted of assignments that teachers preplanned, presented, collected, and graded. This prior experience may get in the way of doing things differently now that you are responsible for guiding young children's growth. The truth is that teaching children to care about the quality of their work is not always supported by practices in early childhood settings. Children are routinely encouraged to answer quickly, dash off a painting, move rapidly from project to project, or write a story hastily. It is almost like a production line where workers' productivity is evaluated by piecework and they are rewarded for the sheer number of things that they produce. Under these conditions, quality often suffers as workers struggle to crank out as many items as possible. In educational settings, children are similarly pushed and prodded to produce by tests, grades, and promises of higher education.

Commitment to craft is learned through the arts.

We are reminded of a sign that was posted on the wall of a prekindergarten classroom in an area where family members congregated to pick up the children. It read: "Please remember that children's learning is not measured by the weight of their backpacks!" Because most parents recall stacks of papers when they were students and associate them with "real" schoolwork, early childhood educators often have a difficult time convincing parents that children learn better through hands-on activities. Some teachers continue to rely on paper-and-pencil tasks, and well-intentioned parents will sometimes insist that their child be transferred from the setting where the children "just play" to the old-fashioned setting where the children "really work" (Isenberg & Jalongo, 1997).

Yet if you are going to depart from routine teaching, you have an obligation to educate parents, families, and the community at large about what you are doing and why. Often it is helpful to make these communications very concrete and directly related to families' lives. You could, for example, begin by asking parents if they have had any frustrating experiences with shoddy merchandise that had to be returned or items that were not repaired even after they had been in the shop and were supposedly fixed. After parents have shared several examples, you can make the connection between craftsmanship in society and craftsmanship at school very concrete. Show them a typical worksheet versus a project that the children really worked on and ask them to compare/contrast the two in terms of what the child needed to be able to do. You could, for instance, show an anonymous child's hastily scribbled coloring page, then show a child-made game and ask, "What is the quality of thinking behind these two tasks? What skills did children have to apply? What are they really learning about work?" Then, return to your original topic of craftsmanship in society. Ask them to think about how mindlessly plowing through papers might affect their child's views of work, effort, and craftsmanship. Usually, they will see your point. In your interactions with parents, try to show rather than tell and make certain that they understand "where you are coming from."

Too often, teachers yield to external pressures, and the long process of refining a work until it is representative of the child's very best effort is often abandoned in favor of "covering" more material in the class. The arts teach attention to craft by encouraging children to problem-solve and refine a form. "It is in wrestling with the wonders and uncertainties of life that we come to know it and love it most. From this direct knowledge and care, imagination springs and a concern for the well-made thing is born" (London, 1994, p. xii). That is how young children acquire a commitment to craft.

BECOMING AN ARTS ADVOCATE

$\mathcal{E}$arly childhood educators must make a conscious effort to become advocates for the arts. "If the schooling of young children is to evolve in positive ways, changes in caregivers' and teachers' values, beliefs, and skills must first occur" (Baker, 1990, p. 24). As the saying goes, actions speak louder than words. The most important prerequisite in becoming an arts advocate is making a commitment to the child as artist. Before reading on, turn to pages 238–239 and complete the self-assessment. What insights did you gain about your perspectives on the arts and how these might affect your work with young children? In order to lead them to the arts, you will have to appreciate not only the work that they produce, but also the problem-solving processes that they use to get there.

This sort of self-appraisal is important for early childhood educators because, as arts expert Susan Stinson (1992) reminds us, "regardless of subject, how we teach is also what we are teaching—about self, others, and the world we share" (Stinson, 1992, p. 27). After you have made children the focal point of your arts program, there are several other things that you can do to demonstrate your commitment to aesthetic education. They include valuing processes as much as products, working to build support for the arts, extending your own background in the arts, confronting your own biases, and recognizing the multicultural potential of the arts.

Value Processes as Much as Products

One of the dangers of our era is ignoring processes and rushing to products. Drew's experience offers a good example. His teacher was playing a musical selection and inviting the children to draw pictures in response to the music. But Drew just sat

In the arts, the process is as important as the product. These three children find measuring and mixing the dough as exciting as fashioning an object from it.

there, crayon poised, with a frown on his face. His teacher asked what was wrong, and Drew replied that he couldn't "think of anything to draw." When the teacher urged him to just let his hand and arm move to the music, Drew refused because "if it doesn't look like somethin', my mommy won't put it on the refrigerator."

As early childhood educators, we have a special responsibility to counteract the view that representational art, drawings that "look like something," are the only appropriate response. The teacher spoke with Drew's mother and emphasized the concept of originality in art. She explained it this way: "When teachers use patterns and copies, they are doing the work *for* the children. Then one child's work looks just like everybody else's. Eventually, children begin to doubt their own abilities, and they resort to doing what a great number of older children do—trace and copy rather than create something original. If we work together to build Drew's confidence in his own ideas, we can help Drew to avoid seeing himself as many American adults do, as 'uncreative.'"

Strive to Build Administrative and Parental Support

Teachers who are convinced that the arts are valuable often find themselves in conflict with the administration. Unenlightened administrators sometimes base their judgments of educational programs on standardized test scores or on how quietly the children work. A supervisor might visit an early childhood setting and ask, for example, "Why are they drawing during writing time?" If the teacher cannot supply a sound rationale for this practice, it will continue to be challenged. Part of the responsibility of early childhood teachers is to educate others about why we do what we do. A good response might be "As you know, very young children look at both writing and drawing as 'marks on paper.' Encouraging children to experiment with both symbol systems enables them to make more concrete connections between their experiences and pictures that represent those experiences. The use of pictures as symbols leads to the use of more abstract symbols, like letters and words. Studies have shown that the children who perform well academically are also the best at drawing (Baker, 1992). That result occurs because they are learning to master complex symbol systems."

Parents frequently challenge the value of creative expression and play as well. A parent may say disparagingly of sociodramatic play, "They're just jumping around. They can do that at home." Once again, the teacher's responsibility is to make it clear why dance is important, to describe how, through dance, children become aware of their bodies, learn how their bodies move, coordinate their actions with those of the group, and problem-solve as they try to accomplish a particular goal. Citing concrete examples from the child's learning through dance, noting the connections between childhood dance, coordination, and wellness, or discussing the role of dance in celebrations all help parents to understand why dance is significant in young children's lives.

Work to Build Your Background in the Arts

Ask early childhood educators if the arts are important and they will surely say, "Of course!" But ask most American early childhood teachers if they have had thorough preparation in the arts, and the answer is a resounding "No." Providing aesthetic experiences begins with you, the adult. When you show children that you value the arts by showing interest, displaying enthusiasm, and finding the time, it lets children know that you think the arts matter. Ramon Cortines (1994), the chancellor of New York City public schools, reminds us that

> many adults are scared of the arts—we were told as kids that we had two left feet, couldn't carry a tune, mixed pigments gracelessly, colored outside of the lines.
>
> Whether communicated by words, actions, jokes, raised eyebrows, or simple fact of expenditures of funds, the message was that we were not worthy, and that pursuit of the arts was not important in the real world. . . . But despite the damning denunciation of creativity that most of us so unfortunately experienced, we now live adult lives that are enriched immeasurably by the beauty of music, motion, color, and the communicative power of the arts. (p. 8)

Most American teachers would be rather surprised to see the teacher preparation programs in other countries. Elsewhere, the arts hold a far more respected place than they do in the United States, both in traditional and in contemporary culture. As a result, a significant portion of the teacher preparation curriculum is devoted to dance, drama, and music. In many other countries, there is a national commitment to aesthetics, one that considers the arts to be not only an educational basic, but also an essential component of good citizenship. Prospective teachers in England, China, Russia, and Latino countries are routinely required to take entire courses in painting, singing, drama, dance, and instrumental music. English and Japanese teachers, for example, are coached in the construction of "beauty areas" in early childhood classrooms. Such areas include flowers, sculpture, and natural objects designed to develop an awareness of aesthetic elements such as color, line, shape, texture, arrangement, harmony, balance, proportion, and simplicity.

Meanwhile, American teacher preparation programs typically offer a single creative activities course as the prospective teacher's or caregiver's sole preparation for bringing the arts into the classroom. Some teacher preparation programs include a complete course devoted to music and art, but often these courses focus on teachers' ability to perform music or function as artists themselves rather than the teacher's role as a facilitator of *children's* musical or artistic abilities. American teacher education courses or experiences in drama for children are rare. Rarer still are courses or experiences in guiding young children's development in dance or song or instrumental music. Yet, all of the children in every classroom need to express themselves through language, song, movement, and craft because the arts are for every child, not only the exceptionally talented or socially elite.

As a result of teachers' inadequate preparation in the arts, public elementary school teachers often gratefully surrender total responsibility for the arts to special programs with specialist teachers. Such an approach is in direct opposition to the idea of integrated curriculum. It divorces the arts from other ways of learning and further isolates music and art teachers from their colleagues, treating them like second-class citizens rather than the resource people they are.

Access to the services of arts specialists for preschool teachers, on the other hand, is virtually nonexistent. Good preschool teachers recognize that they have major responsibility for introducing young children to aesthetics, yet they often have limited backgrounds in the arts. Opportunities for children's participation in the expressive arts are too important to leave to chance or to be reserved for one brief class period per week (Jalongo, 1990). For all these reasons, most early childhood educators must actively seek in-service education in the arts throughout their careers.

Confront Personal Biases and Embrace Diversity

As teachers, we need to examine our own prejudices about the arts. Do we, for example, communicate the message that the arts are equated with snobbery? Do we stereotype all artists, expecting them to be "temperamental," "impractical," or, if male, "effeminate"? Are we intolerant of children who are free-spirited rather than conformists? To further examine your attitudes and confront your biases about the arts, return to the self-evaluation questions on pages 238–239 of this chapter. Far too often, genius is dismissed as a form of eccentricity or even as borderline madness. But genius is a positive trait, a trait that must be recognized and cultivated in every child. Classrooms should develop those special aptitudes of children that define them as unique people, and schools should be places where children can know subject matter in the deepest sense—by being creative with it (Eisner, 1991b).

After you have confronted biases, you can begin to embrace diversity and regard the arts as a rich resource for multicultural education. If you doubt that art is a cultural force, imagine yourself standing on Easter Island, exploring Egyptian ruins, visiting the Sistine Chapel, examining cave paintings created by ancient Australian Aborigines, or studying one of Diego Rivera's huge murals depicting the people of Mexico. These artifacts demonstrate the power of art. Art not only communicates ideas, but also preserves cultural ideals by giving younger generations the opportunity to see what others have deemed worthy of maintaining. During early childhood, children are forming the foundation of their cultural identity. They are at a starting point where a basic sense of self and others is formed.

Until teachers lead the way in overcoming stereotypes about the arts, emphasizing processes, building arts backgrounds, educating administrators and parents, and integrating the arts throughout the school day, aesthetics education will remain marginalized in our schools. Figure 8.4 provides an overview of the abilities you will need to develop in order to become an arts advocate.

AWAKENING TO THE ARTIST IN YOU

*A*s instructors who teach undergraduate- and graduate-level courses in creativity, the arts, and aesthetic education, we frequently encounter teachers and caregivers who doubt their own creativity. These early childhood educators approach a course in creativity and the arts with all the anxiety with which other people approach mathematics or public speaking. They are hoping for the reassurance of a pattern to copy, correct answers to memorize, and instructions so explicit that every student's work is essentially the same. Yet none of these things will enable them to become more creative. In fact, these approaches will further undermine their trust in their own abilities. Until they learn to relax, to play with ideas, to trust in young children, and to believe in themselves, they will remain dependent on others for ideas about what to do. Under these conditions, teachers become desperate for direction and turn to textbooks or whatever is available. They also become very protective of ideas that they find because they fear that if another teacher uses "their" idea, there will be nothing to replace it. Naturally, such attitudes lead to worry, isolation, and frustration. The solution lies, not in laying claim to a few ideas that can be repeated year after year, but in freeing your mind from the one-right-answer mentality, opening your life to the possibilities of art, and

Figure 8.4   **How to Become an Arts Advocate**

In *To Become a Teacher: Making a Difference in Children's Lives,* William Ayers (1995), the book's editor, gives advice on how to rise above ordinary, business-as-usual teaching. We apply that advice here to becoming a teacher of the arts.

In order to become a strong advocate for the arts, you will need to

- have the courage, vision, and determination necessary to integrate the arts into the curriculum.
- find allies in your quest for teaching practices that support the arts and aesthetic education.
- maintain a vision of teaching that is vibrant, dynamic, intellectual, ethical.
- keep students at the center of your practice.
- "teach against the grain" and be hypervigilant about habit and routine.

seeking a dynamic form of collegiality that will enable your creativity to flourish. Look around you with the wide-awakeness of children, and believe in brainstorms. We often ask our students to really pay attention to what they see and make the familiar new by coming up with interesting combinations. Here are some of the ideas that they shared in their journals in response to a task we call "I had a brainstorm!":

- My little sister, who will be in second grade next year, is fascinated by ticktack-toe, and she is just beginning to understand the strategy behind it. One morning, while I was eating cereal, I had a brainstorm! I could save the caps from one-gallon plastic milk jugs, and we could make a permanent ticktacktoe game. We drew Xs and Os on the caps with a permanent felt-tip marker and made a game board out of cardboard. She loves it.
- I had the rather depressing job of undecorating the Christmas tree. We usually throw away the tinsel, and some of the garland had broken. I almost threw it away too, but then I had a brainstorm! This stuff would make terrific hair for puppets or add textural interest to collage. I took it to preschool, and the children used it in their arts projects.
- I saw a rug in a store window that was printed to look like a road, and I had a brainstorm! I got a piece of heavy cardboard and made it into a parking lot. It had numbered spaces, directional arrows, stop signs, and so on. I added a small box for the parking lot attendant. Then I got self-adhesive dots, wrote numbers on them corresponding to the numbers on the spaces, and stuck them on small plastic cars. The children got very excited and wanted to make their own games that they could drive the cars through. So far I have seen an amusement park, a zoo, a playground, a circus, a jungle, and a farm.
- I was taking plastics over to recycle, and I had a brainstorm! I thought about how we might use some of these things at the day care center. Spray-can lids make good containers for water or sand. A half-gallon jug cut diagonally on the bottom makes a good sand scoop. Different types of containers are good for molding sand. I have one that a Jell-o salad comes in that creates a circular shape with a ropelike edge. As I browsed through a catalog of early child-hood materials, I saw other things that I could replicate with recycled materials. Most of the teachers use baby-food jars for paints, but they can break and tend to tip over easily. Plastic jars with lids for tempera paints can be bought, but I use a hand cream that comes in a jar that is much sturdier than

the ones sold in stores. I put strips of plastic tape on the outside that are the color of the paint on the inside. Our crayons were sorted into boxes of eight different colors, but I took them all out and asked the children to help me sort them by color, and then we put them in plastic cups with the color name written on the outside. This gives the children the colors they need and leaves them free to talk about something important.

- I know it isn't a new idea to make a large cardboard box into a house, but I had a brainstorm! The house we moved into had a couple of rolls of wallpaper in the attic that we would never use, so I brought them to school, and we papered the inside of the box. The children used smaller gift boxes to make frames for pictures to hang up on the wall. I added a carpet remnant for the floor, and the children made pillows. It turned out to be a very attractive and popular play item. When the weather gets better, we have plans for an outdoor playhouse.

- Instead of giving my first graders a snowflake pattern to cut out, I let them go outside to look at snowflakes with a magnifying glass. We also watched a film that showed close-ups of snowflakes. Then I had a brainstorm! I would give them choices about how to represent their snowflakes—let *them* choose. I provided white crayons, white paint, doilies, bits of lace, pieces of yarn, soap flakes, scissors, glue, a paper punch, toothpicks, and so forth. You would be amazed by what they came up with. It was much more interesting than the cutout pattern I saw in a book. I did the same thing when it was time to go outside. Instead of saying, "Okay, let's build a snowman," I asked, "What would you like to build out of snow?" We voted and agreed upon a dinosaur—diplodocus, to be exact—and it was the talk of the entire school.

As these examples illustrate, once you start to think creatively, you begin to imagine all sorts of possibilities. When you share those ideas with others, even more ideas are born. When teachers ask what they can do to become more creative and what they can do to support the arts, Alejandro (1994) suggests, "We can always keep the quest for understanding and making beauty at the heart of our curriculum. . . . We can always strive for meaning that matters to us. . . . We can imagine anything for ourselves. I can keep screaming at my district, '*Never* remediate. *Always* enrich. Treat students as if they were all gifted and talented, and they will show you that in some way, or many ways, they are'" (p. 20).

CONCLUSION

𝒯hroughout this chapter and throughout this book, we have emphasized the notion that the arts are important for every child. "Growth in the ways persons know the world and themselves is, after all, the point and purpose of schooling and education. If the young people who pass through our schools are to learn how to realize their full humanity, then opportunities for aesthetic growth must be provided. The development of artistic and aesthetic ways of knowing must become part of the basic education of all students" (Reimer, 1992, pp. xi–xii). This is particularly important for young children whose sense of wonder is so alive and whose sense of self is at such a formative stage. The great educational philosopher John Dewey put it this way: "Children are people. They grow into tomorrow only as they live today." When you work with young children, resolve to make the arts and aesthetics part of that today so that children will become tomorrow's creative adults.

Learning about the Arts from Children

Profile of Burkely, a Budding Naturalist

When Burkely was two and a half, she saw a caterpillar out in her backyard. Because her parents are science teachers, Burkely had seen them use a field guide to identify plants, animals, reptiles, and insects many times. Burkely rushed back into the house, told her parents about it, found the book, and located the section on caterpillars. She tried to visualize exactly how the caterpillar looked and persisted until she found a drawing of the very caterpillar that she had seen. To confirm her hypothesis, Burkely took the book outside and looked again.

She was thrilled when her mother and father agreed that this was indeed the right caterpillar.

Burkely lives in a rural area, and her family has two horses, three dogs, and a cat. Caring for and playing with these animals is a major part of her life. Because her parents model inquisitiveness, Burkely's natural curiosity has been developed even further. Her mother created a butterfly garden and keeps a hummingbird feeder on the porch, and Burkely observes these areas frequently. Her father hunts deer and has stocked the stream with some fish, and as they take walks together, they look for wildlife and admire their surroundings. All this emphasis on the natural world is reflected in Burkely's drawings as well. At age three and a half, she drew a ladybug family with her family's names (1). At age four, she drew a blueberry bush (2), and a camel lying on a pillow (3). At four, one drawing challenge that she spontaneously undertook after a trip to the beach was to show what a horse might look like if it were wearing water wings and swimming in the ocean

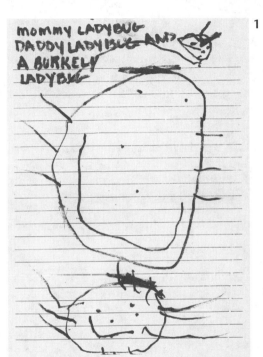

(4). When Burkely was four and a half, she drew a self-portrait that showed her in striped pants (5).

Now that Burkely is nearly five, she has learned to read independently well in advance of most of her peers. She keeps a reading log on the refrigerator door and revises it regularly to keep it up to date.

Burkely's favorite film is a home video she calls "jeeps in mud." An area in their field gets very muddy after a heavy rain and her father likes to drive his jeep there. When her father's jeep got stuck in the mud, he and his friend made a film of it. Now Burkely uses it for entertainment. She tries to get

1

MOMMY LADYBUG DADDY LADYBUG AND A BURKELY LADYBUG

2   **3**

LOVE BURKELY

Camel laying on a pillow

others to sit down and watch the tape with her, laughs delightedly when the tires spin and spray mud everywhere, and offers a running commentary on the incidents that have been recorded on film. Evidently, there is something very funny about adults enjoying themselves just as much as she does by playing in the mud.

When Burkely went trick-or-treating, she dressed in a cat costume. Afterward, she drew a picture of a ghost and the sounds it makes. Then she wrote the words, "Dad and Burkely woo woo woo woo" (6).

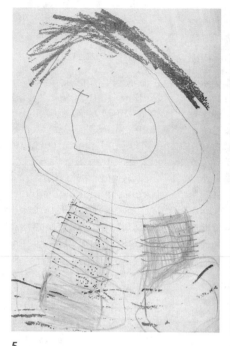

5

6

Discussion Questions

• How have Burkely's interests been shaped by her environment?
• What habits of mind and values have been taught to Burkely through her parents' examples?

• If Burkely was the only child in your class who was drawing representationally, how would you avoid making the other children feel inadequate while at the same time acknowledging and encouraging her talents?

The Artist in You

A Self-Assessment

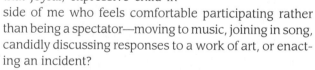

Use the following questions to examine your attitudes and confront possible biases toward the arts.

1. Evidence of high-quality art forms

Would visitors to my classroom routinely see such things as prints of work by famous artists, recordings of quality music of various types, award-winning picture books, and work by children that is distinctive and original? Would they observe children exploring, discovering, inventing, building, and responding through the arts? Do I really believe that "caring about the whole child means caring about arts education" (Feierabend, 1990, p. 19)?

2. Examining biases

Do I avoid stereotyping artists, expecting them to be temperamental or eccentric? Do I regard the arts as an equally worthy activity for boys and girls, as a legitimate career for men and women? Am I open to art and able to

respond freely to it, rather than being overly concerned about the opinions of other adults? Do I strive to maintain contact with that joyful, expressive child inside of me who feels comfortable participating rather than being a spectator—moving to music, joining in song, candidly discussing responses to a work of art, or enacting an incident?

3. Presence of authentic art activities

Do I avoid activities that require excessive adult intervention in order for children to participate and succeed, such as scripted drama, patterns and models for children to copy, or elaborate crafts projects? Is my classroom well stocked with materials that support children's artistic expression, even though these materials can be messy or create clutter—things like paints, clay, crayons, simple musical instruments, dramatic play props, books, records, and tapes? Are there activities in all the arts—music, creative dance, drama, the visual arts, and the language arts?

4. Modeling enthusiasm

Do I cultivate my own interests in the arts by such things as attending concerts and plays, visiting galleries and museums, supporting local craftspeople, or supporting the arts? Do I seek out and take advantage of opportunities for my students to experience the arts and meet real artists?

5. Equity and the arts

Do I remember the fundamental goals of public education by defending every child's right to the expressive arts, rather than focusing all of the attention on children who appear to be gifted and talented in the arts or who can afford special programs, private lessons, and expensive resources?

6. Classism and the arts

Do I tend to associate the fine arts with the upper class and highest income levels? Am I eclectic in my outlook about the arts? Do I appreciate folk art, such as carving or quilting or storytelling, and value its contributions as much as sculpture or tapestry making or poetry?

7. Contributions of the arts

Do I really view the arts and academic subjects as equally important? Do I make the assumption, for example, that 30 minutes of art or music all week is sufficient for a typical school-age child yet feel that 90 minutes a day is not enough to build emerging language abilities?

8. Responsibility for the arts

Do I accept my responsibility for the arts and aesthetics in early childhood even though I am not a performing artist? Am I willing to

- share a song even though I am not a professional musician?
- include creative movement even if I do not have dance training?
- incorporate creative dramatics even though I have no acting experience?
- talk about works of art even if I am not well educated about the classics?

Have I clearly defined my role in bringing children and the arts together?

Situations and Solutions

Seeking Professional Development in the Arts

Situation 1

Miguel sees an announcement that the student affiliate of a professional organization is offering a one-day workshop on children's music. He would like to develop his skills in this area but is inclined not to go because he might have to sing and dance in front of his peers. What would you say or do to counteract Miguel's fear?

Situation 2

After Lisa presents a big book that she made for toddlers to her creative activities class, the instructor asks her if she would be willing to share the book at the "Read-in" sponsored by the local public library. Lisa begs off, saying that she cannot find the time, but actually she is worried that she might be unsuccessful. What could she do to build her confidence?

Situation 3

Jody worked hard during her initial practice teaching experience in second grade and earned an A. After the student teaching assignments for next semester were posted, Jody was disappointed with her assignment. She will be student teaching in a prekindergarten class for four-year-olds and is concerned that so little of her work in second grade will be of any help with this age group. When Jody meets the teacher with whom she will be working, he tells her that her duties during the first week are to observe for the first two days, then take over circle time and story time. Now Jody really panics because she has always avoided singing in public, something that is a part of circle time. If you were Jody, what strategies would you use to plan for circle time and story time?

Situation 4

One of your instructors has reviewed a draft copy of your professional portfolio. In her comments about your philosophy statement, she writes in the margin, "You need to be clearer about how your teaching supports creative expression, promotes the arts, and celebrates diversity." How could you state your ideals in a sentence or two?

Integrating the Arts

Children's Museums and Multicultural Experiences

Australian Donald Horne (1992) has said that museums give us a glimpse of ourselves because they encourage us to more closely examine the social and cultural contexts in which we live. In other words, a museum tells you what a group of people care about and what they think is worth saving. If you have not visited a museum lately or if you think of a museum as a dusty collection of artifacts, you will be pleasantly surprised by contemporary museums, particularly children's museums. Peter Sterling (1993), president of Children's Museum of Indianapolis, explains the emerging philosophy of children's museums: "We are redefining how places of learning can serve people who want to learn" (p. 431). Today's children's museums are more stimulating, interactive, and user-friendly than ever before (Blenz-Lucas, 1993). Three significant trends in children's museums are (1) the use of simulations, (2) multicultural exhibits, and (3) educational resources.

Simulations

One of the more controversial types of exhibits makes life-size or larger-than-life models available for patrons to explore. Milwaukee County Museum has, for example, a diorama of the rain forest. Other children's museums have larger-than-life replicas of portions of the human body, such as a human heart that children can walk through. This is a controversial trend because all the objects in these simulations are replicas and museums have been traditionally associated with real objects (Boyd, 1993). Nevertheless, children (and adults) respond favorably to the opportunity to experience a different environment even if it is not a genuine historical artifact.

Cultural Immersion

Children's museums support the goals of multicultural education as well. At the Boston Children's Museum, for example, you can visit two permanent exhibits that enable you to become fully immersed in another culture's homes. The first is a full-scale, traditional Japanese merchant's house from Kyoto's silk-weaving district. The second permanent exhibit enables you to visit a life-size fully equipped seventeenth-century wigwam as well as a contemporary Native American home. The exhibit was cooperatively planned with Native Americans and is called "We're Still Here: Indians in Southern New England." Their goals are for children to learn about and value their own race and ethnicity, view cultural diversity as an enrichment of their lives, and try to work against racism, discrimination, and prejudice.

The Boston Children's Museum also has traveling exhibitions that support the goals of multicultural education. One is called "The Kids' Bridge" program. As it tours various cities, community advisers contribute the cultural identity of their cities to the program. A portion of the exhibit is called "Neighborhood Windows," a collection of dioramas that depict different holiday traditions. Another part of the program is "Speak to Me," an interactive video program that gives children opportunities to speak in Spanish, Khmer, Canton Chinese, Haitian Creole, and English (Riechers, 1994).

Resources for Educators

Increasingly, museums are offering support to teachers through materials that can be borrowed, in-school programs, and short-term professional development seminars. One item that is available on loan from the Newark Museum in New Jersey is "The Colonial Living Box." It includes a working miniature loom, an old wood carving, miniature rooms and furnishings from the era, and quilt samples. Such collections can be checked out for two weeks for a small fee. One advantage of borrowing these boxes, trunks, and other collections of artifacts is that after children have seen them, they often become excited about creating one of their own related to a topic that they have studied.

Many museums also have in-school programs where representatives of the museum visit the school. These visits sometimes take the place of a museum visit or prepare children for a field trip to the museum.

Other resources for educators include the inexpensive short seminars for teachers and other patrons. When the King Tut exhibit came to Pittsburgh, for example, there was a special seminar about it that furthered participants' understandings about Egyptian times. Along similar lines, the Smithsonian Institution has a summer seminar for teachers on exploring African American art.

Making Your Own Museum

Museum experiences, either real (actual field trips) or vicarious (through videos or in-school programs) can serve as a stimulus for creating a simulated museum in school. For infants, the museum might consist of a follow-the-leader type of activity over different textured fabrics and small obstacles. For the very young, it might be as simple as displaying works of the visual arts in a museum-like way. As children move into the primary grades, they can create a guided tour, complete with an audio or video cassette. Such projects form a natural bridge between the arts and other subject areas like math, science, social studies, and the language arts.

Wallach and Callahan (1994) point out that after children have become involved in visiting and evaluating museums, they can apply those understandings to create an interactive museum of their own. In their project with first graders, the children created a plant museum. Some of their ideas for activities were

- a giant floor puzzle that helps to illustrate farming around the world.
- using pattern blocks to design a garden.
- videotaped dances and musical numbers that interpreted the life cycle of plants in their natural habitats.

Likewise, Diffily (1996) described a rock museum created by kindergartners. The children made floor plans, arranged furniture, labeled specimens, constructed the displays, and created signs and an advertising brochure. They built pedestals out of wood to display their rocks, planned a trip to the geology department of a local university, gathered facts about rocks, and painted a mural that showed their data-collection process. They also produced charts and graphs. For more on constructing simulated museums with older children, see *Make an Interactive Science Museum* (R. Gardner, 1995).

Discussion Questions

- Is there a children's museum where you live? Investigate the resources that they have available.

- How do some of the children's museum activities described here (or others you are aware of) support the goals of aesthetics as well as the goals of multicultural education?
- What museum-type activities can you imagine doing with your students? What simulations, boxes/trunks, or other projects do you envision?

Children's Books about Museums

Bjork, C. (1987). *Linnea in Monet's garden.* New York: Farrar, Straus, & Giroux.

Brown, L. K. (1986). *Visiting the art museum.* New York: Dutton.

Kremetz, J. (1987). *A visit to Washington, D.C.* New York: Scholastic.

Mayers, F. C. (1986). *The Museum of Fine Arts, Boston: ABC.* New York: Abrams.

Mayers, F. C. (1986). *The Museum of Modern Art, New York: ABC.* New York: Abrams.

Mayers, F. C. (1988). *Egyptian art from the Brooklyn Museum: ABC.* New York: Abrams.

Micklethwait, L. (1992). *I spy: An alphabet in art.* New York: Greenwillow.

Micklethwait, L. (1996). *A child's book of play in art.* New York: Dorling Kindersley.

Vincent, G. (1986). *Where are you, Ernest and Celestine?* New York: Greenwillow.

Individual and Group Projects for Teachers

Learning What It Means to Be Artful

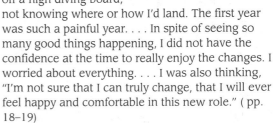

How adaptable and flexible are you? When you are called upon to make a significant change in your behavior, how do you usually respond? Is it with butterflies in your stomach, but a smile on your face? Is it with teeth gritted, grumbling under your breath? Is it full of enthusiasm and hopeful dreams that the changes you institute will be for the better?

As adults, one of the biggest projects you will ever undertake is making changes in yourself. In fact, you are working on it right now. If you are not yet a teacher, your project is to become one. If you already are, your project is to become an even better teacher. Here is how Humphrey (1989) candidly described her struggle to transform her class to a more child-centered, developmentally appropriate environment:

Never having coped well with sudden decisions and change, I was an emotional wreck. I felt physically

ill, out of control, and I pictured myself jumping off a high diving board, not knowing where or how I'd land. The first year was such a painful year. . . . In spite of seeing so many good things happening, I did not have the confidence at the time to really enjoy the changes. I worried about everything. . . . I was also thinking, "I'm not sure that I can truly change, that I will ever feel happy and comfortable in this new role." (pp. 18–19)

This teacher was also concerned about criticism from administrators and parents as she moved away from a rigid, academically oriented curriculum and toward a play-based curriculum that would give children choices and opportunities for creative expression:

What would the principal think if he walked in and saw these children playing and moving freely from one activity to another? What would parents think when these children proudly brought home these odd-looking creations they made on their own. . . . What would first grade teachers think when they found out I was no longer "getting children ready" for first grade? It was an exciting but worrisome year, and I felt as though I were involved in some sort of subversive activity. (Humphrey, 1989, pp. 18–19).

This is one type of "self-work" that teachers do—rethinking the curriculum. Even more fundamental is refashioning ourselves, not only as teachers but also as artful human beings. Stephens (1994) speaks to this issue when she writes:

Even though I am 46 years old . . . I have just begun, in the last two or three years, to understand what it means to be artful. My parents could have taught me, of course, if they themselves had known. But they did not. As a child, I never went to a concert, heard an orchestra, saw a ballet, or went to an art gallery. My teachers could have taught me, of course, if they themselves had known; but because they did not do so, I suspect that they were ignorant of art, that they did not know what it meant to be artful.

And so I stand here today—feeling artless . . . (p. 34)

Perhaps you too have felt "artless" in one or more areas of the arts. Think about all of the expressions we use to exclude and excuse ourselves from art:

"I can't draw a straight line."
"I have two left feet."
"I must be tone deaf."
"I'm just not creative."
"I can't carry a tune."
"I'm artistically challenged."
"I get stage fright."
"I'm not very cultured."

Interestingly, the vast majority of preschoolers do not say that they cannot or do not know how to draw, dance, sing, or dramatize. They assume that they can do or learn to do these things and are willing to give the arts a try. By the time most children enter the primary grades, things change. Now children have picked up the message that they will be criticized, compared, and found lacking. As teachers of young children, we have to undertake the project of letting go of some of our own negative experiences in the arts so that they do not seep into our classrooms and get passed on to the young child. A teacher who recalls that her paintings were seldom good enough to be put on the bulletin board can go one of two ways: she can vow never to do the same thing in her class, or she will perpetuate the practice of judging her students' work. A teacher who recalls feeling awkward during dance can go one of two ways: he can ignore dance out of his own discomfort or strive to change his outlook in the interest of enabling his students to have pleasurable associations with dance experiences. Every early childhood educator must resolve to give the young children in her or his class high-quality arts experiences. "The children in our classrooms deserve to understand about art and about being artful, and we, their teachers, need to teach them, even if what that means is that, as teachers, we learn along with them" (Stephens, 1994, p. 34).

Discussion Questions

- Reflect upon your early memories of school. What arts experiences, both good and bad, do you recall? What will you do to make the arts come alive for the children in your classes?
- In what areas of the arts curriculum will you need to "learn along with" the children?
- Try to conceptualize an action plan for becoming more artful. What will your long-range goals be? What short-range goals will you need to accomplish in order to get there? Design a drawing, map, staircase, or chart that depicts your journey to becoming more artful.

REFERENCES

Alejandro, A. (1994). Like happy dreams—integrating visual arts, writing, and reading. *Language Arts, 71*, 12–21.

Ayers, W. (1995). Joining the ranks. In W. Ayers (Ed.), *To become a teacher: Making a difference in children's lives* (pp. 1–9). New York: Teachers College Press.

Baker, D. W. (1990). The visual arts in early childhood education. *Design for Arts in Education, 91*, 21–25.

Baker, D. W. (1992). *Toward a sensible education: Inquiring into the role of the visual arts in early childhood education.* Urbana, IL: ERIC Document Reproduction Service No. ED356080.

Blenz-Clucas, B. (1993). Bring the museum to the media center. *School Library Journal, 39*, 150–153.

Bluestein, J. (comp.). (1995). *Mentors, masters, and Mrs. MacGregor: Stories of teachers making a difference.* Deerfield Beach, FL: Health Communications.

Boyd, W. L. (1993). Museums as centers of learning. *Teachers College Record, 94*(4), 761–770.

Boyer, E. L. (1995). *The basic school: A community for learning.* Washington, DC: Carnegie Foundation for the Advancement of Teaching.

Cortines, R. C. (1994). *The arts: Partnerships as a catalyst for educational reform.* Sacramento: California Department of Education.

Csikszentmihalyi, M. (1993). *The evolving self: A psychology for the third millennium.* New York: HarperPerrenial.

Csikszentmihalyi, M., & Csikszentmihalyi, I. S. (Eds.). (1988). *Optimal experiences: Studies of flow in consciousness.* New York: Cambridge University Press.

Csikszentmihalyi, M., & Schiefele, U. (1992). Arts education, human development, and the quality of experience. In B. Reimer & R. A. Smith (Eds.), *The arts, education, and aesthetic knowing* (pp. 169–191). Ninety-first yearbook of the National Society for the Study of Education (Part 2). Chicago: University of Chicago Press.

Diffily, D. (1996). The project approach: A museum exhibit created by kindergartners. *Young Children, 51*(2), 72–75.

Eisner, E. W. (1991a). What the arts taught me about education. *Art Education, 44*(5), 10–19.

Eisner, E. W. (1991b). *The enlightened eye.* New York: Macmillan.

Feierabend, J. (1990). Music in early childhood. *Design for Arts in Education, 91,* 15–20.

Gardner, R. (1995). *Make an interactive science museum.* New York: McGraw-Hill.

Giroux, H. (1992). *Border crossings: Schools and the politics of education.* New York: Routledge.

Greene, M. (1978). *Landscapes of learning.* New York: Teachers College Press.

Greenman, J. (1994). Institutionalized childhoods: Reconsidering our part in the lives of children. *Child Care Information Exchange, 100,* 63–67.

Horne, D. (1992, January). Look at museums and find yourself. *The Weekend Australian,* January 4–5, Adelaide.

Humphrey, S. (1989). The case of myself. *Young Children, 45*(1), 17–22.

Isenberg, J. P., & Jalongo, M. R. (1997). *Creative expression and play in early childhood.* Englewood Cliffs, NJ: Merrill/Prentice Hall.

Jalongo, M. R. (1990). The child's right to the expressive arts: Nurturing the imagination as well as the intellect. *Childhood Education 66*(4), 195–201.

London, P. (1994). *Step outside: Community-based art education.* Portsmouth, NH: Heinemann.

May, R. (1972). *Power and influence.* New York: W. W. Norton.

Naisbitt, J. (1992). Futurist forsees arts renaissance. *ASCD Update, 34*(5), 5.

Reimer, B. (1992). What knowledge is of most worth in the arts? In B. Reimer & R. A. Smith (Eds.), *The arts, education, and aesthetic knowing* (pp. 20–50). Ninety-first yearbook of the National Society for the Study of Education (Part 2). Chicago: University of Chicago Press.

Riechers, M. (1994). A place of their own: Boston's Children's Museum. *Humanities, 15*(1), 32–35.

Sapon-Shevin, M. (1995). Building a safe community for learning. In W. Ayers (Ed.), *To become a teacher: Making a difference in children's lives* (pp. 99–112). New York: Teachers College Press.

Sarason, S. B. (1995). *Parental involvement and the political principle: Why the existing governance structure of schools should be abolished.* San Francisco: Jossey-Bass.

Stephens, D. (1994). Learning that art means. *Language Arts, 71,* 34–37.

Sterling, P. (1993). In Cammack, N. Rex's lending center a roaring success. *American Libraries, 24,* 428–431.

Stinson, S. W. (1992). Reflections on student experience in dance education. *Design for Arts in Education, 93*(5), 21–27.

Stubbs, T. (1992). *An ascension handbook.* Livermore, CA: Oughten House.

Veale, A. (1992). Arts education for young children of the 21st century. South Australia ERIC Document Reproduction Service No. ED351124.

Wallach, C., & Callahan, S. (1994). The 1st grade plant museum. *Educational Leadership, 52*(3), 32–34.

Children's Books and Recordings

Ginsburg, M. (1987). *Four brave sailors.* New York: Greenwillow.

The Child's Bill of Rights in Music

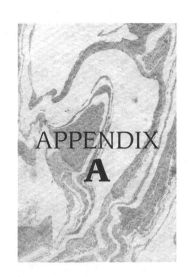

Music Educators National Conference 1991

The Music Educators National Conference believes that every American child should have the following rights to instruction in music and urges that these rights be recognized and guaranteed by educational funding authorities, school administrators, and the public:

1. As their right, all children at every level must have access to a balanced, comprehensive, and sequential program of music instruction in school taught by teachers qualified in music.

2. As their right, all children must be given the opportunity to explore and develop their musical abilities to the fullest extent possible through instruction that is equal to that provided in the other basic subjects of the curriculum and is responsive to the individual needs of each child.

3. As their right, all children must receive the finest possible education in music, every child must have an equal opportunity to study music, and the quality and quantity of children's music instruction must not depend upon their geographical location, social status, racial or ethnic status, urban/suburban/rural residence, or parental or community wealth.

4. As their right, all children must receive extensive opportunities to sing, play at least one instrument, compose, improvise, and listen to music.

5. As their right, all children must have the opportunity to study music of diverse periods, styles, forms, and cultures, including samples of the various musics of the world and music that reflects the multimusical nature of our pluralistic American culture.

6. As their right, all children must have the opportunity to develop their abilities to analyze music with discrimination, to understand the historical and cultural backgrounds of the music they encounter, to make relevant critical judgments about music and performances, and to deal with aesthetic issues relevant to music.

7. As their right, all children must have the opportunity to grow in music knowledge, skills, and appreciation so as to bring joy and satisfaction to their lives, challenge their minds, stimulate their imaginations, and exalt their spirits.

How to Teach a Song to Young Children

Basically, there are two types of singing that should be encouraged in the early childhood classroom: spontaneous and structured. Spontaneous singing occurs when children sing in a playful, improvisational manner and adapt or invent songs to suit an activity. A child who sings an answer to a question, singsongs a phrase from a story, or invents a song lullaby while rocking a baby doll is singing spontaneously. In structured singing, the child is expected to imitate a predetermined song's pitch, rhythm, harmony, lyrics, gestures, and so forth. Learning to do something as apparently simple as singing "Eency Weency Spider" with the accompanying gestures is a complex skill. Therefore, if children are to learn to sing, teachers must teach them to sing rather than expecting them to "pick up" a song on their own from hearing it played in the background (Phillips, 1993). Before attempting to teach a song, the teacher should consider the following points:

1. **The song must appeal to the children.** Generally speaking, young children prefer songs with

   • a clear rhythm, rhyme, and/or repetition.
   • a physical activity (e.g., gestures or body movements) or musical accompaniment (e.g., a rhythm band).
   • a pleasing melody that they can at least approximate.
   • a topic that is familiar or one that stimulates the imagination.

2. **The teacher should be thoroughly familiar with the song.** You should select songs that you enjoy, songs that you are excited about sharing with the children, and songs that you can sing well. If you are certain that you cannot sing "on key," use a good-quality recording. Be sure that you have practiced presenting the song until there is no chance of forgetting the words or the melody. If you intend to use a recording, assemble the equipment and figure out the procedures in advance so that you do not need to leave the children waiting while you fumble around trying to locate the song on record, tape, or CD. We recommend planning a program of two to five songs (depending on the children's stage of development and the difficulty of the material). Your musical program would

typically consist of one song that is new to the children and others that are already familiar. Consider copying the specific songs you will use onto a ten-minute blank cassette tape designed specifically for this purpose. (A package of four of these blank tapes is available for $4.50 from World Class Tapes at 1–800–365–0669.)

3. **The song should be developmentally suited to the children.** Most preschoolers, for example, would find it difficult to learn a lengthy song with several verses, so using short songs or inviting them to sing only the chorus while you sing the verses would be more appropriate. Vocal range is another important consideration—a young child cannot sing along with a female soprano voice. Haines and Gerber (1996) report that very young singers do best in the range from middle C up to A. Most of the songs that are found in songbooks for young children are within this range. As more accurate singing develops during kindergarten and first grade, most children's vocal range is expanded downward to B and upward to the B' octave. If you do not understand music, ask someone who does to evaluate a particular song that you have in mind.

   When you have a singing session with young children, pay attention to how they respond to the songs that you share. Do they move their bodies? Try to sing along? Ask to sing the song again? Request the song at a later time? Keep some observational notes and consider audio- or videotaping some of your singalong sessions so that you can assess the children's responses (Jalongo & Collins, 1985).

4. **There should be a compelling purpose for teaching this song.** Ask yourself, why teach this song to a particular group of children at a specific time? It is not enough to teach a song simply because it happens to mention a squirrel and you are teaching a unit on the fall! Nor can you assume that a song is automatically a good choice for your students simply because it was taught to you as a child. Some sound reasons for teaching songs to children are as follows: because learning the songs is an important part of culture and tradition (e.g., Ruth Seeger's American folk songs for children), because the songs will delight children and enhance their enjoyment and appreciation of music (e.g., teaching children "Bingo" using a hand puppet with a dog and a letter on each finger and thumb), or because the song develops a musical concept (e.g., using "John Jacob Jingle-heimer Schmidt" to teach loud and soft).

5. **Have a careful plan for introducing the song as well as the procedure to be used in teaching it.** There is no single way to teach a new song to children, and most experts recommend a procedure such as the following:

   Focus the children's interest. Begin with a real object, pictures, recorded music, a musical instrument, or something remarkable about the song. You could introduce "I Know an Old Lady Who Swallowed a Fly" with a cardboard cutout of the lady and a plastic bag "stomach" that includes pictures of every animal she devours, for instance. You might use a big book of a song and discuss the pictures before singing it. Children could be asked to close their eyes and listen or to identify certain words (rhyming, silly words, days of the week, etc.). A child who has special knowledge about a song can also be invited to share. A child who speaks Spanish might be asked to provide some of the words in the Spanish version of "Today Is Monday" (e.g., "Hoy, Hoy Es Lunes" in Haines & Gerber, 1996, p. 140).

   Sing and/or play the song. If the children are young or the song is generally unfamiliar, you may want to present one line at a time or teach the children to sing just the chorus.

   Establish a starting pitch. Begin the song at a pitch that is low enough for most children to sing. Hum the pitch (or play it on a small keyboard or glockenspiel), then cue the children by saying, "One, two, ready, sing," in the same tempo as the song.

Repeat the song. After the children have heard the song and sung it, try adding movement, gestures, or simple rhythm instruments. Here are several strategies for repeating a song without making it tedious:

- Hum the tune so that children can concentrate on just the melody, for example, playing a pretend horn to the tune of "Baby Beluga." (Raffi uses this technique on his video *A Young Children's Concert with Raffi,* 1984.)
- Add children's names to the song; for example, use magnetic name cards to sing "Pawpaw Patch" with various children's names inserted.
- Add motions to the song, for example, the gestures to go with "The Wheels on the Bus."
- Sing the song faster or slower, more loudly or softly; for example, sing "The Ants Go Marching" with second graders in a lively fashion before reading Chris Van Allsburg's (1988) *Two Bad Ants,* then sing it slowly after the ants return from their adventure. Try Joe Scruggs' (1995) medley of songs and chants on his album *Ants.*
- Ask children to listen for parts that are alike or repeated, for example, the chorus of the Russian song "May There Always Be Sunshine" (Cockburn & Steinbergh, 1991).
- Clap or play a rhythm to the beat or pulse of the song, for example, snapping fingers to "Head 'n' Shoulders, Baby" or a train chugging to Sweet Honey in the Rock's version of "Little Red Caboose."
- Look at a published picture-book version of the song or at a song chart or big book created by the teacher while listening to the recording again, for example, Tom Glazer's (1977) parody of "On Top of Old Smokey" called "On Top of Spaghetti."
- Play accompanying chords on an autoharp or omnichord (electronic autoharp), or play the melody on a music maker (a stringed instrument with picture cards to follow) or toy xylophone, for example, playing a simple Mother Goose song like "Baa Baa Black Sheep."
- Use toys and equipment, for example, a pond made of a plastic basin and six bath-toy ducks to sing "Six Little Ducks" or a rocking horse to mark the rhythm of and dramatize "Froggie Went a-Courtin'."
- Use a story map to accompany a repetition of a song, for example, "Over the River and through the Woods."
- Create word and/or picture cards to remind children of the verses, for example, the animals' names, numbers, and actions in "Over in the Meadow."

REFERENCES AND RECOMMENDED RESOURCES

Andress, B., & Walker, L. (Eds.). *Readings in early childhood music education.* Reston, VA: Music Educators' National Conference.

Bayless, K. M., & Ramsey, M. (1991). *Music: A way of life for the young child* (4th ed.). Columbus, OH: Merrill.

Campbell, P. S., & Scott-Kassner, C. (1995). *Music in childhood.* New York: Schirmer.

Cockburn, V., & Steinbergh, J. (1991). *Where I come from! Poems and songs from many cultures.* Chestnut Hill, MA: Talking Stone Productions.

Glazer, T. (1977). *Let's sing fingerplays.* New York: CMS Records.

Graham, R. M., & Beer, A. S. (1980). *Teaching music to the exceptional child.* Englewood Cliffs, NJ: Prentice Hall.

Haines, B. J. E., & Gerber, L. L. (1996). *Leading young children to music* (5th ed.). Englewood Cliffs, NJ: Prentice Hall.

Hallworth, G. (Ed.). (1996). *Afro-Caribbean rhymes, games, and songs for children.* New York: Scholastic.

Jalongo, M. R., & Collins, M. (1985). Singing with young children! Folk singing for nonmusicians. *Young Children, 40*(2), 17–21.

McDonald, D. T., & Simons, G. M. (1989). *Musical growth*

and development: Birth through six. New York: Schirmer.

Phillips, K. H. (1993). Back to basics: Teaching children to sing. *General Music Today, 6*(3), 30–31.

Raffi (Producer), & Devine, D. (Director). (1984). *A young children's concert with Raffi* [Videotape]. Hollywood, CA: A&M/Troubadour.

Scruggs, J. (1995). *Ants* [Cassette]. Austin, TX: Educational Graphics.

Van Allsburg, C. (1988). *Two bad ants.* Boston: Houghton Mifflin.

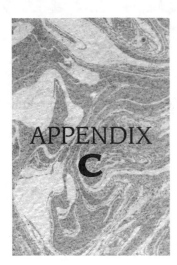

Recorded Music and Rhymes for Young Children

Nonmusician teachers often find songbooks to be of limited value. If you are like most early childhood educators and cannot read music or play an instrument, the recordings listed in the appendix will enable you to quickly revive your knowledge of singing and listening favorites for children. As you scan through the list, you will probably recognize many of the titles, recall some of the words, and remember a few melodies. For other songs, you will find that you remember them only after you have heard them sung. For still other songs and rhymes, learning them will be an exciting new discovery. Keep working on building your repertoire of songs that you can sing and rhymes that you can recite with the children.

Unfortunately, most high-quality children's recordings will not be found at your local record store. You probably will need to use mail-order sources or a bookstore that specializes in materials for children or teachers in order to locate good sources. The difficulty with ordering sight unseen and sound unheard is that you often do not know what songs are on each album or whether you will like the recording. In order to aid you in this process of locating traditional and familiar songs, we recommend the following artists and albums. You will find that a few carefully selected albums may be sufficient to reactivate or begin building your song repertoire. For your basic lullaby collection, try Pat Carfa, Priscilla Herdman, Linda Arnold, and the Music for Little People lullaby collections. To build your basic action song collection, include Ella Jenkins (especially her videos *For the Family* and *Live! at the Smithsonian*), Hap Palmer (*So Big*), and Tonya Weimer (*Fingerplays and Action Chants*); for contemporary music, try Joe Scruggs, the Roches, and Bill Shontz (*Animal Tales*); for traditional folk music and new variations, include Pete Seeger, Burl Ives, John Langstaff, John McCutcheon, and Fred Penner; for albums that offer a wide array of musical styles, try Steve Rashid (*Fidgety Feet*) and Sharon, Lois, and Bram. To start your classical collection, consider John Schaefer (*Klassix for Kids*), and for opera, Luciano Pavarotti (*My Favorite Showstoppers* and *My Favorite Opera for Children*). For access to the largest number of songs performed with simple accompaniments, try the Wee Sing books, tapes, and videos or Sesame Street's Bob McGrath, and for strong harmonies, consider The Chenille Sisters' *1, 2, 3 for Kids*. The list that follows shows you where to find specific songs, fingerplays, and action rhymes that are generally a part of the early childhood curriculum.

ADVANTAGES OF RECORDED MUSIC

Recorded music can make important contributions to teachers' and children's musical experiences. Donna Brink Fox (1992) enumerates several advantages of recorded music that are elaborated on here:

1. Recorded music provides examples of songs that we can sing ourselves and models of how to sing expressively, and it illustrates how the same song can be presented in a unique style. Recorded music often demonstrates (particularly in the case of live concert tapes or videos) recommended ways of learning a song.
2. Recorded music supplies a wide array of musical styles and accompaniments that offer excitement and invite listeners to join in the singing. Children can hear music they might not otherwise encounter in their environments—authentic music from other cultures or lands such as a mariachi band or a kalimba (thumb piano) from Africa. When young children listen to recorded music, they can encounter various kinds of singing—a soloist, an *a capella* group, a chorus of children, or a trio who sing in three-part harmony.
3. Recorded music enables young children to make deliberate choices of music, listen to favorite selections as often as they wish, and participate in singing along as a part of their everyday activities.

Here are some of our favorite musical recordings for young children along with a list of specific songs you might want to include in your singalong repertoire:

Linda Arnold

Arnold, L. (1994). *Lullaby land*. Hollywood, CA: A&M Records.
Starlight, Starbright
Twinkle, Twinkle Little Star
Hush, Little Baby
Brahms' Lullaby
All through the Night

Arnold, L. (1995). *Sing along stew*. Hollywood, CA: A&M Records.
Six Little Ducks
She'll Be Comin' Round the Mountain
Wheels on the Bus
This Old Man
We're Off to See the Wizard
High Hopes
This Little Light of Mine
Down by the Bay
De Colores
Day-O
Yankee Doodle
Camptown Races
Turkey in the Straw
If I Had a Hammer

Hoyt Axton

Axton, H. (1995). *Jeremiah was a bullfrog!* Available from Wilmington, NC: Educational Record Center.
Oh, Susannah!

On Top of Spaghetti
Happy Trails
Arkansas Traveler

Joanie Bartels

Bartels, J. (1990). *Sillytime magic*. New York: Discovery/BMG Music.
The Name Game
The Alphabet Song
Do Your Ears Hang Low?
Swinging on a Star
Supercalifragilisticexpialidocious
This Old Man
Animal Crackers in My Soup
Mairzy Doats

Pamela Conn Beale and Susan Hagen Nipp

Beale, P. C., & Nipp, S. H. (1994). *Wee sing around the world*. Los Angeles: Price Stern Sloan.
Going over the Sea (Canada)
Eentsy Weentsy Spider (USA)
Tingalayo (West Indies)
El Coqui (Puerto Rico)
Chi Chi Bud (Jamaica)
Brown Girl in the Ring (Guyana)
Los Pollitos (Peru)
Wee Falorie Man (Ireland)
Frère Jacques (France)
Alle Meine Entlein—All My Little Ducklings (Germany)
Zum Gali Gali (Israel)

Beale, P. C., & Nipp, S. H. (1987). *Wee Sing America*. Los Angeles: Price Stern Sloan.
You're a Grand Old Flag
Three Cheers for the Red, White, and Blue
America
Yankee Doodle
Dixie
When Johnny Comes Marching Home
Sweet Betsy from Pike
The Old Chisolm Trail
Git Along, Little Dogies
The Boll Weevil
Pick a Bale of Cotton
Cape Cod Chantey
Blow the Man Down
Erie Canal

Buckwheat Zydeco

Buckwheat Zydeco (1994). *Choo choo boogaloo*. Redway, CA: Music for Little People.
Get on Board
Iko Iko
Cotton Fields (The Cotton Song)
Crawfish Song
I've Been Working on the Railroad
Skip to My Lou
Little Red Caboose

Michael "Beausoleil" Doucet

Doucet, M. (1992). *Le hoogie boogie: Louisiana French music for children*. Cambridge, MA: Rounder Records.
Le Hoogie Boogie (Louisiana French version of the Hokey Pokey)

Tom Glazer

Glazer, T. (1977). *Let's sing fingerplays*. New York: CMS Records.
Grandma's Spectacles
The Barnyard Song
The Bear Went over the Mountain
Bingo
Charlie over the Water
Eye Winker, Tom Tinker, Chin Chopper
Five Little Ducks
Go in and out the Window

Jerry Garcia and David Grisman

Garcia, J., & Grisman, D. (1993). *Not for kids only*. Available from Redway, CA: Music for Little People. (Acoustic disc)
Jenny Jenkins
Freight Train
Arkansas Traveler
Teddy Bears' Picnic

Ladysmith Black Mambazo

Ladysmith Black Mambazo. (1994). *The gift of the tortoise*. Redway, CA: Music for Little People.
Mbube (The Lion Sleeps Tonight)

John Langstaff

Langstaff, J. (1995). *Making music with children (ages 3 to 7)*. Berkeley, CA: The Langstaff Video Project. (Videotape)
Jeremiah, Blow the Fire
Jim Along, Josie
The Muffin Man
Sally Go 'Round the Moon

Cheryl Warren Mattox

Mattox, C. W. (1986). *Shake it to the one you love the best: Play songs and lullabies from Black musical traditions*. Nashville, TN: JTG.
Little Sally Walker
Mary Mack
Hambone
Kumbaya
Shortnin' Bread

John McCutcheon

McCutcheon, J. (1988). *Mail myself to you*. Appalseed Records.
Over in the Meadow
Mail Myself to You
I'm a Little Cookie
Somos El Barco
Hambone
Turn Around

Bob McGrath (from Sesame Street)

McGrath, B. (1984). *If you're happy and you know it sing along with Bob*. New York: Kids' Records.
The Farmer in the Dell
Happy Birthday
I'm a Little Teapot
Looby Loo
She'll Be Comin' Round the Mountain
Hush Little Baby
Frère Jacques
John Jacob Jingle Heimer Schmidt
Mary Had a Little Lamb
You Are My Sunshine
Oh Susanna

Lisa Monet

Monet, L. (1986). *Circle time*. Redway, CA: Music for Little People.
If You're Happy and You Know It
Five Little Speckled Frogs

Here Is the Beehive (fingerplay)
Little Red Caboose
Little Teapot
Head and Shoulders
The More We Get Together
Teddy Bear (action rhyme)
Five Little Seashells (fingerplay)
Baa Baa Black Sheep
This Old Man
Here Is a Bunny (fingerplay)
Two Little Blackbirds (fingerplay)
ABC Song
One, Two, Buckle My Shoe

Maria Muldaur

Muldaur, M. (1993). *On the sunny side*. Redway, CA: Music for Little People.
Side by Side
Mockingbird Hill
Would You Like to Swing on a Star?

Music for Little People (various artists)

Music for Little People. (1990). *Family folk festival*. Redway, CA: Author.
Skip to My Lou (John McCutcheon)
Little Red Caboose (Sweet Honey in the Rock)
Puff the Magic Dragon (Amber McInnis)
Grandfather's Clock (Doc Watson)
I Had a Rooster (Pete Seeger)

Music For Little People (1992). *A child's celebration of showtunes*. Redway, CA: Author.
Do Re Mi (Julie Andrews)
Whistle a Happy Tune (Alan Amick and Constance Towers)
My Favorite Things (Julie Andrews)
I Won't Grow Up (Mary Martin)
Getting to Know You (Constance Towers and Chorus)
Consider Yourself (Michael Goodman and Bruce Prochnik)
Put On a Happy Face (Dick Van Dyke and Janet Leigh)
Music for Little People (1992). *A child's celebration of song*. Redway, CA: Music for Little People.
Polly Wolly Doodle (Burl Ives)
This Old Man (Pete Seeger)
Skip to My Lou (John McCutcheon)
Over the Rainbow (Judy Garland)
Baby Beluga (Raffi)
The Banana Boat Song (Taj Mahal)
Wynken, Blynken, & Nod (The Doobie Brothers)

Tom Paxton

Paxton, T. (1984). *The marvelous toy and other gallimaufry*. Los Angeles: Linden Tree Books and Records.

Englebert the Elephant
The Marvelous Toy
Going to the Zoo
My Dog's Bigger Than Your Dog

Fred Penner

Penner, F. (1989). *Collections*. Los Angeles, CA: A&M Records.
If I Knew You Were Comin' (I'd Have Baked a Cake)
The Cat Came Back (chant)
Car Car Song
A House Is a House for Me (from Mary Ann Hoberman's book)
Ghost Riders in the Sky
Marvelous Toy

Peter Paul and Mary

Peter, Paul and Mary. (1971). *Peter, Paul & Mommy*. Burbank, CA: Warner Brothers.
The Marvelous Toy
Day Is Done
All through the Night
It's Raining
Going to the Zoo
Boa Constrictor
Puff the Magic Dragon

Raffi

Raffi. (1976). *Singable songs for the very young*. Hollywood, CA: A&M Records.
The More We Get Together
Brush Your Teeth (chant)
Aikendrum
Must Be Santa
Mr. Sun
Baa Baa Black Sheep
Going to the Zoo
Raffi (1977). *More singable songs for the very young*. Hollywood, CA: A&M.
Who Built the Ark?
Shake My Sillies Out
Working on the Railroad
Six Little Ducks
You Gotta Sing
Raffi (1985). *One light, one sun*. Hollywood, CA: A & M
Apples and Bananas
Take Me Out to the Ballgame
Tingalayo
De Colores
Twinkle, Twinkle Little Star

Kevin Roth

Roth, K. (1994). *Train songs and other tracks*. Unionville, PA: Marlboro Records.

The City of New Orleans
If I Had a Hammer
I've Been Working on the Railroad
New River Train
Five Hundred Miles
Theme from Shining Time Station

Sharon, Lois, & Bram

Sharon, Lois, & Bram (1979). *Smorgasboard*. Toronto, ON: Elephant Records.
Peanut Butter (chant)
Head 'n' Shoulders, Baby
Jenny Jenkins
Michael Finnegan
Little Sally Saucer
Train Is a-Comin'
Sharon, Lois, & Bram (1980). *Singing 'n' swinging*. Toronto, ON: Elephant Records.
Charlie over the Ocean (play rhyme)
All Hid (chant)
Doctor Knickerbocker (action rhyme)
The Ants Go Marching
The Muffin Man
The Cat Came Back (chant)
Sharon, Lois, & Bram (1984). *Mainly Mother Goose*. Toronto, ON: Elephant Records.
Humpty Dumpty
Simple Simon
This Is the Way the Ladies Ride (play rhyme)
Yankee Doodle
The Three Little Kittens
Hickory, Dickory Dock
Pease Porridge (chant)
Pop! Goes the Weasel
Rain, Rain Go Away
Oh, Dear What Can the Matter Be?
Old Woman, Old Woman
Sharon, Lois, & Bram (1986). *Elephant show record*. Toronto, ON: Elephant Records.
One Elephant Went Out to Play
London Bridge
Ten in the Bed
Rig-a-jig-jig
Take Me Out to the Ballgame
The Wheels on the Bus
Going to the Zoo
There's a Little Wheel a-Turning in My Heart
Sharon, Lois, & Bram (1987). *Stay tuned*. Toronto, ON: Elephant Records.
We're Gonna Shine
Do Your Ears Hang Low?
Little Liza Jane
A-tisket, A-tasket
How Much Is That Doggie in the Window?

The Hokey Pokey
Miss Lucy (The Lady with the Alligator Purse)
Sharon, Lois, & Bram. (1995). *Sing around the campfire*. Toronto, ON: Elephant Records.
Bingo
Mister Sun
"A" You're Adorable
Do Your Ears Hang Low?

Judith Steinbergh and Victor Cockburn

Steinbergh, J., & Cockburn, V. (1991). *Where I come from! Poems and songs from many cultures*. Chestnut Hill, MA: Talking Stone Productions. (Distributed by Troubadour: 617–734–1416)
De Colores (accompanied by an authentic mariachi band)
May There Always Be Sunshine
Various American playground chants and chants from other lands
London Bridge
Train Is a-Comin'
Cancion de Pedro
Abrazos (Hugs)
Somos el Barco

Tickle Tune Typhoon

Tickle Tune Typhoon (1983). *Circle around*. Seattle: Tickle Tune Typhoon.
Bear Hunt
Clap Your Hands
Magic Penny

Doc Watson

Watson, D. (1990). *Doc Watson sings songs for little pickers*. Waterbury, VT: Alacazam.
Mole in the Ground
Froggy Went a-Courtin'
Sing Song Kitty
The Crawdad Song
Shady Grove
The Riddle Song
The Green Grass Grew All Around
Liza Jane

ADDITIONAL RESOURCES

Anthony, R. M. (1990). *Fun with choral speaking*. Englewood, CO: Teacher Ideas Press.
Brady, M., & Gleason, P. T. (1994). *Art starts: Music, movement, puppetry, and storytelling activities*. Englewood, CO: Teacher Ideas Press.
Brown, M. (1980). *Finger rhymes*. New York: Dutton.
Brown, M. (1985). *Hand rhymes*. New York: Dutton.

Cohn, A. L. (1993). *From sea to shining sea: A treasury of American folklore and folk songs*. New York: Scholastic.

Cole, J., & Calmenson, S. (1991). *The eentsy, weentsy spider: Fingerplays and action rhymes*. New York: Mulberry.

Cole, J., & Calmenson, S. (1992). *Pat-a-cake and other play rhymes*. New York: Mulberry.

Drew, H. (1993). *My first music book*. New York: Dorling-Kindersley.

Fox, D. B. (1992). A guide to recorded music for young children. *General Music Today, 6*(1), 27–29.

Glazer, T. (1974). *Eye winker, Tom Tinker, Chin chopper: Fifty musical fingerplays*. New York: Doubleday.

Glazer, T. (1980). *Do your ears hang low? Fifty more musical fingerplays*. New York: Doubleday.

Green, J. (1989). *Green book: Songs classified by subject* (3rd ed.). Smyrna, TN: Professional Desk References.

Guilmartin, K. (1992). *Music and your child: A guide for parents and caregivers*. Princeton, NJ: Music and Movement Center. (Tape, songbook and guide)

Honig, A. S. (1995). Singing with infants and toddlers. *Young Children, 50*(5), 72–78.

Jarnow, J. (1991). *All ears: How to choose and use recorded music for children*. New York: Penguin.

Jenkins, E. (1966). *The Ella Jenkins song book for children*. New York: Oak Publications.

Kleiner, L. (1995). *Kids make music music music*. Redway, CA: Music for Little People. (Instructional video that shows how to teach children basic music skills)

Krull, K. (1992). *Gonna sing my head off! American folk songs for children*. New York: Knopf.

Lax, R., & Smith, F. (1989). *The great song thesaurus* (2nd ed.). New York. Oxford University Press.

Levine, D. B. (1993). *Music through children's literature: Theme and variations*. Englewood, CO: Libraries Unlimited/Teacher Ideas Press.

MacDonald, M. R. (1995). *Bookplay: 101 creative themes to share with young children*. Seattle: Library Professional Publications/Shoestring Press.

Mattox, C. W. (1993). *Let's get the rhythm of the band: Music from African-American culture with history and song*. Nashville, TN: JTG.

Oppenheim, J., & Oppenheim, S. (1996). *The best toys, books, and videos for kids*. Oppenheim Toy Portfolio.

Reid, R. (1995). *Children's jukebox: A subject guide to musical recordings and programming ideas for songsters ages one to twelve*. Chicago: American Library Association.

Schwann record and tape guide. Schwann compact disc guide. Published monthly.

Snow, A. (1988). *Index of songs on children's recordings*. Eugene, OR: Staccato Press.

Weikart, P. S. (1985). *Movement plus music: Activities for children ages 3–7*. Ypsilanti, MI: High/Scope.

Weikart, P. S. (1987). *Movement plus rhymes, songs, and singing games*. Ypsilanti, MI: High/Scope.

Catalog Sources for Records, Tapes, and CDs

Educational Record Center
3233 Burnt Mill Drive Suite 100
Wilmington, NC 28403–2655
1–800–438–1637

Music for Little People
P.O. Box 1720
Lawndale, CA 90260
1–800–727–2233

Picture-Book Versions of Songs, Chants, Fingerplays, and Action Rhymes

Adams, P. (1973). *There was an old lady*. New York: Child's Play.

Adams, P. (1975). *This old man*. New York: Child's Play.

Adams, P. (1979). *There were ten in the bed*. New York: Child's Play.

Aliki. (1968). *Hush little baby*. New York: Prentice Hall.

Aliki. (1974). *Go tell Aunt Rhody*. New York: Macmillan.

Aruego, J., & Dewey, A. (1989). *Five little ducks*. New York: Crown.

Aylesworth, J. (1991). *Old black fly*. New York: Henry Holt.

Barbaresi, N. (1985). *Frog went a-courtin'*. New York: Scholastic.

Baum, S. (1992). *Today is Monday*. New York: Harper-Collins.

Brett, J. (1986). *The twelve days of Christmas*. New York: Putnam & Grosset.

Bonne, R. (1961). *I know an old lady*. New York: Scholastic.

Bozylinsky, H. H. (1993). *Lala salama: An African lullaby*. New York: Putnam Philomel.

Buffet, J., & Buffet, S. L. (1988). *The jolly mon*. Fort Worth, TX: Harcourt Brace Jovanovich.

Bullock, K. (1993). *She'll be comin' 'round the mountain*. New York: Simon and Schuster.

Carle, E. (1992). *Today is Monday*. New York: Scholastic.

Child, L. M. (1974). *Over the river and through the wood*. New York: Coward.

Christelow, E. (1989). *Five little monkeys jumping on the bed*. New York: Trumpet.

Conover, C. (1976). *Six little ducks*. New York: Crowell.

Dale, P. (1988). *Ten in the bed*. Martinez, CA: Discovery Toys.

Glazer, T. (1982). *On top of spaghetti*. New York: Double-day.

Glazer, T. (1990). *The more we get together*. Forth Worth, TX: Harcourt Brace Jovanovich. (Big book)

Gurney, J. S. (1992). *Over the river and through the woods*. New York: Scholastic.

Hale, S. J. (1990). *Mary had a little lamb*. New York: Scholastic. (Photos by Bruce McMillan)

Hurd, T. (1984). *Mama don't allow*. New York: Harper & Row.

Ipcar, D. (1971). *The cat came back*. New York: Knopf.

Ivmey, J. (1990). *Three blind mice*. Boston: Little, Brown.

Jeffers, S. (1974). *All the pretty horses*. New York: Scholastic.

Jones, C. (1990). *This old man*. Boston: Houghton Mifflin.

Jorgensen, G. (1988). *Crocodile beat*. New York: Aladdin.

Karas, G. B. (1995). *I know an old lady*. New York: Scholastic.

Keats, E. J. (1971). *Over in the meadow*. New York: Scholastic.

Kellogg, S. (1984). *There was an old woman*. New York: Macmillan.

Kennedy, J. (1983). *The teddybears' picnic*. La Jolla, CA: Green Tiger Press.

Kovalski, M., (1987). *The wheels on the bus*. New York: Trumpet. (Big book)

Kovalski, M. (1988). *Jingle bells*. Boston: Little, Brown.

Langstaff, J. (1963). *Old Dan Tucker*. Boston: Harcourt.

Langstaff, J. (1974). *Oh, a-hunting we will go*. New York: Atheneum.

Lawson, C. (1991). *Teddy bear, teddy bear*. New York: Dial.

McCarthy, B. (1987). *Buffalo girls*. New York: Crown.

Pearson, T. C. (1985). *Sing a song of sixpence*. New York: Dial.

Paparone, P. (1995). *Five little ducks: An old rhyme*. New York: North-South.

Paxton, T. (1990). *Englebert the elephant*. New York: Morrow.

Peek, M. (1981). *Ten in the bed*. New York: Clarion.

Peek, M. (1985). *Mary wore her red dress and Henry wore his green sneakers*. New York: Clarion.

Quackenbush, R. M. (1973). *She'll be comin' 'round the mountain*. New York: Lippincott.

Quackenbush, R. M. (1974). *Clementine*. New York: Lippincott.

Quackenbush, R. M. (1975). *Skip to my Lou*. New York: Lippincott.

Quackenbush, R. M. (1988). *There'll be a hot time in the old town tonight: The great Chicago fire of 1871*. New York: Harper.

Rae, M. M. (1988). *The farmer in the dell*. New York: Viking/Kestrel.

Raffi. (1987). *Down by the bay*. New York: Crown.

Raffi. (1987). *Shake my sillies out*. New York: Crown.

Raffi. (1988). *One light, one sun*. New York: Crown.

Raffi. (1989). *Everything grows*. New York: Crown.

Reid, B. (1992). *Two by two*. New York: Scholastic. (Includes song "Who Built the Ark?")

Rojankovsky, F. (1955). *Frog went a-courtin'*. New York: Scholastic.

Rounds, G. (1967). *The boll weevil*. New York: Golden Gate.

Rounds, G. (1968). *Casey Jones: The story of a brave engineer*. New York: Golden Gate.

Rounds, G. (1973). *Sweet Betsy from Pike*. New York: Children's Press.

Rounds, G. (1989). *Old MacDonald had a farm*. New York: Holiday House.

Seeger, P. (1986). *Abiyoyo*. New York: Aladdin.

Seeger, P., & Seeger, C. (1973). *The foolish frog*. New York: Macmillan. (Also available on video from Weston, CT: Weston Woods Studios 1–800–243–5020)

Simon, P. (1991). *At the zoo*. New York: Doubleday.

Spier, P. (1961). *The fox went out on a chilly night*. New York: Doubleday.

Staines, B. (1989). *All God's critters got a place in the choir*. New York: Puffin.

Wadsworth, O. A. (1985). *Over in the meadow*. New York: Puffin.

Weiss, N. (1987). *If you're happy and you know it*. New York: Greenwillow.

Westcott, N. B. (1987). *Down by the bay*. New York: Crown.

Wescott, N. B. (1987). *Peanut butter and jelly: A play rhyme*. New York: Dutton. (Big book version available from Trumpet Book Club)

Westcott, N. B. (1989). *Skip to my Lou*. New York: Trumpet.

Westcott, N. B. (1990). *There's a hole in the bucket*. New York: HarperCollins.

Winter, J. (1988). *Follow the drinking gourd*. New York: Knopf.

Wolff, A. (1990). *Baby Beluga*. New York: Crown.

Zelinsky, P. O. (1990). *The wheels on the bus*. New York: Dutton. (Pop-up book)

APPENDIX E

Sources for Toys, Materials, and Equipment That Support the Arts

Animal Town
Toys, games and books for cooperative learning
1–800–445–8624

Back to Basics Toys, Games, and Hobbies
Traditional toys and high-quality resource materials
1–800–356–5360

Chime Time Movement Products
An extensive collection of materials for creative movement and physical activity
1–800–477–5075

Constructive Playthings
A wide assortment of sturdy and bright play equipment and materials
1–800–448–4115

Creation Station
Resources for creative expression and play
1–206–775–7959

Creative Educational Surplus
Inexpensive and recycled materials that support art projects and children's creative expression
1–612–884–6427

Getty Trust Publications
Beautiful books that feature works of art and books about art history
1–800–223–3431

Hand-in-Hand Professional
An assortment of equipment, furniture, toys, and curriculum resources for teachers of young children
1–800–872–3841

HearthSong
Children's toys, games, and materials, especially those that are part of folk traditions
1–800–325–2502

Metropolitan Museum of Art
Museum quality gifts, books, prints, calendars, note cards, and videos
1–800–468–7386

Museum of Fine Arts, Boston
A source for high-quality art prints, children's books, and activities
1–800–225–5592

Parents' Choice
A nonprofit consumer guide to children's toys, and print and nonprint media
1–617–965–5193

PlayFair Toys
Nonviolent educational toys, games, and equipment
1–800–824–7255

Music for Little People
High-quality recordings and music materials for young children
1–800–727–2233

UNICEF
Note cards, calendars, and other materials featuring children's and professional artists' work from around the world
1–800–553–1200

Woodbine House: The Special Needs Collection
Specializing in toys and materials for children with special needs
1–800–843–7323

APPENDIX
F

Professional Organizations and Journals That Support the Arts in Early Childhood Education

American Alliance for Health, Physical Education, Recreation, and Dance
1900 Association Drive
Reston, VA 22091
Journal: *Journal of Physical Education, Recreation, and Dance*

American Council for the Arts
1 East 53rd Street
New York, NY 10022–4201
1–212–223–ARTS
Publications and resources

Association for Childhood Education International
11141 Georgia Avenue, Suite 200
Wheaton, MD 20902
Journal: *Childhood Education*

Educational Resources Information Center/Early Childhood Education (ERIC/ECE)
805 West Pennsylvania Avenue
Urbana, IL 61801
Disseminates information about early childhood programs, curriculum, and issues

The Getty Center for Education in the Arts
401 Wilshire Boulevard, Suite 950
Santa Monica, CA 90401–1455
1–310–395–6657
Publications emphasize visual arts and discipline-based arts education

Human Sciences Press
233 Spring Street
New York, NY 10013
Journal: *Early Childhood Education Journal*
Publishes articles about children's creativity and the arts

Music Educators National Conference
1902 Association Drive
Reston, VA 22091
1–703–860–4000
Journal: *Music Educators Journal*
Various books, brochures, copies of national standards, position papers

National Art Education Association
1916 Association Drive
Reston, VA 22091–1590
1–703–860–8000
Periodicals and other resources

National Assembly of State Arts Agencies
1010 Vermont Avenue, NW
Suite 920
Washington, DC 20005
1–202–347–6352
Information about various art groups in your state

National Association for the Education of Young Children
1509 16th Street, N.W.
Washington, DC 20036
Journal: *Young Children*

National Endowment for the Arts
Division of Education Programs
1100 Pennsylvania Avenue, NW
Room 602
Washington, DC 20506
1–202–682–5426
Information about education in and through the arts

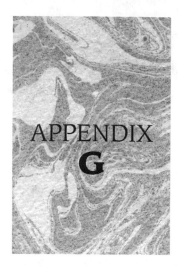

APPENDIX
G

Creating a Documentation Panel

What Is Documentation?

Have you ever noticed an impressive display of panels approximately 4 by 6 feet exhibited in public places such as banks, airports, shopping malls, libraries, museums, professional conferences, or job fairs? Individuals, programs, businesses, and organizations often hire graphic artists to depict their goals and achievements on three or four of these display panels. The idea is to capture the essence of whatever is being documented, to represent the concepts succinctly, and to allow onlookers to come away with a clear idea of what the display is all about.

How Are Documentation Panels Used in Early Childhood Education?

The idea of documentation has been borrowed from the beautiful traveling exhibit of the schools of Reggio Emilia, Italy. Documentation panels from Reggio Emilia use the same techniques used in professional displays—a combination of photographs, children's work, descriptive captions, and collage-style samples of various materials to represent the process of learning. The materials are artistically arranged using basic principles of graphic design so that they are eye-catching and communicate well. Documentation panels can be used by early childhood educators to characterize many different things, such as

- the overall philosophy and mission of a program (e.g., building self-esteem)
- the general principles of the curriculum (e.g., active learning)
- the life cycle of a project undertaken by the children (e.g., a study of a construction site near the school)
- the early childhood program's response to an issue of concern (e.g., violence prevention)
- the professional development experiences of the teachers (e.g., learning in a children's literature course).

How Do Documentation Panels Differ from Bulletin Boards?

Documentation panels differ from the usual bulletin board displays in several ways:

1. Bulletin boards usually have a brief title; documentation panels use words to tell the story behind the pictures.
2. Bulletin boards often consist of a few purchased or traced decorative items; documentation panels highlight significant issues and events that are unique to the particular program.
3. Bulletin boards usually feature seasons or holidays; documentation panels show the learners in action and include samples of their work.
4. Bulletin boards consist of a one-color background with students' papers or decorations stapled on top; documentation panels use a variety of art media to create different colors, textures, and arrangements that result in a truly beautiful product.

How Is a Documentation Panel Constructed?

Carter and Curtis (1996) suggest the following sequence, which we elaborate on here:

1. Take photographs. First, obtain a model release for every child or adult who will appear in the photographs. (A sample form appears at the end of this Appendix.) Use a 35-mm camera (a disposable camera is fine). Take several shots and shop around for a good price on developing the photographs. If you plan to make a large documentation panel (rather than a small one for your teaching portfolio), you will find it necessary to enlarge the photographs. The least expensive way to do this is to make color copies. Once again, shop around for the best price.

2. Collect materials. Gather samples of children's art and writing, your notes and sketches, quotations from books and professional articles, covers from picture books or other books, and items that could be used to create a collage effect.

3. Select a story line or theme. Choose the motif for your documentation panel and the best images and background to support that theme. If the purpose of the panel is to show the value of the visual arts in early childhood, for example, you might want to use background papers that have bright primary colors, such as those found in tempera paints or crayons. If you are documenting a project that took place in the fall, you might want to include some leaf rubbings, and so forth. Choose a title for your panel. Write a brief introductory statement to set viewers' expectations for the panel.

4. Assemble the panel. Go through your notes and write the script for your panel. If you can print very artistically, hand letter the text. If not, type the words and print them out in boldface print on a laser quality printer in a font that is large, simple, and easy to read from a few feet away (Arial Bold is a good choice). Spread out all the materials you have collected and experiment with different arrangements until you decide upon the one that is most aesthetically pleasing. Graphic artists often recommend a "Z" pattern that draws the eye first to the upper left-hand corner, across the top, down through the center and finally over to the lower left-hand corner. Make sure that your display is not too cluttered.

FOR FURTHER INFORMATION

Carter, M., & Curtis, D. (1996). *Spreading the news: Sharing stories of early childhood education*. St. Paul, MN: Redleaf Press.

Goldhaber, J., & Smith, D. (1997). "You look at things differently": The role of documentation in professional development. *Early Childhood Education Journal, 25.*

Rinaldi, C. (1993). The emergent curriculum and social construction in the *Hundred Languages of Children*. In C. Edwards, L. Gandini, & G. Forman (Eds.), *The Reggio Emilia approach to early childhood education* (2d ed.) (pp. 101–112). Norwood, NJ: Ablex.

My signature below indicates that I grant permission for photographs depicting me and/ or my child engaged in school activities to appear in books, articles, videos, brochures, displays, and so forth. I understand that these photographs will be used for the purpose of training teachers and the public about early childhood education. I further agree that I am to receive no compensation for my child's appearance in these photographs nor for my own appearance in the photographs. I also understand that my participation and/or my child's participation in these photographs confers no ownership rights to the photographs or negatives whatsoever.

Please print the following information.

Child's Name _____

Parent's or Guardian's Name _____

Address
Street _____ Apt. or Box No. _____

City, State, Zip Code _____

Telephone with Area Code _____

Please sign your name.

_____

Date: _____

Sample Model Release

What to Do with a Masterpiece

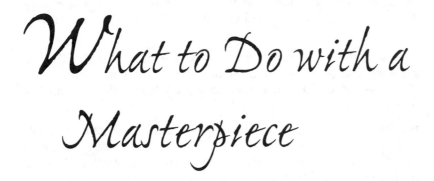

Early childhood educators are sometimes uncertain about how to get children involved in the fine arts. Look through these ideas, then brainstorm additional ideas in your class.

- As you look at these prints of works by famous artists, try to imagine how the artist created a particular effect. How could you create a similar effect? What materials and tools would you try? Why?

- Listen to this picture-book story without seeing the pictures and try to imagine them in your mind. After the story is finished, look at the pictures. How are they alike or different from what you imagined?

- How do artists change the way that we look at things? To answer these questions, let's look at three books: *Large as Life* (Finzel, 1991), *Zoom* (Banyai, 1996), and *Artistic Trickery* (Capek, 1996).

- Look in silence at this artist's work for 60 seconds. Search for colors. Now search for shapes. What feelings do you have as you look at the picture? Let's write your comments on this chart paper (Ernst, 1996).

- Artists almost always give their work a title. Let's look at these prints of artists' work and give them a title. I will write your ideas on sentence strips and post them underneath. Then we will look at the title the artist chose and try to figure out why.

- How do artists mix colors? Let's read the big book of *Mouse Paint* (Walsh, 1989) and try to guess what color is produced when two colors are mixed. Later, we can use M & M's to make color equations (e.g., yellow + red = ?), then eat the candy for a snack.

- Now that we have looked at the work of Picasso, let's have a shape day! I'm thinking that we might have a shape city (a wall-sized town made of shapes), a shape graph (a pictograph that shows the results of class survey on favorite shapes), a wearable-shapes center (a place where children can make hats, necklaces, or t-shirts that feature brightly colored shapes), a shape game (a child-constructed variant of Twister that uses different shapes and colors), a shape-block center (using attribute blocks—red, blue, and yellow circles, squares, and triangles that are small, medium, and large as well as thick or thin—to classify and categorize and create sets and subsets, and hula hoops to make categories and Venn diagrams). We could also have shape snacks (e.g., tortilla chips for triangles, graham crackers for square and rectangle, cookies for circles) (Novelli, 1993).

• Look at all these reprints of artists work (Living Arts Seminars, 1992). All of us, including me, will be choosing one work of art to investigate. When it is your turn to share, talk about why you selected a particular piece of art. What did the artist do that interested you? (Ernst, 1996)

• [First, make a poster of poor quality photographs out of snapshots of pets collected by you and the children.] Let's look at the book *Without Words* with photographs by Barbara Sonneborn (1995) and the Humane Society calendar. Now let's look at the photographs that we took. What makes a good picture of a pet?   Now let's look at a book called *Looking at Photographs: ANIMALS* (Coleman, 1995). When we are finished looking, we will be making a comparison chart.

• Even though the museum is too far away for a field trip, I have borrowed videodiscs that will show us the art that is inside famous museums (Voyager, 1993). With this program, you can create your own scrapbook of the art you like best, then share it with the class.

• Today I brought Pat Cummings' (1994–1996) books, *Talking with Artists*. These books tell us about the illustrators who created the pictures in many of the books that we have heard during story time. The books also show us what their artwork looked like when they were children. Both of these books will be on display all week. When you have time, I want you to look through the books and think about an answer to these questions that I have written on chart paper: How did the artist's work change as she or he grew up? What do you notice about this illustrator's work?

• Now that you have heard *The Tangram Magician* (Ernst, 1990), I want you to create your own ending to the story using the tangram shapes.

• Let's look at this painting and make a class list of all the words we can think of to describe it. Now let's cluster our words into a map or web of ideas and put those words that go together into categories (e.g., shape words, feeling words, etc.).

• I'm going to demonstrate how Japanese artists fold paper. This paper folding is called origami and I am going demonstrate how to make a bird called a crane. This week you will be hearing stories about origami (Bang, 1985; Say, 1991; Small, 1987). You will also get to try origami following the directions in a book (Temko, 1993).

• [Use museum postcards of various works of art. Let the child who is doing the describing be the only one who sees the postcard. Then, after it has been described, pass around the postcard and add more to the description.] Pretend that you just bought this piece of art. Use this toy telephone to call someone in the room and tell that person about it.

• Consider using *Good Times, Good Rhymes* (Hopkins, 1995) as a source for poems.] As I read this poem out loud, I want you to listen carefully and then draw the pictures that were in your head [for older children].

• People are often the subject of paintings and photographs. What makes a good photograph of a person? This book, *Looking at Photographs: PEOPLE* (Lowe, 1995) will help to answer that question. Later, we will be looking at *Portraits* (Delafosse, 1996).

• [Use *Landscapes* (Delafosse, 1996) as a resource for this activity.] Imagine that you can walk inside this picture. What would you hear? Touch? Taste? Smell?

- [The basic story line of *Lucy's Picture* (Moon, 1995) is that Lucy makes a collage for her blind grandfather so that he can "see" Lucy's picture with his fingers.] Now that all of you have made a texture collage, I have an interesting story for you. In this book, Lucy makes a very special collage for someone she loves. As we read the story about Lucy's collage, think about why her collage is the perfect gift for that person.

- [Use poster-sized art prints or slides borrowed from the library.] Select your favorite print from the ones on display. Pretend that you are selling this piece of artwork to us. How would you convince us to buy it?

- As I play this music (e.g., "Flight of the Bumblebee" by Rimsky-Korsakov, "Royal March of the Lion" from *The Carnival of the Animals* by Saint-Saëns, *The Nutcracker Suite* by Tchaikovsky, "Music Box Waltz" by Shostakovich), I want you to move your paintbrushes in the way that the music makes you feel.

REFERENCES AND RESOURCES

Bang, M. (1985). *The paper crane*. New York: Greenwillow.

Banyai, I. (1996). *Zoom*. New York: Viking.

Burroughs, L. (1988). *Introducing children to the arts: A practical guide for librarians and educators*. Boston: G. K. Hall.

Capek, M. (1996). *Artistic trickery: The tradition of trompe l'oeil art*. New York: Lerner.

Coleman, A.D. (1995). *Looking at photographs: ANIMALS*. San Francisco: Chronicle.

Cummings, P. (1994–1996). *Talking with artists (Vols 1–2)*. New York: Simon & Schuster.

Delafosse, C. (1996). *Portraits* (First Discovery Art Books). New York: Scholastic.

Delafosse, C. (1996). *Landscapes* (First Discovery Art Books). New York: Scholastic.

Ernst, K. (1996, January). Lessons from literature and art. *Teaching K–8*, pp. 34–36.

Ernst, L. C. (1990). *The tangram magician*. New York: Abrams.

Fine art books for young people [series]. Champaign, IL: Garrard.

Finzel, J. (1991). *Large as life*. New York: Lothrop, Lee, & Shepard.

Hopkins, L. B. (1995). *Good rhymes, good times*. New York: HarperCollins.

Living Arts Seminars (1992). *Meet the masterpieces: Strategies, activities, and posters for understanding great works of art*. New York: Scholastic.

Lowe, J. (Ed.). (1995). *Looking at photographs: PEOPLE*. San Francisco: Chronicle.

Moon, N. (1995). *Lucy's picture*. New York: Dial.

Novelli, J. (1993). Teaching with technology: Special needs, special project. *Instructor, 103*(2), 38, 42–43, 45–46.

Richardson, W., & Richardson, J. (1991). *The world of art through the eyes of artists*. Chicago: Childrens Press.

Say, A. (1991). *Tree of cranes*. Boston: Houghton Mifflin.

Small, D. (1987). *Paper John*. New York: Farrar, Straus, & Giroux.

Sonneborn, B. (1995). *Without words*. San Francisco: Sierra Club Books.

Temko, F. (1993). *Origami magic*. New York: Scholastic.

Voyager Company (1993). *With open eyes; The Louvre: Thousands of masterpieces; The Orsay Museum*. 1–800–446–2001.

Walsh, E. (1991). *Mouse paint*. (Scholastic Big Books). New York: Lothrop, Lee, & Shepard.

Photo Credits

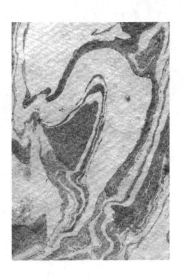

Index

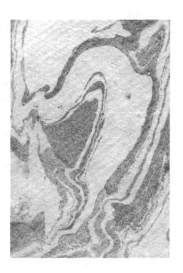